A HISTORY OF THE STAINED GLASS OF ST GEORGE'S CHAPEL, WINDSOR CASTLE

HISTORICAL MONOGRAPHS RELATING TO ST GEORGE'S CHAPEL

General Editor: The Reverend Canon John A. White.

VOL. 1. THE KNIGHTS OF THE GARTER, 1348–1939, WITH A COMPLETE LIST OF THE STALL PLATES IN ST GEORGE'S CHAPEL
By the Rev. E. H. FELLOWES, C.H., M.V.O., MUS.DOC. (1939)

VOL. 2. THE PLATE OF ST GEORGE'S CHAPEL, WINDSOR CASTLE
By E. ALFRED JONES, M.A., F.S.A. (1939)

VOL. 3. ORGANISTS AND MASTERS OF THE CHORISTERS OF ST GEORGE'S CHAPEL IN WINDSOR CASTLE
By the Rev. E. H. FELLOWES. 2nd edn. (1979)

VOL. 4. THE MILITARY KNIGHTS OF WINDSOR, 1352–1944
By the Rev. E. H. FELLOWES. (1944)

VOL. 5. THE VICARS OR MINOR CANONS OF HIS MAJESTY'S FREE CHAPEL OF ST GEORGE IN WINDSOR CASTLE
By the Rev. E. H. FELLOWES. (1945)

VOL. 6. ST GEORGE'S CHAPEL, WINDSOR, 1348–1416, A STUDY IN EARLY COLLEGIATE ADMINISTRATION
By A. K. B. ROBERTS, B.A., PH.D. (1947)

VOL. 7. THE INVENTORIES OF ST GEORGE'S CHAPEL, WINDSOR CASTLE, 1384–1667
By MAURICE F. BOND. (1947)

VOL. 8. FASTI WYNDESORIENSES: THE DEANS AND CANONS OF ST GEORGE'S CHAPEL
By the Rev. S. L. OLLARD, D.LITT., F.S.A. (repr. 1999)

VOL. 9. THE WOODWORK OF THE CHOIR
By M. R. JAMES, O.M., LITT.D. (repr. 1985)

VOL. 10. THE BAPTISM, MARRIAGE AND BURIAL REGISTERS OF ST GEORGE'S CHAPEL, WINDSOR
By the Rev. E. H. FELLOWES and ELISABETH R. POYSER, M.A., M.LITT. (1957)

VOL. 11. THE MANUSCRIPTS OF ST GEORGE'S CHAPEL
By the Rev. J. N. DALTON, K.C.V.O., C.M.G., LL.D., F.S.A. (1957)

VOL. 12. THE MONUMENTS OF ST GEORGE'S CHAPEL
By SHELAGH M. BOND, M.A., F.R.HIST.S. (repr. 1999)

VOL. 13. THE CHAPTER ACTS OF THE DEAN AND CANONS OF WINDSOR, 1430, 1523–1672
By SHELAGH M. BOND. (1966)

VOL. 14. THE MUSICAL MANUSCRIPTS OF ST GEORGE'S CHAPEL, WINDSOR CASTLE: A DESCRIPTIVE CATALOGUE
By CLIFFORD MOULD. (1973)

VOL. 15. A CATALOGUE OF PRINTED BOOKS (PRE-1751) IN THE LIBRARY OF ST GEORGE'S CHAPEL, WINDSOR CASTLE
By JOHN CALLARD, B.A. (1976)

VOL. 16. THE ORDER OF THE GARTER: ITS KNIGHTS AND STALL PLATES, 1348–1984
By GRACE HOLMES. (repr. 1999)

VOL. 17. ST GEORGE'S CHAPEL, WINDSOR, IN THE LATE MIDDLE AGES
Edited by COLIN G. RICHMOND and EILEEN SCARFF

Historical Monographs relating to
St George's Chapel, Windsor Castle, Volume 18

A HISTORY OF THE STAINED GLASS OF ST GEORGE'S CHAPEL, WINDSOR CASTLE

Edited by

Sarah Brown

Publication of this book has been made possible by a donation in memory of
Eileen Joan Burgess, 1928–2000.
She loved St George's Chapel and enriched the lives of her friends.

WINDSOR 2005

Published by the Dean and Canons of Windsor

ISBN 0–9539676–3–8
978–0–9539676–3–6

A catalogue record for this book is available from the British Library

Paperback front cover illustration: St George in the Deanery Chapel, as restored in 1982 (SGC © Deans and Canons of Windsor)

Paperback back cover illustration: A late seventeenth-century portrait of Charles II on enamel-painted glass in the Edward IV Chantry, based on an engraving by David Loggan. Glass painter unknown

Produced by Maney Publishing
Hudson Road Leeds LS9 7DL UK

CONTENTS

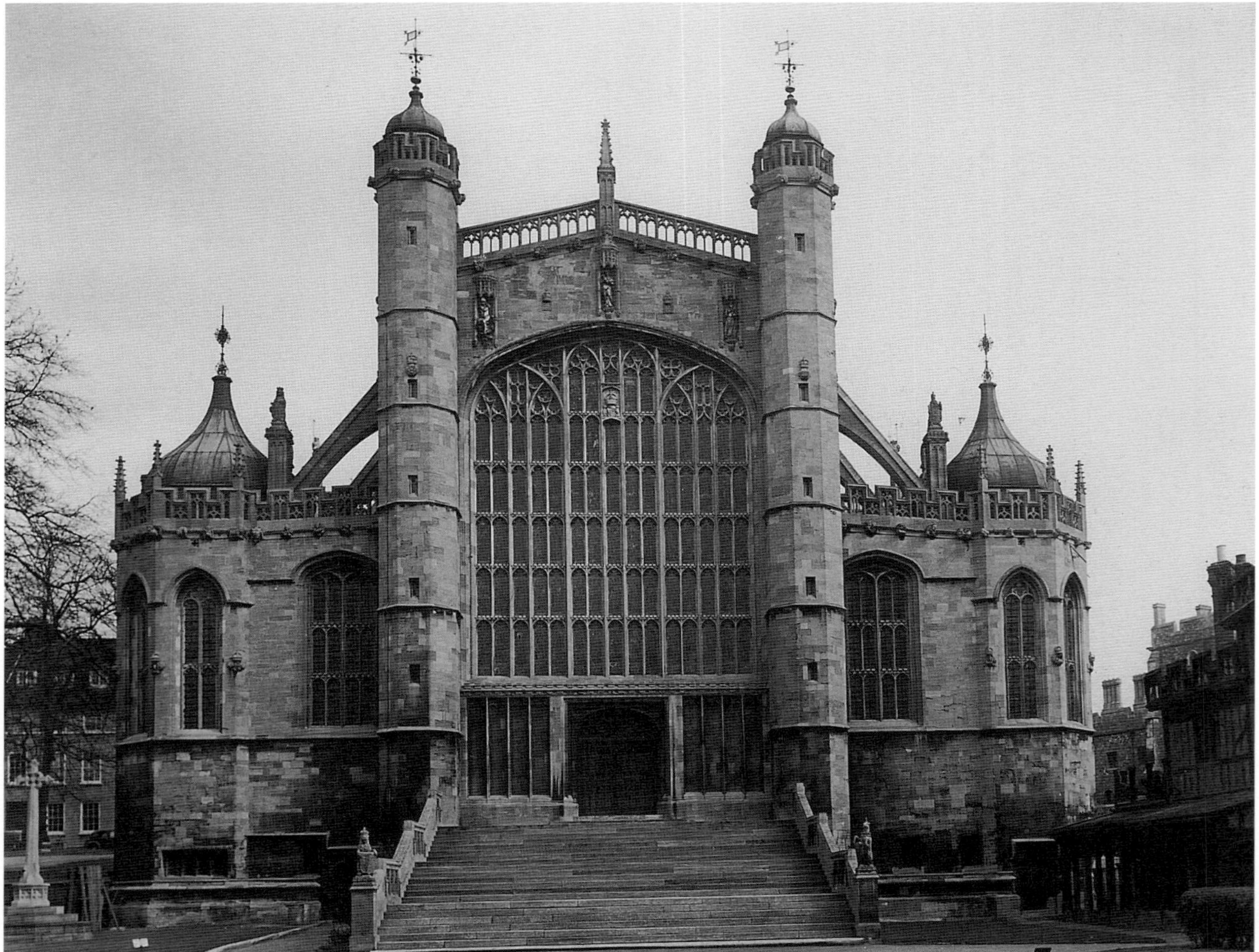

The west front of St George's Chapel, Windsor Castle (SGC © Dean and Canons of Windsor)

ACKNOWLEDGEMENTS

Perhaps our greatest debt of gratitude is to the late Maurice Bond, who first conceived this volume and assembled a team whose expertise could make it a reality. Over the many intervening years the commitment of the late Peter Begent, who knew the chapel so well and was so willing to share his heraldic knowledge, remained unshaken, despite delays and difficulties. It is a great sadness that neither Maurice nor Peter lived to see the publication of the book. We hope they would have been proud of it. Equally important has been the assistance and wise guidance of Dr Eileen Scarff, whose unmatched knowledge of the chapel archives has been at the disposal of us all. I would also like to thank Enid Davies for her many kindnesses.

Those institutions and archives that have supplied illustrations, together with permission to reproduce them, are detailed in the main text. However, special thanks are due to Dr John Crook, who took many new photographs especially for this publication, and to the National Monuments Record for allowing us to reproduce many images from its extensive record of the choir clerestory.

Finally, on behalf of the authors I would like to join the General Editor in thanking Miss Phyllis James for her generous donation in memory of Eileen Joan Burgess.

SARAH BROWN

ABBREVIATIONS AND SHORTENED TITLES

Architectural History	W. H. St. John Hope, *Windsor Castle: An Architectural History*, 2 vols and plans, London 1913
BL	London, British Library
Collegiate Chapel	Thomas Willement, *An Account of the Restoration of the Collegiate Chapel of St George, Windsor*, London 1844
CPR	Calendar of Patent Rolls
CVMA	Corpus Vitrearum Medii Aevi
Fasti Wyndesoriensis	S. L. Ollard, *Fasti Wyndesoriensis; The Deans and Canons of Windsor*, Historical Monographs relating to St George's Chapel, Windsor Castle, volume 8, reprinted Windsor 1999
Friends Report	*Annual Report of the Society of Friends of St George's and the Descendants of the Knights of the Garter*
JBSMGP	*Journal of the British Society of Master Glass Painters*
SGC	Windsor, St George's Chapel Archives
V&A	London, Victoria & Albert Museum

GENERAL EDITOR'S FOREWORD

This major contribution to the monograph series was conceived by Maurice Bond, then general editor of the Monograph series, some thirty years ago. Since that time it has gradually and painfully come to birth. But the strength of his original vision and the clear need for a scholarly study of the glass of the Chapel has kept the project alive despite what sometimes appeared, to the present general editor, apparently insurmountable obstacles. In the presence of the finished work the satisfaction in achievement is somewhat diminished by the realization that the original editor and three contributors, William Cole, Peter Begent and Hilary Wayment, did not live long enough to enjoy seeing their work in print. I hope that the volume will be understood to be an appropriate tribute to their memory. Particular thanks must be extended to all those early contributors who displayed commendable patience whilst important final editorial details were accomplished. For example, Peter Begent had left his Heraldic Schedule incomplete and Hubert Chesshyre and Robert Harrison had the arduous task of checking through the whole of Peter's text. A general editor can be counted fortunate if the majority of contributions in such a volume have reached an equally high standard. With this monograph the quality of the scholarship and presentation is consistent throughout and for this thanks are due to all the scholars who have fulfilled the task set with academic diligence and recognizable enthusiasm. But to Sarah Brown must go an additional accolade, for she accepted the editorship of this monograph at a time when we were beginning to wonder if our hopes of publication were ill-founded. She has brought together the text, the illustrations and the layout to produce what we believe to be a signal volume in our attempt to make the St George's monographs conform to present-day standards, thus opening them to a wider readership. Perhaps the silver lining to the dark cloud of the thirty years' delay is that we have been able to use all the advantages of modern technological advance which the decades have brought into being. We feel confident that the important photography of Dr John Crook is now reproduced at a level commensurate with his skill. The staff of Maney Publishing have continued to show their accustomed care and attention to delaying and demanding clients and are to be wholeheartedly commended for the quality of the finished work. It would be a grave omission on my part to conclude this introduction without special mention of Dr Eileen Scarff, the College archivist whose personal support and informed enthusiastic encouragement continues to engage the Dean and Canons' desire to develop these publications. With her I must couple her excellent colleagues who have furnished to all involved in this major project information and advice 'at the drop of a hat' with admirable cheerfulness and accuracy. We are all especially grateful for the generous donation made towards this work by Miss Phyllis James, in memory of her friend. Perhaps the lesson to be learned from the history of this volume is that a fine thing is truly worth waiting for.

THE REVEREND CANON JOHN A. WHITE LVO

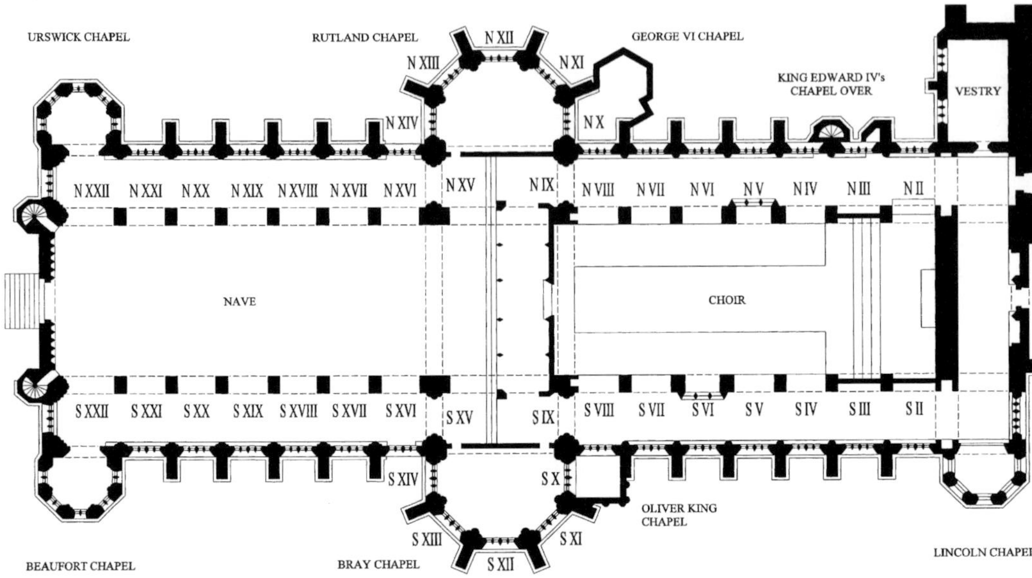

UPPER WINDOWS

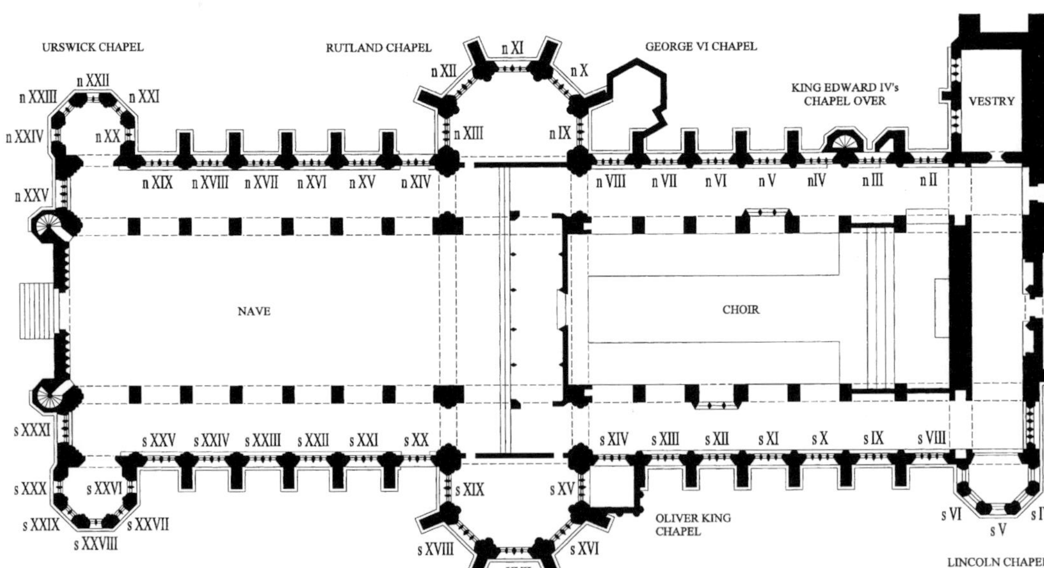

LOWER WINDOWS

Ground plans of St George's Chapel, with windows numbered according to the notation of the Corpus Vitrearum (Drawn by Andy Donald)

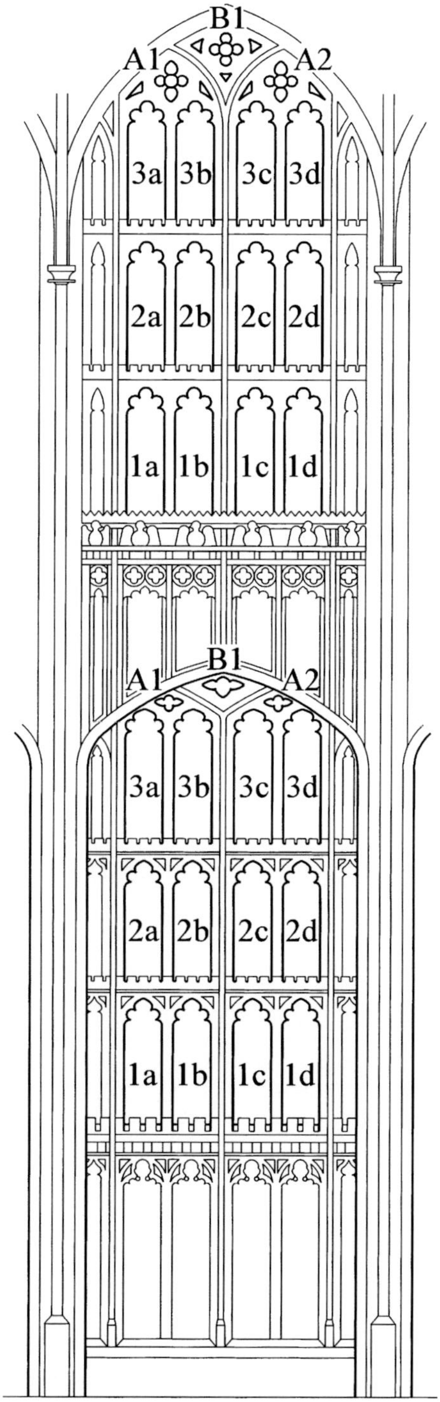

Aisle and clerestory window panel numbers
(Drawn by Andy Donald)

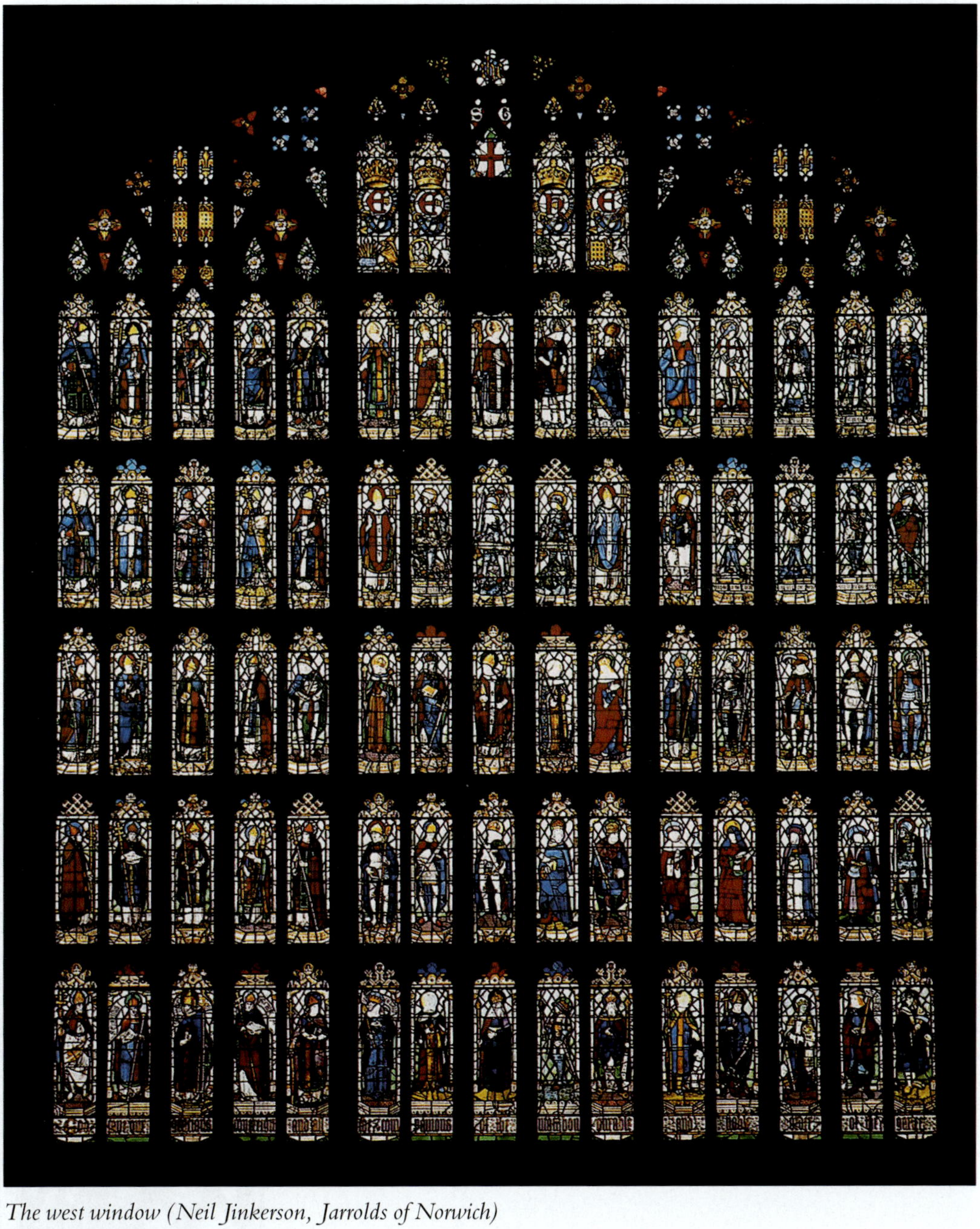

The west window (Neil Jinkerson, Jarrolds of Norwich)

PLATE II

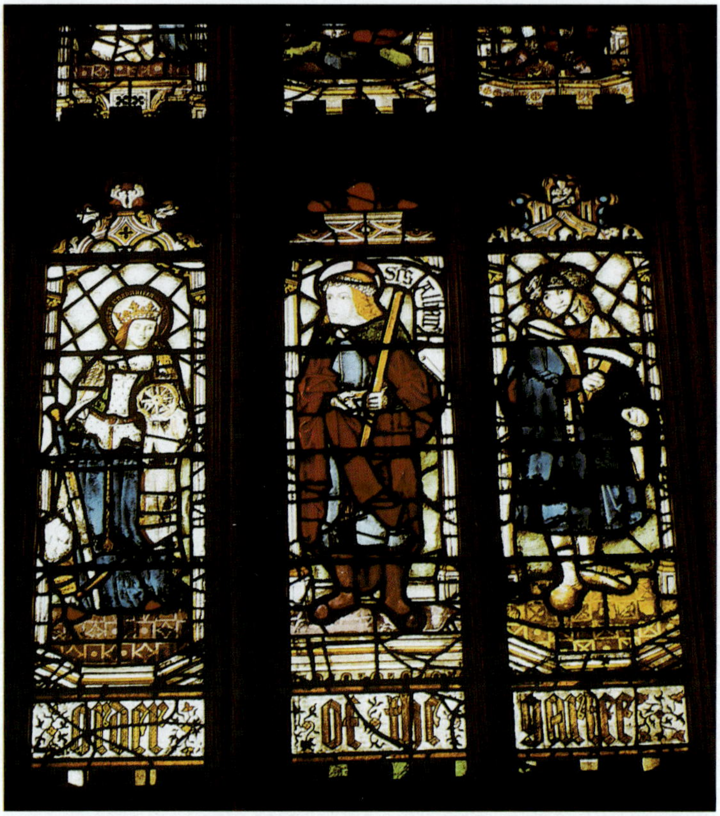

A. *The west window, St Catherine, St Alban and the Master Mason (1m–1o) (© Dean and Canons of Windsor)*

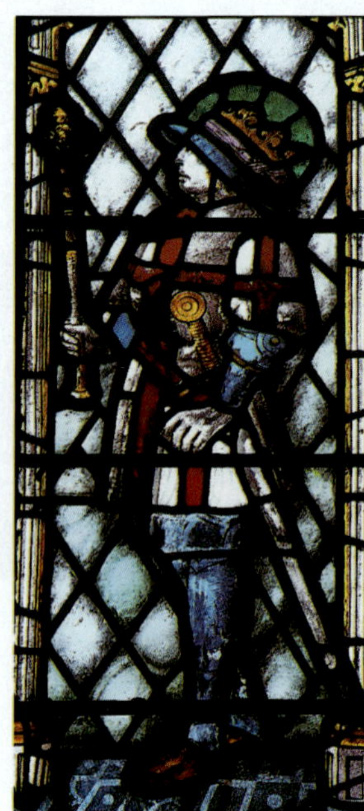

B. *The west window, St George (1i) (Photo John Crook, © Dean and Canons of Windsor)*

PLATE III

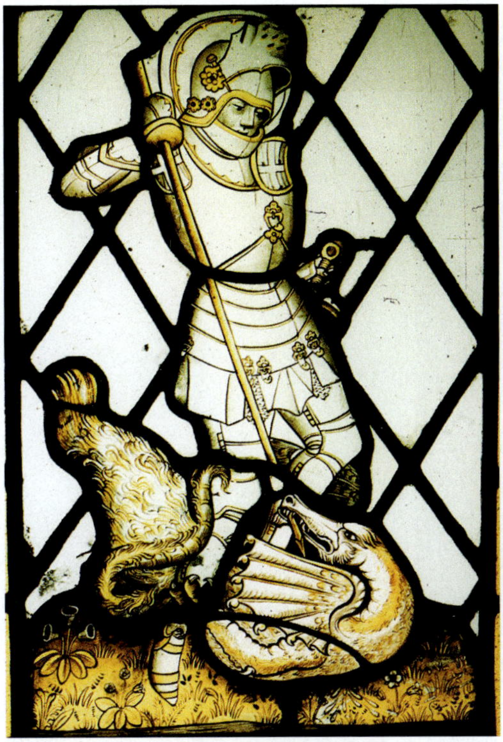

A. *Deanery Chapel, figure of St George as restored in 1982 (SGC © Dean and Canons of Windsor)*

B. *Deanery Hall, the arms of Canon Thomas Magnus (1520–47) (H.G. Wayment)*

C. *The Deanery dining room, the arms of Henry VIII and Catehrine Howard,* c. *1540 (H.G. Wayment)*

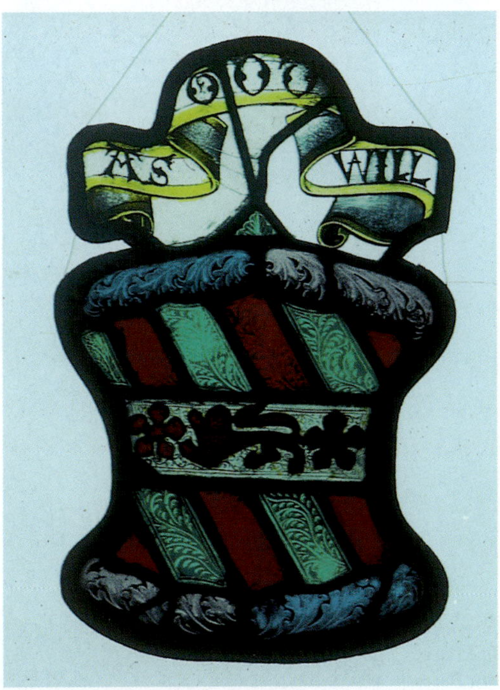

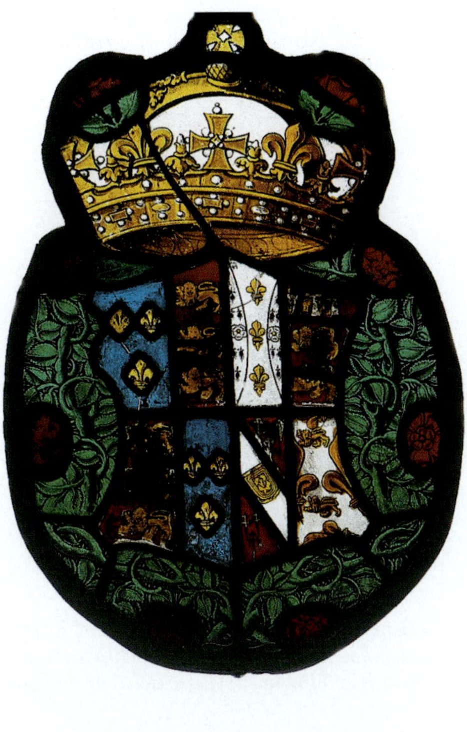

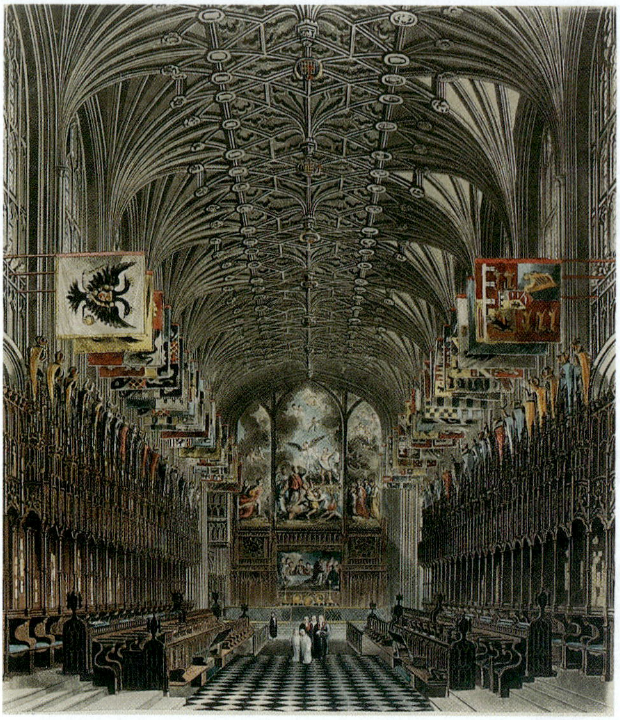

A. *T. Sutherland after a drawing by C. Wilde. The choir of St George's Chapel. Aquatint engraving from W.H. Pyne,* History of the Royal Residences, *I (1819) (Photo © Cambridge University Library)*

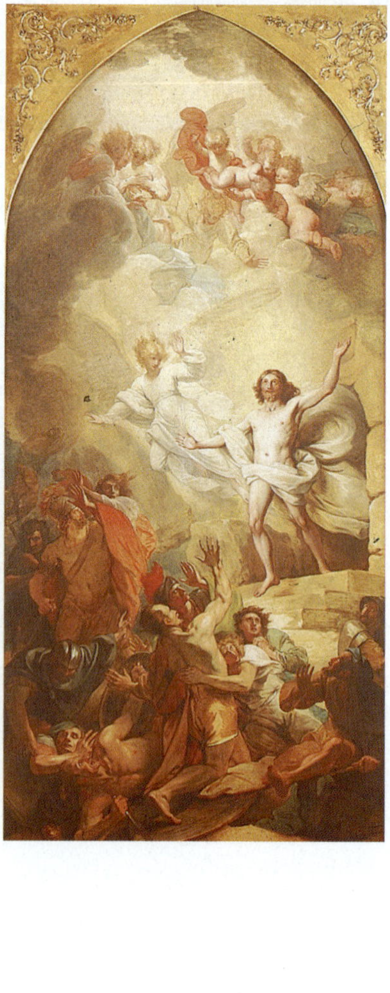

B. *Benjamin West, 'The Resurrection',* c. *1782, oil design for east window of St George's Chapel, Museo del Arte de Ponce, Puerto Rico (Photo © Museo del Arte de Ponce, Puerto Rico)*

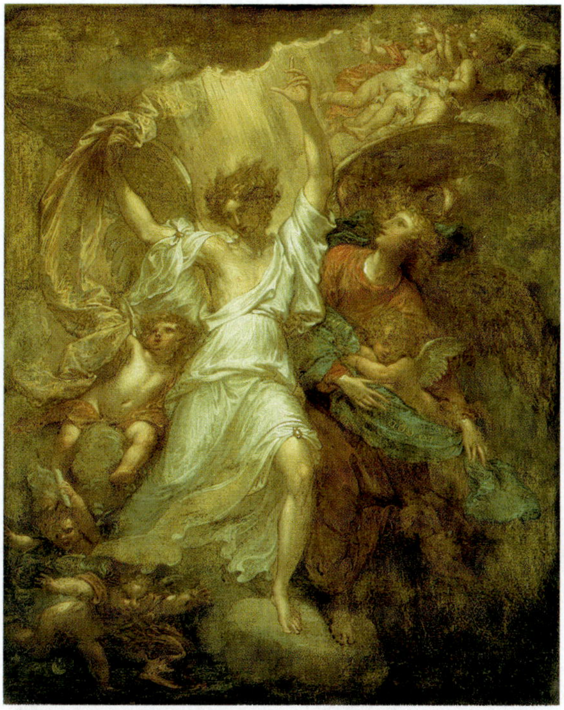

A. *Benjamin West, 'The Angel appearing to the Shepherds', oil design for east window of the south aisle, St George's Chapel. Private collection (Photo © Christie's New York)*

B. *Watercolour drawing, of the unfinished 'Crucifixion' window, St George's chapel,* c. *1807, SGC XVII.61.18 (A) (Photo John Crook, © Dean and Canons of Windsor)*

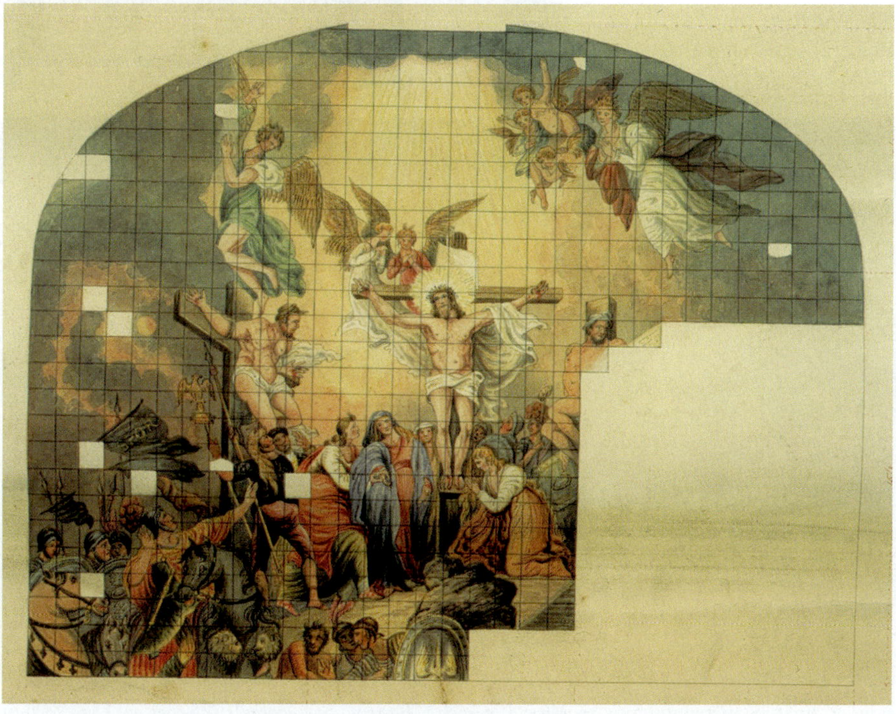

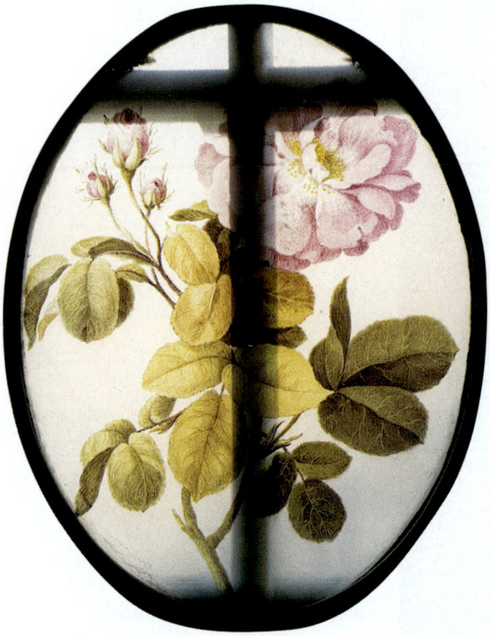

A. *Thomas Jervais, rose panel in the Edward IV Chantry, c. 1782 (Photo John Crook, © Dean and Canons of Windsor)*

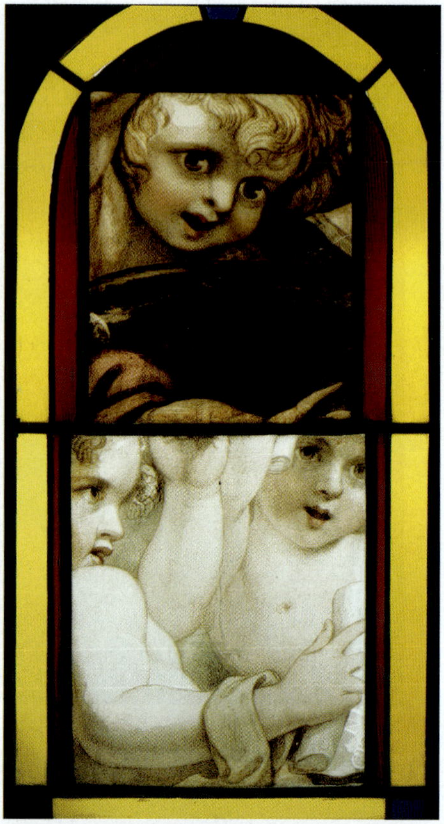

B. *?Charles Forrest/Benjamin West, cherubs. Fragments of a lost window from St George's Chapel, c. 1790 (Photo © Dean and Canons of Windsor)*

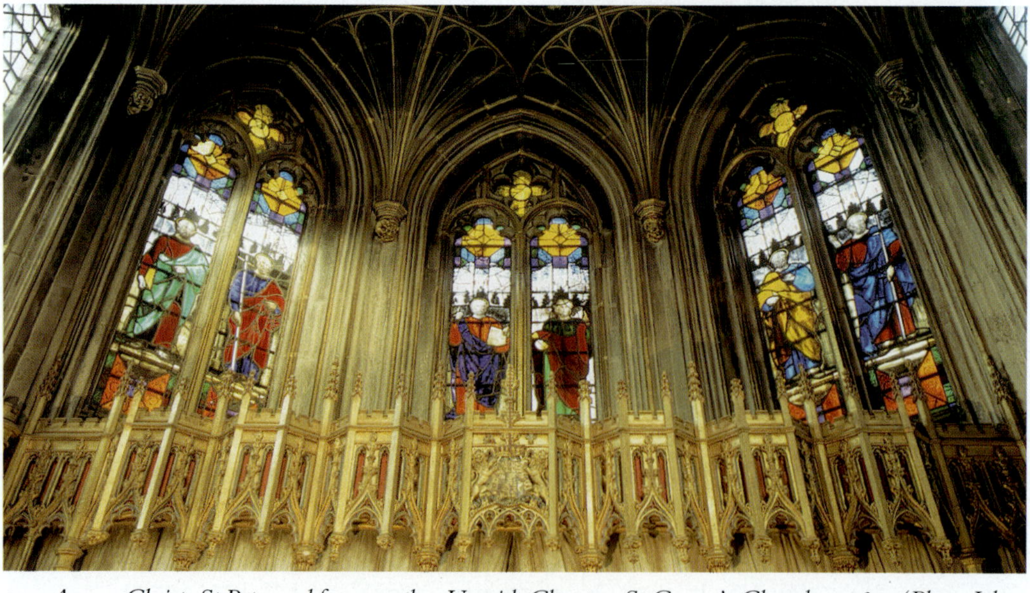

C. *Anon., Christ, St Peter and four apostles, Urswick Chantry, St George's Chapel, c. 1830 (Photo John Crook, © Dean and Canons of Windsor)*

PLATE VII

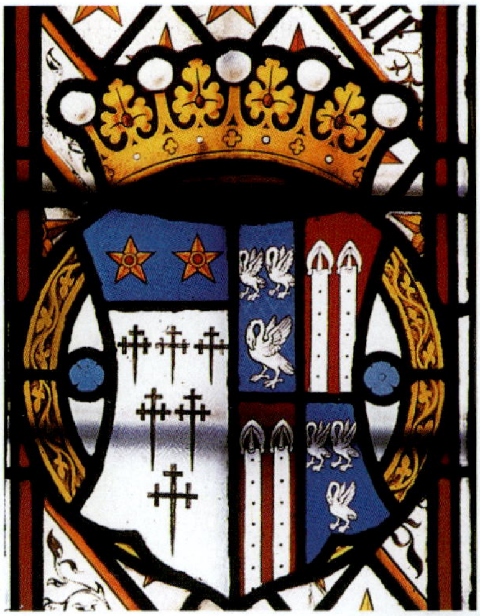

A. *Heraldic glass by Thomas Willement in the Lincoln Chantry, sV, 1848 (Photo John Crook, © Dean and Canons of Windsor)*

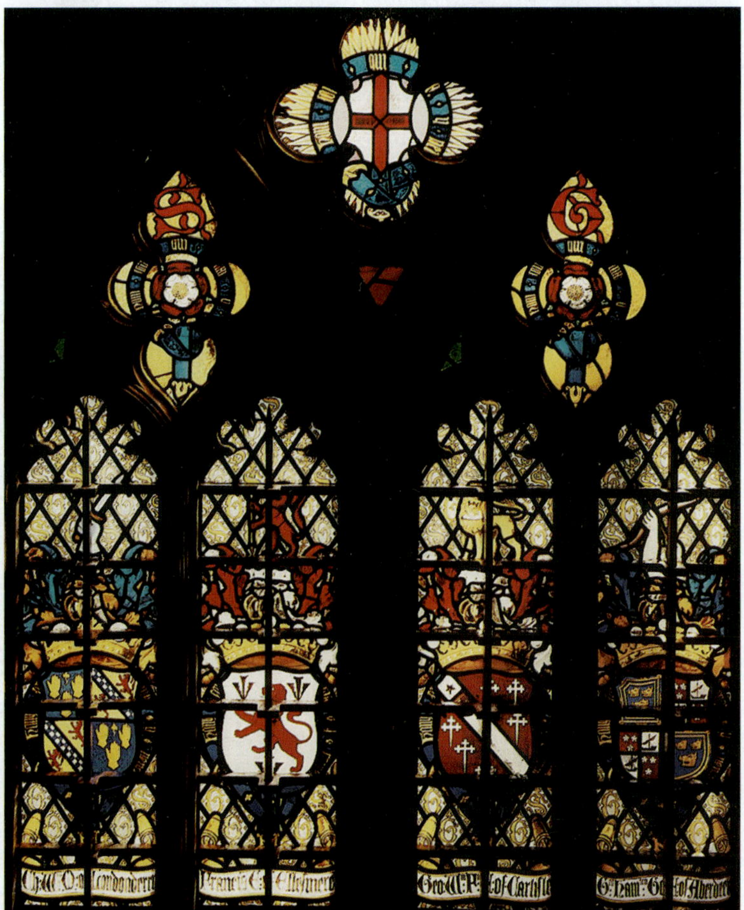

B. *Heraldic glass by Thomas Willement, SVII, 1856 (© Crown Copyright. NMR)*

PLATE VIII

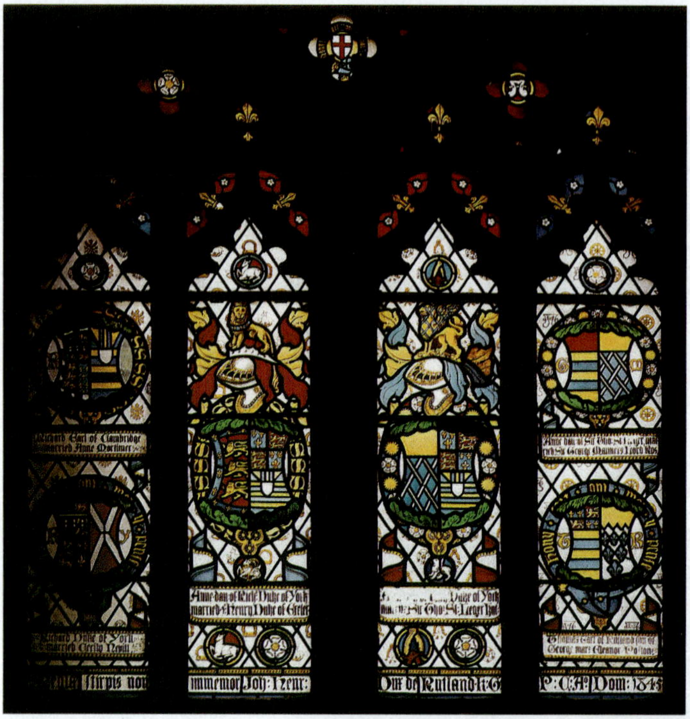

A. *Memorial to Ann, Duchess of Exeter, by Thomas Willement, nIII, 1845 (© Crown Copyright. NMR)*

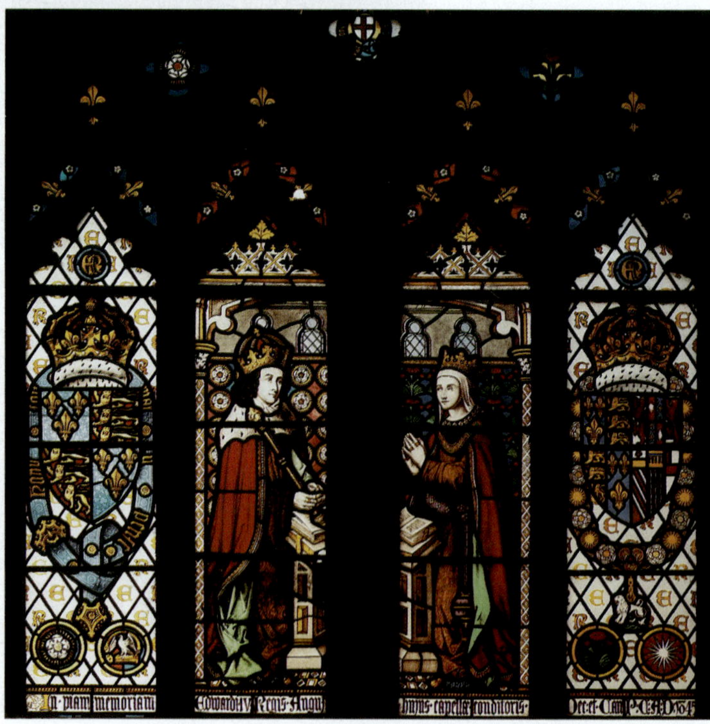

B. *Edward IV and Elizabeth Woodville by Thomas Willement, nII, 1845 (© Crown Copyright. NMR)*

PLATE IX

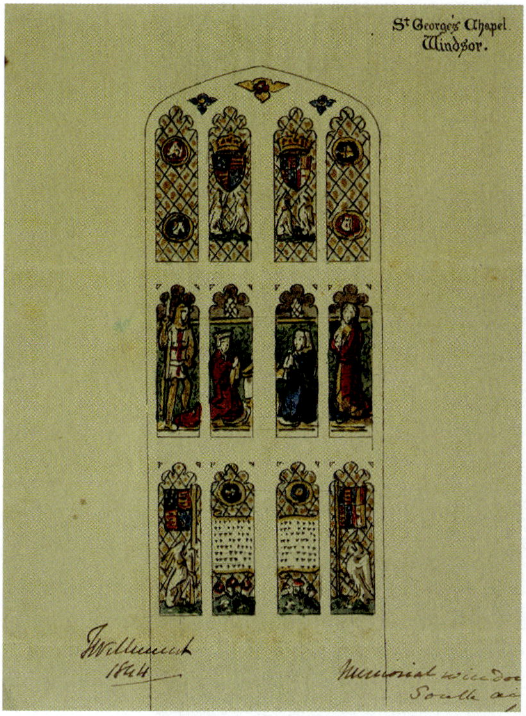

A. *Sketch design by Thomas Willement of the Henry VI and Margaret of Anjou window, sIX, 1844 in the SGC archives, XIV (Photo John Crook, © Dean and Canons of Windsor)*

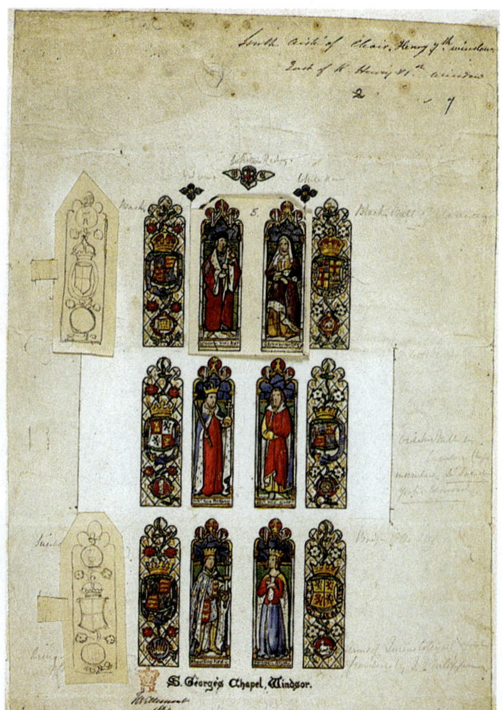

B. *Sketch design by Thomas Willement of the Edward III and Henry VII window, sVIII, 1846, British Library Add. MS 34872, f. 7 (Reproduced courtesy of the British Library)*

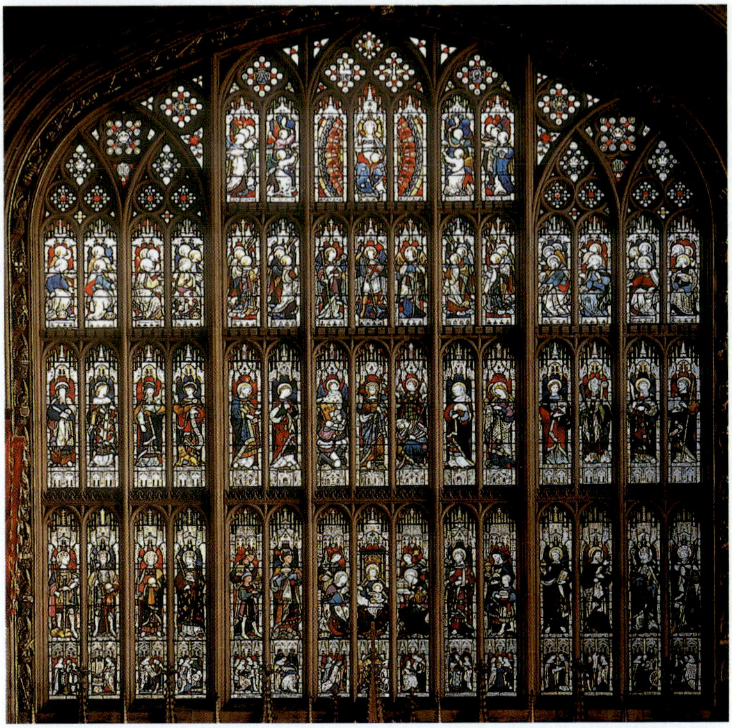

A. *The east window of the choir, the Prince Consort Memorial. Clayton & Bell, 1862–3 (Photo John Crook, © Dean and Canons of Windsor)*

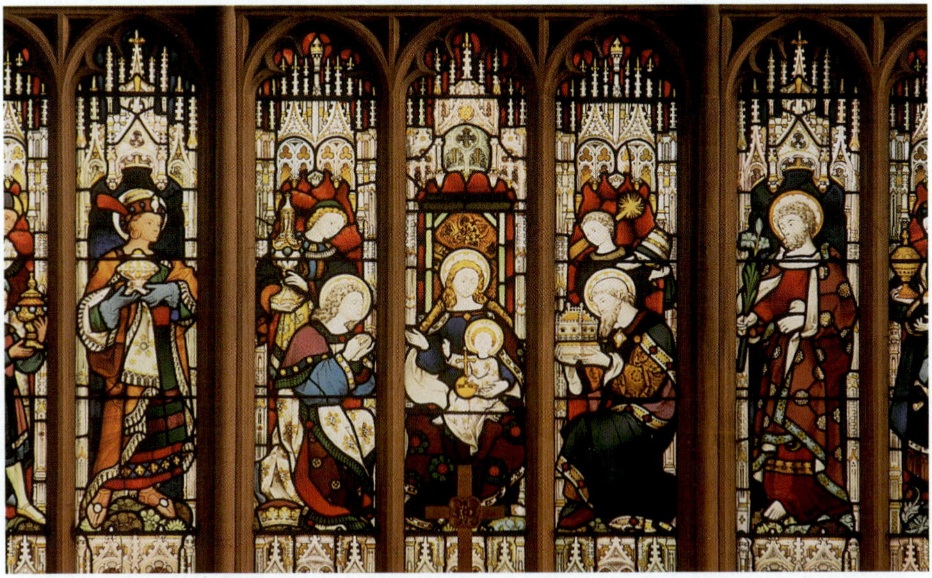

B. *The Adoration of the Magi in the east window by Clayton & Bell, 1862–3 (Photo John Crook, © Dean and Canons of Windsor)*

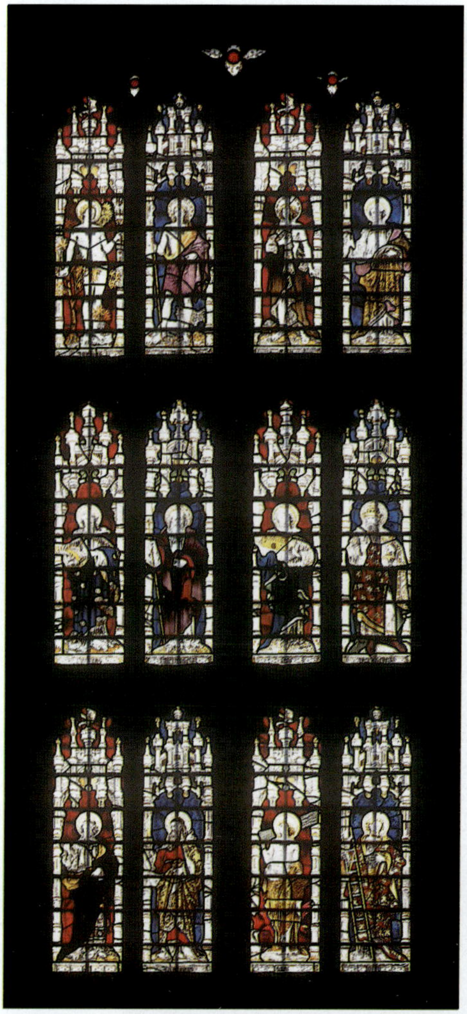

A. *Patriarchs and Prophets, nXXV, Clayton & Bell 1870 (Photo John Crook, © Dean and Canons of Windsor)*

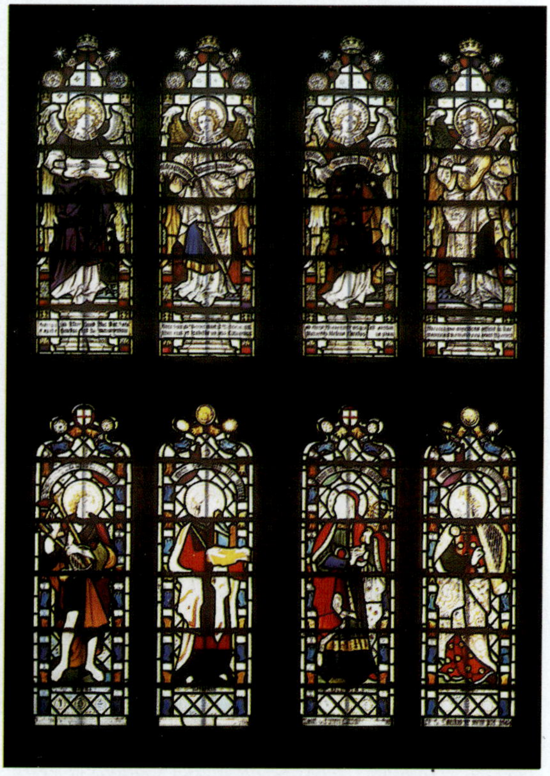

B. *The Rutland Chapel (nXI), Clayton & Bell 1865 & 1894 (Photo John Crook, © Dean and Canons of Windsor)*

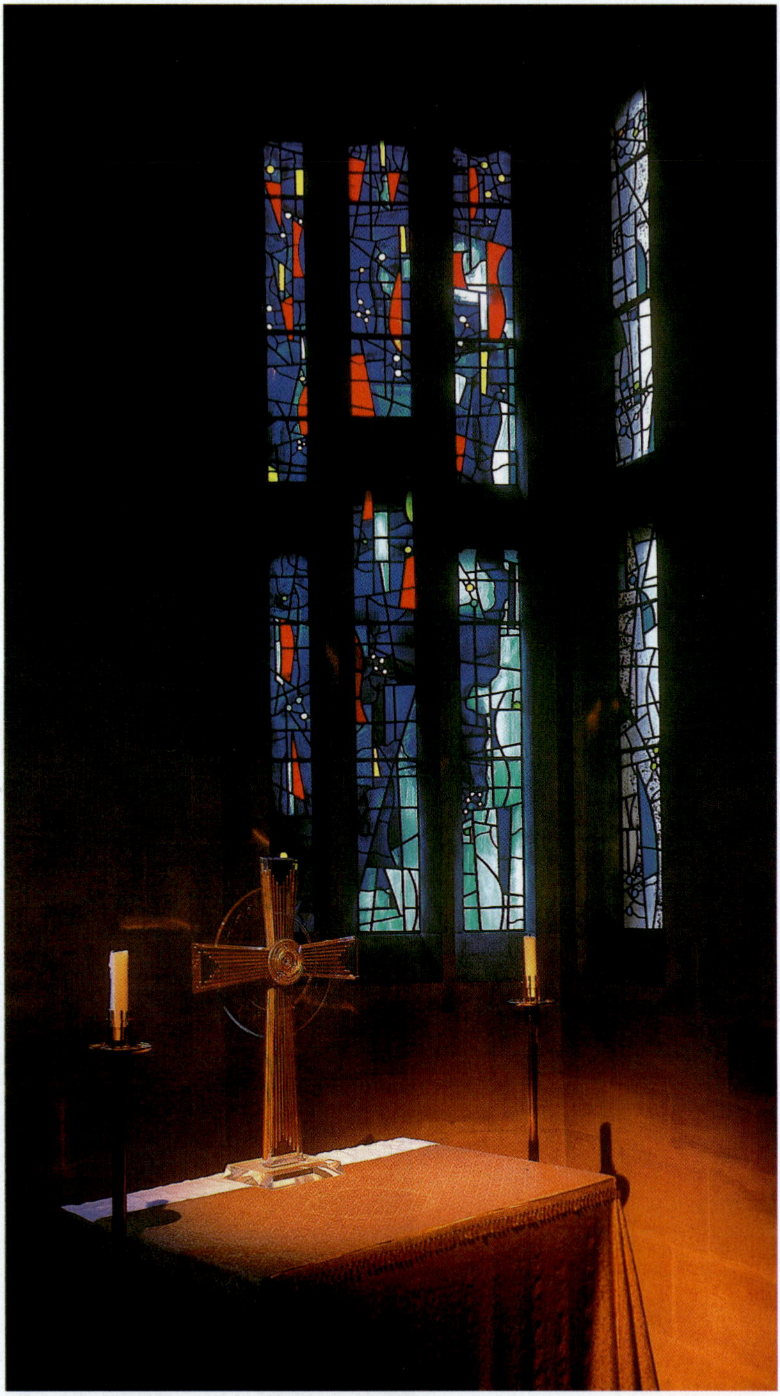

Interior of the George VI memorial chapel with windows by John Piper (Photo John Crook, © Dean and Canons of Windsor)

The Medieval Stained Glass

HILARY G. WAYMENT

THE GLAZING OF THE EARLIER CHAPEL BUILDINGS

The first chapel built on the site of the present Albert Memorial Chapel, dedicated to St Edward the Confessor, was erected by Henry III as part of a scheme of work in the lower ward begun in 1240. In 1248 Brother William the painter, monk of Westminster, was paid 100s for the painting of the chapel.[1] Nothing is said of the glazing of the chapel, although it is known that in 1236 the Queen's Lodging in the upper ward had been graced with a Tree of Jesse in the south gable window.[2] However, a survey of 1327 found that the chapel windows needed repair at an estimated cost of 200l, and this might suggest that there was figural glass in the window already.[3] No record of any actual repairs survives, however, and it may well be that nothing was done until after Edward III's return in 1347 from Crécy and the siege of Calais. It seems probable that it was in the summer of 1348 that he established the Order of the Garter; but between the autumn of that year and the end of 1349 the plague known as the Black Death raged, and is believed to have halved the country's population. So it was not until the spring of 1350 that the reconstruction of the chapel for a College of Canons and the spiritual home of the new Order could begin. The work included the building of a chapter-house and vestry. Meanwhile a team of glaziers impressed from the whole of southern England and the Midlands tackled the glazing of St Stephen's Chapel in the Palace of Westminster.[4] When this was finished, in March 1352, the team turned its attention to the painting of glass first for the chapter-house (much of it incorporated in the drawing room of the present deanery), and then for the chapel proper.[5] Roughly a score of glaziers worked on the chapel glass between June and December 1352, one or two at 'drawing of glass' or 'ordering of the glazing' at 12d a day, five to ten painting glass at 7d a day or 6½d a day and a dozen or so breaking, setting out and fixing it at 6d a day. In March 1353 the panels were packed at Westminster in boxes lined with hay and straw; about Michaelmas of the same year they were brought by barge to Windsor, and installed during the five weeks following. In all, the glazing of the chapel proper cost about 135l, not including the chapter-house, on which about 60l was spent. The total is suspiciously close to the estimate of 1327, and may well suggest that there was in fact no coloured glass in the windows before the mid-fourteenth century.

1. Virginia Jansen, 'Henry III's Windsor: Castle-building and residences', in Laurence Keen and Eileen Scarff, eds, *Windsor: Medieval Archaeology, Art and Architecture of the Thames Valley*, British Archaeological Association Transactions, Leeds 2002, pp. 102–5; *Architectural History*, i, p. 56.

2. *Architectural History*, i, p. 64.

3. *Architectural History*, i, p. 107.

4. L.F. Salzman, 'The Glazing of St Stephen's Chapel, Westminster 1351–2', *JBSMGP*, 1 (1926–7), pp. 14–16, 31–5, 38–41.

5. *Architectural History*, i, pp. 141–3; L.F. Salzman, 'Medieval Glazing Accounts', *JBSMGP*, 2 (1927–8), pp. 120 and 188.

In 1493–4 all but the lower parts of the west and north walls of this chapel were demolished at the orders of Henry VII. Between 1494 and 1498 a Lady Chapel and tomb chapel was rapidly constructed; it has been suggested that as the windows of this chapel were given pointed rather than Tudor heads, the fourteenth-century glass was transferred to them.[6] A few fragments of it may perhaps be identified in the east window of the former vestry, now the Deanery Chapel.

THE WEST WINDOW

All the surviving figural glass of medieval date in the chapel proper is now concentrated in the great west window (Fig. 1, Pl. I). How much of it was made for the window is open to question. This is one of the largest windows in any English church, measuring as it does 36ft in height and 29ft in width, and comprising just over 500 sq. ft (or nearly 50 sq. m) of stained glass, not including the tracery. The main lights contain seventy-five full-length figures in five rows of fifteen each. Sixty-eight are of late medieval origin, while seven date from the mid-nineteenth century. The canopies, side-shafts and pedestals, together with the backgrounds of the figures, the inscription at the foot of the window, and all the glass in the tracery, except a single coat of arms, are of the same date. The width of all the lights is 42 cm; in the lowest register the height of the openings is 179 cm and in all the others 153 cm.

The History of the Glass

Work on the new chapel had begun in the spring of 1477.[7] By the death of Edward IV in April 1483 the new choir was nearing completion, and in the following year, when the body of Henry VI was transferred to the south side of the sanctuary, the choir had been roofed but not vaulted and the choir stalls had been constructed. A partition wall separated the choir and its aisles from the unfinished nave. No further substantial progress was made until the period 1494–8 when a new Lady Chapel was constructed to the east. In 1498 plans to make this the site of Henry VI's shrine and Henry VII's tomb were abandoned in favour of ambitious plans for the Lady Chapel of Westminster Abbey. Consequently work on the main chapel was resumed. Some time in the 1490s the decision to build the nave one bay shorter than planned in 1475 had been made. The completion of the work owed much to the generosity of Sir Reginald Bray, close friend of Henry VII. In his will of August 1503, Sir Reginald had instructed his executors to draw on his assets and the income from his extensive estates for the completion of 'the werke of the new werkes of the body [i.e. the nave] of the church of the college . . . Within the Castell of Wyndesore . . . according and after the fourme and entent of the fundacion thereof as well in stone werke, tymbre, ledde, Iron, glasse and all other thinges necessary and requisite for the utter

6. Tim Tatton-Brown, 'The constructional sequence and topography of the Chapel and College buildings at St George's', in Colin Richmond and Eileen Scarff, eds, *St George's Chapel, Windsor, in the Late Middle Ages*, Historical Monographs relating to St George's Chapel, Windsor Castle 17, Windsor 2000, p. 16; John Harvey, 'The Architects of St George's Chapel. Part 2, The Fifteenth and Sixteenth Century', *Friends Report* (1962), p. 95.

7. The following account is indebted to Tatton-Brown, 'Constructional Sequence', cited in note 6 above.

performance of the same'.[8] Sir Reginald had already been concerned in a number of important glazing campaigns from 1480 onwards, in particular the west window of Peterborough Cathedral and the royal window of *c.* 1500 in the façade of the north transept at Great Malvern Priory.[9]

The nave was structurally complete and the vault in hand by 1506, for on 5 June of that year John Hylmer and William Vertue signed a contract to build the choir vault 'according to the roof of the body of the said College', undertaking to complete it by Christmas 1508.[10] At the time of Henry VII's death in April 1509 only the crossing remained unvaulted. The installation of the stained glass is unlikely therefore to have started before 1506 in the nave and 1509 in the choir, though the choir aisle windows might have been glazed some years earlier.

No records of the subsequent history of the glass before the later eighteenth century are available; but it may be surmised, from the survival of the figures of over twenty popes and the complete absence of any original canopy-work or side-shafting, that all the figures were hastily removed and stored away during the Civil War.[11]

Apart from the mention of the glazing in Bray's will, the earliest documentary evidence about the glass dates only from 1767. A decision of the Chapter on 18 April of that year reads:

> The great Western window of the Chapel being out of repair, order'd that the Stone-work be made good, and the window repair'd with such Painted Glass, as can be collected from the other parts of the chapel.[12]

The work was entrusted to one William Kimberley, twice mayor of Windsor, under the direction of Canon John Lockman. Kimberley had, in fact, begun the work on 30 March; he finished it on 10 October and submitted his bill.[13]

To new leading repairing and making Good 69 Figures for the West Window with Coloured Glass some new to the Borders and Pedistals to D° at £1 3sh p. Figure	£79. 7. 0
To 10 Lights[14] made with the Arms for the sides of the West Window new Coloured Glass for the Borders and some pieces of ornament to D° at £1 5sh a piece	£12.10. 0
To 79 crockets made all of new Coloured Glass for the Tops of the Figures and Lights with the Arms to D° at 7 sh a piece	£27.13. 0
To making good and filling and Gothic Work at Top of the West Window with new Coloured Glass 62 lights	£20

The total amount, exclusive of Kimberley's other work in the chapel, amounted to £139 10s 0d. This account shows that there were sixty-nine intact figures available, with pedestals (alluding probably only to the tiled grounds), but without canopies, which were made up by Kimberley. Four of the figures were evidently set in the four top openings, in the sixth register, leaving ten, or two full lights, to be garnished with heraldic pieces

8. *Architectural History*, ii, p. 384.
9. R.C. Marks, 'The Stained Glass Patronage of Sir Reginald Bray', *Friends Report* (1974), pp. 199–202.
10. *Architectural History*, ii, pp. 460–1; Tatton-Brown, 'Constructional Sequence', pp. 18–23.
11. A.C. Deane, 'Notes on the West Window', *Friends Report* (1940), pp. 8–9.
12. *Architectural History*, ii, p. 454, from Register of Chapter Acts.
13. SGC XVII.61.10.
14. Kimberley uses this word in the sense of 'openings', or spaces bounded by stonework; the present practice of architectural historians is to use the word 'light' of the whole space between two millions, as far as the spring of the arch, however many openings it may comprise.

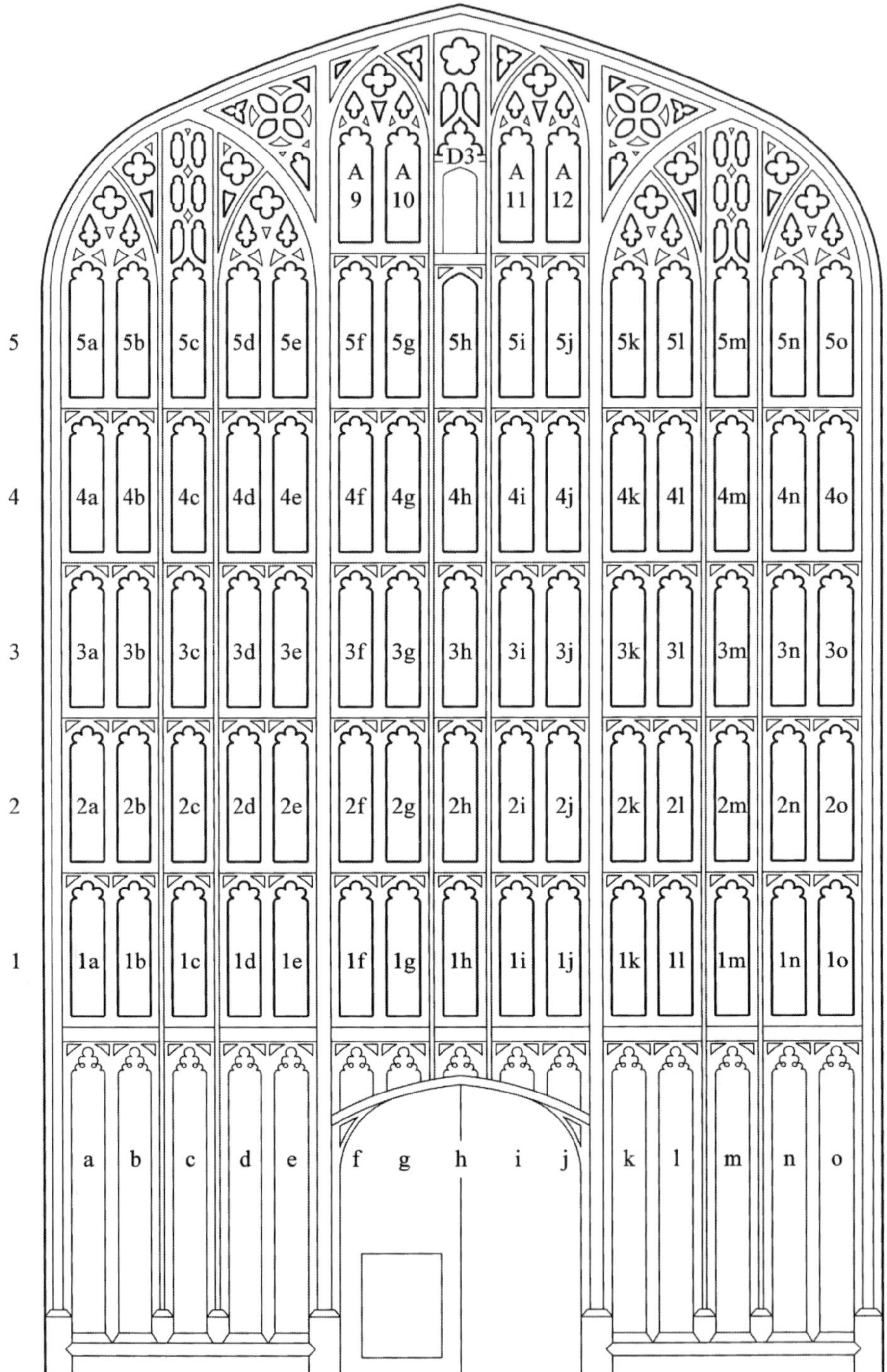

Fig. 1. *The west window. Notation of window openings (Drawn by Andy Donald)*

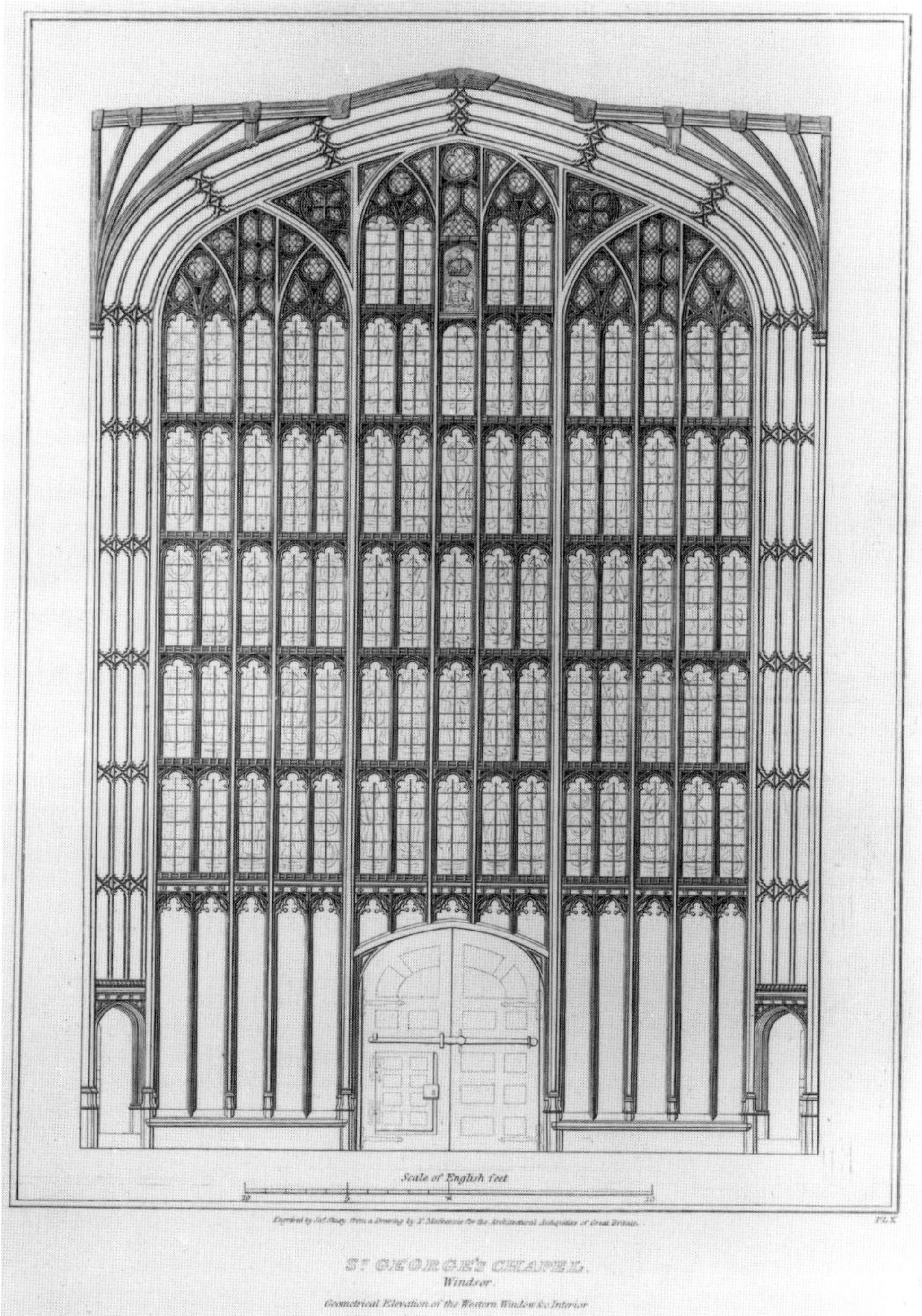

Fig. 2. *West window. Engraving of elevation by James Shury from a drawing by F. MacKenzie, 1 July 1820 (© Crown Copyright. NMR)*

('Arms'), as is in fact implied in the words of the Chapter Act 'such Painted Glass as can be collected from the other parts of the chapel'. These may, however, have been eked out by brash new glass, as will be seen from a later account. Kimberley had working with him an assistant named Spicer, an apprentice and (at most) three labourers.[15] The Dean and Chapter considered Kimberley's charges excessive and in 1768 secured estimates from two other glaziers, Nathaniel Stephens and Robert Crook, which were between £50 and £60 lower; they confirm, incidentally, that Kimberley did install sixty-nine figures. Then Kimberley's lawyer sends a stiff letter, and two further estimates are sought, which prove to be less categorical. The Dean describes Kimberley as 'a rascal and a rogue', but recommends that he should be paid only £12 less than he demanded; and there the matter ends.

An early nineteenth-century engraving,[16] however (Fig. 2), shows only fifty-nine figures, not sixty-nine, and twenty openings, or four lights out of the fifteen, filled apparently with heraldic arrangements. The ten missing figures may well have been taken out in 1777 by the anonymous glazier whose estimate for further repairs, amounting to £15 18s 3d, was accepted by the Chapter on 25 August of that year.[17] Then, about 1796, George III proposed to replace the glass in the window by a Crucifixion designed by Benjamin West; the work was entrusted to a glazier named Forrest, who died before finishing the window, so that it was never installed.[18] By 1841, however, the stonework was in need of repair, and the window had to be removed. In the following year Thomas Willement devised and installed a new scheme, at a cost of £520;[19] he described the new arrangement as follows:

> The glass occupying the openings, was of the time of king Henry VII, consisted partly of fifty-nine figures of saints, prophets, kings, and knights, all of which had been removed to this window from various parts of the chapel in 1774[a] by the Rev. Dr. Lockman, canon, who had placed the figures on a ground of clear white glass; the remaining openings were filled by reticulated patterns in common and glaring colours, placed also on clear glass.[b] Still, with all its defects, this window, particularly towards the time of sunset, had from its great dimensions a very imposing and pleasing effect. The removal of the glass being necessary previous to the renewal of the stone work, it was thought desirable to make some considerable alterations in its arrangement. It was found that *ten* more of the ancient figures still remained in the stores of the chapter;[c] with these, and by the addition of six new effigies,[d] the glaziers' patterns were excluded,[e] and every opening became then occupied by a whole length figure. The plain ground of white was removed, and superseded by ancient diaper patterns in a quiet tone of drab; rich canopies, columns, and bases were added to each figure, and on a scroll which now runs through the whole of the bases of the lowest compartments is inscribed the prayer peculiar to the service in this chapel: *God save our gracious sovereign, and all the companions of the most honourable and noble Order of the Garter.* The arched part of the window head has been filled by royal badges on grounds of rich colour, with four large compartments in the centre containing the devices of king Edward III, king Edward IV, king Henry VII, and queen Elizabeth; all of whom were particularly connected with the architectural history of the chapel and castle of Windsor.[f]

15. SGC XVII.61.10(B).

16. Engraved by James Sherry from a drawing by F. Mackenzie for the *Architectural Antiquities of Great Britain* and published on 1 July 1810.

17. *Architectural History*, ii, p. 454. The sum was included with an estimate for the repair of the stonework of the window, amounting to £250 18s 7d; it was presented by Henry Emblin, or Emlyn, the carver (Hope, Index, *s.v.*).

18. Discussed by D.R. Baylis in Chapter 3.

19. SGC XVII.61.21.

This passage requires some detailed comment:

[a] Dr Lockman's scheme was carried out, as we have seen, in 1767.

[b] The words 'reticulated patterns in common and glaring colours' may imply that the 'Arms' Kimberley installed were eked out with brash modern glass, such as that still to be found in the north windows of the Edward IV Chantry and the east window of the Annex to it. This was evidently installed (by an anonymous glazier) in 1782 (see p. 57 below).

[c] Willement was clearly unaware that these ten figures had been included in the arrangement of 1767, and subsequently removed.

[d] There are in fact seven new figures of nineteenth-century date. Willement must have cannibalized one defective figure; several of those at present in the window are composite. The four original figures previously in the large openings above the spring of the arch were re-set in the main lights, so as to make up the number to seventy-five.

[e] That is, the 'reticulated patterns' mentioned above were removed.

[f] The third royal badge above the spring of the arch is inscribed *H VIII*; but the devices at the foot refer to Henry VII, in accordance with Willement's expressed intention. The *VIII* must be the glazier's error for *VII*.

Willement's arrangement of the figures was clearly intended to give the window as much variety as possible by alternating the different categories; and this scheme was maintained when the glass was replaced after removal during the war of 1914–18.

In 1929, however, the Provost of Eton, Dr M.R. James, put forward what he considered a more logical arrangement, which would bring all the popes together in the five southern lights, and keep the other categories grouped as far as possible in the central and northern lights, while setting the more interesting and identifiable figures low down in the window.[20] This proposal, coming from such an eminent authority, proved acceptable, and was largely put into effect in 1930. Ten years later, towards the end of 1940, the glass was removed by Wilfred Drake; when he replaced it, in November 1945, he completed James's scheme, with only minor modifications. Before re-installation each panel was photographed separately by S.A. Pitcher, and many of his photographs are reproduced in the present book.

Description

The window as it is today combines a certain monotony in composition with outstanding brilliance and variety of colour. Of the seventy-five figures, twenty-five (or twenty-six) represent popes, seventeen are kings, eleven (or twelve) are knights, ten are archbishops or bishops, and eight are saints, of whom two are female and six male. These seventy-two are all nimbed. There remain three civilians, of whom one (2i) has been fitted with the nimbed head of a king (Fig. 11).

Something needs to be said about the costume of the main groups of figures. The knights wear variants of the standard early Tudor armour: cuirass, taces, mail skirt, cuisses, genouillieres and jambs; sabatons or round-toed shoes, and either mantles or tabards with the cross of St George, and even the Garter with motto. The kings wear mantles and often

20. Letter of 29 March (Good Friday) 1929 to the architect Harold Brakspear, SGC M.29.

ermine cape-collars over full-length robes, and carry sceptre or sword; in three or four cases they have attributes by which they can be identified.

Among the popes St Peter stands out, wearing only a plain white tunicle belted in and hitched up under his cope so as to reveal the bare feet of an apostle (1a, Fig. 3). The rest, with but one or two exceptions, wear tiara, tight-sleeved alb, richly coloured dalmatic or tunicle and cope joined by a morse or plain band; in many cases the amice of fur can be seen at the neck. One surprising exception is the martial pope (3n, Fig. 4), who wears Tudor armour under his cope, brandishes a sword in one hand, and carries a book in the other.[21]

Of the archbishops only one original figure (3h) wears the chasuble and the pallium (plus two of Willement's creation); most of them wear copes over their dalmatics. One bishop, like the martial pope, wears Tudor armour and a princely helmet, while carrying both book and crozier (2f, Fig. 5).

The colour in the original glass, as indeed in the restorations, is varied, and there is none of that excessive reliance on paint and stain which was so common in the general run of English fifteenth-century glass. Potmetal and flashed glass are lavishly used: both crimson and vermilion ruby; plum, puce and lilac-pink; blue, rich or dull, light or dark, and much grey-blue; amber, dark or light, with brown and yellow potmetal; and many shades of green, rich, drab or pale, with light or dark olive and lime-green as well. Apart from the backgrounds, which are Willement's, white glass is used in moderation, with many shades of yellow stain for crowns, tiaras, crosses and accoutrements. The general effect is exceptionally rich and satisfying.

The glass has in the course of nearly five centuries suffered not inconsiderable damage and decay. To this not only the composite figures such as the king at 1j bear witness, but also the heads with features erased, such as King Edmund's at 1g, or the extensive stop-gaps, as for instance in the robes of Edward the Confessor (1h, Fig. 9). The stop-gaps are the main, if not the only, surviving evidence of the eighteenth-century restoration.

Then in 1842 Willement introduced not only seven new figures, but also twenty new heads and numerous other additions to clothes or limbs. Of these, three figures and nine heads (including 2f, Fig. 5) are by the 'wide-eyed' glazier, as he is here called, eight heads (e.g. 2g, by the 'delicate' glazier, and two figures and three heads (e.g. 3j, Fig. 6) by the so-called 'meagre' glazier. Some at least of the new heads must have followed the design of fragmented originals which were copied and then discarded (e.g. 1m). Of the seven modern figures one is a king (3f), three are archbishops (4f, 4j, and 5f), two are knights (3o and 5l), and one a saint (5k); five of these copy other, original figures, and two archbishops (4f, Fig. 43, and 4j) were no doubt designed and painted by Willement himself.

Drake, in 1940, discovered a series of graffiti scratched on the outside of the window, as follows:

T Tozer Exeter F Burrow Lancaster
G Lingley London E Colegate Faversham
B Gilestone Braintree T Healey London
Glaziers London Sept 1842
T Willement Esq Master

21. Another figure, 2g, may represent either a knight or a second martial pope.

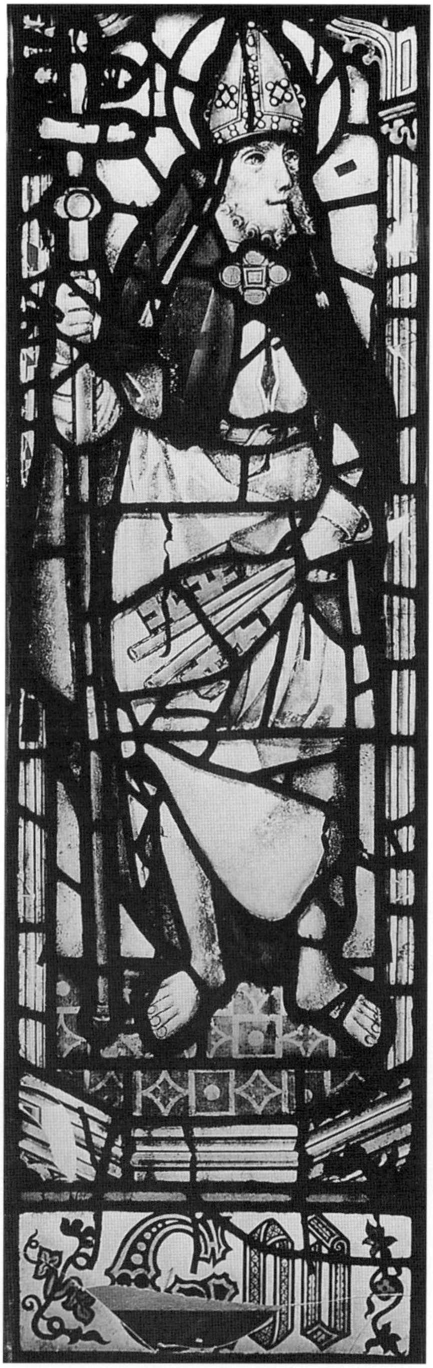

Fig. 3. *1a, St Peter as Pope (Photo by Sydney Pitcher, c. 1940, © Dean and Canons of Windsor)*

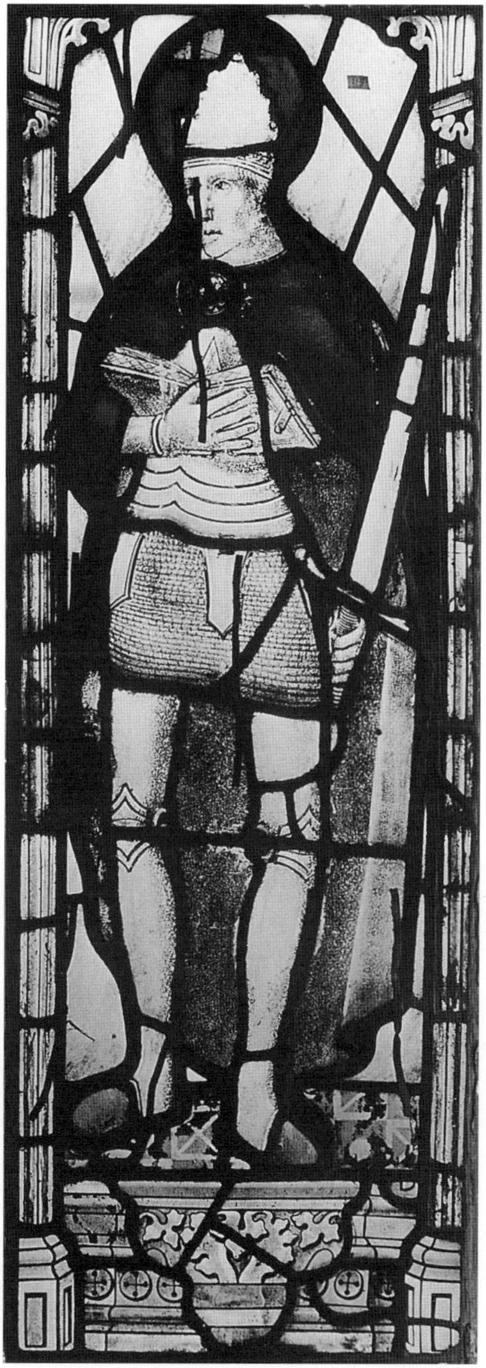

Fig. 4. *3n, martial pope (Photo by Sydney Pitcher, c. 1940, © Dean and Canons of Windsor)*

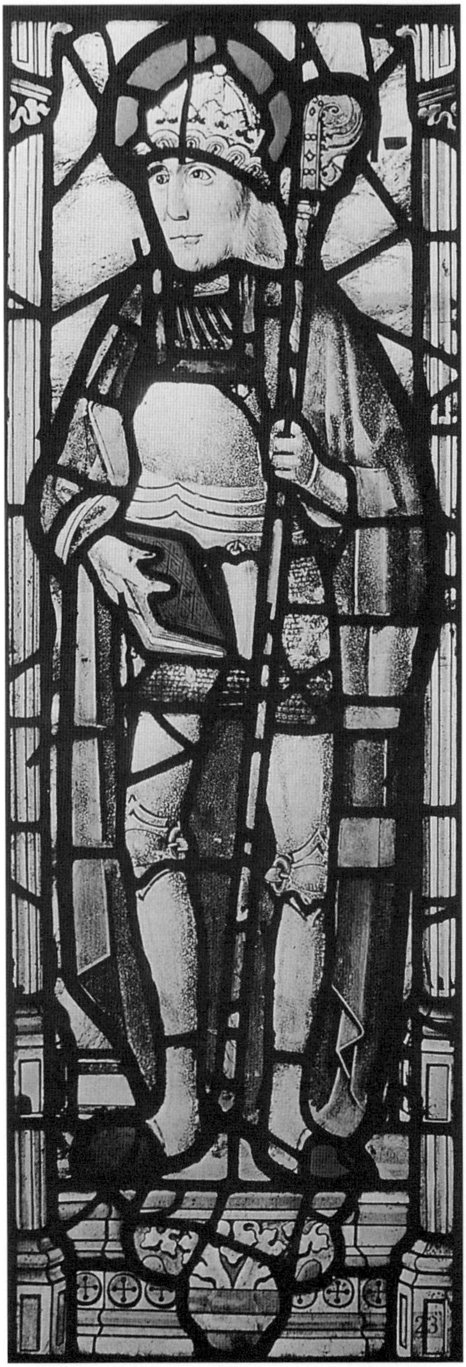

Fig. 5. *2f, martial prince-bishop (Photo by Sydney Pitcher,* c. *1940, © Dean and Canons of Windsor)*

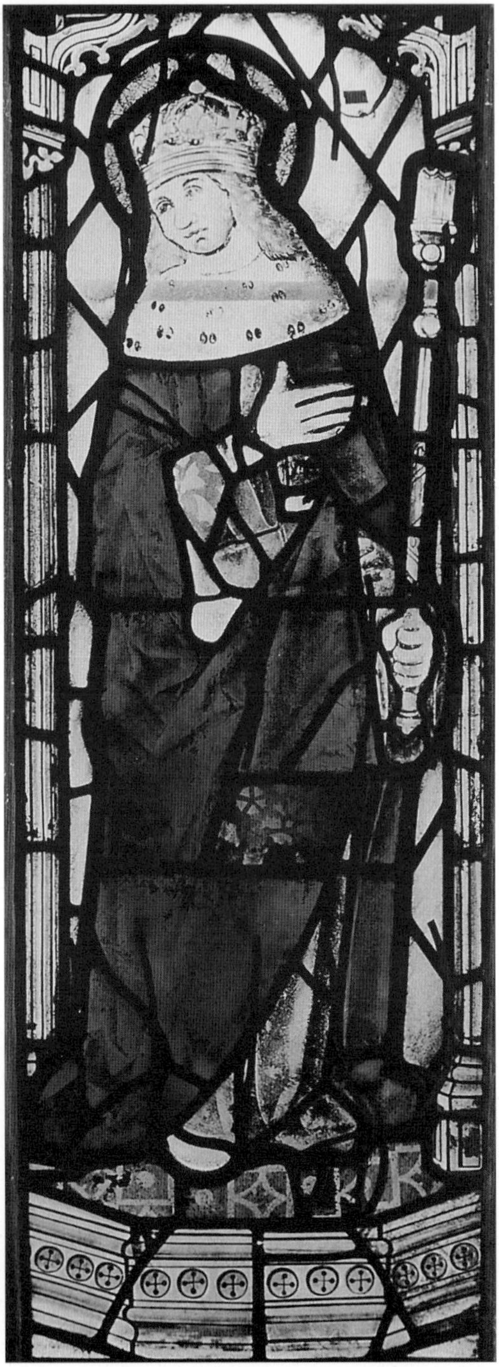

Fig. 6. *3j, king (Photo by Sydney Pitcher,* c. *1940, © Dean and Canons of Windsor)*

and in another place; 'T Healey Glazier fixed this window 1842'.[22] Which of these signatories, however, were responsible for painting the restorations there is nothing to indicate. Intrusions and restorations probably amount to about a quarter of the glass composing the actual figures.

Design, Style and Dating

Discussion of the design, style and dating of the figures must largely be based on comparisons with the surviving work from two glazing campaigns which cover a period from the last year or two of the fifteenth century to the summer of 1509: the first at St Mary's Fairford, and the second in Christ's College Chapel, Cambridge. The royal figures at Christ's must have been delivered by the summer of 1509, when Lady Margaret Beaufort, foundress of the college, died; later in the year her executors made a payment to a certain 'Simon Glasier', and this Simon has been shown to be identical with Simon Symondes, an Englishman from the provinces who with Francis Williamson, a leading Flemish immigrant, contracted in 1526 to glaze four windows in King's College Chapel, Cambridge, that are still extant.[23] For the glass at Fairford, by contrast, no firm dates can be given, since no documents survive which even mention the windows before 1630; but it seems probable that the early glass there, comprising the histories of Christ and of Mary, together with the west windows, the *Persecutors* in the north clerestory and the Creed series of apostles, was completed in a speedy campaign about the time of Prince Arthur's wedding to Catherine of Aragon on 14 November 1501.[24]

At St George's Wilfred Drake claimed to see early work in five figures, two popes and three of the kings,[25] Deane described six figures (which he does not specify) as being smaller than the rest and attributes them to James Skynke, who in 1481 was paid a year's fee of 10l as glazier to the college.[26] However, the five figures singled out by Drake are painted by five different hands, and the six shortest prove to be a very mixed lot indeed. It is in fact possible to distinguish a number of stylistic groups, several of which are related to work at Fairford and Cambridge. Some of these consist of only one or two items, while others are much larger.

1. The king at 3g, holding a book in his right hand, and a sword, point grounded, in his left (Fig. 7). This is the work of the so-called Judas master, who later painted the figure of Judas in the north clerestory at Fairford (Fig. 8), and was also responsible for the twelve apostles in the south aisle, a series which he evidently left unfinished, since one whole figure and four heads had to be added by four other glaziers, two of whom also worked on the Windsor glass.[27] The combination of straight hair in the beard with ringlets in the hair

22. SGC XVII.43.30. These names were rediscovered and photographed from an exterior scaffold in May 2000.

23. R. Willis and J.W. Clark, *Architectural History of the University of Cambridge*, Cambridge 1886, ii, p. 195; Hilary Wayment, *The Windows of King's College Chapel, Cambridge*, Corpus Vitrearum Medii Aevi, Great Britain, Suppl. Vol. i, London 1972, pp. 1, 15, 25.

24. Hilary Wayment, *The Stained Glass of the Church of St Mary, Fairford. Gloucestershire*, Society of Antiquaries, Occasional Paper, ns, v, London 1984, pp. 94–6.

25. SGC XVII.43.30.

26. Deane 'Notes on the West Window', p. 9; *Architectural History*, ii, p. 403.

27. NVb: Wayment, *Fairford*, pp. 78, 89, 93 and pls XXXVII and LVa.

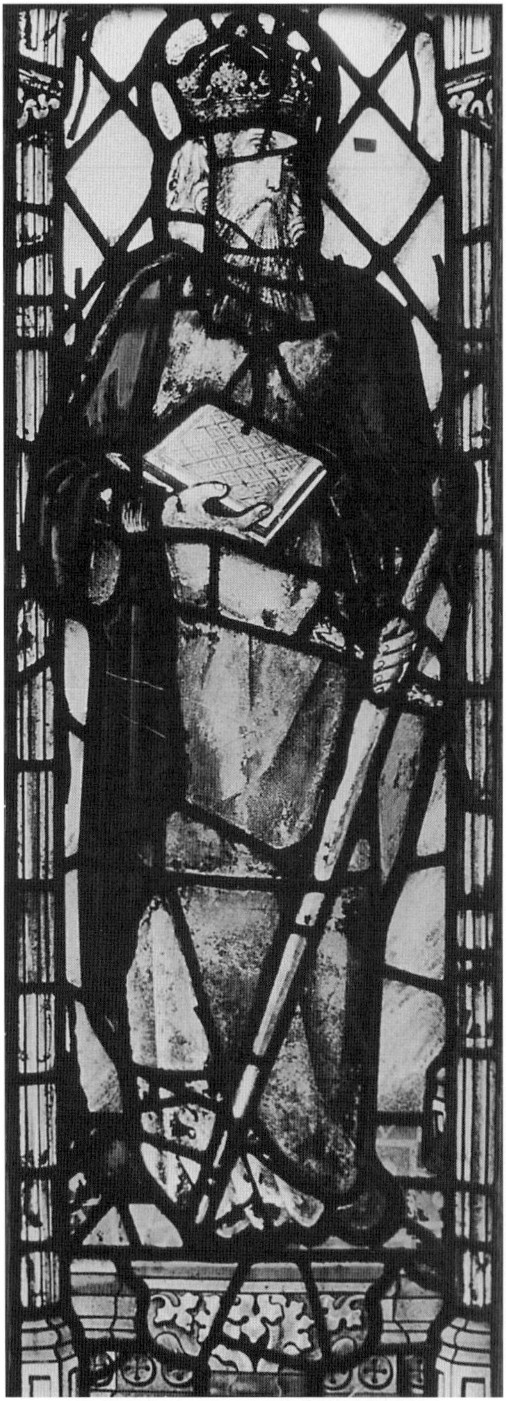

Fig. 7. *3g, king (Photo by Sydney Pitcher, c. 1940, © Dean and Canons of Windsor)*

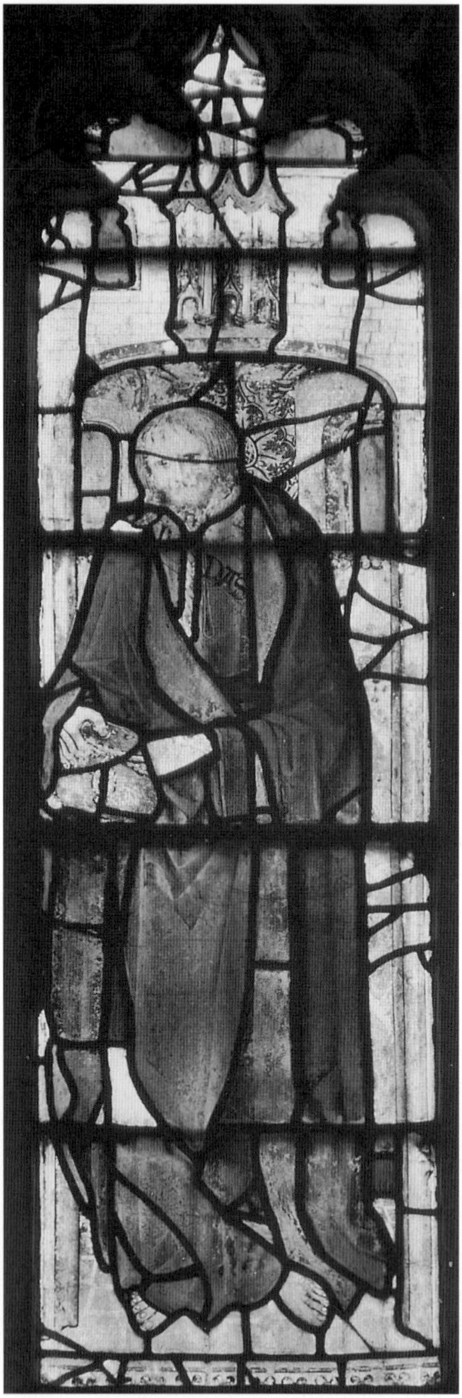

Fig. 8. *St Mary, Fairford, NV, Judas (© Crown Copyright. NMR)*

establishes this royal figure as his earliest extant glass, since at Fairford straight hair and curls are more skilfully integrated.[28] This glazier may be identical with the Cornelius Meelys, evidently a Netherlander, who is mentioned three times in the accounts of Thomas Warley referring to work done at Westminster Palace and in the City in the years 1500–2.[29] The flaying-knife of St Bartholomew at Fairford has a C inscribed on its blade, and in Warley's list, which probably includes most of the glaziers of the Southwark/Westminster School who were active at that time, Meelys is the only one with a first name beginning with C. He appears to have been less important than the two outstanding glaziers who follow. The only other trace of his work at Windsor is in the feeble feet attached to the anonymous saint at 50. The apostles' windows at Fairford all carry ostrich feathers with *ich dene* in the tracery, and it seems not unlikely that they were hastily finished about the time of Arthur and Catherine's wedding, which took place on 14 November 1501, or possibly after Arthur's death on 2 April 1502, as a memorial to him. The king's figure and the saint's feet at Windsor probably date from the last year or two of the fifteenth century.

2. A far more important group is that for which the author of the St Edward the Confessor (1h, Fig. 9) was responsible. He must also have painted the upper part of the king at 1j (Fig. 32) and the head attached to the civilian at 2i (Fig. 11). In addition, his designing hand is readily discernible in the figures of at least nine knights,[30] of a pope (3n, Fig. 4) and of a martial figure (2f, Fig. 5) who wears a princely crown and carries a crozier (both restored). The figures carrying swords pointed upwards at the ready (2g, 2o, Fig. 10, 3e, 3m, 3n, Fig. 4, and 4k) seem to precede and anticipate the vigorous figures of persecutors in the north nave clerestory at Fairford (Fig. 12), while their slender bandy legs and splayed feet, with knees set almost at right angles, seem to be at least as early as the standing figures in the eastern windows there. On the assumption that the early glass at Fairford, including the interwoven histories of Christ and of the Virgin Mary, was designed and painted to celebrate the forthcoming marriage of Arthur and Catherine, a plausible, not to say probable date for the design of the east and west windows there would be 1500. The figure of Edward the Confessor (1h, Fig. 9) and the bearded heads in 1j and 2i (Figs 32 and 11), which must be attributed to the master himself, seem to be roughly contemporary with the head of St James the Great which he must have contributed, probably before April 1502, to the series of apostles at Fairford (Fig. 13).

These four heads exhibit a new technique for rendering grey hair: instead of painting each lock of hair separately, and then lightening it with a stick or needle, as was usual up to this time, the glazier covers the whole area with a wash and then lines out the locks with a scrub or worn-out brush, thus letting much more light pass through the glass. It must have been some years afterwards, perhaps *c.* 1508, that he designed the figure of the mason (Figs 17 and 35): some of the most robust and impressive of the popes probably date from the next decade, *c.* 1514–15 (1b, 1e, 2a (Fig. 14), 2d (Fig. 15), 2e and 3a).

28. For example, in the 'hybrid Apostle' of sVIII.

29. A. Oswald, 'Barnard Flower, the King's Glazier', *JBSMGP*, xi, 1 (1951–2), pp. 10–12.

30. Of the nine knights six have lost their heads, and one is entirely modern. The two which survive more or less intact are 2o and 4k. The first was painted by the St Peter glazier, and the second by the painter of the mason (Io).

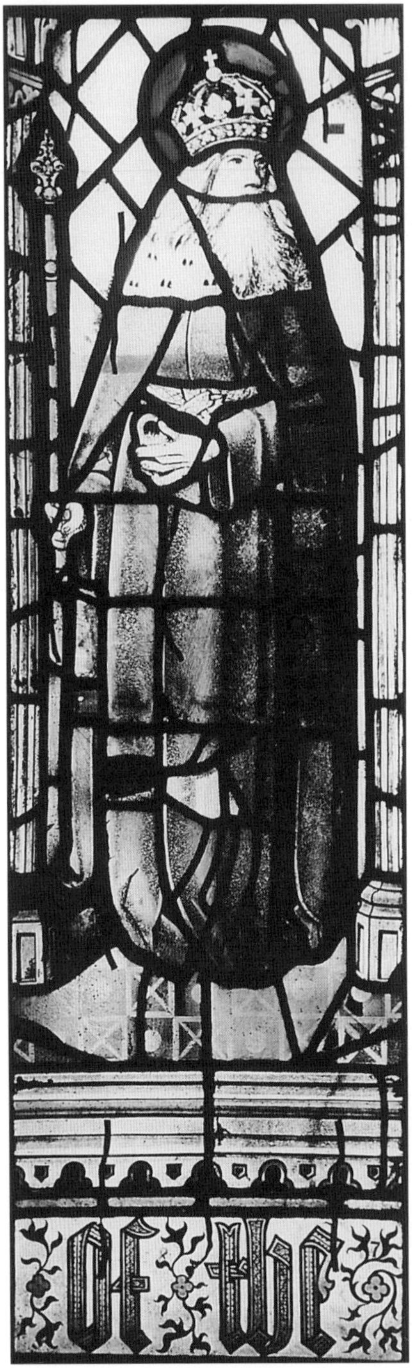

Fig. 9. *1h, King Edward the Confessor (Photo by Sydney Pitcher, c. 1940, © Dean and Canons of Windsor)*

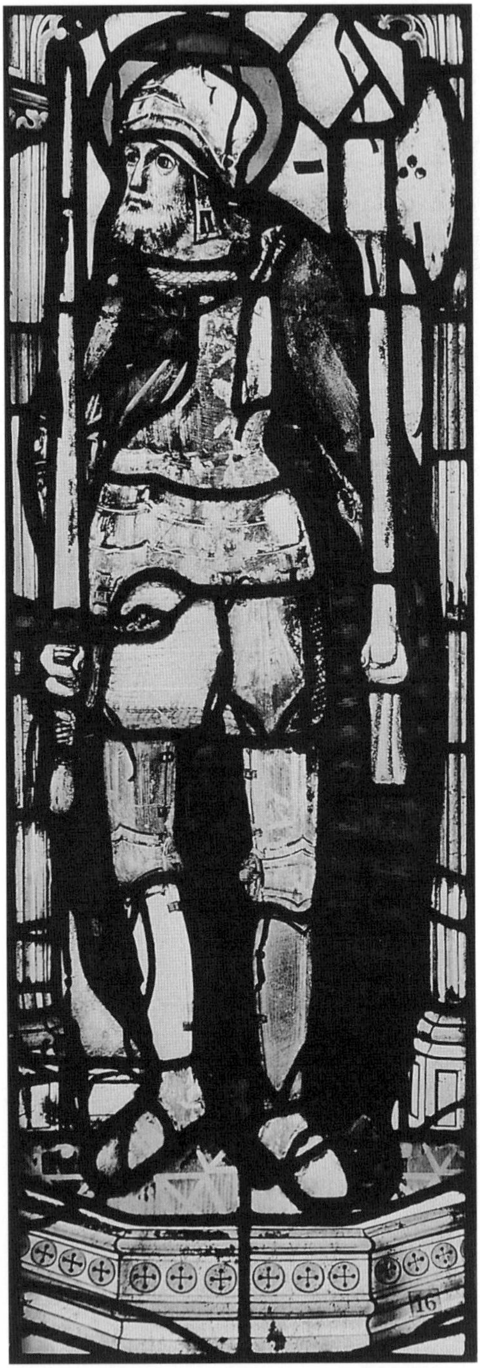

Fig. 10. *20, knight (Photo by Sydney Pitcher, c. 1940, © Dean and Canons of Windsor)*

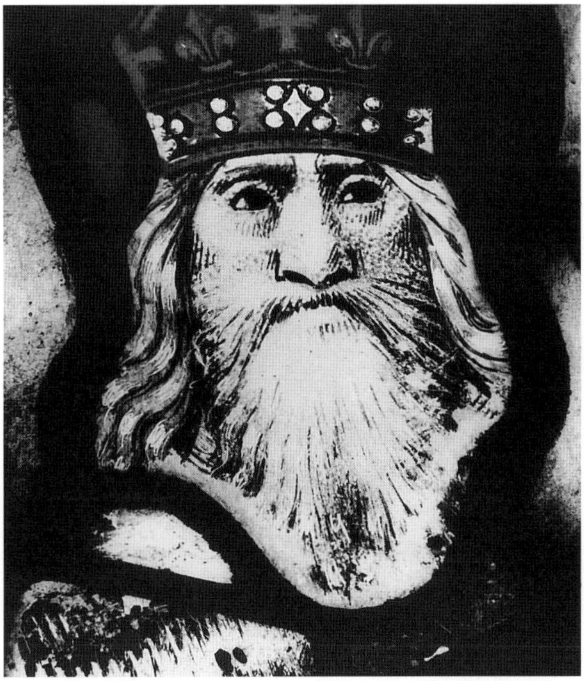

Fig. 11. *2i, intruded head of a king (© R.C. Marks)*

This designer-glazier is probably to be identified with the man who is cited five times in Warley's accounts of 1500–2, in particular as the provider, together with the king's glazier, Barnard Flower, of 280 ft of Normandy glass for the adornment of the hall of the bishop of London's palace on the occasion of the banquet held there after the wedding of Arthur and Catherine.[31] His name is given as 'Adrian Andrew'; this is almost certainly an English corruption of Adrian Vandenhoute, the name of a glazier from Mechlin who lived from about 1459 until 1521 and who appears to have been the outstanding designer/glazier of his time in the Netherlands.[32] After his visit *c.* 1500–2 he can be traced about 1505–6 in Rouen; but he probably came to England twice more, in 1508–9 and in 1515. There are such close stylistic links between the early glass at Fairford on the one hand, and in King's College Chapel on the other, that his responsibility for the designs used at Cambridge in the first period of glazing, 1515–17, can be assumed. But the work at Cambridge was itself linked closely with an earlier series now lost, which stood in the upper windows of the Henry VII Chapel at Westminster Abbey, and is known from the king's will, to have been designed before April 1509.[33] Flower, in 1515, had contracted to tell 'the Story of the olde lawe and of (the) newe lawe after the fourme maner goodenes curyousytie and clenelynes in every poynt of the glasse wyndowes of the kynges newe Chapelle at Westmynster',[34]

31. Oswald, 'Barnard Flower', p. 10.

32. Wayment, 'A rediscovered master: Adrian van den Houte (*c.* 1459–1521) and the Malines/Brussels School, i, A solution to the "Ortkens" problem', *Oud Holland*, lxxxii (1967), pp. 172–202. The 'ou' in 'houte' was pronounced to rhyme with route and not rout.

33. T. Astle, *The Will of King Henry VII*, London 1775, p. 6.

34. Wayment, *Windows of King's Chapel*, p. 124.

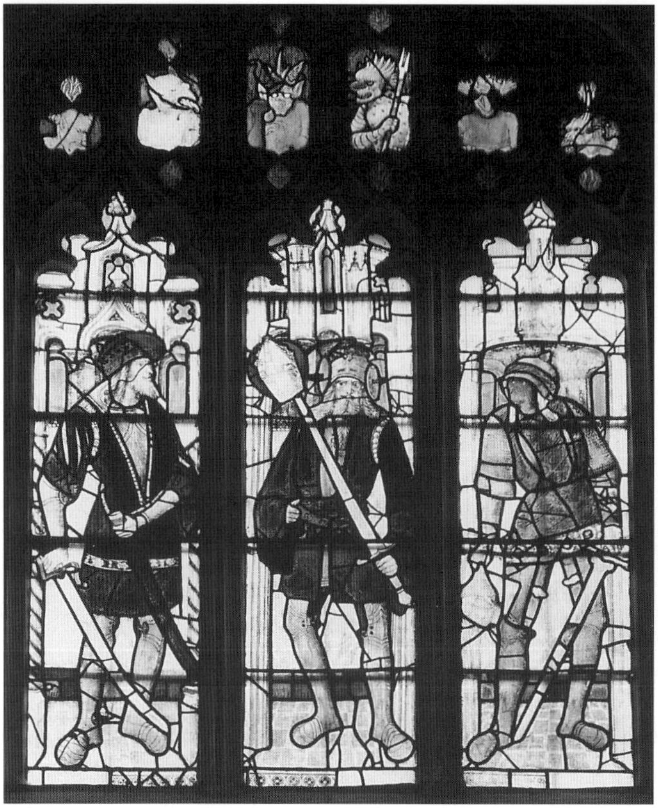

Fig. 12. *St Mary, Fairford, NIII, The Persecutors of the Faith (© Crown Copyright. NMR)*

Fig. 13. *St Mary, Fairford, sVI, St James the Great, detail (H.G. Wayment)*

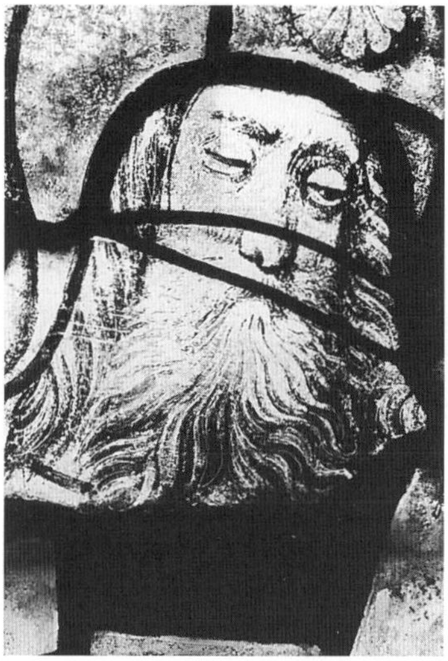

and there could be no better way of beginning this task than to secure designs from the same source.

There are two series of figures at Windsor which are much more solid and robust than the early bandy-legged knights, and may well have been designed a decade or more later. The first, by far the more numerous, includes the mason (10), the pope in profile (2a, Fig. 14). Pope Cornelius (1e, Fig. 24) and an anonymous pope at 3a. These have as a rule over-large circular eyes, and their drapery falls in long, straight, weighty folds; they may well be dated *c.* 1508–9. In addition there is a group consisting of only two surviving figures, a pope at 2d, (Fig. 15), and the bishop at 5g, which are even more sophisticated and full of movement. These are close to the style of certain figures in a series of windows now in the transepts of Tournai Cathedral, on the history of the city and its bishopric (Fig. 16); the first scene of the series, a battle scene, is prominently signed AM (most probably for Adrian of Mechlin).[35] The Tournai glass can be confidently dated to 1513–14, the first year of the English occupation following the Battle of the Spurs. The two Windsor figures may well date from the year 1515, when, as we have seen, Adrian was probably in Westminster designing the early glass for King's College Chapel.

35. Wayment, 'A rediscovered master'.

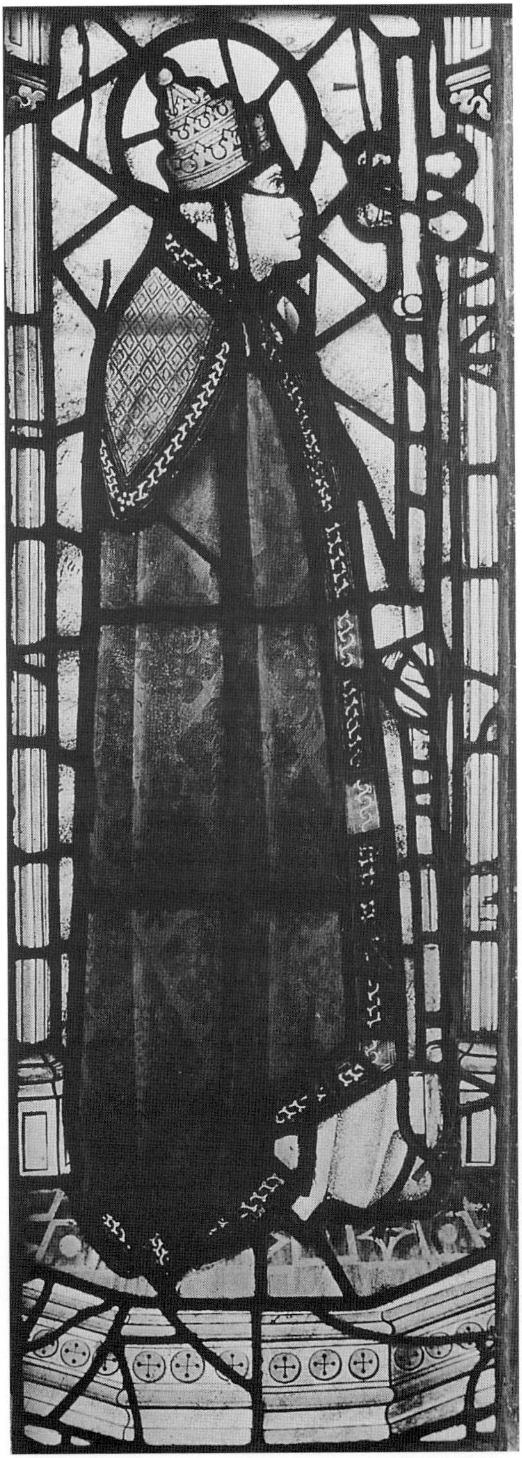

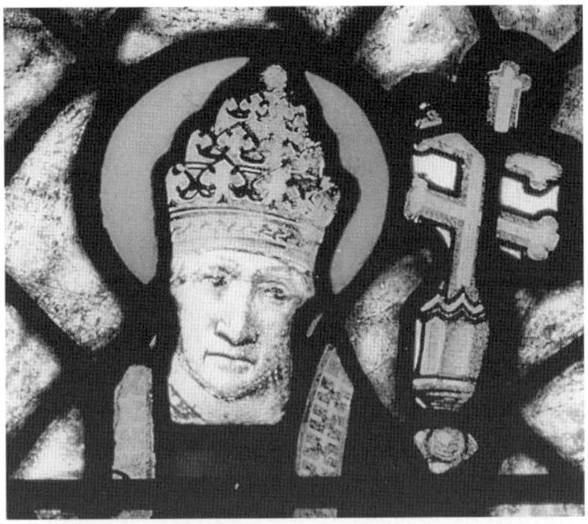

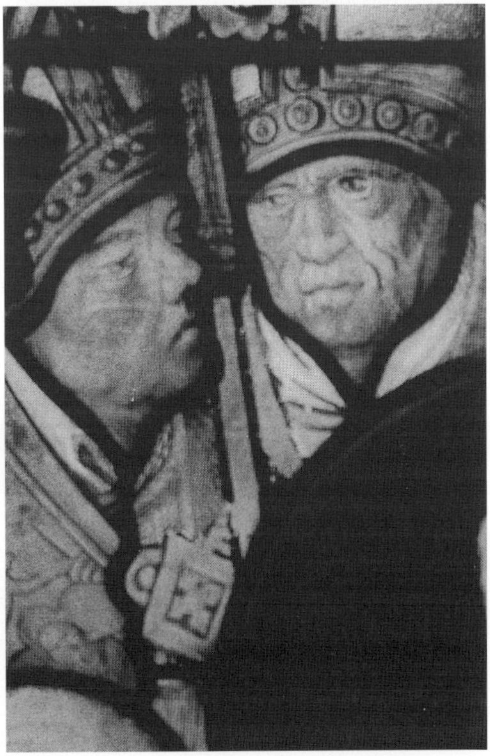

Fig. 14. *2a, pope (Photo by Sydney Pitcher, c. 1940, © Dean and Canons of Windsor)*

Fig. 15. *2d, pope, detail (H.G. Wayment)*

Fig. 16. *Tournai Cathedral, north transept, Canon Letbert received by the Pope, detail (© ACL Bruxelles)*

3. The third distinct stylistic group consists of five figures: (1) the mason (10, Figs 17 and 35), (2) another civilian who wears a floppy bonnet, a fur-lined robe, and a purse hanging from his belt (2n). These may well have been designed by AM, as the set of their feet suggests, though, if so, some years later than the early group of knights; the execution is masterly and individual. (3) A third (2i wears a long gown, fur-cuffed and collared, and carries a scroll in his hand; his head has gone, but has been replaced by that of a bearded king (Fig. 11). (4) and (5) St Cosmas and the presumed St Damian (2k and 2l). In three of the four surviving heads, as in Adrian's, the hair is lightened with the scrub, but without undue flourish or display. The paint of all the faces except the mason's is badly worn. The hands are either shown with knuckles bent and with deep shadows between the fingers, or else the thumb or the two shortest fingers are folded in front of the others in the manner of Van der Weyden, to foster a sense of depth. The rayed nimbus in 2l also suggests a Netherlandish hand (cf. the saints at 4k and 5e). The drapery folds tend to be long, heavy and rather deep, with strong gatherings on the arms, and give dignity to the figures.

At Fairford Adrian's energy as a designer is balanced by the skill and poise of an outstanding glass-painter who influenced almost all the others. In the mason's figure in particular can be discovered the traits which distinguish this artist's more advanced work at Fairford: the round eyes with dark pupils and full upper eyelids, the firm lines of the mouth and jaw, the slightly pendulous nose, all of which are seen for instance in the second Magus at Fairford (n III, 1c, Fig. 18). It is difficult not to recognize in him Adrian's collaborator in the glass for the royal wedding, the king's glazier Barnard Flower, who is now known to have been a subject of the duke of Burgundy, that is to say, almost certainly, a Netherlander.[36] It would be natural for the king's glazier to honour his colleague, the master mason, by painting him with his own hand, just as, for instance, in thirteenth-century France, at Vendôme, the master sculptor carved the mason's bust in

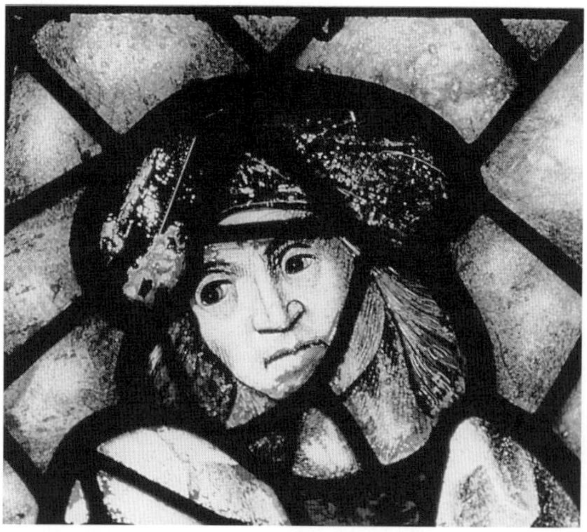

Fig. 17. *10, the master mason (detail) (H.G. Wayment)*

36. Angela Smith, 'Henry VII and the appointment of the King's Glazier', *JBSMGP*, xviii, 1 (1988), pp. 59–61. See also Wayment, 'The quest for Barnard Flower, King's Glazier to Henry VII and VIII', *JBSMGP*, xix, 1 (1989–90), pp. 24–37.

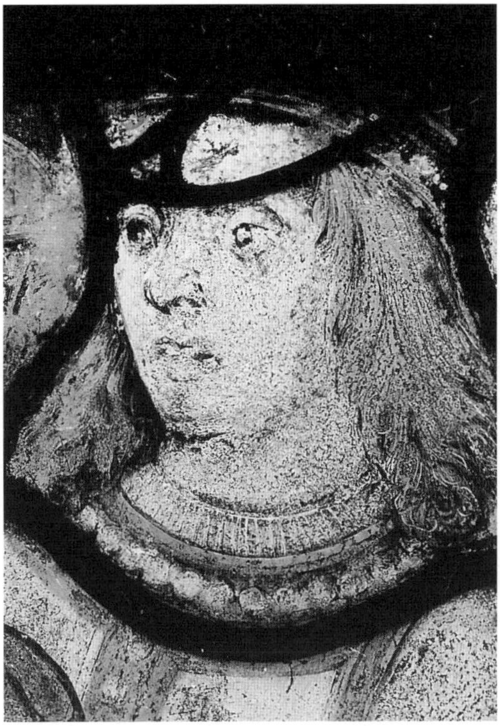

Fig. 18. *St Mary, Fairford, nIII, 1c, the second Magus from the Adoration of the Magi (H.G. Wayment)*

stone, with compasses in his hand.[37] John Harvey points to an even closer parallel in the late fourteenth-century *Tree of Jesse* in Winchester College Chapel, replaced by copies in the 1820s: at the foot of the lights are shown not only Edward III, Richard II and William of Wykeham, the founder (twice), but the clerk of works, the mason, the carpenter, and, beneath Jesse's feet, the glazier, Thomas of Oxford himself.[38] Harvey recognized in the mason William Vertue, who with John Hylmer was responsible for the building of the nave fabric and the vaults of both nave and choir. The two other civilians (2i and 2n) may well have been officers bearing some responsibility for the building operations.

The date of these five figures lies probably towards the end of the first decade of the century.

4. The fourth group consists only of three figures: two kings and one female saint. Those of St Edmund (1g) and St Louis (3i, Fig. 19) face half-right in an almost identical pose, with robes falling in long, quiet, curving folds, while the edges of their ermine-lined mantles flow gently over their wrists. The St Catherine (1m, Fig. 34) must have been the most splendid of the three; her head has had to be repainted, but the restorer probably had

37. North-west corner of north transept, second quarter of thirteenth century: L. Schreiner, *Die frühgotische Plastik sudwestfrankreich*, Cologne and Graz 1963, pp. 93 and 203.

38. Harvey, 'Architects', p. 92. James (see n. 14) called the figure St Adrian, but it is neither nimbed nor in armour. For the Winchester glass see J.H. Harvey and D.G. King, 'Winchester College Stained Glass', *Archaeologia*, ciii (1971), pp. 149–77, esp. pl. 67.

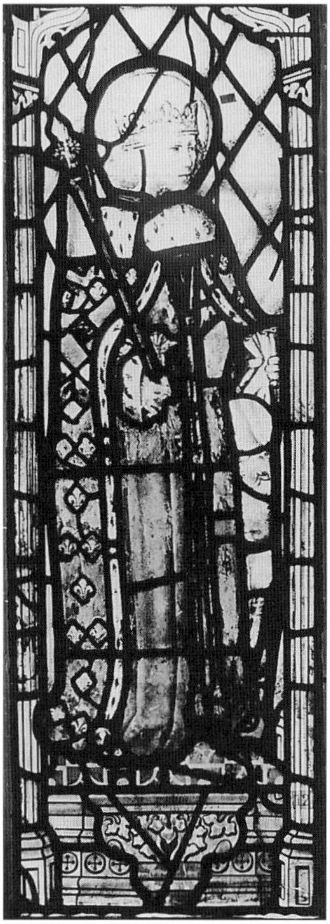

Fig. 19. *3i, St Louis (Photo by Sydney Pitcher, c. 1940, © Dean and Canons of Windsor)*

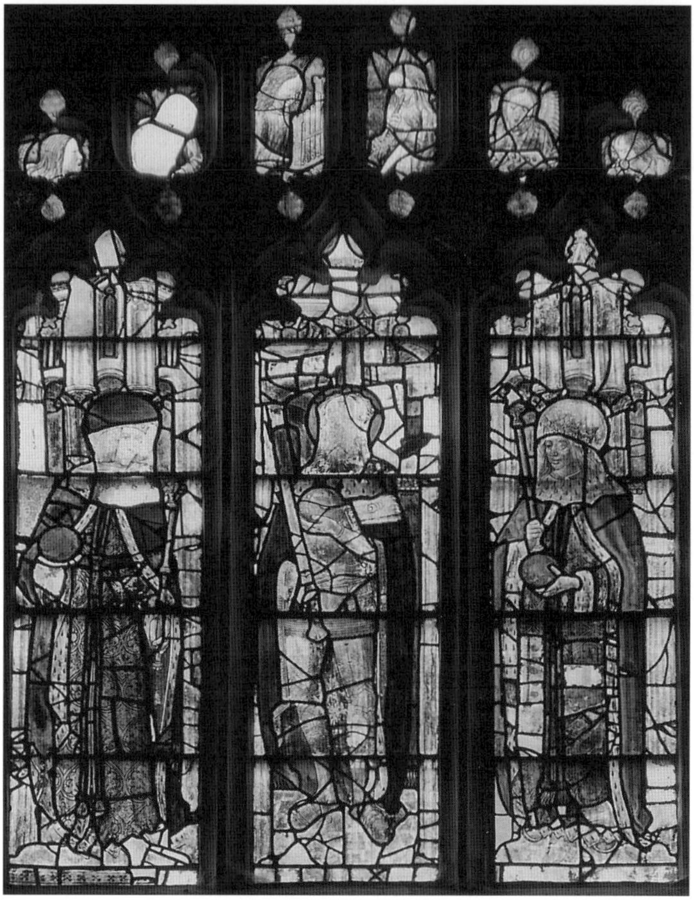

Fig. 20. *St Mary, Fairford, SIV, emperor between two royal saints (© Crown Copyright. NMR)*

the fragments of the original in front of him, and has skilfully recreated the style of the master. He is traceable in the south clerestory at Fairford where *c.* 1502 he painted Saints Dorothy and Margaret (SIIa and SIIIb),[39] and also the figures (though probably not the heads) of those presumed to represent St Edward king and martyr and Henry VI in SIV (Fig. 20).[40] The Saints Louis and Catherine are, however, his most accomplished figures, and appear to date from about 1505. The St Louis master evidently designed for himself the figures he painted; his was a gentle, well organized talent of somewhat limited range.

5. Apart from the group of seven knights designed, probably, at the very end of the fifteenth century by AM, there is also a later group of nine knights and martial princes, eight of whom still retain their original heads. These are not from AM's designs. They

39. Wayment, *Fairford*, pp. 71 and 73, pls 31 and 33.
40. *Ibid.*, p. 74 and pl. 34: Henry's head appears to be Flower's work.

take vigorous but more or less realistic stances; they are at rest, but alert for action. They seem to be the work of several glass-painters working together; in one case two royal Knights of the Garter are based on the same design but painted by different hands, one gentler, one more vigorous. The first of these hands (in 4m, Fig. 21) seems to be that of Simon Symondes, who in or before 1509 painted the figures of Henry VI and Elizabeth of York (Fig. 22), which are still in the chapel of Christ's College, Cambridge.[41] Symondes' style has here reached the same point of development as at Christ's College; his figures can scarcely date from before 1508–9, and may well be later.[42]

6. The twenty-five popes[43] form by far the largest set of all, or 40 per cent of the original figures. Two are singletons: the pope at 2d, painted probably by AM (and an assistant) about 1514 (Fig. 15), and the composite figure at 4d. One has a paint-worn head, another's head is intruded, and three have modern heads. The remaining eighteen can be divided into three groups:

(1) The first comprises six figures. The St Peter (1a, Fig. 3) must have been designed by AM about 1500, as the bandy legs and feet at right-angles imply. His large staring eyes and dark, semicircular upper eyelid are repeated in two profile figures, the awkward archbishop at 5j (Fig. 48) and the magnificent pope at 2a (Fig. 14). Four other popes, Saints Evaristus and Cornelius (1b, Fig. 23, and 1e, Fig. 24), and those at 2e and 3a, share the same robust dignity, and a similar treatment of the light drapery of the alb suggests that these are later work from the same source. The designs for the last five recall a bishop already mentioned (5g) and a pope (2d, Fig. 15) and may well have been prepared by Adrian more than a decade after that of the St Peter.

(2) St Eleutherus (1c, Fig. 25) must give his name to the second group of eight popes. These vary as much as those of the first group in maturity and no doubt in date, from the anxious boy-like figure at 3c to the confident, urbane, compelling young men at 2b (Fig. 26) and 4c (Fig. 27).[44] All have long, thin noses with small nostrils, but the mouth, at first a rather weak Cupid's bow, broadens in the maturer examples and develops a full lower lip. These eight are all from the same hand, but again the last may well be ten years or so later than the first.

(3) The third group, which consists of four popes, 1d (St Calixtus, Fig. 28), 3b, 3k, and 5d (Fig. 29), is closely allied to the second.

This glazier's angular drapery folds and too-sharp chin are also recognizable in a bishop, St Dunstan (1l), though the head is evidently a nineteenth-century copy from a damaged original.

All three groups must have been produced in close proximity, since they share certain special characteristics. Both of the first two groups develop a notable use of stipple and

41. See p. 11 above, and n. 23.

42. Wayment, *Windows of King's Chapel*, pp. 24–5. For Symondes' earlier (and indeed immature) work, see *id.*, *Fairford*, pp. 92–3.

43. If the figure at 2d is included, there are twenty-six popes: see n. 14.

44. The others are 2c, 3d, 3n (Fig. 4) and 5c.

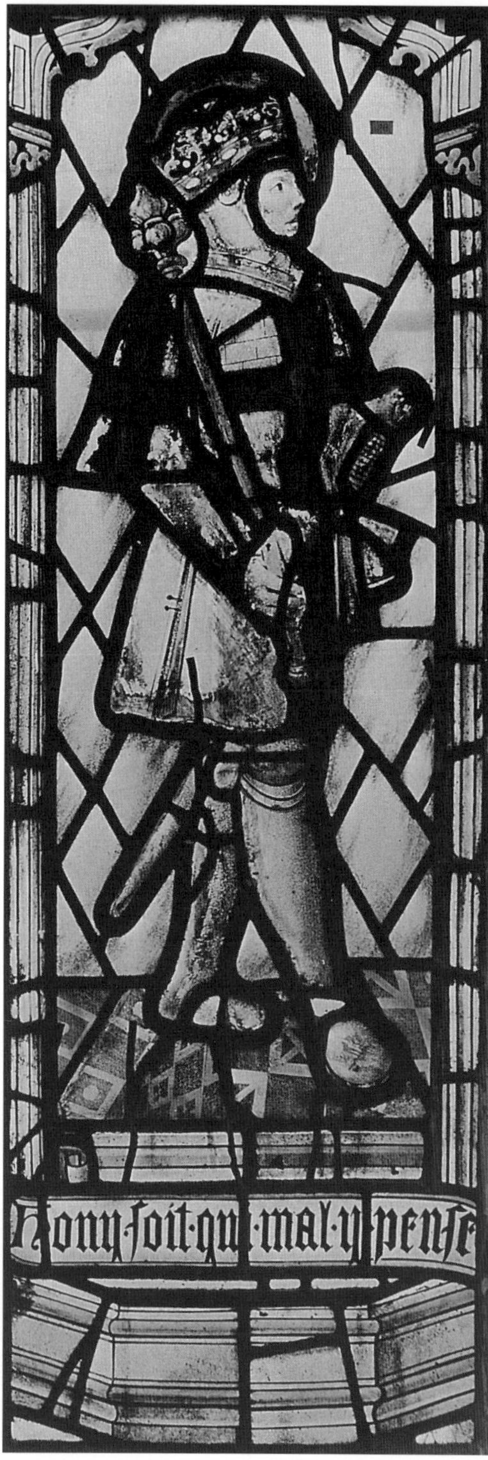

Fig. 21. *4m, princely knight (Photo by Sydney Pitcher,* c. *1940, © Dean and Canons of Windsor)*

Fig. 22. *Cambridge, Christ's College Chapel, Queen Elizabeth of York (H.G. Wayment)*

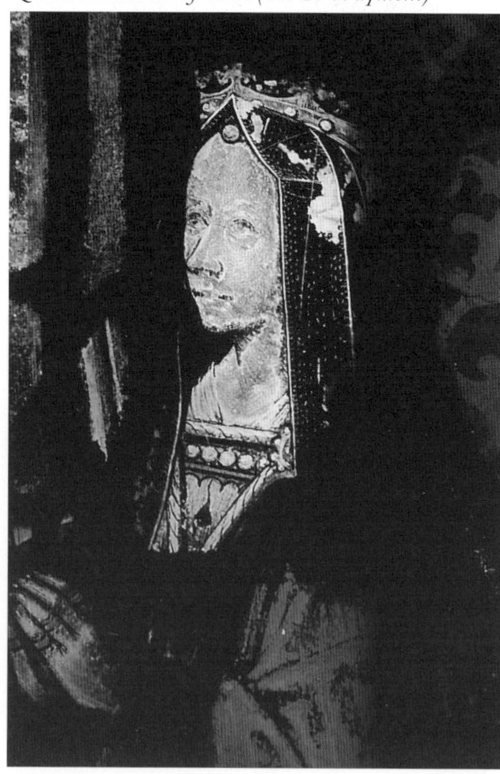

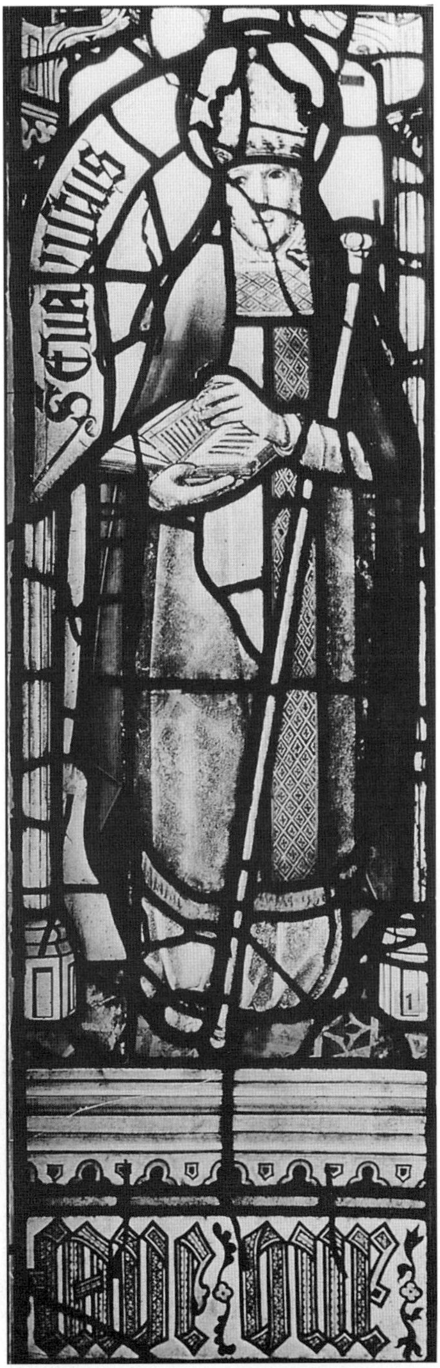

Fig. 23. *1b, Pope Evaristus (Photo by Sydney Pitcher, c. 1940, © Dean and Canons of Windsor)*

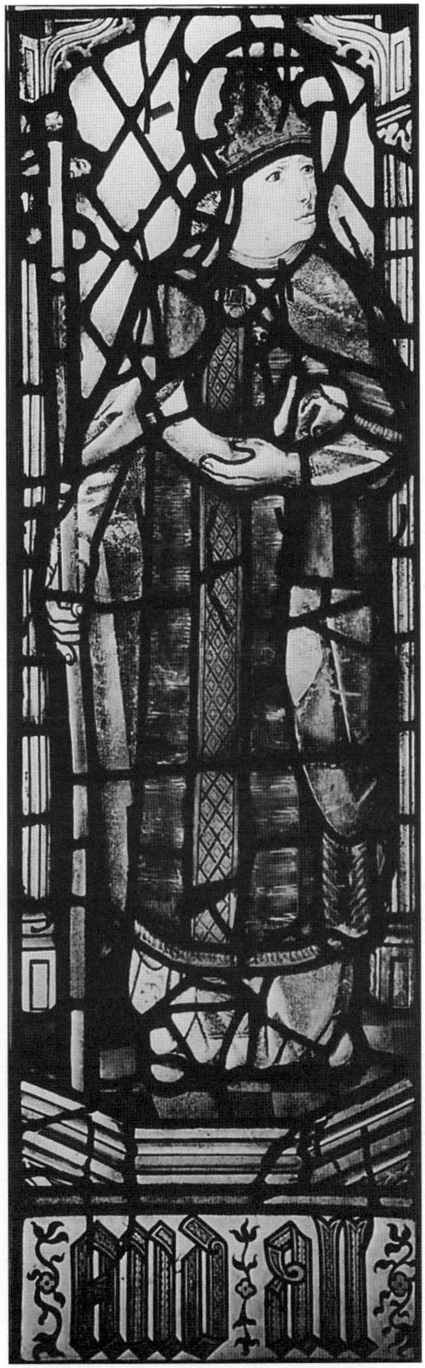

Fig. 24. *1e, Pope Cornelius (Photo by Sydney Pitcher, c. 1940, © Dean and Canons of Windsor)*

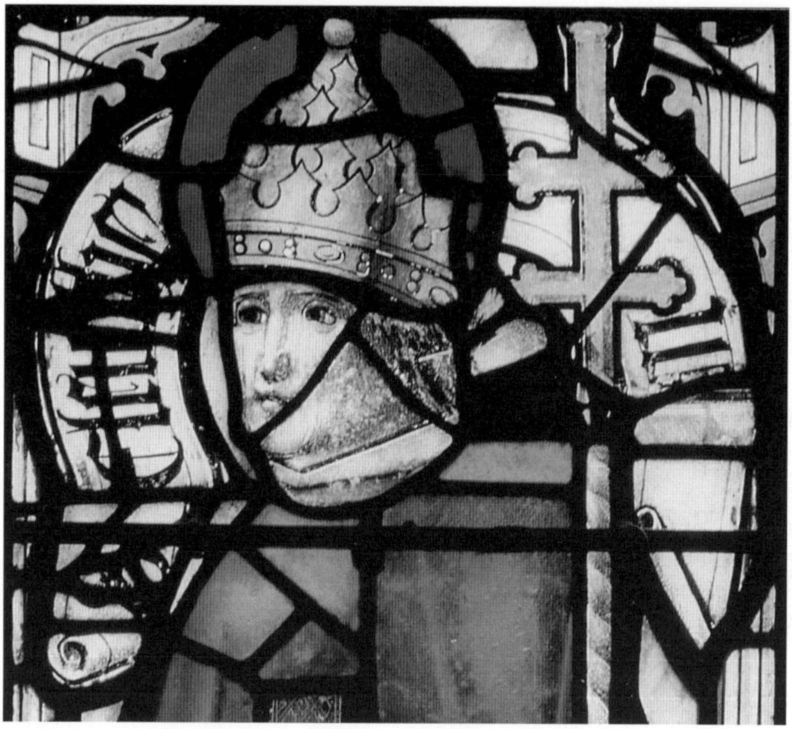

Fig. 25. *1c, St Eleutherus, head (H.G. Wayment)*

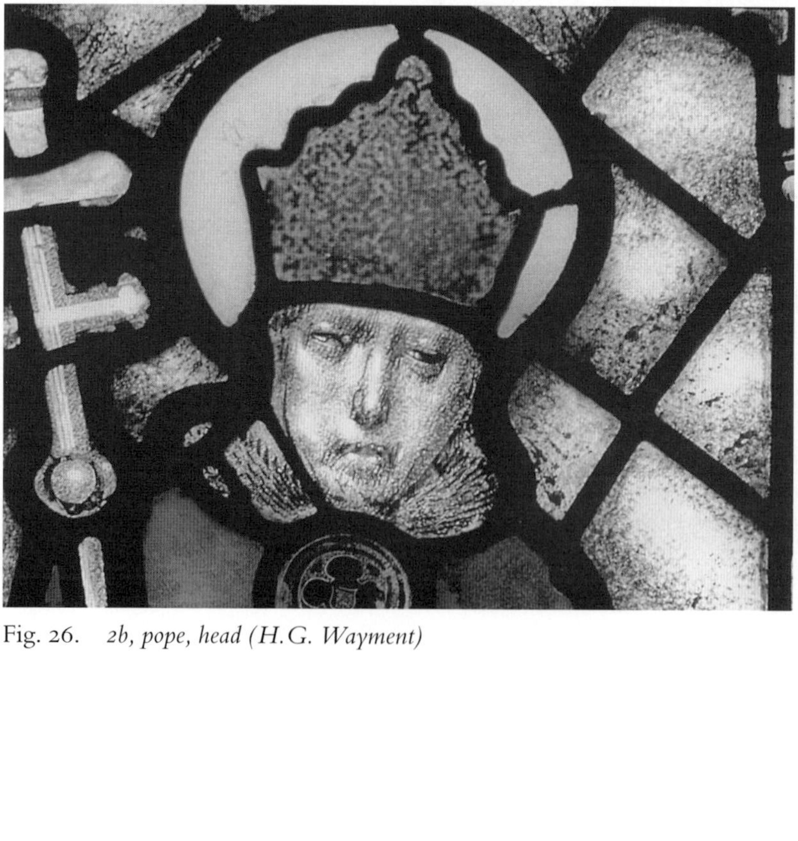

Fig. 26. *2b, pope, head (H.G. Wayment)*

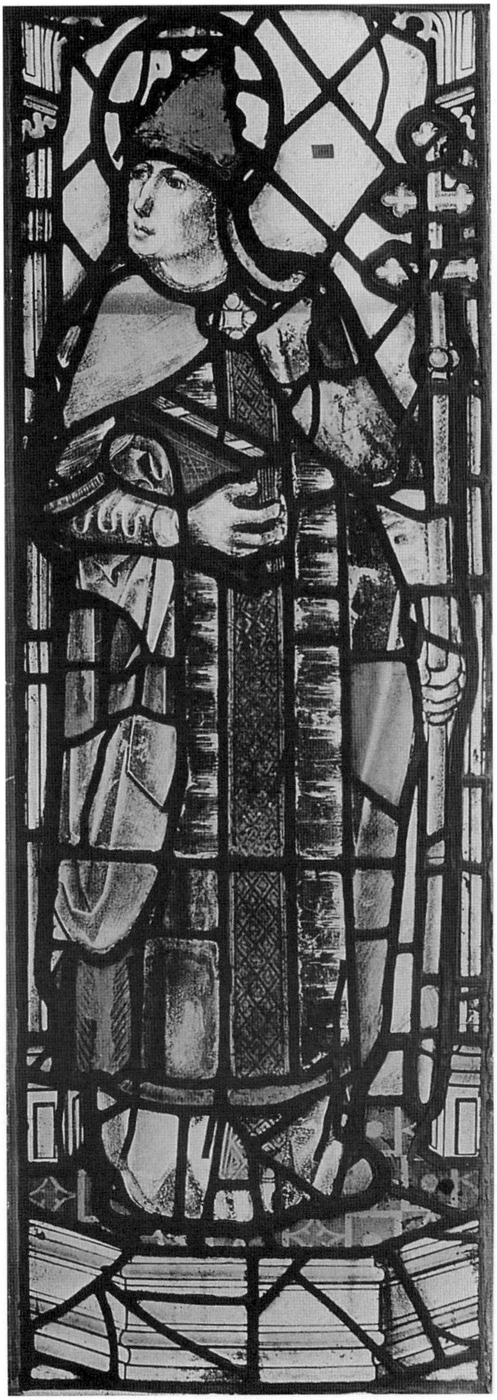

Fig. 27. *4c, pope (Photo by Sydney Pitcher, c. 1940, © Dean and Canons of Windsor)*

(Fig. 26) this even results in a kind of fudge which gives the popes concerned an air of wise benevolence. Though the third glazier uses the stipple skilfully, he is basically a linear artist, and relies heavily on line in all his faces except one (3b). In figures belonging to all three groups a peculiar repeat pattern, like a distorted capital T or I set diagonally, is used for fringes (2a, Fig. 14, 2e, and 3a, from the first group, 2c from the second, and 5d, Fig. 29, from the third); the same pattern is found, in a slightly more sophisticated form, on the tiara of the pope at 2d (Fig. 15). The remarkable contrast between the awkwardness of the early figures and the assurance of the later, by all three glaziers, suggests that they spent a number of years on the job, perhaps from 1500 until after the completion of the choir vault in 1511. None of the three glaziers seem to be traceable elsewhere; they appear to have formed a self-contained group based on one or more independent workshops, most probably in Southwark or Westminster, but conceivably in Windsor itself. The listing of James Skynke as glazier to the college in 1481 has already been mentioned; and again in 1533 Galyon Hone, the king's glazier, was to pass on responsibility for certain glazing works in the royal chambers to a local glazier, Hubberd Tysseburt.[45] It is uncertain whether there was a continental immigrant among them or not; but their initial *naïveté* suggests that they may all have been English.

Nevertheless the late figures attributed to the St Peter and St Eleutherus glaziers exhibit qualities of poise and solidity which characterize the best work of the pre-Renaissance in the Netherlands; they are on the whole more natural and convincing than those of Simon Symondes and his colleagues. It may not be too far-fetched to compare their maturer work with the fine sculptured

45. *Architectural History*, ii, p. 483; i, p. 251.

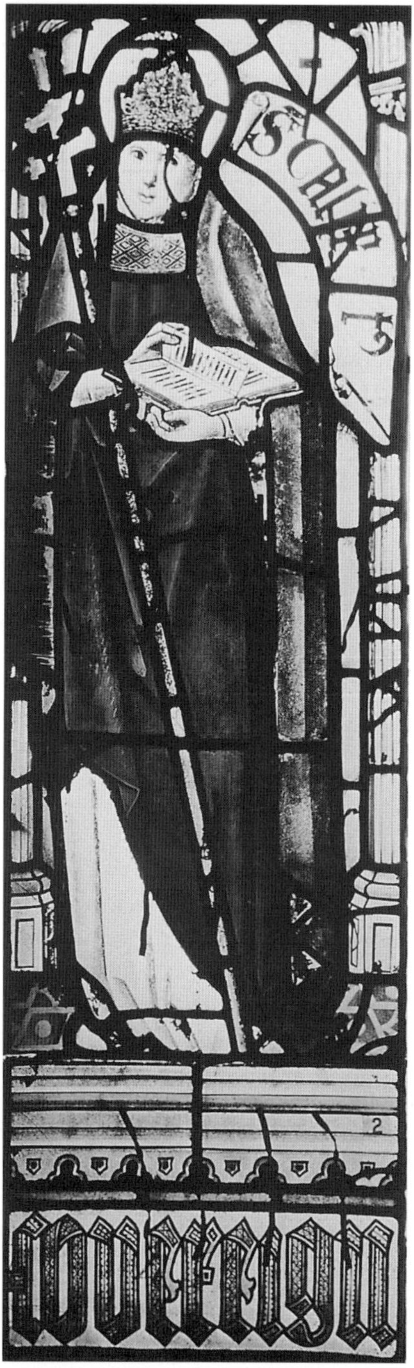

Fig. 28. *1d, St Calixtus (Photo by Sydney Pitcher, c. 1940, © Dean and Canons of Windsor)*

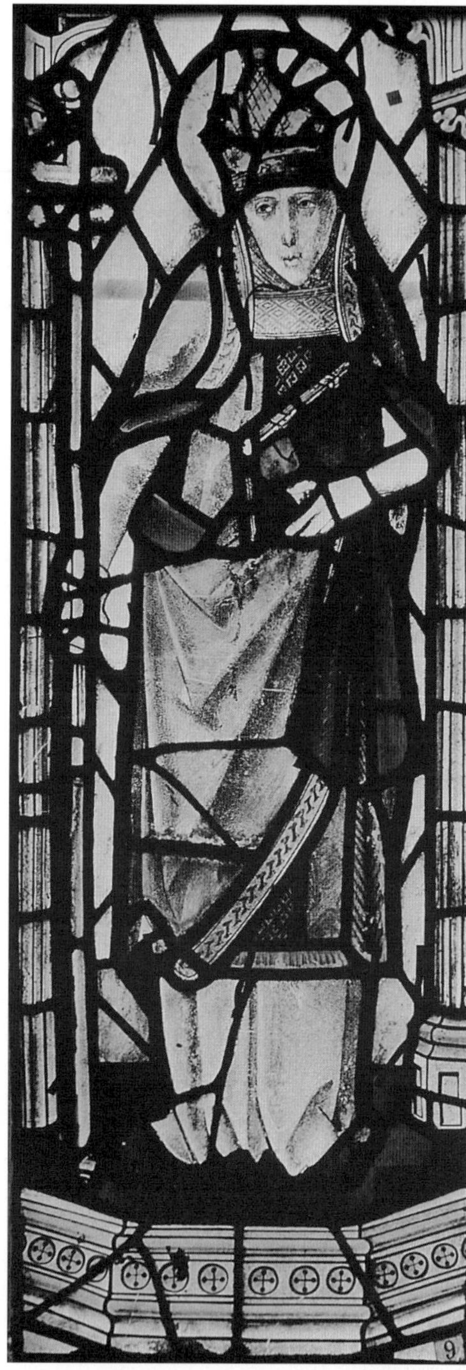

Fig. 29. *5d, pope (Photo by Sydney Pitcher, c. 1940, © Dean and Canons of Windsor)*

light hatching in place of line for the outlines of faces; in 1b (St Evaristus, Fig. 23) and 2b figures in the Henry VII Chapel at Westminster, which are to be dated 1505–15, especially the St Jerome and the so-called Philosophers.[46]

This study of the different glaziers, and groups of glaziers, who contributed to the painting of the figures now in the west window of St George's, based as it is on tentative deductions from evidence often imprecise, is put forward with every necessary reserve. It may, however, suggest certain general conclusions:

(1) That the glazing work was begun at the very beginning of the sixteenth century, if not before, and continued until the middle of the second decade.
(2) That the original nine kings were perhaps the first group to be started, by a team including Adrian of Mechlin, the Judas glazier, and a third glazier who had worked with them on the Fairford glass (the St Louis master).
(3) That the bishops and archbishops also constitute a relatively early group, though only three original heads remain to suggest this.
(4) That the saints are a heterogeneous group of the early and middle years of the first decade, two of them being probably from the same hand as the three civilians (perhaps Barnard Flower's).
(5) That there are two groups of knights, one of seven figures designed by Adrian and evidently early, another of seven bearing either scrolls with chivalrous inscriptions or the cross of St George (in one case both); these seem to date from the end of the first decade of the sixteenth century or the beginning of the second.
(6) That the series of popes was largely executed by a separate group of glaziers, apparently from the beginning of the first decade to the middle of the second.

Installation and Siting

Although a building, or a part of it, could be glazed as soon as it was roofed, it would be most unwise to install painted glass and add vaulting afterwards; the glass would be almost certain to get damaged.[47] At Windsor there is a notable contrast between the order of building and roofing the different parts of the chapel, and the order of vaulting them. The choir was built and roofed between 1477 and 1484; but although the choir aisles had probably been vaulted 1498–1500 the choir vault was not added until 1506–9. Meanwhile the nave, the construction of which had lagged behind the choir, was finished and vaulted by June 1506.[48] The question is, which of these two uncoordinated processes determined the order of glazing?

It is important here to distinguish four different stages: the planning, design, painting, and installation of the glass. The only document we have to guide us is Bray's will. This

46. *St Jerome*: L. Tanner and R.P. Howgrave-Graham, *Unknown Westminster Abbey*, Harmondsworth 1948, fig. 62. The '*Philosophers*': Royal Commission on Historical Monuments (England), *London* I, London 1924, p. 65 and pl. 124. See also Helen Dow, *The Sculptural Decoration of the Henry VII Chapel, Westminster Abbey*, Soham 1992.

47. F. Perrot in 'Le vieux marché de Rouen', *Les Amis des Monuments Rouennais, Bulletin* (1978–9), pp. 57–9; P. Curnow, 'The east window of the chapel of Hampton Court Palace', *Architectural Review*, 27 (1984), pp. 5–6.

48. Tatton-Brown, 'Constructional Sequence', fig. 8.

seems to imply that before he died, in August 1503, there was a concerted plan for the 'utter perfourmance' of the nave, not only in stonework, but also in timber, lead, iron, and glass. In view of Bray's experience of glazing programmes elsewhere, it is likely that he had at least given general directions for the iconographical scheme. In several windows of the nave clerestory, on both north and south sides, and in the north-west window of the south transept, above the entry to the south aisle of the nave, the cusping of the main lights, at top or middle level, contains a total of thirteen examples, some damaged and some intact, of Sir Reginald's badge, the hemp-brake or bray.[49] There are also a number of these carved in the stonework of the nave vault and in both transepts; they occur again in the parish church of Shere (Surrey), where Bray had a manor.[50] Here they prove that the clerestory windows concerned were glazed by Bray's executors after his death in August 1503, and no doubt after the completion of the vault in June 1506. Conversely, any glass now in the west window which can be shown with any degree of probability to have been either designed or executed before his death in 1503, when the nave remained incomplete, is likely to have been destined for the eastern arm of the chapel, and to have been designed and painted in accordance with a comprehensive scheme established before the end of the fifteenth century, though little of it, if any, can have been actually installed before the completion of the choir vault in 1509.

It is probable, then, that the work of the Judas glazier and the St Louis glazier, together with the early work of AM, whether as glass-painter or designer, was intended for windows in the choir. These comprise six kings (1g, 1h, 1j, 2h, 3g, 3i), together with a seventh whose head alone survives (2i) and the St Oswald and St Catherine, whose heads are modern (1f and 1m), and also eight knights with spindly legs from early designs by AM (2f, 2g, 2o, 3e, 3l, 3m, 4k, 4o), only two of which have their original heads (2o, Fig. 11, and 4k, Fig. 46), and the martial pope at 3n (Fig. 4). To these must be added the figure of St Peter (1a, Fig. 3) and probably also four or five other popes whose tentative style suggests early dates (1c, 1d, 3c, 5b, 5c). In all, out of the sixty-eight original figures, just over a third appear to date from the turn of the fifteenth century, or a little later, while a roughly equal number are unlikely to be earlier than the middle of the first decade of the sixteenth and some of them might date from as much as a decade later; the rest, amounting to a quarter of the total, are doubtful. There are in fact signs of a renewal of the glazing campaign about 1508, when AM's work, both in designing and painting, again becomes evident, and when the hand of the St Peter glazier, for instance, seems traceable in a group of papal figures far more sophisticated than his early work. The late group of knights, nine in number, including seven in Garter tabards, seems likely to date from about 1510 or later, and is quite distinct in style from the early group. Thus the evidence, such as it is, encourages the view that the sixty-eight ancient figures now in the west window came from both parts of the chapel; that some of the glass destined for the choir was designed and painted before, and some after that intended for the nave; and that the main windows of the choir may well have been the last to be installed; but which of the figures, if any, were in the west window originally it is impossible to tell.

49. NXX, A1; NXXi, 2c; NXXII, 2b and 2d; SXV, 3b and 3c; SXVIII, 2b, 2c, 3b; SXX, 1b, 2b, 3c; and SXXI, 3c.

50. J. Aubrey, *The Natural History and Antiquities of the County of Surrey*, London 1718, p. 46; Marks, 'Patronage of Sir Reginald Bray', p. 201.

Conclusion

Although the glass surviving in the chapel from the late fifteenth and early sixteenth centuries consists, apart from heraldic pieces, exclusively of single figures, it must not be supposed either that these represent at all accurately the original proportion of the various categories, or that there were never any biblical or sacred subjects in the windows. In the mid-fourteenth-century east window of Gloucester Cathedral, for instance, the two lowest tiers which are fully visible contain fourteen abbots and bishops and fourteen saints, while in the tier above the two central openings are occupied by a *Christ and the Virgin in Majesty*, with the twelve apostles ranged on either side.[51] In York Minster, at about the same time, the west window was glazed with the figures of eight archbishops in the lowest tier, twelve apostles in the next, and five sacred scenes in two shallower tiers above.[52] In clerestory windows single figures have always been found appropriate, from the eleventh-century prophets at Augsburg onwards.[53] At Bourges, in the thirteenth-century windows of the clerestory, nineteen prophets face nineteen apostles and disciples on either side of the Virgin and Child (Ecclesia) and St Stephen, patron of the church, in the east.[54] In England, unfortunately, the programmes into which such figures fitted have nearly always to be reconstructed from the scattered remnants of glass remaining. At Winchester Cathedral, for instance, it can be deduced that three separate campaigns of the fifteenth and early sixteenth centuries established figures of prophets, apostles and saints in both nave and choir clerestories.[55] At Fairford, fortunately, the eight clerestory windows of the nave still contain groups of three figures each: Champions of the Church on the south side, and Persecutors on the north; these remain separate even when linked to each other iconographically.[56] It has been conjectured that at Gloucester as many as forty kings and/or biblical ancestors of Christ filled the main lights of the choir clerestory;[57] but this is a guess. In the west choir clerestory of York Minster there are eight early fifteenth-century windows containing in all thirty-eight single figures in the main lights, where seven popes are flanked by kings, archbishops and saints, with at least five more popes amongst numerous such figures in the traceries.[58] There is no reason to suppose that St George's formed an exception to the traditional arrangement. Thus the concentration of the figures of popes, on the advice of M.R. James, may be misleading; they are just as likely to have taken their place, as examplars and sponsors of the Order, amongst the kings, knights, bishops, archbishops, and saints. Beyond a certain point, however, speculation is idle; we

51. D. Welander, *The Stained Glass of Gloucester Cathedral*, Gloucester 1985, pp. 11–19.

52. T. French and D. O'Connor, *York Minster, The West Windows of the Nave*, CVMA Great Britain, iii, 1, Oxford 1987, pp. 15–18.

53. E. von Witzleben, *Farbwunder deutscher Glasmalerei aus dem Mittelalter*, Augsburg 1965, p. 91 and col. pls ii–v.

54. M. Aubert *et al.*, *Le vitrail français*, Paris 1958, p. 139*a*, pls 48 and 103.

55. J.D. Le Couteur, *Ancient Glass in Winchester*, Winchester 1920, pp. 25–6, 28–35.

56. Wayment, *Fairford*, pp. 71–84.

57. C. Winston, 'The Great East Window of Gloucester Cathedral', *Archaeological Journal*, 20 (1863), p. 247; G. McN. Rushforth, 'The Great East Window of Gloucester Cathedral', *Transactions of the Bristol and Gloucester Archaeological Society*, 44 (1922), pp. 303–4. See also J. Kerr, 'The East Window of Gloucester Cathedral', in *Medieval Art and Architecture at Gloucester and Tewkesbury*, British Archaeological Association Conference Transactions, vii, Leeds 1985, pp. 116–29.

58. F. Harrison, 'The west choir clerestory windows in York Minster', *Yorkshire Archaeological Journal*, 26 (1920–2), pp. 353–73.

can only be grateful for the battered but cherished remnants of what must have been, even in the sixteenth' century, an exceptionally brilliant and impressive array of saints and patrons.

CATALOGUE

In the following description figures are described as presently constituted and only restorations to the medieval figures are noted; the backgrounds, canopies and side-shafts are all Willement's work, together with the simulated stone-work of the bases, though most of the tile-work, which closely resembles that in the clerestory lights at Fairford, seems to be original. The notes on restoration should not be regarded as definitive. They are based primarily on Drake's notes of 1945, but also on Richard Marks' observations at the time of the cleaning of the glass in 1976, and the writer's long-range observation through binoculars in 1990. A full description will only be feasible when the window is again scaffolded for cleaning or repair.

Some of the terms used may need explanation. 'Yellow' refers to yellow potmetal only, and 'stained' to yellow stain, applied as a rule to the back of the glass. 'Ruby' is used to describe red glass, made by combining (flashing) a layer of white or yellow glass with one tinted almost to black by copper oxide. The word 'flash' is used sometimes to denote glass so treated: other potmetals, especially blue, can be lightened in the same way. 'Murrey' is a term used by glaziers to denote a dullish purple, maroon or plum; but it can also resemble a dull pink. The notes on colour and costume are not necessarily exhaustive.

The words 'intrusion' and 'intruded' are used to denote fragments of medieval glass intended to replace lost original pieces, while 'replacement' or 'restoration' indicate the use of modern glass for the purpose. The term 'insertion' is explained under 3i.

The capitals L and R indicate the spectator's view, while 'left' and 'right' are reserved for the parts of the figure itself. Inscriptions are black-letter unless otherwise stated. In their transcription an upright line stands for a lead-line or mend, round brackets for expanded contractions, and square for conjectural completions; a dot underneath a letter means that only part of it is in fact visible.

All figures are nimbed except two civilians (at 10, Fig. 17, and 20) and the much restored figure of a knight (3e) which has lost its original head; the saintly status of the remaining figures is not always specified in the catalogue. Many of the popes wear amices of fur, which are visible at the neck only, and are rarely mentioned below; the vestment worn below the cope (or chasuble) is usually described as a dalmatic, which, however, cannot always be distinguished from the tunicle.[59] Shoes or sandals are always round-toed, and their colour is not often given. The tiling, as at Fairford, is normally painted without any attempt at perspective, usually in lime-green or pink-murrey.

1a SAINT PETER as POPE (Figs 3 and 30)

Stands full-square looking half R and holding a pontifical cross-staff in his right hand and two massive keys in his left. He wears a ruby cope with pale green lining, held by a morse, and a blue

59. The tunicle (*dalmatica minor*) was originally white, but by 1500 had become much more elaborate, and is often indistinguishable from the dalmatic. Both could be worn together, the tunicle below the dalmatic, but there seems to be no example of this practice here.

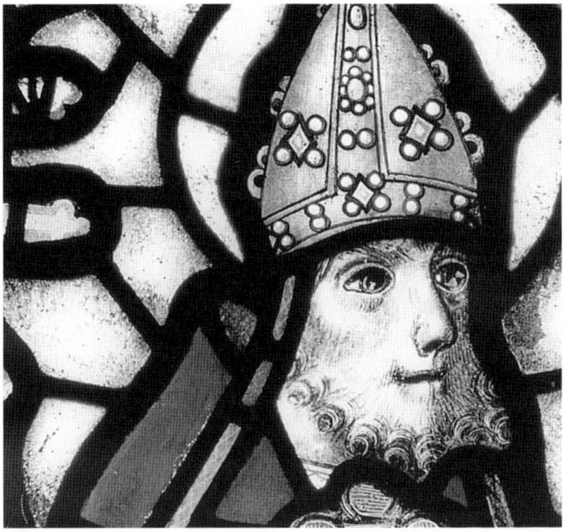

Fig. 30. *1a, St Peter as pope, detail (H.G. Wayment)*

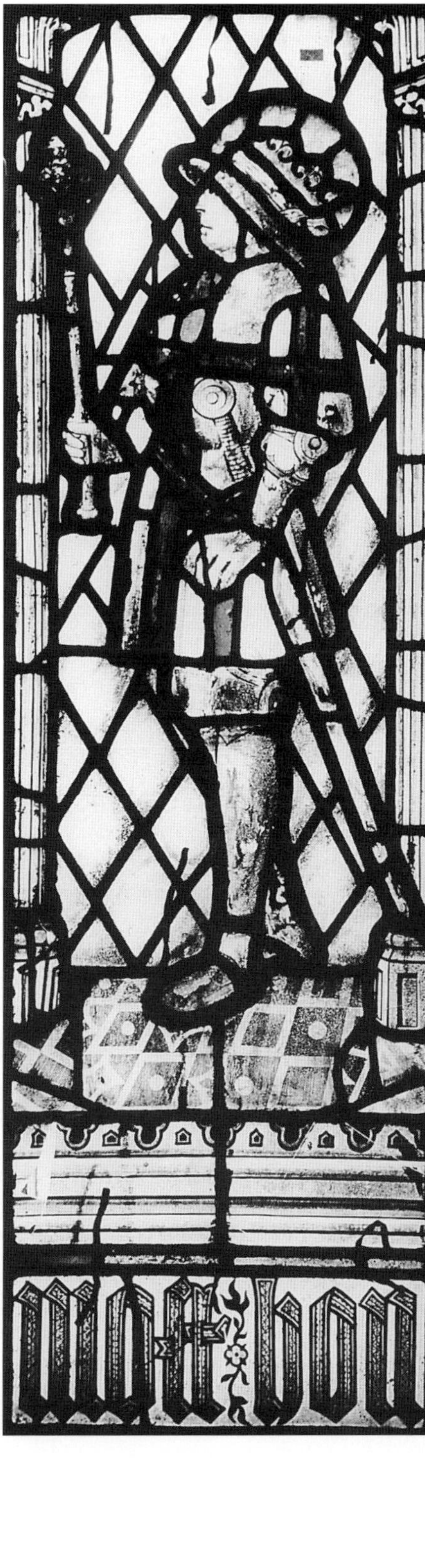

Fig. 31. *1i, princely knight (Photo by Sydney Pitcher, c. 1940, © Dean and Canons of Windsor)*

Fig. 32. *1j, king, detail of head (H.G. Wayment)*

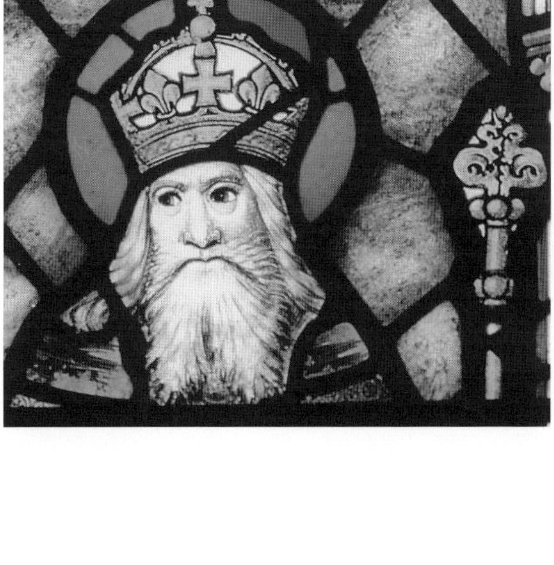

girdle over a white alb which is looped up to reveal the bare shins and feet of an apostle. His yellow-stained mitre (with green lappets) is set off against a light blue nimbus.

Condition good: some lead-mending; toes of both feet and parts of the pink-murrey tiling restored. The design is no doubt by AM. The painting of the head scarcely conforms, except in the curls of the beard (which are somewhat stylized) with the traditional image of the saint as a robust, rather elderly countryman. Painted probably in the early years of the sixteenth century.

St Peter is reliably assumed to have been executed under the Emperor Nero *c.* A.D. 64, and from about A.D. 200 was regarded as the first bishop of Rome.

1b POPE EVARISTUS (Fig. 23)

Inscription on scroll curving L of the right shoulder: /S(anctus)Eua/ristus/. Stands full-square with a benign expression holding an open book in both hands towards his right, with a staff leaning against the crook of his left arm. He wears a ruby cope with yellow band over a damasked blue dalmatic with yellow orphrey and green fringe, and below that an alb. His yellow tiara is set against a green nimbus.

Condition good, apart from a few cracks lead-mended in the head. Fluent stippling for shadow, and also for facial outlines (cf. 2b below).

St Evaristus was regarded as the fourth or fifth bishop of Rome (*c.* 100–*c.* 109).

1c POPE ELEUTHERUS (or Eleutherius) (Fig. 25)

Inscription on scroll circling behind his head: /S/Eleu/t/her/us/. He faces half L, raising his right hand in blessing and holding his pontifical cross-staff erect with his left. Blue cope with green lining over ruby dalmatic with yellow orphreys and fringes; white apparelled alb over ruby shoes. Yellow tiara against murrey nimbus. The rather pinched face points to a tentative but prolific member of the workshop, whose later work can be seen at 5c, 3n (Fig. 4), 3d, and finally 4c (Fig. 27). Damage lead-mended in head and scroll, and at foot.

St Eleutherus was Pope *c.* 174–89; he appears at least twice in the windows of York Minster.

1d POPE CALIXTUS (or Callistus) I (Fig. 28)

Inscription on scroll curving R of left shoulder: /S(anctus) Cali/x/t(us)/. He stands full-square, leaning both head and body gently R, and holding an open book in both hands, with a double cross-staff in the crook of his right arm. He wears a blue cope with yellow band and green lining over a full-length ruby tunicle hitched up in the crook of his right arm to reveal the alb over his ankles. His eyes, slanted R, his rather prim mouth and pointed chin give him an arch expression, and the plain stippled folds of the drapery, as it follows the curve of his body, add a certain elegance. Apart from a mending-lead across the face, and another in the scroll, there are few repairs.

St Calixtus was Pope from 217–22; he may have died in a riot, without being, strictly speaking, a martyr. His figure appears in the east window of York Minster (panel 1g), and in a tracery light of *c.* 1470 at Wiggenhall St Mary, Norfolk.

1e POPE CORNELIUS (Fig. 24)

He stands full-square with head turned half R, holding a horn (Lat. *cornu*) in his left hand and a pontifical cross-staff in his right. He wears a pink-murrey cope, joined by a pale green and stained morse over a blue dalmatic with yellow orphrey and green fringes, and an apparelled alb almost covers his pink-murrey shoes. Cross-staff, morse and tiara are all yellow, the nimbus dark blue. Some peripheral mending-leads. His finely painted face expresses clear-sighted defiance.

Cornelius was Pope from 251 to 253. His figure appears at Wiggenhall St Mary (see 1d).

1f SAINT OSWALD

He leans L with his head turned in three-quarter profile, holding a sceptre in his right hand and making a gesture of exposition with his left. A scroll curving behind his nimbed head and over his left shoulder reads: /S(anctus)/Oswald/(us)/. His blue robe falls in straight folds (cf. 1h), and his cloak and shoes are ruby. His head, coronet and ermine cape-collar are restored (by the 'wide-eyed' glazier).

St Oswald, king of Northumberland from 633 to 641, was an ardent champion of Christianity and died fighting against the pagan king of Mercia. His figure is found in glass at Cockayne Hatley, Bedfordshire, and in the west choir clerestory of York Minister.

1g SAINT EDMUND

He turns half R, holding an arrow erect in his left hand and a short staff in his right (perhaps the remains of a sceptre). Over his yellow gown the ermine lining of his ruby mantle curves gently across his wrists, and long blue cords hang down to his ankles. He was evidently bearded, but his other features, and almost all but the stained outlines of his closed crown, are effaced. No doubt designed and painted by the St Louis glazier (see p. 00).

St Edmund was king of East Anglia from 855 to 890, in which year he was captured by the Danes and shot to death with arrows. He appears frequently in English glass, for example, at Tong in Shropshire.

1h KING EDWARD THE CONFESSOR (Fig. 9)

He holds a sceptre erect in his right hand and a ring in his left (both stained) as he seems to turn half L, but his fine bearded head faces half R. He wears a closed crown of England (stained) against ruby nimbus, an ermine cape-collar over a murrey mantle, and under that a blue robe belted at the waist and falling in long, wide, gently curving folds. Condition good, apart from a few mending-leads and damage to the robe below the knees. The drapery, together with the hair and beard picked out with the scrub, and the entangled fingers point to the master AM as designer and painter; the date is *c.* 1502. The king's identity is established by the ring, which he was believed to have given to St John the Evangelist, disguised as a beggar, and to have received back again later through a pilgrim returning from Jerusalem. He was king of the English from 1042 to 1066, and patron saint of the English monarchy until 1348, when Edward III replaced him by St George. He appears frequently in English glass, notably in a narrative series at Ludlow.

1i A PRINCELY KNIGHT (Fig. 31)

He is shown in profile to the L, apparently moving forward with sceptre held in his right hand and sheathed sword by his left. He wears a blue helmet with murrey kerchief and stained coronet against a green nimbus, and a white tabard with the ruby cross of St George over light blue plate armour on knees, shins and feet. The chiselled features of his face (delicate open nostril, firm mouth with full lower lip) suggest one of the Simon Symondes group (see p. 21). Note the perspective effect in the tiling, which at Windsor is rare. Date: probably after 1510.

1j A KING (Fig. 32)

Composite figure, of which the upper, main part shows a nimbed and bearded king wearing a closed crown of England, with alternate crosses and fleurs-de-lis,[60] a blue robe and a ruby cloak with green cords and cape-collar. In his left hand he holds a sceptre erect, and with his right he makes an expository gesture. Intruded glass connects this upper part with a pair of legs bare at the knees, but wearing green hose and ruby buskins, with slippers stained on the abraded flash; behind is seen the lower part of an ermine lining. Legs and torso may well come from separate figures, both by the master AM. The hair and beard are similar in technique and aspect to those of 1h, and the set of the legs resembles that of some of the figures in the north clerestory at Fairford.

60. Cf. the crown of Edward the Confessor (1h, Fig. 9), the normal form of the sovereign's crown to this day.

1k SAINT MARTIN OF TOURS

On the border of his stained nimbus, either side of his mitred head, is inscribed in Roman capitals: /SANCTVS/MARTIVS/ [*sic*]. At his feet R is a stunted beggar to whom he holds out a purse with his left hand while his right supports a pontifical cross-staff. He wears a green cope over a blue dalmatic, both with yellow orphreys, and a dark blue cassock (for black) over green shoes. Paint worn in head and mitre; intrusions in cassock. The identifying gestures is less common than the cloak cut in half, but nevertheless occurs quite frequently.[61]

1l SAINT DUNSTAN OF CANTERBURY (Fig. 33)

He stands collected, gripping the ruby-coloured devil at his feet with tongs held in his left hand, while raising his right hand to exorcise it, with his cross-staff erect in the crook of his arm. He wears a deep blue chasuble over a murrey dalmatic with green fringes. His nimbus is pink-murrey, his mitre stained. The head is modern (the 'delicate' glazier), but no doubt follows a damaged original by the glazier of 3b, 3k and 5d. Dunstan was born in 929, and was Archbishop of Canterbury from 959 to 988. He appears in several English windows, including one at All Souls' College, Oxford.

1m SAINT CATHERINE OF ALEXANDRIA (Fig. 34)

She carries a small wheel in her left hand and holds in her right the blue grip of a drawn sword, which rests point downwards on the ground. Her blue skirt almost covers her ruby shoes, and she wears a green robe under a sideless surcoat of ermine. From her belt, inscribed /SAN/CTA CA/, a pomander hangs on a long chain. Over her white cloak, held by a chain at the neck, fails long hair stained to gold. Her head, coronet and halo are restored; on the border of the halo, picked out in stained capitals, is /SANCTA CAA / HARINA VIRGO/ [*sic*]. This piece, however, is evidently a faithful copy of the destroyed original, since a fragment in the west window at Fairford (probably also representing St Catherine) shows very similar traits. Both figures are to be attributed to the St Louis master (see p. 20 and note). The saint was much venerated in the Middle Ages as the 'bridge' of Christ.

1n SAINT ALBAN[62]

A scroll behind his left shoulder reads: /S(an)c(tu)s/Alban(us)/. In restless folds round his shoulders hangs a ruby cloak with green collar. His stocky figure, the short staff held over his left shoulder, his right hand gripping the belt round his plain blue coat, and his murrey-booted feet firmly set at right-angles all contribute to give a truculent expression which is enhanced by the tension of his circleted head, as he looks out half L. The set of the legs suggests a design by AM. The head and a large part of the cloak are modern.

Saint Alban, protomartyr of England, was a Romano-British citizen who was converted to Christianity and executed about the middle of the third century at Verulamium. He is seen, notably, as a knight, following the late fourteenth-century life by Thomas of Walsingham, in the east window of the Beauchamp Chapel in St Mary's, Warwick.

1o THE MASON (Figs 17 and 35)

His compact frame and his right arm holding a hammer are turned half R, while his small head and his dark wide-open eyes follow the line of his leading foot, to the L. He wears a dark blue cloak with white collar and lining over a ruby robe, seen only at neck, elbow and cuff. A loose black bonnet covers the shoulder-length hair, which is stained and lined out with the scrub. His hands have firmly drawn knuckles, and his feet are set at more than right-angles to each other, with white

61. E.g. in the Master of Frankfurt's *Altarpiece of the Holy Kindred*, Frankfurt, Historisches Museum; M.J. Friedländer, *Early Netherlandish Painting*, vii, Leyden 1971, no. 129, pl. 101.

62. The author acknowledges the assistance of Dr Eileen Roberts in the iconographic content of this entry.

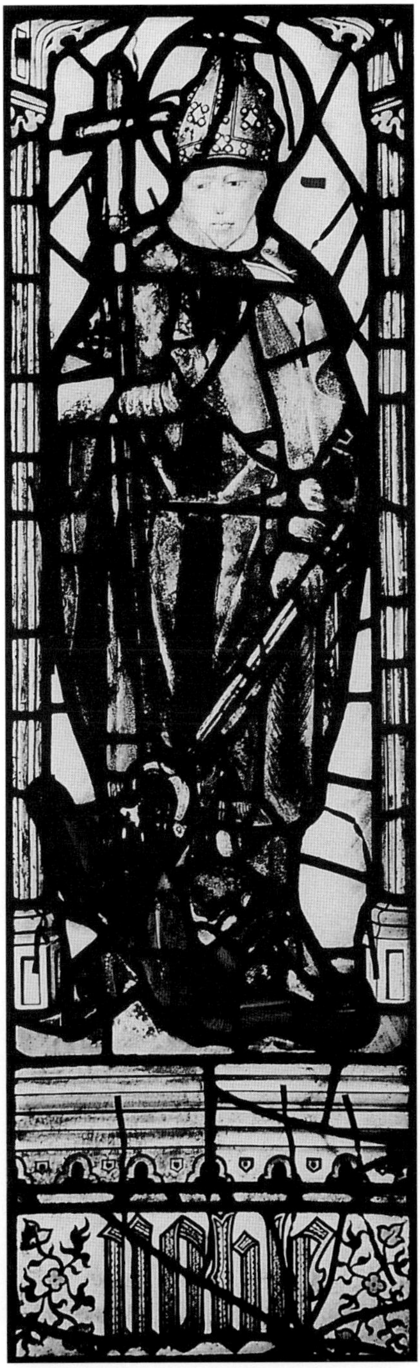

Fig. 33. *1l, St Dunstan (Photo by Sydney Pitcher, c. 1940, © Dean and Canons of Windsor)*

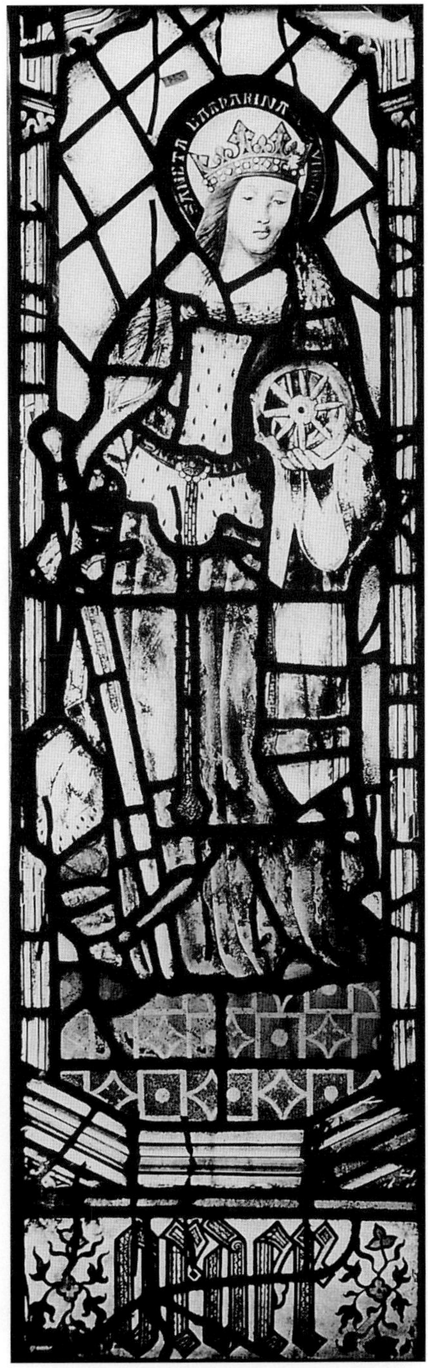

Fig. 34. *1m, St Catherine (Photo by Sydney Pitcher, c. 1940, © Dean and Canons of Windsor)*

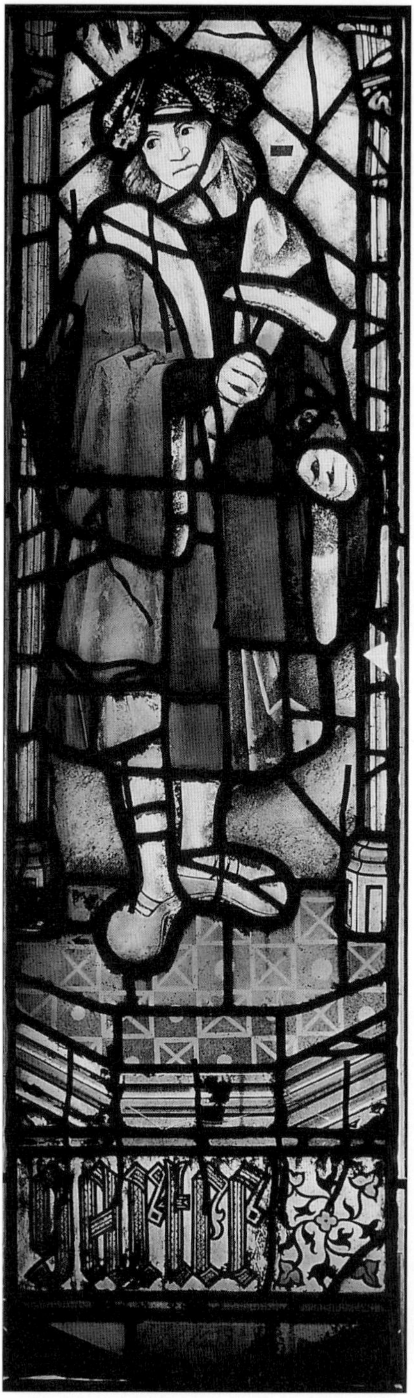

Fig. 35. *10, the master mason (© Crown Copyright. NMR)*

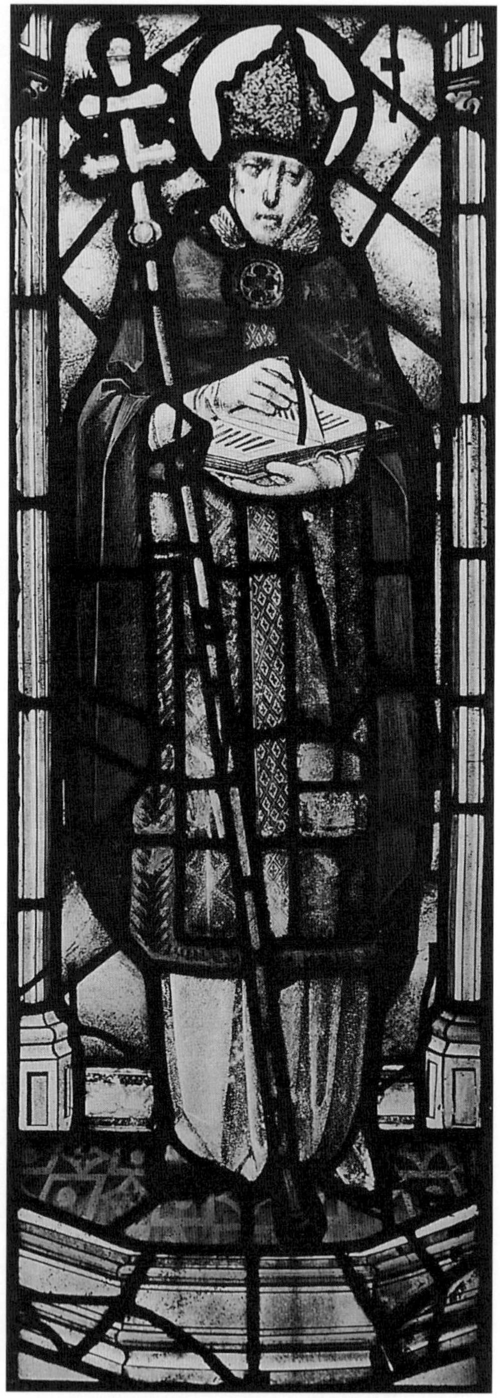

Fig. 36. *2b, pope (Photo by Sydney Pitcher, c. 1940, © Dean and Canons of Windsor)*

hose and broad stained shoes. An intrusion in the head, a few mending-leads, and one or two new places of blue in the drapery. Canon A.C. Deane saw Henry Janyns in the mason, but the date of the figure must be later than 1503, when William Vertue took charge, first with Robert Janyns, then with John Hylmer.[63] Most probably it is Vertue who is represented. The set of the feet may suggest a relatively late design by AM, and the style of painting suggests Barnard Flower and a date towards the end of the first decade of the century. A fourteenth-century stonemason, William Campiun, is to be seen in a north window at Helmdon, Northants.[64]

2a A POPE (Fig. 14)
He stands in full profile R, holding his double cross-staff in front of him, and showing to advantage not only the long folds of his damasked ruby cope, but also its yellow hood on his shoulders (cf. 5j). He wears a yellow tiara with green lappets, and his nimbus is blue. The dignity of the stance, the firm structure of the head, and the patterns on silks and orphreys link this figure with 3a above. For the design see p. 00. Condition excellent, though the tiara is probably modern; date *c.* 1505–10.

2b A POPE (Figs 26 and 36)
He stands full-square, leaning his head slightly R and holding an open book in his hands, with a double cross-staff in the crook of his right arm. He wears a murrey cope with green morse over a damasked blue dalmatic with green edgings and painted orphrey. Yellow tiara against a blue nimbus; amice visible at the neck. The head gains warmth and power from the use of stippled contours as opposed to line. Condition good; date *c.* 1505–10.

2c A POPE
Looks half R, holding his cross-staff in his right hand and a ruby-covered book in his left. His murrey cope is gripped over his amice by a ruby morse, and his dalmatic is blue with green edgings and stained orphrey. His alb has fur cuffs. Yellow tiara against ruby nimbus; ruby shoes on lime-green tiling. A few intrusions in the drapery.

2d A POPE (Fig. 15)
He looks a little to the R, holding a ruby book by its envelope in his right hand and a double cross-staff in the crook of his left arm. His ruby cope, with stained orphreys and a green lining, is held by a ruby band; but the whole of its L side, from the right shoulder downwards, is missing. His dalmatic is blue with stained orphrey and green fringes. Blue nimbus, stained tiara. A few intrusions in the drapery. Late work, probably designed by AM and painted by Flower, *c.* 1514; hands by an assistant, cf. 5g.

2e A POPE
Faces half L holding his double cross-staff across his body. He wears a ruby cope with yellow orphrey, and a green dalmatic, also with yellow orphreys, and in addition a violet fringe, over an alb. His tiara with its lappets is yellow, the nimbus pink-murrey. The right arm is made up of intruded pieces, and there are replacements in the cope. Resembles 2a and 3a in style.

2f MARTIAL PRINCE-BISHOP (Fig. 5)
He wears a closed crown of strawberry leaves over a rimmed war-hat, against a ruby nimbus, and white plate armour, painted and stained, with mail skirt and ruby shoes; in his right hand is a ruby-covered book and in his left a crozier. From his shoulders falls a blue mantle. His face is by the

63. Harvey, 'Architects', p. 92.

64. Richard Marks, *The Medieval Stained glass of Northampronshire*, Corpus Vitrearum Medii Aevi, Great Britain, Summary Catalogue 4, Oxford 1998, p. 104, pl. 9.

'wide-eyed' glazier and the crozier's head may also be modern. There are a number of intrusions and mending-leads. The thin, bandy legs imply a design by AM from the turn of the century.

2g A KNIGHT or MARTIAL POPE

He holds up a large sword across his body, gripping it by the stained pommel in his right hand, and supporting the blade with his left. He wears plate armour and mail skirt, as 2f, under a ruby mantle with pale blue lining and green clasp. His face is modern (the 'delicate' glazier) and he wears a tiara which is fitted awkwardly into the leading of the blue nimbus, but may be *in situ* (cf. 3n). Design, style and date as 2f.

2h A KING

He wears Tudor plate armour and a mail skirt, holding his sword in his left hand point upright across his body. His cloak is blue with ruby lining, and he wears a green cape-collar with stained edging. His shoes and the grip of his sword are also green. Design and style as 2f. The head, crown and nimbus are modern (the 'meagre' glazier).

2i CIVILIAN with intruded head

A king's head, bearded and crowned,[65] full-face, with green nimbus has been set on the figure of a civilian turned half L, wearing a long blue robe with fur collar and cuffs and holding a scroll in his left hand. The robe has a false sleeve at the left shoulder, and is gathered up from the lime-green tiling to show his ruby hose. The head was no doubt painted by AM *c.* 1502. The scroll suggests that the figure may represent the clerk of works.

2j AN EMPEROR (Fig. 37)

The figure seems to be stooping forward, as if with the weight of the globe he carries in his left hand and the upturned sword in his right. He wears a blue robe stained to green at the border, and a ruby belt with yellow clasp, a murrey cloak and green hose. His head and closed crown are modern (the 'wide-eyed' glazier), and there are intrusions here and there. None of the other kings carries a globe, which, with a sword, is the attribute of both Charlemagne (742–814) and Henry of Bamberg (972–1024). St Henry was a cripple and was called in Germany 'Henry the lame' or 'the limper'; the stooping figure may perhaps be an allusion to this disability; Charlemagne, though, might seem more likely to appear in this martial context. St Henry appears in a window in Antwerp Cathedral, dated 1503, as name-saint of Henry VII, the donor, and very probably in a south clerestory window at Fairford (SIV); no medieval figure in glass of Charlemagne is recorded in England. The drapery is rather tortured, and the date may lie in the second half of the first decade of the sixteenth century.

2k SAINT COSMAS

A civilian in an ankle-length ruby gown with white fur cuffs, an ermine cape-collar and a murrey doctor's cap against a blue nimbus. He moves half R but looks full at the spectator holding up a grey-blue urinal in his left hand, and raising his right in a reassuring gesture.

Saints Cosmas and Damian were said to have been martyred in 287 under Diocletian; they seem to have competed with, and eventually supplanted, Castor and Pollux, and churches dedicated to them replaced the temples of Aesculapius. The paint of the face is worn, and the nose and mouth are almost obliterated; a few mending-leads and intrusions of old glass.

Perhaps by Barnard Flower *c.* 1506.

65. See n. 60.

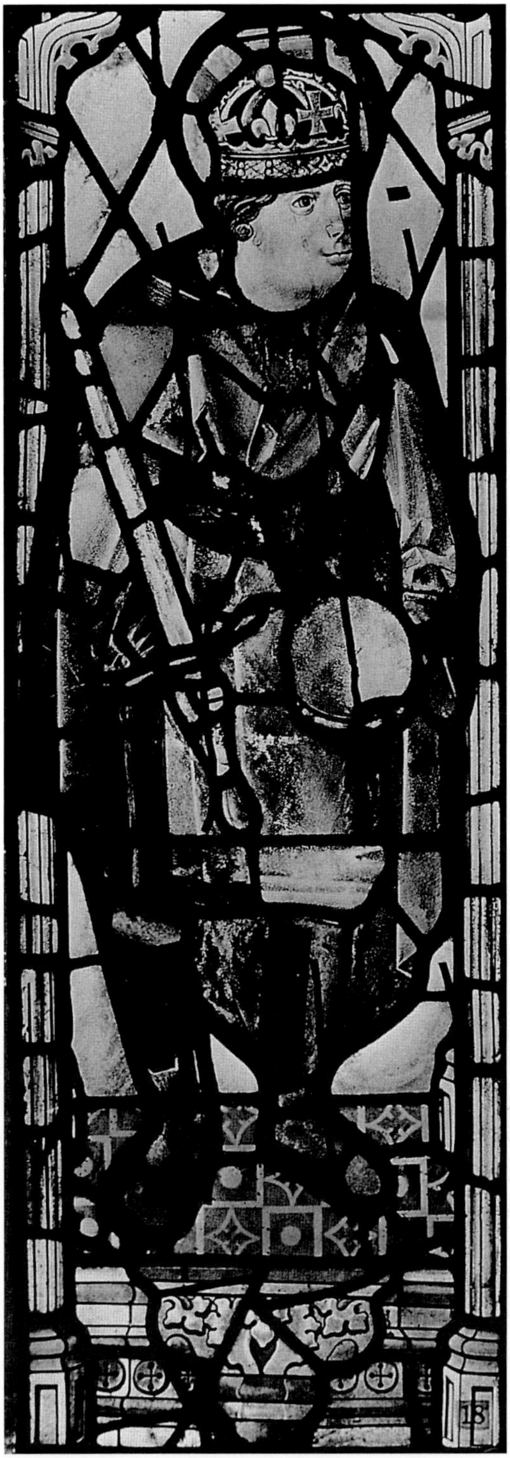

Fig. 37. *2j, emperor (Photo by Sydney Pitcher, c. 1940, © Dean and Canons of Windsor)*

Fig. 38. *2o, knight, detail (H.G. Wayment)*

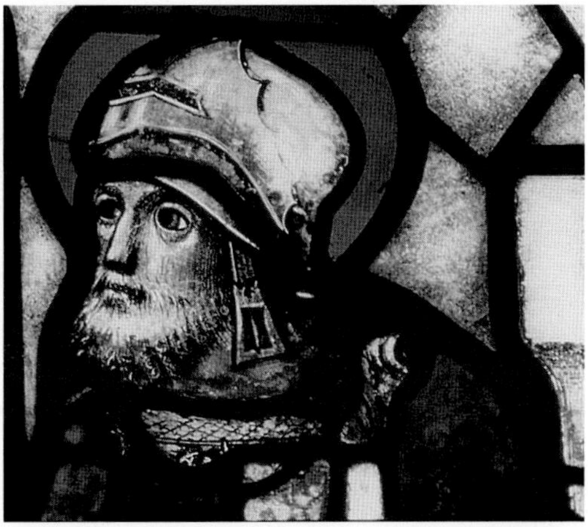

2l SAINT DAMIAN

Moves half R in a long ruby gown with green cuffs, raising both hands in front of him waist-high; but he looks out half L, wearing a grey doctor's cap covered with a blue hood. His rayed nimbus is yellow. Paint worn in face and hands; numerous mending-leads and intrusions in drapery.

For artist, style and date, see 2k.

2m A DOCTOR

He faces half L, raising his left arm to his waist. Over a white robe with stained girdle he wears a long blue cloak with yellow fastening, and a murrey hood and cap against a blue nimbus. His small, bearded head is largely effaced, and there are a few intruded pieces. The belt inscribed /STEADER/ is an intruded fragment.[66]

2n A CIVILIAN

He stands looking half L with one hand raised deprecatingly, and the other holding a blue scarf which falls from his left shoulder. His ruby cap sports a long blue plume, and his ruby cloak is trimmed with pink-murrey fur at the cuffs and from shoulder to ankle. At his belt hangs a pale blue purse. His feet in green hose are set wide apart at an obtuse angle. The face is almost obliterated, but the hair, which is picked out with the scrub, and the hands are in the style of Barnard Flower. The figure is in fact linked with those of the other two civilians, the mason (1o) and the presumed clerk of works (2i) and probably represents a third person concerned closely with the completion of the chapel. Date *c.* 1506.

2o A KNIGHT (Fig. 38)

He wears full armour of Tudor style, all in pale blue; sallet with raised visor, cuirass, skirt of taces over mail, and tuille on his left leg, the other being replaced by a intrusion; he holds erect a sword in his right hand and a battle-axe in his left. His murrey cloak has a ruby lining, and his nimbus is of a lighter ruby. The design can be attributed to AM, and the painting to the St Peter glazier (see 1a).

3a A POPE

He faces half R, with a double cross-staff in his right hand and a book in his left. His tiara is yellow, with green lappets, against a blue nimbus, and his ruby cope with green lining is gripped by a large quatrefoil morse. He wears a damasked blue dalmatic with yellow orphrey and green border, over an alb. An impressive figure by the same painter as 2a below.

3b A POPE (Fig. 39)

He is seen full-face, leaning his head slightly forward and to the L; he raises his right hand in blessing and holds a ruby book in his left, while the double cross-staff leans against the crook of his arm. He wears a yellow tiara against a murrey nimbus, a blue cope with ruby lining over an amice seen at the neck, and a green dalmatic with stained fringe over an alb and green sandals. The figure is notable for a sophisticated use of the stipple, combined with unobtrusive hatching and line-work; the sharp drapery folds are characteristic of the St Calixtus glazier (1d), cf. 3k and 5d.

3c A POPE (Fig. 40)

His right hand holds a book, and his left supports a double cross-staff. He wears a grey-blue cope over and a ruby dalmatic with yellow orphreys over an alb with an amice barely visible at the neck, and murrey shoes. Some mending-leads, and intrusions in the drapery.

The figure has a timid, haunted look, and is no doubt an early work by the St Eleutherus glazier; cf. 1c and 5c.

66. Drake in SGC XVII. 43. 30.

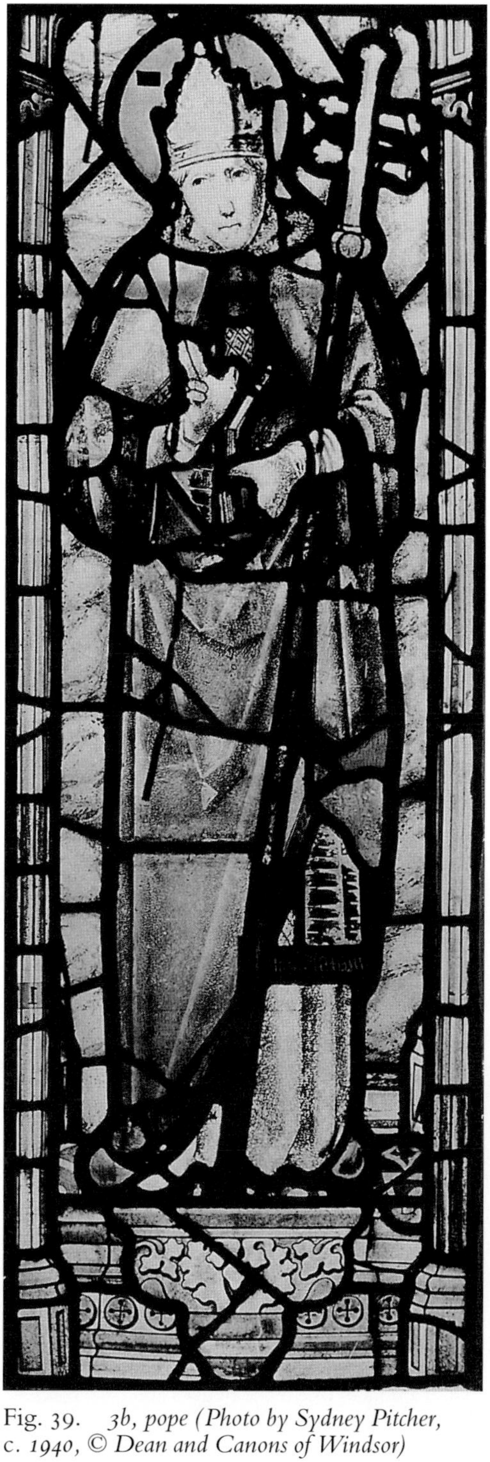

Fig. 39. *3b, pope (Photo by Sydney Pitcher, c. 1940, © Dean and Canons of Windsor)*

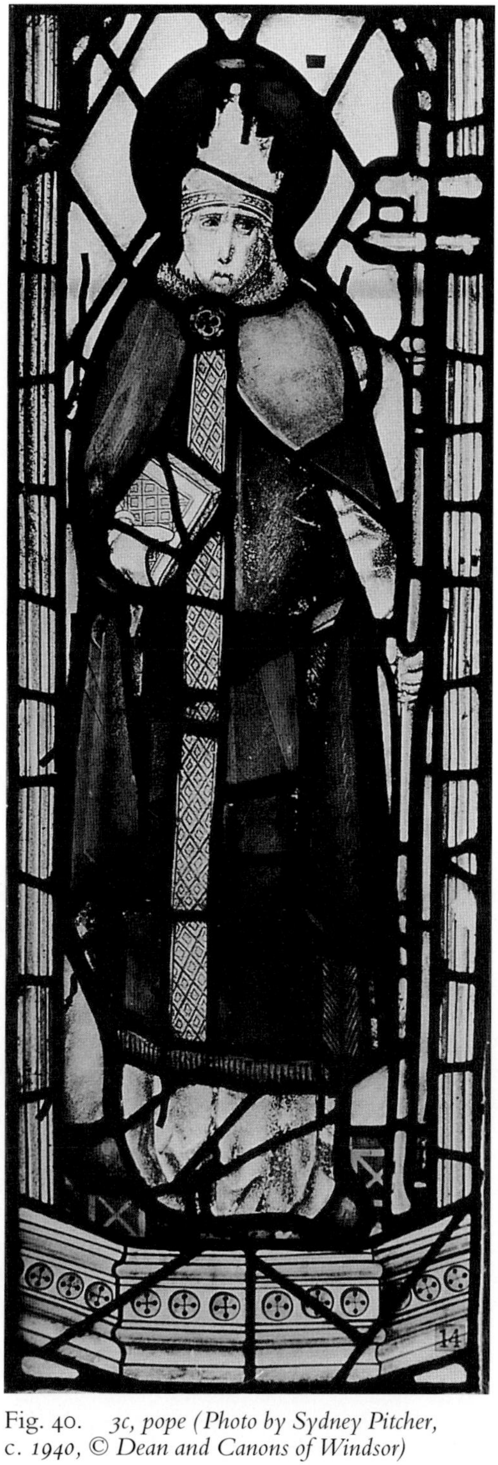

Fig. 40. *3c, pope (Photo by Sydney Pitcher, c. 1940, © Dean and Canons of Windsor)*

3d A POPE

He stands in three-quarter profile to the L, raising his right hand in blessing and holding a double cross-staff across his body in the left. His ruby cope has a pale green lining, and his blue dalmatic a green fringe and painted and stained orphrey. His tiara is stained, against a green nimbus. By the St Eleutherus glazier (1c).

3e A KNIGHT

He looks half L, holding his sword in his right hand with the point across his left shoulder. A blue mantle with green lining falls from elbows held akimbo, and a ruby girdle from his waist. He wears a stained war-hat with ruby ribbon. His head is by the 'wide-eyed' restorer, and there are many replacements elsewhere, especially in the armour on arms and legs. Design as 2f and 2g.

3f A KING

A copy (in reverse) of St Edmund (1g) by the 'meagre' glazier. He holds two sceptres, one in each hand. Green mantle with ermine cape-collar and lining over yellow robe. A blue under-robe can be seen at neck and cuffs. From under his cape-collar ruby cords fall to his ankles.

3g A KING

Looks half R as he holds a sword point downwards in his left hand, and a stained book in his right. Blue gown over white under-gown, and ruby cloak with green lining. His closed crown is yellow, against a blue nimbus. For style, glazier and date see p. 11. The ringleted piece over the right ear is intruded.

3h AN ARCHBISHOP

He stares out three-quarter L, holding a cross-staff against his left shoulder in one hand and a stained book in the other. Ruby chasuble with white pallium over green dalmatic and alb. The head and stained mitre are by the 'wide-eyed' restorer, but the murrey nimbus and blue lappets to the mitre (with green tassels) are original.

3i SAINT LOUIS (Fig. 19)

Clothed strikingly in a blue mantle set with stained fleurs-de-lis and edged in ermine, with an ermine cape-collar, and blue cords falling across an ochre-yellow robe to his ankles; he carries a stained sceptre in his right hand and against his right shoulder, and holds a pair of white gloves in his left. Several of the fleurs-de-lis were inserted in the blue glass, which in one case remains intact.[67] The head, the open fleur-de-lis crown and the nimbus were originally on one piece of glass now broken and lead-mended, with paint worn. A few intrusions. The painter, who also designed the figure, is a prolific member of the Southwark/Westminster school whose work is also found at Fairford (see p. 20).

3j A ROYAL SAINT

He turns his head over his right shoulder while his hand points in the other direction towards the heavy sceptre which he holds in his left hand. His cloak is ruby, and the robe beneath it blue. His head, his closed crown with crosses and fleurs-de-lis and his ermine cape-collar are all painted and stained on a single piece of glass by the 'meagre' restorer, but his green nimbus is original. Intrusions in the drapery.

67. This operation was a notable test of skill. The glazier makes a hole in one piece of glass and fits a piece of another colour into it; the technique is frequently used in heraldic work. The weakened base often splits and has to be strapped with lead, but there is one fleur-de-lis here, at knee level, which remains islanded.

3k A POPE

Stands full-face, with eyes glazed, his right hand raised in benediction, the other holding a double cross-staff. His dalmatic is ruby, with green fringe and grey painted orphrey, under a blue cope. The paint in both line and stipple remains fresh. Tiara modern; one or two minor intrusions. By the St Calixtus glazier (1d), cf, 3b and 5d.

3l A KNIGHT (Fig. 41)

He looks upwards to his right, body almost square to the spectator, with a globe in his right hand and a lance in his left. He wears an Italian sallet and a murrey mantle with yellow lining over full plate armour of pale blue, stained here and there to green, with a ruby cross on his breastplate and a sword hanging from a baldrick in front of his skirt of mail. His thin, rather bandy legs and ruby shoes set at an obtuse angle betray AM's designing hand. The 'delicate' restorer has given him an almost feminine face with curling locks which may be justified by fragments remaining on the left shoulder. Date *c.* 1505.

The figure may perhaps represent the Emperor Charlemagne's nephew, Roland, who was indeed rumoured to be not only his sister's son, but his own. Taken together with the globe, sword, and cross, the lance may be interpreted as an allusion to the legend of the budding lances: on the eve of the battle against the Saracens at Roncevaux the lances of those men of Charlemagne's army who were doomed to fall were said to have flowered, including his nephew's. Roland occasionally appears nimbed, as in several scenes of the early thirteenth-century Charlemagne window in the apse at Chartres.[68]

3m A KNIGHT

An elegant figure wearing a ruby hat with blue plume against a yellow-ochre nimbus, and a ruby mantle with green lining. He holds a sword point upwards in his right hand and grips his stained girdle with the other. Early design by AM; head by the 'delicate' restorer.

3n A MARTIAL POPE (Fig. 4)

He wears Tudor armour, as for instance 2g, and holds a bare sword point upwards in his left hand, but in the other an open book; on his head, as he looks out half L, is a stained tiara against a ruby nimbus. From his shoulders falls a ruby mantle lined with blue. Condition good, some paint-loss in tiara, and an intrusion in the nimbus.

There is no reason to doubt the authenticity of the tiara (as M.R. James may have done, in excluding him from the group of popes on the L of the window), and the figure may well represent a martial pope such as Damasus I (*c.* 305–84), who in 366 led an armed struggle against the anti-pope Ursinus; he wrote epitaphs on many of the early martyrs, and commissioned Jerome to prepare a new Latin translation of the Bible. Early design by AM, executed by the St Eleutherus glazier(1c).

3o A MARTIAL KING

As 2o reversed, but the painter has given him a sceptre instead of a battle-axe. Armour of pale blue flash stained in places to green, mantle ruby with yellow-ochre lining. By the 'wide-eyed' restorer.

4a A POPE (Fig. 42)

He looks half R over his left shoulder, holding a ruby-covered book in his right hand and a yellow crozier across his body with his left. His dalmatic is murrey, with yellow orphrey and green fringe,

68. Y. Delaporte and E. Houvet, *Les vitraux de la cathédrale de Chartres*, Chartres 1926, i, pp. 313–19, and iii, pls CVI–CVIII; C. Manhès-Deremble, *Les vitraux narratifs de la cathédrale de Chartres*, Paris 1993, pp. 261–7 and 308 (window 7, 14).

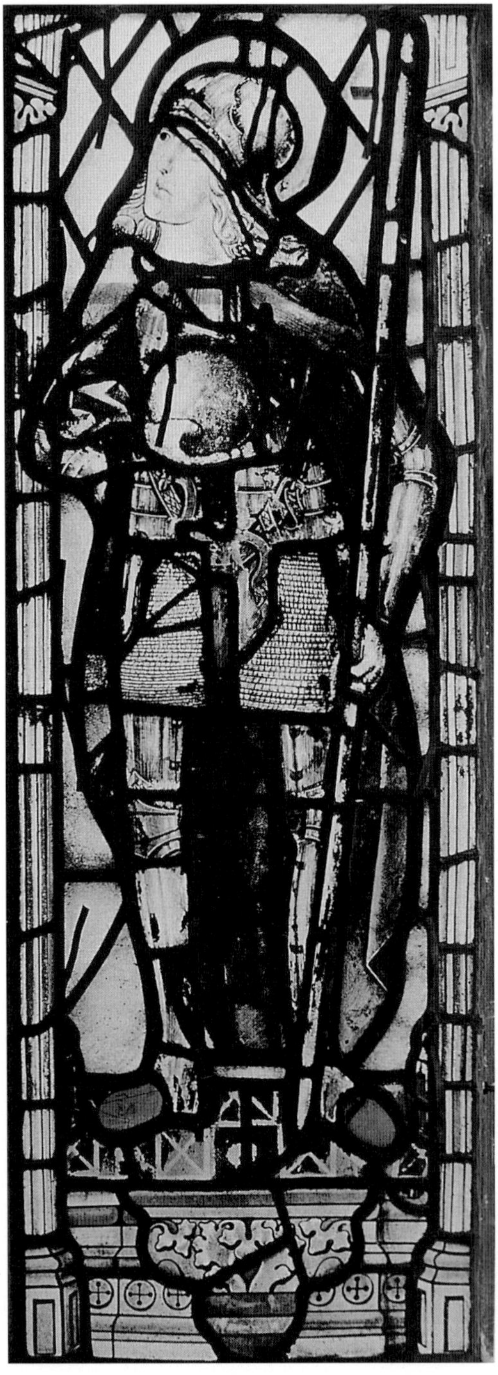

Fig. 41. *3l, princely knight, probably Roland (Photo by Sydney Pitcher, c. 1940, © Dean and Canons of Windsor)*

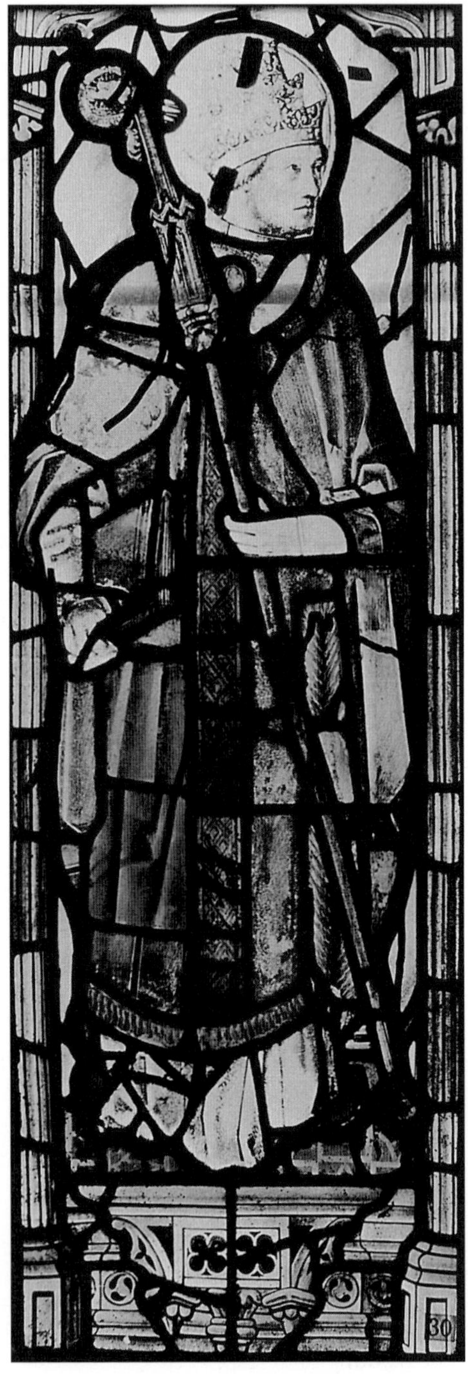

Fig. 42. *4a, pope (Photo by Sydney Pitcher, c. 1940, © Dean and Canons of Windsor)*

and his cope blue with green lining. The head, tiara and nimbus are painted and stained on a single piece of plain glass now lead-mended. Intrusions in the drapery.

4b A POPE

He stands full-face holding a stained open in his hands, and a double cross-staff in the crook of his left arm. His dalmatic is blue, with plain painted orphrey and green fringe, his cope ruby with yellow band and lining. The paint on the face (and the main part of the tiara) is effaced. The blue pieces covering his right upper arm are no doubt intrusions, replacing ruby. Probably middle period.

4c A POPE (Fig. 27)

His head, with yellow tiara against a blue nimbus, is turned sharply to the L over his right shoulder, and over a ruby-covered book which he holds in his right hand, while his left arm is stretched out to the R, in the opposite direction, to hold erect his double cross-staff. His cope is pink-murrey, over a blue dalmatic with green fringes and yellow orphrey, and below that an apparelled alb. Intrusions in the drapery.

A mature work with notable *contrapposto*, by the St Eleutherus glazier (cf. 1c, 1e, 5c, 3n, 3d). Date probably after 1510.

4d Composite figure: POPE/BISHOP

He faces half R, holding an open book in front of him with both hands, while a double cross-staff leans across his body against his right shoulder. His blue cope has stained orphreys decorated with crosses, and a green lining. The green-fringed tunicle is embroidered all over with crossed lozenges in golden stain. The face is an intrusion, and there are several others in the drapery; indeed, the head of the staff may itself be intruded, since it seems to begin as a crozier head, and the tiara may also be a stop-gap.

4e A POPE

He faces half L, holding his double cross-staff across his body and against his left shoulder. Ruby cope with yellow band and lining over blue dalmatic with plain orphrey and green fringe; below that an alb. Face by the 'wide-eyed' restorer; the stained tiara is original, against a blue nimbus with modern intrusions.

4f AN ARCHBISHOP (Fig. 43)

Ruby chasuble with blue lining and white and painted pallium over. Below this are a green dalmatic with yellow fringes and an apparelled alb. The whole figure is by Willement, to the same design as 4j.

4g A MARTIAL SAINT, probably St George (Fig. 44)

An inscribed scroll across his thighs is much damaged, but may perhaps be read: /Justic[ie]/ Martuisat[e]/ for *Martirisate* (Be martyrs for Justice), the corruption being due in all probability to the misreading of the letters 'ir' as 'u' by the glazier. The Garter motto below was added by Willement. The knight faces half L in full armour, bearing the cross of St George on the tabard which covers his breastplate and upper arms; a sheathed sword hangs from a baldrick at his left side, and at his feet lies a snarling amber dragon.

The painting of the face corresponds closely with that of the head of Elizabeth of York in Christ's College Chapel, Cambridge, which must be attributed to Simon Symondes (see p. 21 and Fig. 22). He was clearly not the designer of the figure, however, for he has misinterpreted the helmet, and locked the visor under the comb. Date *c.* 1510 or a little later.

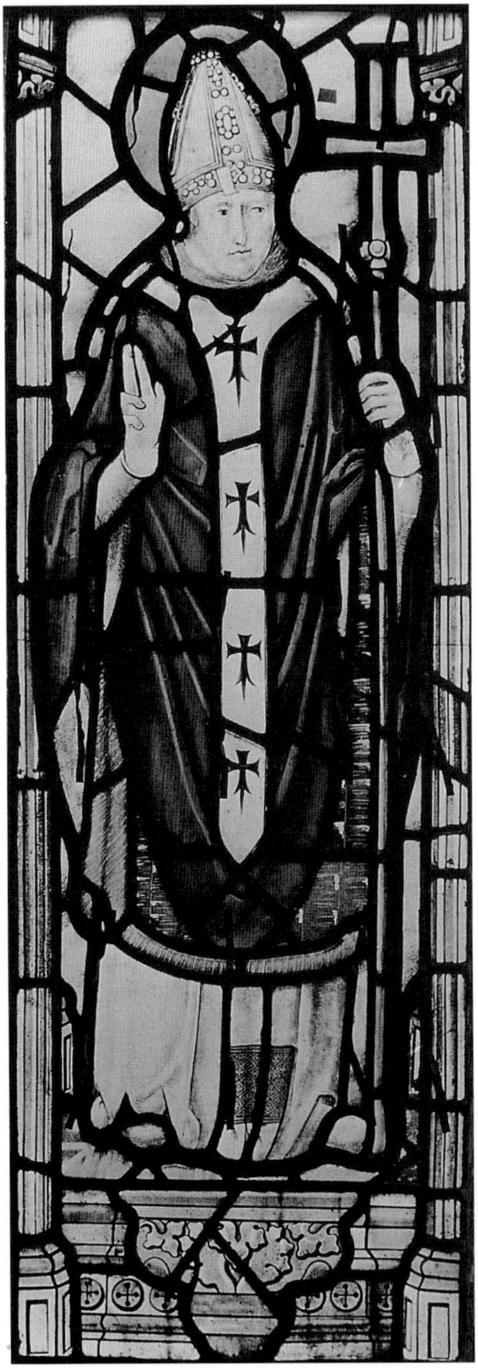

Fig. 43. *4f, archbishop (Photo by Sydney Pitcher, c. 1940, © Dean and Canons of Windsor)*

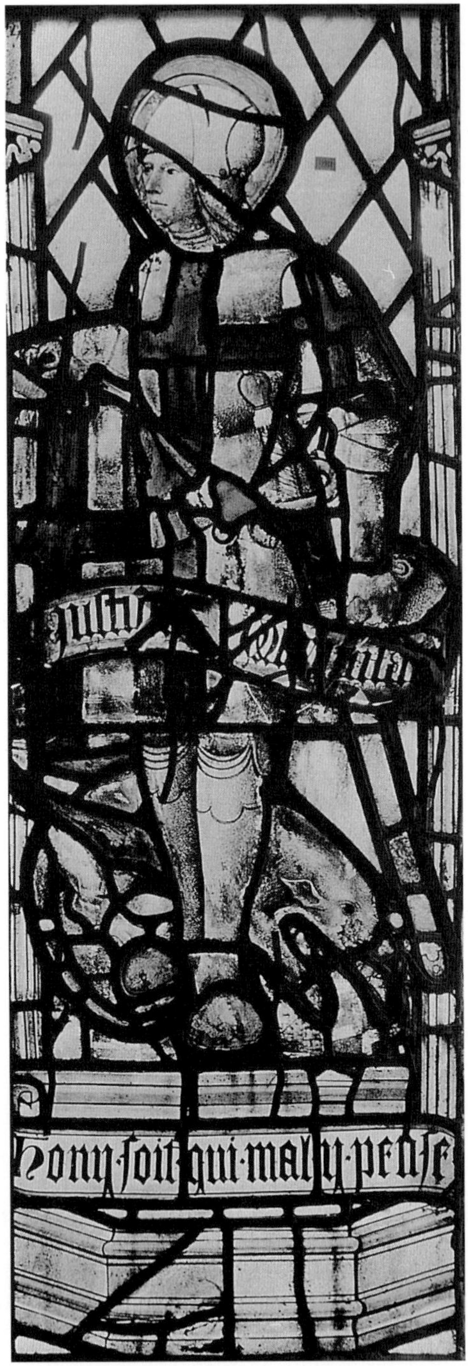

Fig. 44. *4g, martial saint, probably St George (Photo by Sydney Pitcher, c. 1940, © Dean and Canons of Windsor)*

This figure, showing a nimbed warrior bearing *argent a cross gules* and trampling on a dragon, has a better claim than any other to represent St George, the patron saint of the order and of England.

4h A MARTIAL SAINT (Fig. 45)
Inscribed scroll:/fidem•/s(er)uate•/('Keep the Faith'), legible in Pitcher's photograph, but now damaged and lacking the middle of the second word.

He faces half L holding his drawn sword point upwards in his right hand, and the end of the scroll in his left. The scabbard hangs from a baldrick at his left thigh, and he wears full plate armour, all of blue flash, except for his ruby shoes and the painted mail skirt under his tuilles. Blue helmet with blue, green and ruby plumes against a stained nimbus. A violet dragon curls under his feet. Style as 4g, but less mature both in design and in execution; date *c.* 1505.

4i A MARTIAL SAINT
On a central scroll: /Rebelles/castig/[e]lis/. The last piece is restored, and the original must have read: /etis/ (You are to punish rebels).

Based on the same cartoon as 4h, but the knight's sword (with green grip) is in the scabbard on his left thigh, and in his right he carries an anklet or cuff.

Head restored by 'delicate' glazier.

4j AN ARCHBISHOP
As 4f, by Willement. Blue chasuble over ruby dalmatic.

4k A KNIGHT (Fig. 46)
Leans to R, and looks over his left shoulder, holding his sword point upwards in his right. Ruby cloak and shoes, blue surcoat with yellow girdle, plate armour on legs. Hair and rayed nimbus stained, features worn. A yellow linked chain round his neck. The set of his knees and feet, at right angles to each other, suggests a design by AM; the sophisticated head, the rayed nimbus and the poise of the body point to a continental executant, *c.* 1505.

4l A PRINCELY KNIGHT
He moves half R, holding a sceptre over his right shoulder and the grip of his sheathed sword in his left hand. Wears a yellow strawberry-leaf coronet against a murrey nimbus, and a tabard with ruby cross on breast and arm; pale blue plate armour is visible on his forearms and legs. Face damaged and lead-mended; intrusions at right wrist. The motto /H/ony soit/qui•mal•/y•pense•/ was added by Willement.

Painted by one of Simon Symondes' colleagues.

4m A PRINCELY KNIGHT (Fig. 21)
As 4l, with slight variations, but probably painted by Symondes himself, *c.* 1508–10.

4n A PRINCELY KNIGHT (Fig. 47)
He looks half L, holding his sword, which hangs from a baldrick, in both hands by pommel and sheath. He wears a blue helmet combined with yellow coronet against a green nimbus, and a tabard as 4l and 4m; on his left jamb, just below the knee, is a garter on which/hony s/ can be read. Intrusions at right elbow and shin. A compact figure, with a rather grim, determined look; related in style to 4l. Garter motto below by Willement.

4o A KNIGHT
He looks half R, holding a drawn sword across his body with his right hand, and with his left arm hitching up a ruby, green-lined mantle. Plate armour, with mail skirt and ruby shoes. The placing

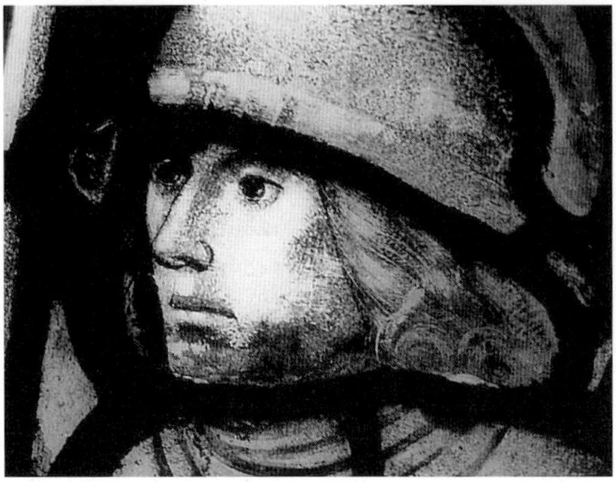

Fig. 45. *4h, martial saint, detail of head (© R.C. Marks)*

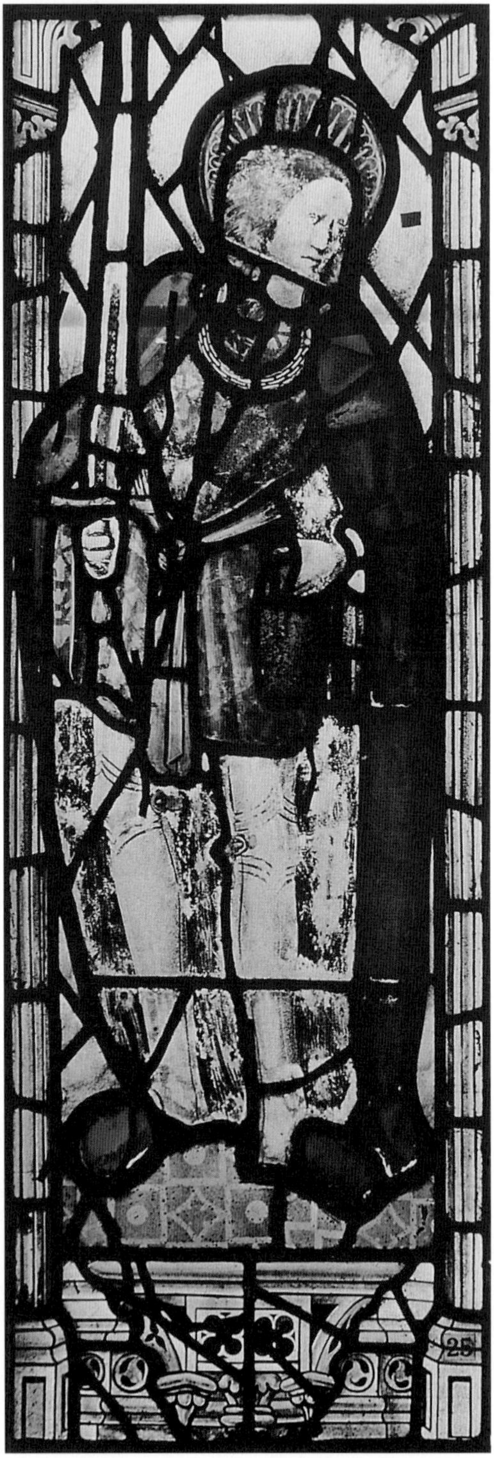

Fig. 46. *4k, knight (Photo by Sydney Pitcher, c. 1940, © Dean and Canons of Windsor)*

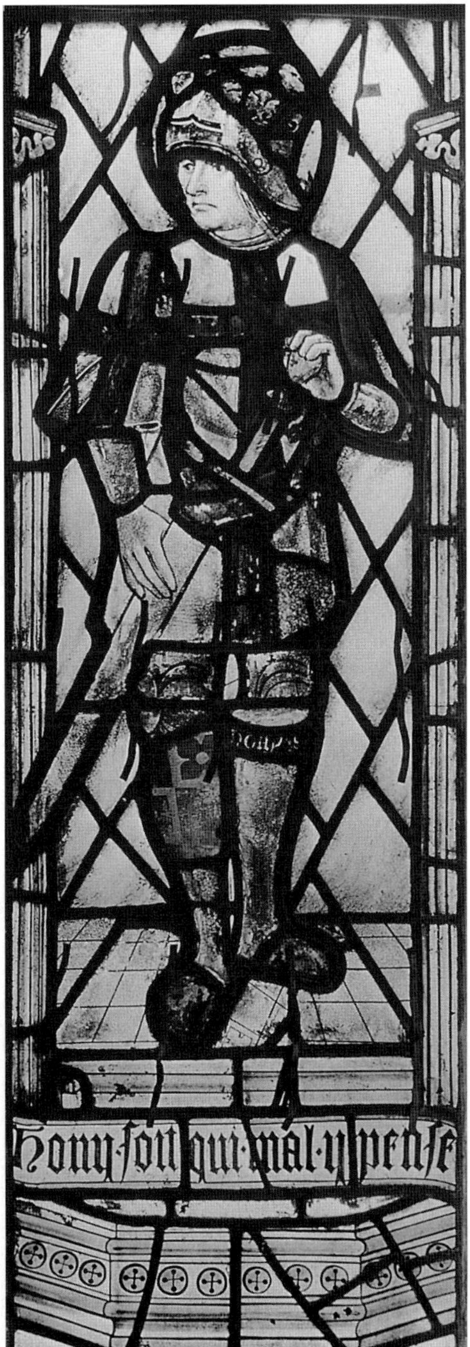

Fig. 47. *4n, princely knight (Photo by Sydney Pitcher, c. 1940, © Dean and Canons of Windsor)*

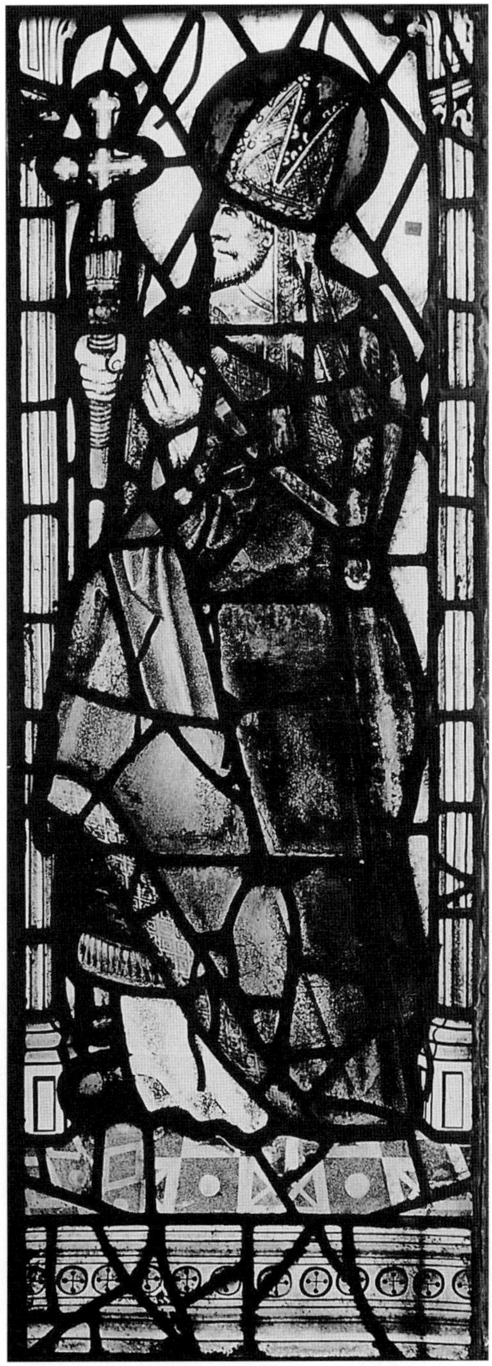

Fig. 48. *5j, archbishop (Photo by Sydney Pitcher, c. 1940, © Dean and Canons of Windsor)*

of head and nimbus (by the 'wide-eyed' restorer) give him a stoop; several intrusions. The slender legs and feet at right angles suggest an early design by AM, but the deep cross-folds of the drapery may well imply a later date of execution, perhaps *c.* 1505.

5a A POPE

He looks half R, holding a double cross-staff across his body with his left hand, and a ruby book in his right. He wears a blue cope, a green dalmatic with yellow orphreys, an amice, and an alb. The head and the stained tiara, which are both modern (by the 'wide-eyed' restorer), are set against a fragmented and lead-mended murrey nimbus.

5b A POPE

He holds a pontifical cross-staff in his right hand (displaced and probably intruded); in his left he grips a blue-covered book. Wears a blue, green-lined cope with yellow band over a ruby tunicle and an apparelled alb. His tiara is stained and his nimbus murrey. Head restored (by the 'delicate' glazier) and orphrey replaced with plain glass. The sloping shoulders suggest an early design, *c.* 1500.

5c A POPE

Faces half R with a timid look, wearing a stained mitre against a blue nimbus, a murrey cope with green lining, and a ruby dalmatic with yellow orphrey over an alb with fur cuffs, and ruby sandals. An amice is visible at his neck. He holds a ruby-covered book in his left hand and a double cross-staff in his right. Many repairs and intrusions in the drapery, especially the shoulders of the cope and the orphrey, which below the waist has been replaced with plain glass. An early figure by the St Eleutherus glazier (1c).

5d A POPE (Fig. 29)

He leans his head forward in a fixed, earnest look, holding a ruby book in his left hand and a double cross-staff in his right. His cope is blue with stained orphreys and ruby lining, over a murrey dalmatic with green fringes, an alb and ruby sandals. Condition good, apart from a few mending-leads. The sharp angle of the chin is repeated in the drapery below; cf. St Calixtus (1d), and also 3b and 3k.

5e COMPOSITE FIGURE

Above, a female martyr wearing a black-painted veil against a stained and rayed nimbus, holding a book in her left hand and a palm in her right, over her left shoulder. She wears a three-quarter-sleeved violet robe with green fringes and yellow orphrey. Below the waist the garment turns into a dalmatic, and the orphrey changes its pattern; beneath this are an alb and ruby shoes. The nun's palm has been restored, and there are several intrusions.

5f AN ARCHBISHOP

Blue cope with ruby lining over green dalmatic with yellow orphrey, and green apparelled vestment below.[69] Stained cross-staff in left hand. A Willement figure, reverse of 1k, by the 'meagre' glazier.

5g A BISHOP

Leans head and looks out L, holding crozier in left hand and an open book in right. Ruby cope with stained orphrey, and green dalmatic with pink-murrey fringe and stained orphrey, over alb. Stained mitre against green nimbus. Several intrusions and mending leads. The face, the long folds, and the

69. The glazier seems to have made a mistake here; the garment seen at the archbishop's ankles must have been intended for an apparelled alb, which of course could only be white.

heavy stippling are characteristic of AM, but the face is heavy, and the hands are evidently by an assistant (cf. 2d). Date *c.* 1515.

5h A BISHOP
Turns half R, raising left hand to chest and holding crozier in right. Wears ruby cope, yellow dalmatic with blue fringes and plain painted orphrey, over alb below. Head and nimbus modern (the 'meagre' glazier); intrusions and mending leads in drapery.

5i AN ARCHBISHOP
He stares out half R, holding back his ruby cope with his left hand, and leaning a cross-staff over his right shoulder. Blue dalmatic with yellow orphrey and green fringes, alb and blue sandals beneath. Green nimbus and stained mitre over modern face (the 'wide-eyed' glazier); some intrusions and mending leads.

5j AN ARCHBISHOP (Fig. 48)
He turns his head in full profile over his left shoulder, with his back almost square to the spectator, so as to reveal a green hood over his blue cope (cf. 2a). His arms seem both to be distorted: he holds out a stained cross-staff in front of him with his right hand, and raises his left towards it, so that the folds of his cope reveal a ruby dalmatic with green fringe, and an alb. His nimbus is ruby, and his mitre and lappets stained, with ruby tassels. Many mending-leads and insertions; the arms can never have been very convincing, but they have clearly been disturbed by damage and restorations. The large hooded eye and schematic beard point to the St Peter glazier (see p. 21).

5k A SAINT
Reversed copy of 1n, St Alban. Blue cloak with ruby cape-collar over amber coat. Green nimbus and hose. By the 'wide-eyed' glazier.

5l A ROYAL KNIGHT
Reversed copy of 4n by 'wide-eyed' glazier, with garter inscribed /hony•s/ on left leg, and the full motto below. Murrey nimbus.

5m A ROYAL KNIGHT OF THE GARTER
Stands with feet apart, pointing to the ground with his right hand, and with his left holding the scabbard of his sword, which hangs from a baldrick. He wears pale blue plate armour on his legs, a white surcoat with red cross, a blue cloak over, with Garter emblem on the left shoulder, and a coronet. Pale violet nimbus. Head damaged and lead-mended. Painted *c.* 1508 by one of Simon Symondes' colleagues, cf. 4l; the Garter motto below added by Willement.

5n A ROYAL KNIGHT OF THE GARTER (Fig. 49)
He wears a closed crown (stained) over a blue helmet against an orange nimbus, and faces half R, holding a sceptre in his right hand and raising his left towards the pommel of his sheathed sword, which passes behind him. Tabard, leg armour and garter as 4n below. Condition good, apart from a few mending-leads. Probably painted by Simon Symondes (see p. 21); motto by Willement.

5o COMPOSITE FIGURE
Faces forward and raises one hand above a ruby-covered book which he holds in the other. Wears a black hood which is just visible over a blue cloak with ruby lining, and a pink-murrey robe below. The drapery folds are complex and sophisticated, but the bare feet, in the style of the Judas glazier (see p. 00) are intruded from elsewhere. The head, turbaned and crowned with a coronet together with the ermine choker below, are by the 'delicate' restorer. The turban, the coronet, the hood,

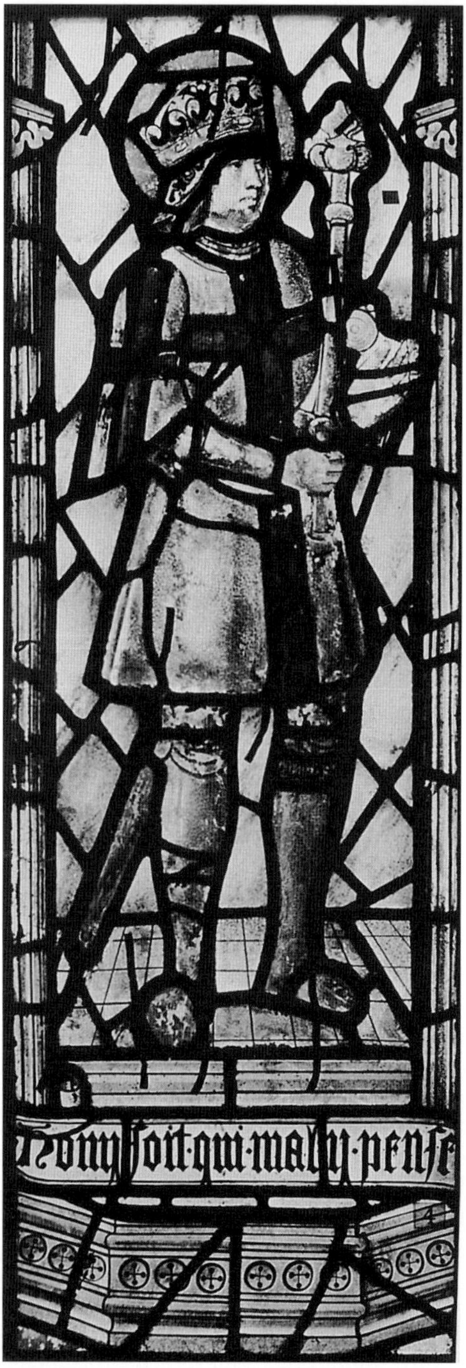

Fig. 49. *5n, royal Knight of the Garter (Photo by Sydney Pitcher, c. 1940, © Dean and Canons of Windsor)*

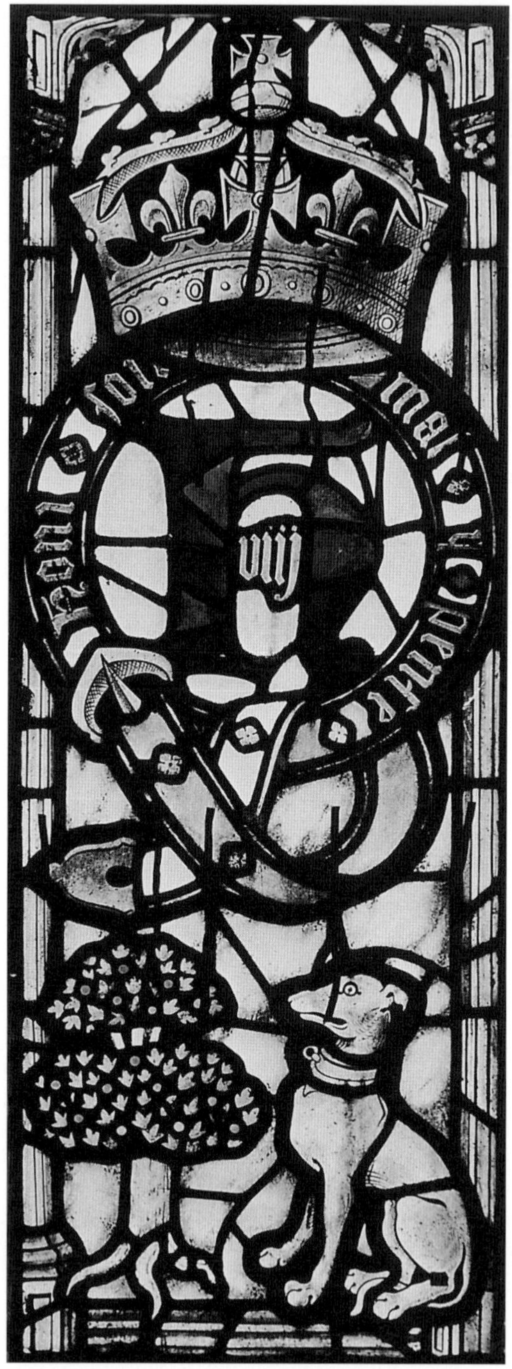

Fig. 50. *A12, cypher of Henry VII (not Henry VIII) (Photo by Sydney Pitcher, c. 1940, © Dean and Canons of Windsor)*

the ermine and the book would seem to suggest an 'oriental' nobleman and scholar. Probably late in the first decade of the sixteenth century.

A9 CYPHER OF EDWARD III within the Garter, ensigned with an open crown, above his badges, sunbeams arising from clouds and a falcon. Willement, 1842.

A10 CYPHER OF EDWARD IV within the Garter, ensigned with a closed crown, above his badges, the falcon within an open fetterlock and the white lion of March. Willement, 1842.

A12 CYPHER OF HENRY VIII (an error for VII) within the Garter, crowned, above the badges of Henry VII, the hawthorn bush and the greyhound collared *or*. Willement, 1842. (Fig. 50)

A13 CYPHER OF QUEEN ELIZABETH within the Garter, crowned, above her badges, the portcullis chained and the falcon crowned and bearing a sceptre fleurdelisé. Willement, 1842.

D3 COAT OF ARMS 45 x 43 cm
Argent a cross gules, for St George, on a green background. Early sixteenth century. This was the only coloured glass left in the window during the war of 1939–45.[70]

SMALL GLASS: SIDE-CHAPELS AND THE DEANERY

As far as possible the same notation is used as for the great west window, except that windows are for the most part designated simply by their orientation (e.g. north-east, south-west). The east window of the Deanery Chapel is a special case (see below).

THE OLIVER KING CHAPEL

Willement conjectured, no doubt correctly, that the painted panels of four royal figures now in the south choir aisle, which carry an *Orate* for Oliver King, were copied from the original glazing of windows in this chapel.[71] The figures represent (from R to L) Prince Edward, son of Henry VI, King Edward IV and his uncrowned son Edward V, and Henry VII, all of whom Oliver King served as principal secretary. The figures stand on pedestals against a background of appropriate heraldic quarries.

The three remaining windows in the chapel now contain heraldic pieces set in medieval quarries. The fourth (sIV, westernmost in the south wall) was blocked up *c.* 1930 in Harold Brakspear's reorganization, and the glass then installed in it was removed to the Schorn Tower before being set up, in 1945, in the north window of the Annexe to Edward IV's chantry. The glass remaining in the chapel was removed for safety by Wilfred Drake in 1940 and replaced in 1945.[72]

I *(East)*

1a COMPOSITE SHIELD 25 cm diam.
Enclosed within a Garter inscribed with the motto of the Order, a waisted shield bearing *France modern and England quarterly* impaling a quartered shield in yellow stain and worn-out paint and sanguine: 1 and 4 *gules a castle or* (Castile), 2 and 3 *argent a lion rampant purpure* (Leon) impaling per

70. See n. 66.
71. *Collegiate Chapel*, p. 19.
72. SGC XVII. 43.30. General description in *Architectural History*, ii, p. 467.

saltire in chief and in base *or four pales gules* and in the flaunches *argent an eagle displayed sable* (Sicily), in base of third quarter *argent a pomegranate proper* (Granada); but the impaled shield has been reversed, for whatever reason, and is back to front. As it stands the shield is no doubt intended to represent Henry VII and Catherine of Aragon.

In the dexter arms the fleurs-de-lis are of amber potmetal inserted in the blue, and the lions are roughly abraded out of the ruby and stained. Date between 1509 and 1533. These may perhaps be the arms seen in the east window by Ashmole in 1666.[73]

1b ST GEORGE 25 cm diam.

A heater-shaped shield bearing *argent a cross gules* within a Garter with the motto of the Order. In the L and upper arms of the cross the ruby has been replaced, while in the other two arms the flashing is worn. Date *c.* 1500.

A shield *argent a cross gules* was signalled by Ashmole in the east window in 1660;[74] but see sIII, 3b.

2a SHIELD OF SIXTEEN QUARTERINGS 21 x 18 cm

For Henry Hastings, third earl of Huntingdon. Potmetal, paint, stain and enamel.

1 *Argent a maunch sable* (Hastings)

2 *Per pale or and sable a saltire engrailed counter-changed* (de la Pole)

3 *Quarterly France modern and England a label of three points argent charged with cantons gules* (for George Duke of Clarence)[75]

4 *Gules a saltire argent a label of three points argent and azure*[76] (for Neville)

5 *Argent three lozenges in fess gules* (Montagu)

6 *Or an eagle displayed sable*[77] (for Monthermer)

7 Azure (repair)[78]

8 *England within a bordure argent* (Edmund of Woodstock)

9 *Gules a fess between six crosses crosslet* (Beauchamp)

10 Azure (repair)[79]

11 *Quarterly argent and gules a fret or over all a bend sable* (Despenser)

12 *Or three chevronels gules* (Clare)

13 *Sable two bars argent and in chief three plates* (Hungerford)

14 *Argent a griffin segreant gules armed azure* (Botreux)

15 Azure (repair)[80]

16 *Or two bars gules in chief three torteaux* (for Wake)[81]

73. Oxford, Bodleian Library MS Ashmole 850, 238.
74. *Ibid.*
76. Most of the azure has turned to black.
75. The red colour of the cantons has in fact disappeared.
77. *Sable* should read *vert armed gules*.
78. The lost coat must have been *azure semy de lis and a lion rampant argent*, for Holand.
79. This should be *checky or and azure a chevron ermine*, for Newburgh.
80. For *paly wavy or and gules* (*Moleyns*).
81. If the field were *argent*, and not *or*, this coat could represent Moels; but Edmund of Woodstock (see 8th quartering) married Margaret, daughter and sole heir of John Lord Wake.

Henry, third earl of Huntingdon (1535–95) was installed K.G. in 1570; he was one of the custodians of Mary Queen of Scots.[82] His stall-plate as K.G. shows the arms of Hastings with 28 quarterings. Here nos 13 to 16 should properly precede no. 2, but such displacement is not unusual in armorial stained glass. Owing to the complication and minute scale of the quarterings certain charges are omitted or misrepresented.

The royal arms in no. 3 are enamelled, while the field of no. 14 is abraded out of flashed ruby and the griffin's break and talons added in blue enamel. Late sixteenth century.

2b SHIELD OF TWELVE QUARTERINGS 21 x 18 cm
For William Brooke, tenth Lord Cobham. Paint, stain and enamel

1 *Gules on a chevron argent a lion rampant sable* (Brooke)

2 *Gules on a chevron or three lions rampant sable* (Cobham)

3 *Argent seven mascles gules three, three, and one* (Braybroke)

4 *Barry nebuly azure and or* (de la Pole)

5 *Gules a fess between six crosses flory or* (Peverell)[83]

6 *Argent a chevron between three eagles' legs sable* (Bray)

7 *Vair three bendlets gules* (Langvale or Bray)[84]

8 *Argent on a bend gules three goats argent armed or* (Hallewell)

9 *Sable a chevron between three bulls' heads cabossed argent* (Norbury)[85]

10 *Gules a fess chequy argent and sable between six crosses pattee fitchee of the second* (Boteler)

11 *Or two bends gules* (Sudeley)

12 *Bendy of ten or and azure* (Montfort)

In the first three quarterings the ruby is abraded.
The tenth Lord Cobham (1558–97) was installed K.G. in 1584.[86] Late sixteenth century.

sII *(South-east)*

1a WAISTED SHIELD WITHIN SCROLLING RUBY AND BLUE ALTERNATING 33 x 18 cm

1 *Sable a lion rampant between eight cinquefoils argent* (Clifton)
2 *Gules three lions passant guardant or* (intruded)
3 *Azure a lion rampant langued queue fourchee or* (Braytoft?)
4 *Argent a fess between three escallops gules two and one* (Kingthorpe?)

Probably for Gamaliel Clifton, D. C. L., Canon 1522–41.[87]
The blue scrolling below is a replacement.
Date *c.* 1530.

82. Grace Holmes, *The Order of the Garter: Its Knights and Stall Plates 1348 to 1984*, Windsor 1984, p. 68.
83. The field should be *azure* and not *gules*: London, College of Arms MS Vincent 172, p. 51.
84. College of Arms MS Vincent 172 gives Langdale, but the arms were also used by a branch of the Bray family, and they appear in other parts of the chapel, as well as no. 6, for Sir Reginald Bray.
85. A fleur-de-lis which normally appears on the point of the chevron has been omitted: *ibid.*
86. Holmes, *Order of the Garter*, p. 80.
87. *Fasti Wyndesorienses*, p. 156. No satisfactory Clifton pedigree has been found, however, by which the two last quarterings could be identified.

1b Heater-shaped shield 30 cm diam.
Enclosed within a Garter and motto *Gules four fusils ermine impaling gules three arches argent capitals and bases or two and one* (Arches). For John, first Lord Dynham, Lord Treasurer 1486–1501, who was installed K.G. *c.* 1487 and died 28 January 1501.[88] Date *c.* 1500; a similar coat is in the annexe to Edward IV's Chantry, N II, 1a.

2a RED ROSE, with crown above
Rose 16 cm diam, crown 19 x 23 cm (separate).
Flashed ruby, paint and yellow stain; seeds of rose amber potmetal. Paint worn. Early sixteenth century.

2b SHIELD WITHIN GARTER 30 cm diam.
Heater-shaped shield bearing *azure a cross flory between five martlets or* for Edward the Confessor, one of the original patrons of the Order. Paint worn; damage at foot of cross, where the fifth martlet has almost disappeared. Date *c.* 1500.

Ashmole saw a similar shield in the east window in 1666; but see annexe to Edward IV's Chantry, north window 1*c*.[89]

sIII *(South-west)*

1a RED ROSE 18 cm diam.
Seeds stained. Date early sixteenth century.

1b RED ROSE 18 cm diam.
Seeds amber potmetal. Date early sixteenth century.

2a HEATER-SHAPED SHIELD 28 cm diam.
France modern and England quarterly, enclosed within a Garter with the motto of the Order. Lions scratched out of wash on white glass yellow-stained. Date *c.* 1515.

2b HEATER-SHAPED SHIELD 28 cm diam.
France modern and England quarterly within a bordure argent, enclosed within a Garter with the motto of the Order, for Henry Stafford second duke of Buckingham.[90] Lions picked out of black paint on white glass yellow-stained, with straps of ruby leaded in.

The second duke of Buckingham (first creation) was installed K.G. in 1474, and executed after an abortive rising against Richard III in 1483. Date *c.* 1525.

3a HEATER-SHAPED SHIELD as 2a 16 cm diam.
Date early sixteenth century.

3b HEATER-SHAPED SHIELD: Order of the Garter 16 cm diam.
Argent a cross gules for St George, within Garter and motto. Date *c.* 1530.

EDWARD IV'S CHANTRY AND ANNEXE

These two rooms stand over nII (annexe) and nIII (chantry). They have both north and south windows and are divided by a glass screen. In 1782 an unknown glazier under the direction of

88. Holmes, *Order of the Garter*, p. 52.
89. Ashmole, as in n. 73.
90. Holmes, *Order of the Garter*, p. 105.

Henry Emlyn installed most of the stained glass now to be seen there (see pp. 00 and 00). The two pieces in the south window of the annexe must have been added later, and those in the north window of the annexe, which had until 1930 stood in the south-west window of the Oliver King Chapel, were set up in their present position in 1945.

The backgrounds of the east window of the annexe and the two north windows of the chantry are enlivened (if that is the right word) by unpainted pieces of red and yellow potmetal, which give a clue as to the origin and nature of the 'brash' work removed from the west window by Willement in the 1840s.

Annexe to Edward IV's Chantry

EAST WINDOW

1 Above door, on a late eighteenth-century background of coloured pieces. Small panel, David's young men visit Nabal (see p. 66).

NORTH WINDOW

See Oliver King Chapel, introduction, para 2, 2nd sentence.

1a SHIELD WITHIN GARTER 39 x 30 cm
Gules four fusils ermine impaling gules three arches argent and or two and one. For John Lord Dinham (1465–1509) K.G., *c.* 1485, cf. Oliver King Chapel (p. 232).

Glass rather dirty, paint of Garter worn. Date *c.* 1520.

1b HOROSCOPE OF EDWARD III 12 x 12 cm (Fig. 51)
Inscribed TER. MAXIMI. REGIS. EDWARD I. TERT II / HUJUS. COLLEGE II. FUNDATOR (IS) / NATIVITAS. ANNO. D. 1312. NOVEMBRIS 13.[91]

Paint only, rather worn. Date *c.* 1600. Origin unknown; in late seventeenth century stood in a window of one of the canons' houses.

1c SHIELD WITHIN GARTER 39 x 32 cm
Azure a cross flory between five martlets or. For Edward the Confessor. Condition good. Date *c.* 1520.

Ashmole saw a similar coat in the east window in 1666; but see Oliver King Chapel sII2b.

2a WAISTED AND SCROLLED SHIELD 27 x 22 cm
Argent a fess nebuly azure between three crescents jessant fleur-de-lis sable, all within a bordure gules. For Richard Sidenor, canon 1519–34, chancellor of the Order 1529.[92] Scrollwork alternating murrey and blue above, blue and ruby below (the last restored). The lower part of the shield has been repaired with a perpendicular slip of white glass across the charge. Date *c.* 1520.

2b RED CROSS CROWNED 34 x 22 cm (Rose 16 cm diam, crown 18 x 22 cm)
Seeds yellow, crown stained and strapped with lead, for Lancaster. Date *c.* 1520–30.

91. 'The nativity of the three times greatest King Edward the third founder of this College, in the year of our Lord 1312, on November 13.' See Lisa Jefferson, 'Edward III's horoscope in a stained glass window', *Friends Report* (1991–2), pp. 95–102.

92. *Fasti Wyndesorienses*, p. 138. The bordure should properly be engrailed.

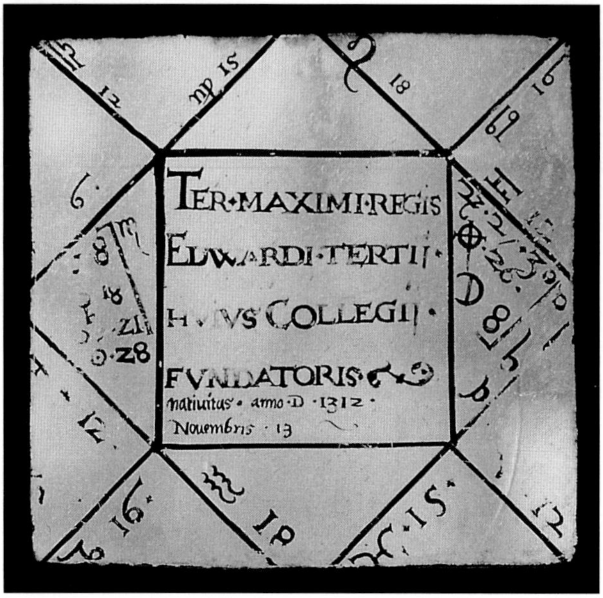

Fig. 51. *Horoscope of Edward III (© Dean and Canons of Windsor)*

2c WAISTED AND SCROLLED SHIELD 27 x 23 cm
France modern and England quarterly within pale ruby and blue scrolling, alternated, with capitals H and R painted and stained on white ground either side at waist, for Henry VIII.

Lions abraded from ruby, then painted and stained. A minor replacement in second quarter; scrolling all restored except upper L. Date *c.* 1535.

Attributed by Wilfred Drake to Galyon Hone, who worked at Windsor in 1533 and 1535, but without any specific justification; the work mentioned in the accounts is confined to the royal lodging.[93]

SOUTH WINDOW

S2a Seventeenth-century enamelled oval, set sideways: *The adoration of the kings* (see p. 66).
S2b Seventeenth-century panel: King Charles II: late seventeenth century.

SCREEN between annexe and Edward IV Chantry

In this glass screen are five small panels described on pp. 65–78.

Edward IV's Chantry

NORTH-EAST

2a Eighteenth-century OVAL WITH ROSE (see p. 103).
2b SHIELD OF ARMS 21 x 15 cm
Within a Garter on ruby ground: *on a field azure* an irregular shield *or*. This may originally have represented the arms of Guileno de Medici, duc de Nemours (brother of Pope Leo X), who was

93. *Architectural History*, ii, p. 251.

nominated on St George's day, 1514, and died 17 March 1516/17. The Medici arms were *or six roundels gules in orle, in chief on a roundel azure three fleurs-de-lis of the first.*[94]

The azure field (like the glass surrounding the Garter and its ruby ground) is no doubt eighteenth century; the paint is much worn.

NORTH-WEST

2b SHIELD OF ARMS 16 x 13 cm

Waisted fragment, *barry gules and vert on a fess argent a lion passant guardant between two cinquefoils of the field*, for Thomas Magnus.[95] Set in eighteenth-century glass. Cf. shields in Deanery, hall and south-east window of landing.

2c RED ROSE WITHIN GARTER 19 x 15 cm

Seeds abraded out of ruby and stained. Section of Garter R centre replaced, and paint much worn. The whole set in eighteenth-century yellow glass.

SOUTH WINDOW

Elliptical panel. *The adoration of the kings* (see p. 66).

THE DEANERY

CHAPEL, formerly Vestry of the earlier Chapel.

EAST WINDOW

Head of window 84 x 130 cm, filled with quarries, within which are nine fragments, numbered L to R, foot to head.

8

7 9

4 5 6

1 2 3

1 FRAGMENTARY FIGURE 30 x 12 cm

Head with yellow curly hair; mid-fourteenth century. Body in white robe with stained undergarment pointing to sword in scabbard at belt; brassy stain, but no doubt mid-fourteenth century. This piece reversed.

Base with seventeenth-century inscription EX FIDE.

The fourteenth-century fragments, together with 3 below, may be all that remains of Edward III's glazing of the earlier chapel (see p. 1).

2, 4, and 6 AGNUS DEI QUARRIES *c.* 12 x 10 cm (Fig. 52)

The lambs carry resurrection banners and are inscribed with 'M'. The scrolls above, inscribed with 'As god will', show that the M forms a rebus for MAGNUS, and imply that the quarries date between 1520 and 1547 (see below, Deanery Hall).

94. This account is based on a letter of 30 March 1994 from the late Sir Colin Cole, Garter Principal King of Arms, to whom the author is indebted for his generous assistance on a number of heraldic problems.

95. *Fasti Wyndesorienses*, p. 100: see below, Deanery, Hall.

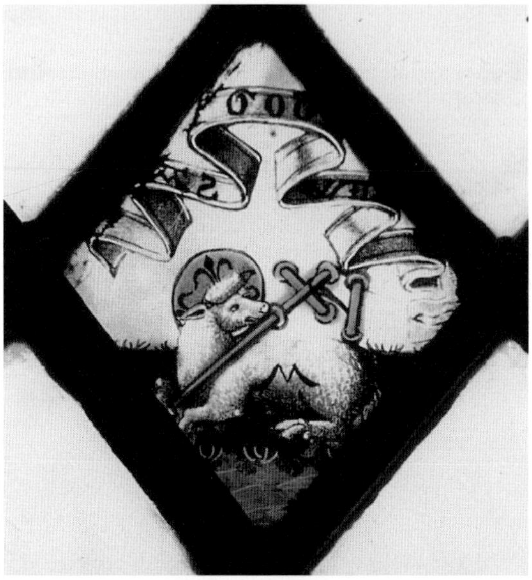

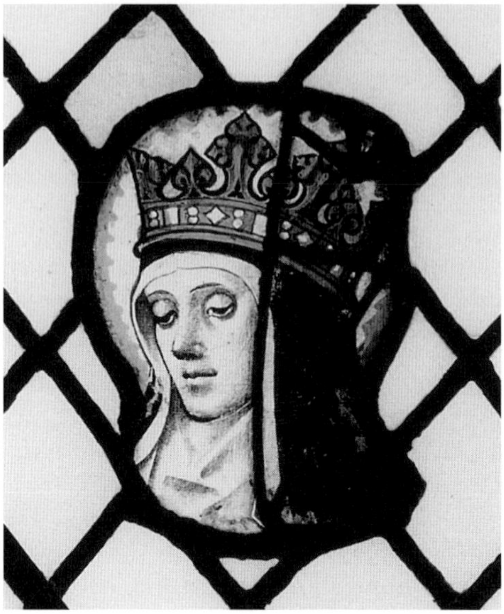

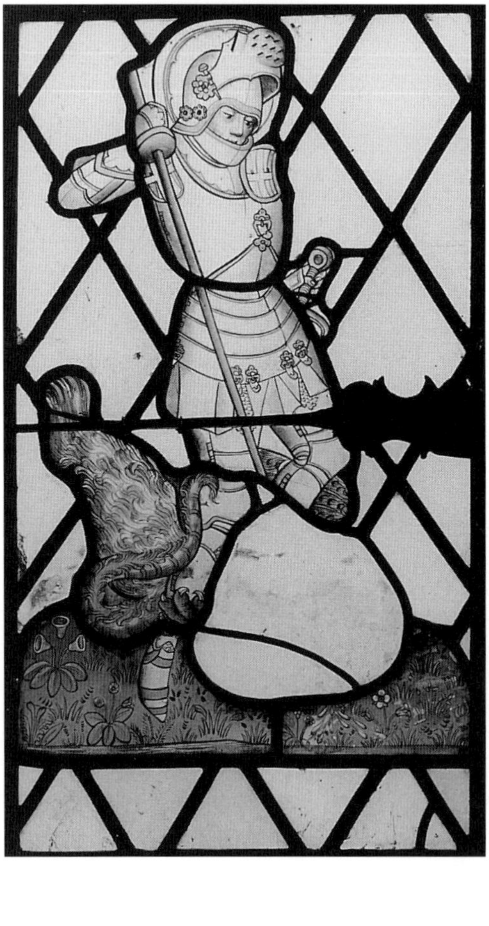

Fig. 52. *Deanery chapel, east window agnus dei quarry (H.G. Wayment)*

Fig. 53. *Deanery chapel, east window, female saint (H.G. Wayment)*

Fig. 54. *Deanery chapel, St George casement as restored in 1966 (Photo © G. King & Sons)*

3 ST STEPHEN 30 x 11 cm
Full-length figure facing three-quarters L.
White robe and nimbus, stained hair and beard. Stained mantle thrown loosely over shoulders. Two grey stones in crook of left arm. Crown glass, mid-fourteenth century. Perhaps a remnant of the earlier chapel glazing. See 1 above.

5 FEMALE HEAD, crowned and nimbed 23 x 15 cm (Fig. 53)
Black veil back-painted, with lighter back-painting behind eyes, mouth and hair.

Anglo-Flemish, early sixteenth century; possibly for St Etheldreda of Ely; cf. the roughly contemporary roundel in the east window of the Deanery Chapel, Ely Cathedral.[96]

7, 8, and 9 Fragments of foliage work leaded up into quarries *c.* 12 x 10 cm; early sixteenth century. The window, with all its glass, is in good condition.

WEST WINDOW

ST GEORGE AND THE DRAGON 48 x 30 cm (Fig. 54 and front cover)
Irregular panel in paint and stain on crown glass, set in the centre of the window. The saint stands on a mound covered with grass and wild flowers, stabbing the dragon through the mouth with a short spear held in his right hand, and holding the hilt of his sword with is left. He is nimbed and wears full plate armour.

Technique: outstanding: delicate stippling on the contours, back-painting, and strict control of yellow stain on the edges of the armour and in the dragon's fur.

Condition: excellent, apart from the dragon's foreparts, which are restored.

History: The panel was found in 1965 in the Catherine Room of the canons' cloister, behind plaster, which had preserved it, probably since the 1640s. It was mounted in a seventeenth-century casement which was cleaned and repaired by G. King & Son of Norwich in 1966 (Fig. 54). In 1982–3 the dragon was restored by the Cathedral Studios at Canterbury and the panel installed in this window, so that it can be seen from either side.[97]

Style, costume and date: There are two distinct ways of estimating the date of the panel. The first is by style. The figure is modelled with a purity and distinction characteristic of the best work in the international style of the early fifteenth century. The panel appears to have been painted by the same glazier as the outstanding fragments at Thenford, Northants, which comprise a figure of St Christopher and parts of those of St Anne and the Virgin. These have been very plausibly attributed to Thomas of Oxford, who is last recorded at both Oxford and Winchester in 1422, and a payment was made to his widow in 1427–8.[98]

The second means of estimation lies in comparison of the saint's costume and armour with dated (or roughly datable) monumental brasses. St George wears plate armour throughout, though mail is visible under the taces and tuilles. He wears a rounded helm and palettes. The taces, only four in number, suggest the early Lancastrian period. Lord Willoughby d'Eresby, of Spilsby, Lincs., already had five taces *c.* 1400, and wore palettes with crosses, as here. The tuille is not shown on surviving brasses before 1424; it must be remembered, however, that Windsor was the very fount of English chivalry, and a figure of the patron saint which was to be displayed there might be expected to wear fully contemporary armour. The date may be put in the first quarter of the fifteenth century, and very probably in the second decade, at the height of the French wars.

96. C.J. Shanks, *St Etheldreda Queen and Abbess*, Ely 1975, cover plate.

97. The recent history of this panel could not have been compiled without the help of the late Dennis King and of Dr Sebastian Strobl.

98. Marks, *Stained Glass in England*, pp. 177–8 and fig. 142.

DEANERY HALL (Pl. IIIb)

Opposite the foot of the stairs, west of yard door.
WAISTED SHIELD WITHIN WREATH, under folded scroll 39 x 24 cm overall, arms 29 x 24 cm
Bendy gules and vert, on a fess argent a lion passant guardant between two cinquefoils of the field for Thomas Magnus. Inscription on scroll of plain glass *As God will.*
The scrolled borders of the shield are blue and pink-murrey above, the reverse below. Condition good, but the R piece of the scroll, with the word 'will', and the border scrolling at lower R are modern replacements.

Canon Thomas Magnus was one of the royal chaplains in attendance on Henry VIII at the Field of Cloth of Gold in June 1520, and held his canonry from that year until 1547. He died on 28 August 1550 at Sessay-in-York.[99] See Edward IV Chantry and Deanery Chapel (p. 59–60), and Deanery Landing (p. 63).

DEANERY, DINING ROOM

SOUTH-EAST WINDOW

SHAPED SHIELD WITHIN A WREATH CROWNED 51 x 30 cm
France modern and England quarterly. Fleurs-de-lis painted and stained, inserted into blue potmetal; lions abraded from ruby, then painted and stained.

Shield and R half of crown original; L half of crown, together with three lateral pieces of wreath and roses enclosed by them, modern. Numerous mending-leads and some unmended cracks.

SOUTH-WEST WINDOW

SHAPED SHIELD WITHIN A WREATH CROWNED 47 x 30 cm (Pl. IIIc)
France modern and England quarterly impaling 1. *argent (for azure) three fleurs-de-lis or between two flaunches ermine on each a white rose* (for red) *seeded or;* 2. *England with a label argent* (Brotherton);
3. *gules crusilly or, on a bend argent the Flodden augmentation;*[100]
4. *argent* (for azure) *two lions passant guardant between four fleurs-de-lis dimidiated or,* for Henry VIII and Catherine Howard.

Bordering the green wreath are six red-blooms, of which that R is modern; above the crown on either side a rose slipped. In the impaled coat not all the tinctures are rendered in the glass; this would have entailed the introduction of many small pieces and excessive leading, or else extensive abrasion of blue and ruby flash. Condition good. Date *c.* 1540.

DEANERY LANDING

SOUTH-EAST WINDOW

1 RED ROSE WITHIN A WREATH, CROWNED 51 x 30 cm overall
The wreath is held by eight clasps set at regular intervals, those at the cardinal points being decorated with grotesques in paint and stain, while those in the diagonals consist of red roses flanked by demi-roses.

99. *Fasti Wyndesorienses*, p. 100.
100. 'A demi-lion pierced in the mouth by an arrow, depicted in the colours for the arms of Scotland, which James, late King of Scots, bore'; A.C. Fox-Davies, *Complete Guide to Heraldry*, London 1951, p. 590. This minute charge is here, of course, shown only schematically.

Condition: The main rose and its white surround, together with two rose clasps (at 2 and 8 o'clock), the upper R section of the crown, and four green pieces of the wreath (at 2, 4, 7 and 11 o'clock) are nineteenth-century work. Four original pieces of the wreath bear the numbers 7 (three times) and 5 scratched on the back; the grotesque clasp L is also numbered 7. The three ancient pieces of green in the wreath of the portcullis at SW1 are also marked 7, and probably stood originally at 2, 4 and 11 o'clock. The seeds of the rose are original potmetal, and so are the five green pricks, which bear the numbers 12, 12, 13, 13 and 15 scratched on the back.

Date *c.* 1535.

2 WAISTED SHIELD WITHIN WREATH, under folded scroll 38 x 24 cm overall, arms 28 x 24 cm

Arms of Thomas Magnus, as wreathed shield in hall. Here again the R piece of the scroll is a replacement, and so is the top L fragment of green glass in the shield.

SOUTH-WEST WINDOW

1 TUDOR ROSE seeded, pricked and crowned 32 x 21 cm

White centre for York with seeds in paint and stain, within five-petalled red rose for Lancaster. The crown is nineteenth-century; although the glass has an uneven surface it is not original, and the stain is clumsily managed.

2 PORTCULLIS WITHIN WREATH, for Beaufort 51 x 30 cm overall

Three green pieces of the wreath (at 11, 2 and 4 o'clock) are early sixteenth-century work; the rest is no doubt Willement's *c.* 1844. The wreath is copied from that surrounding the Lancaster rose in the south-east window.

Repaired by Wilfred Drake 1938. He writes as follows on 12/4/38 to W. McIntosh, Chapel Surveyor:[101]

The only original portions of Galyon Hone's glass remaining in this panel are those three pieces of green foliage each of which was etched [on the back] with a numeral '7', still plainly discernible. Doubtless the original panel was one of a large number painted for the Castle circa 1535: every piece of the various medallions being 'numbered' in this manner, for the convenience of the Tudor glasier who leaded them together. Perhaps other panels at St George's Chapel, and the Deanery, also have these etched numerals?

The attribution to Hone must remain doubtful; for the numbered pieces see entry on *Red rose* above (Deanery Landing SE).

NORTH WINDOW

The two western windows in the north wall, above the second flight of stairs leading from the hall, each have two lights of plain quarries edged with decorative bands, and measure approximately 160 x 47 each. Bands on all four sides 4 cm deep bear alternating red dragons and white greyhounds, each pair set between alternating Tudor roses (white enclosing red) and portcullises, both crowned. On the sides the beasts embrace leafy branches between the two badges, but at head and foot they clamber on them.

Condition excellent, except that the lowest L upright dragon in the easternmost light has been replaced by white glass.

No doubt by Willement *c.* 1844.

101. SGC XVII.9.9.

The Netherlandish Glass in the Upper Chantry of King Edward IV

WILLIAM COLE

The glass in the upper chantry of King Edward IV (also known as the Queen's Closet or Royal Pew), was described by the writer in the *Friends Report* for 1975–6.[1] The present essay contains some slight revisions.[2] The chantry also contains a few medieval fragments, but this account concerns only the Netherlandish glass. Before speculation on its provenance is attempted, it will be described. There are seven panels situated as follows:

IN THE EAST WALL
1. David's young men visit Nabal

IN THE SOUTH WALL
2. The adoration of the Kings

IN THE UPPER PART OF THE SCREEN AT THE NORTH END
3. The return of the Prodigal Son

IN THE UPPER PART OF THE SCREEN AT THE CENTRE
4. The Prodigal Son spending his substance in riotous living

IN THE DOOR IN THE LOWER PART OF THE SCREEN FROM NORTH TO SOUTH
5. The Father awaiting the Prodigal Son
6. Esther being crowned by Ahasuerus
7. St Cornelius with donor

These small pictures have to be seen at close range to be fully appreciated. The three in the door, numbers 5, 6 and 7, and number 2 in the south wall, are easily seen. Number 1 is less easy, number 3 very difficult and number 4, which was hidden at the south end of the screen, has been moved and is now more easily seen.[3] In the description of the panels, measurements are given in centimetres, height followed by width. The attributions are

1. William Cole, 'The Flemish glass in the Upper Chantry of King Edward IV', *Friends Report*, v (1975–6), pp. 285–94. Short descriptions also appeared in the author's *A Catalogue of Netherlandish and North European Roundels in Britain*, Corpus Vitrearum Medii Aevi, Great Britain, Summary Catalogue 1, Oxford 1993, pp. 315–16.

2. Dr Cole completed this essay before his sudden death in 1996. Some small further revisions have been made by the editor, with benefit of sight of the other contributions in this volume which had not been seen by Dr Cole at the time of his death.

3. The original article published in 1976 stated that some of the glass was the wrong way round. Since then this has been put right.

tentative, with the exception of number 1, for which the engraving from which it has been copied has been found, and number 3, which has similarities to a drawing formerly in the Kunstgewerbe Museum in Berlin, apparently destroyed in the Second World War.[4]

1. *David's young men visit Nabal*

Rectangular, 25 x 20.3 cm. Netherlandish, late sixteenth/early seventeenth century. Drawn in black paint and dark yellow stain (Fig. 55).
The detail on this panel is difficult to see because it has become corroded and is also somewhat faded. It is fairly high up on the east wall and is obscured by exterior window bars. The design is after Martin van Heemskerck (1498–1574).[5] Figure 56 shows the engraving from which the glass painting was copied. The story of David and Nabal is recounted in 1 Samuel XXVIII and van Heemskerck illustrated it with five drawings. They are (a) David sending messages to Nabal, (b) Nabal receiving David's messengers, (c) David commanding his servants to arm themselves and destroy Nabal, (d) a man telling Abigail, Nabal's wife, of the danger, and (e) Abigail on her knees before David. One of the most successful scenes is the last, depicting Abigail with her gifts spread about her, kneeling in David's path. The painter was perhaps attracted by the description of Abigail, 'a woman of good understanding and of beautiful countenance' and by the opportunity of a still life picture of all the presents. The Windsor panel is a copy of the second in the series. In the foreground Nabal's men are shearing sheep while Nabal, seated under a tree, is in a position to watch them. In front of him is a basket of food and on his right ewers of wine. On his left are David's young men, and Nabal raises his hand in a questioning gesture. Under the engraving is a description in Latin which may be translated as 'Nabal refuses them and sends them empty away'.

Heemskerck has made the sheep-shearing a prominent part of the scene and it is shown in detail. An interesting feature is the decoration of the ewer on the far left. The glass is a faithful copy of the engraving, and although it appears to be cut down slightly all round, this is the effect of the leading which hides the edges. The engraving and the glass are the same size. There is another in the same series in Glynde Place, East Sussex.[6] It is not mentioned in Kerrich's catalogue (see note 4), but the drawing is in the Print Room at Leyden, Holland. It depicts Nabal's feast.[7]

2. *The adoration of the Kings*

Elliptical, 20.3 x 25.4 cm. Netherlandish, seventeenth century. Drawn in brown/black paint, yellow stain and various coloured enamels (Fig. 57).
This is the latest in date of the Netherlandish pieces. Unfortunately it is broken, the lower circular piece bottom left being an insertion. Otherwise the glass is original. The three kings offer their gifts. The kneeling king offers his casket of gold and takes hold of the

4. This was brought to the author's notice by Dr Karel Boon.
5. T. Kerrich, *A Catalogue of Prints . . . after Martin Heemskerck*, Cambridge and London 1829, p. 22.
6. Cole, *Catalogue*, p. 95, no. 795.
7. Heemskerck was a popular artist among glass-painters and a list is given in William Cole, 'Glass Paintings after Heemskerck in England', *The Antiquaries Journal*, lx, pt ii (1980), pp. 247–67.

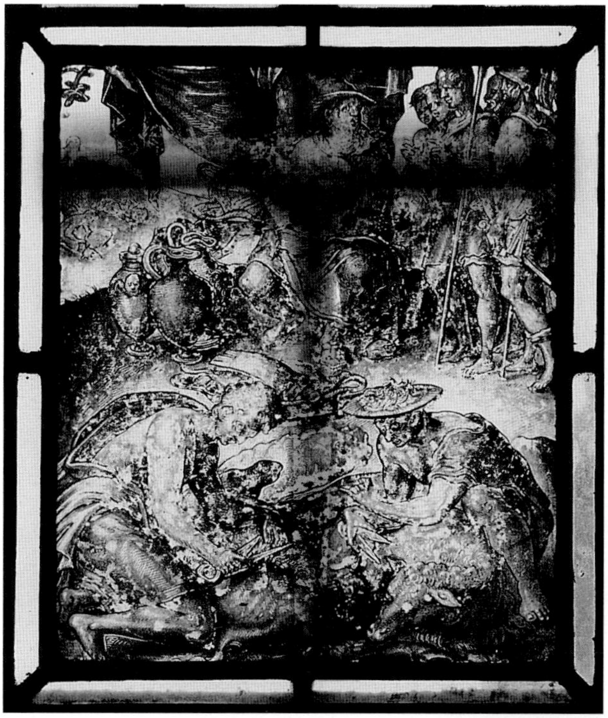

Fig. 55. *David's young men visit Nabal, upper chantry of Edward IV (William Cole)*

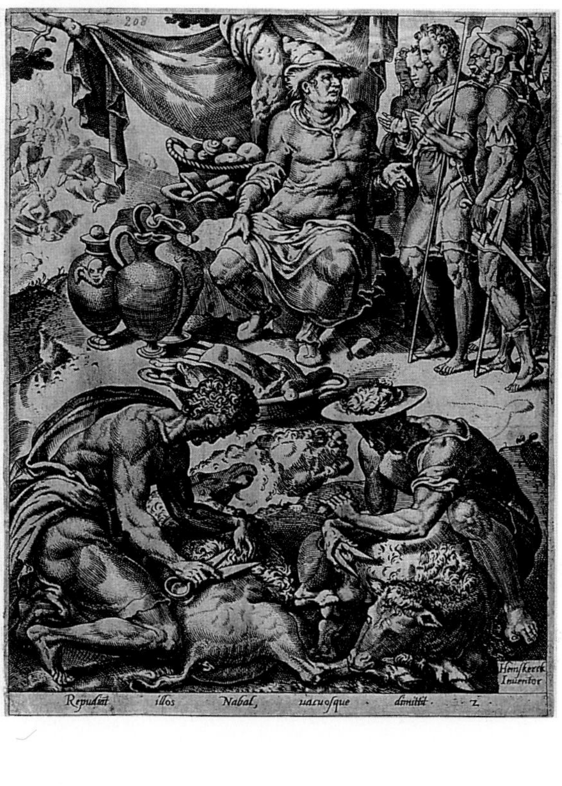

Fig. 56. *David's young men visit Nabal, engraving after Martin van Heemskerck (Courtesy of the British Museum)*

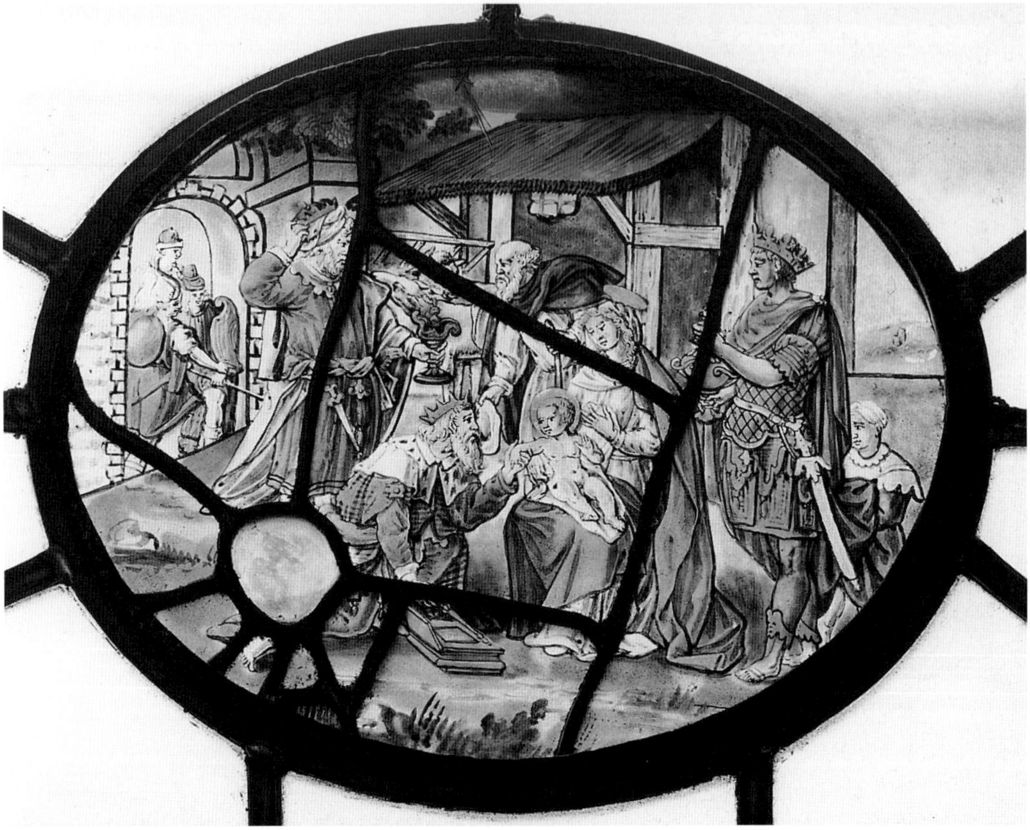

Fig. 57. *The adoration of the Kings, upper chantry of Edward IV (William Cole)*

hand of the Christ Child, who blesses him. The king on the right-hand side is young but is not portrayed as a Moor, as is often the case in Netherlandish paintings of this period.[8] The star is shining over the stable with the ox and the ass in the stall. Joseph, an old man, has respectfully uncovered his head and holds his hat in his hand. There is a secondary scene on the left where three young men enter the stable. They are possibly part of the retinue. The scene of the visit of the shepherds was sometimes combined with the adoration of the kings, but these young men do not look like shepherds. The artist probably felt that the figures would help balance the picture. This panel has been taken from an engraving in reverse.

There is a similar panel in the church of St Nicholas, Wasing, Berkshire.[9] It is not so damaged as the Windsor panel, but the sides are cut off and consequently some of the design is lost. Also, the background is slightly different.

8. G. Schiller, *The Iconography of Christian Art*, London 1971, vol. 1, p. 112.
9. Cole, *Catalogue*, p. 299, no. 2361.

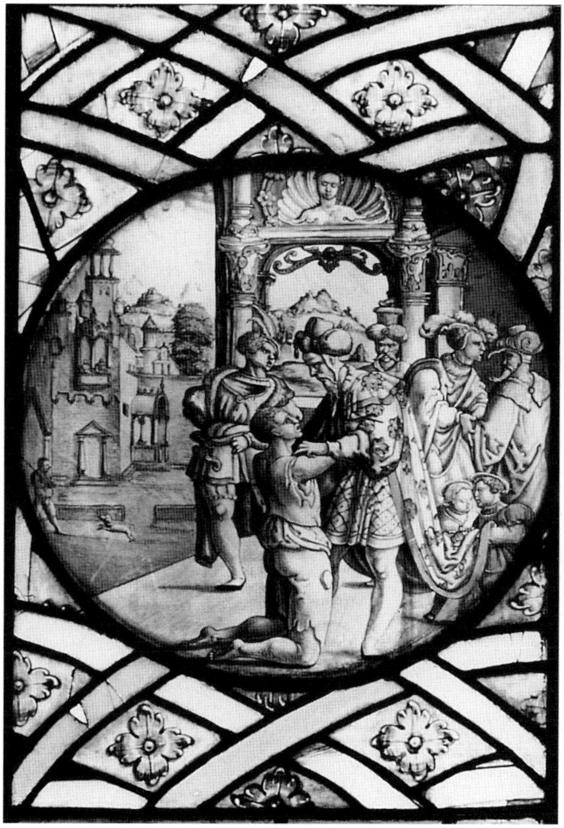

Fig. 58. *The return of the Prodigal Son, upper chantry of Edward IV (William Cole)*

3. The return of the Prodigal Son

Roundel, 25.4 cm in diameter. Netherlandish, mid-sixteenth century. Drawn in black paint and yellow stain (Fig. 58).

The scene is set in the courtyard of a house. The columns of the open doorway have ornate capitals and above them is a mermaid in a shell. Two people look out of a balcony from a house on the left. A dog runs towards a man on the left and in the background is a hilly landscape with buildings. In the foreground kneels the Prodigal Son, poorly dressed, with his father's hand on his shoulder. The father's tunic has a trellis pattern and his robe, which is held by two young pages, has a foliate design. Two men are earnestly talking on the right and there are two others standing, one to the left of the son and the other by the arch. The former is a young gallant while the latter is older and looks morose, presumably the older brother.

The style is that of the Antwerp Mannerists and is reminiscent of Jan Swart von Gronigen who worked *c.* 1522–53. He made many drawings for stained glass and this is probably a copy of one of them. In a panel in the Rijksmuseum, *Esther before Ahasuerus*, said to be by Swart, the latter bears a strong resemblance to the figure of the father in the Windsor panel. Among twenty-three drawings by Swart in the British Museum is a series of the life of Joseph.[10] A glass roundel of Potiphar's wife showing Joseph's cloak to her husband is in the Fitzwilliam Museum, Cambridge. Potiphar's companion is similar to the man standing against the arch in the Windsor panel. There is also a resemblance to Swart in the general appearance of the full, large figures and the way in which they are grouped.

The writer has not found the engraving of the drawing on which this roundel is based. It was presumably one of a series. The most commonly depicted scenes from this parable are the Prodigal Son receiving his patrimony, spending his substance on riotous living, being turned out by the harlots, feeding the swine and being received by his father. Swart, like many other artists, made drawings of the story and a number of original drawings have survived. In the Louvre is a drawing of the Prodigal Son receiving his patrimony[11] and in the British Museum is another version of him received by his father, which included the subsidiary scenes of the killing of the fatted calf and the feast. A small rectangular version of this drawing in glass survives at Glynde Place in Sussex.[12] There are many resemblances to the Windsor panel.

The Prodigal Son was a popular subject with engravers and glass-painters, and the writer has identified over seventy Netherlandish roundels or small panels of the sixteenth and seventeenth centuries in England depicting this subject. The Windsor roundel is one of the best, being of very high quality. No trouble has been spared in the detail and the whole makes a good composition and is carefully drawn.

4. *The Prodigal Son spending his substance in riotous living*

Roundel, diameter from top to bottom 25 cm, diameter across 23 cm. Netherlandish, sixteenth century. Drawn in paint and yellow stain (Fig. 59).

The roundel has been cut off at the sides to fit the screen. When the writer described this panel in 1976, it was located at the southern end of the screen and was dirty, with broken plating. It has since been cleaned and moved to the centre of the screen where it is much easier to see. There is a similar one in the Victoria & Albert Museum, where it has been described as a carousel scene (Fig. 60).[13] As early as the eighteenth century, Knight described the Windsor roundel as depicting the 'dissipation' of the Prodigal Son, and this identification seems reasonable.[14] The two roundels are not identical. Both versions share the same main characters but the V&A version has more figures on the left, and the Windsor panel more on the right. The man with the tambour is missing from the Windsor panel but it shows the whole of the lute player, as well as the man trying to attract her attention. The Windsor panel pushes the main characters to the middle ground, whereas the V&A version puts them in the foreground. The most likely explanation for these differences is that the original drawing was rectangular and the glass-painters have compressed it into a circle in a different way. The alteration of a rectangular design into a circular shape or, in the seventeenth century into an oval, was quite common. In the V&A

10. British Museum, *Catalogue of Drawings by Dutch and Flemish Artists*, London 1932, p. 2, Popham No. 28.
11. Frits Lugt, *Inventaire Général des Dessins des Écoles du nord. Maitres des anciens Pays-Bas*, Paris 1968, pl. 59.
12. Cole, *Catalogue*, p. 99, no. 797.
13. Accession no. 5649–1859.
14. C. Knight, *The Windsor Guide*, Windsor 1799.

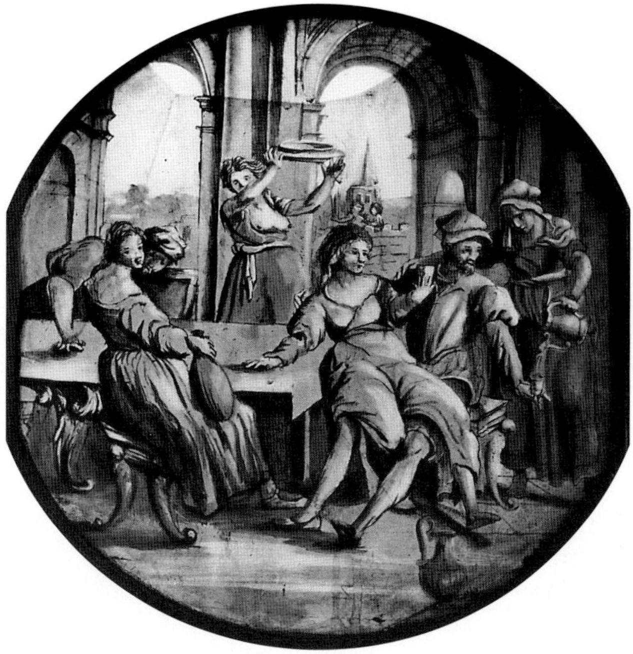

Fig. 59. *The Prodigal Son spends his substance in riotous living, upper chantry of Edward IV (William Cole)*

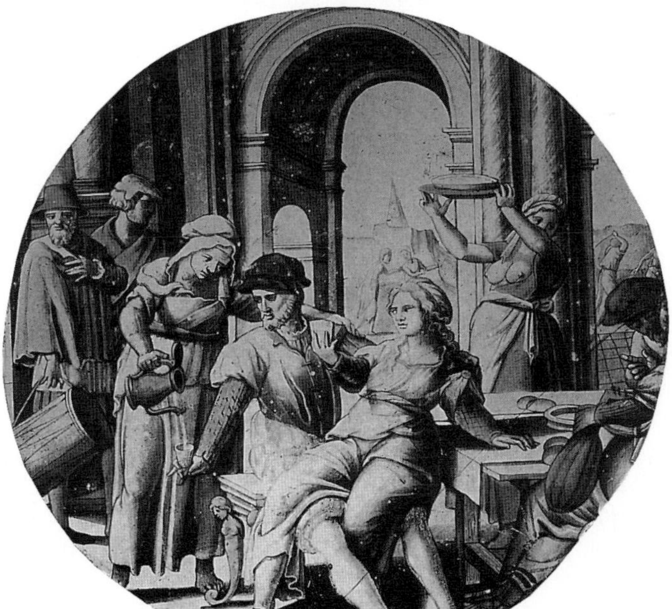

Fig. 60. *The Prodigal Son spends his substance in riotous living, upper chantry of Edward IV (Courtesy of the V&A)*

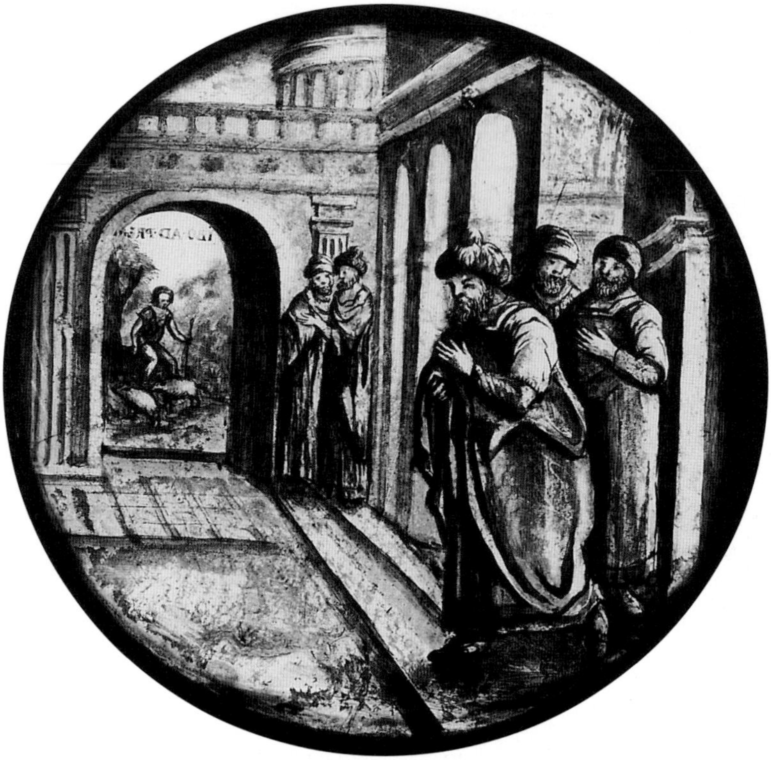

Fig. 61. *The Father awaiting the Prodigal Son, upper chantry of Edward IV (William Cole)*

catalogue Rackham suggested that the drawing 'reflects the manner of Jan Swart'.[15] However, Karel Boon has suggested that this panel is probably of the same series as one or more formerly in the Kunstgewerbe Museum in Berlin. They were attributed by Friedländer to designs by Koecke.[16] Marlier, writing forty years later, is of the same opinion.[17]

5. *The Father awaiting the Prodigal Son*

Roundel, 23 cm diameter. Netherlandish, sixteenth century. Drawn in black paint and yellow stain (Fig. 61).

The inscription, just above the prodigal in the arch at the left-hand side, reads IBO AD P[AT]REM (I will go to father). The whole phrase is taken from Luke's Gospel XV, v.18 (*surgam et ibo ad patrem meum*, I will arise and go to my father). There is very little room for the inscription and the glass-painter manages with nine letters. The roundel is unusual

15. Bernard Rackham, *Victorian & Albert Museum. A Guide to the Collections of Stained Glass*, London 1936, p. 111.
16. Max Friedländer, *Amtliche Berichte aus der Königl. Kunstammlungen*, xxxix, Jahrgang 4 (January 1918).
17. Georges Marlier, *La Renaissance Flamande. Pierre Coeck d'Alst*, Brussels 1966.

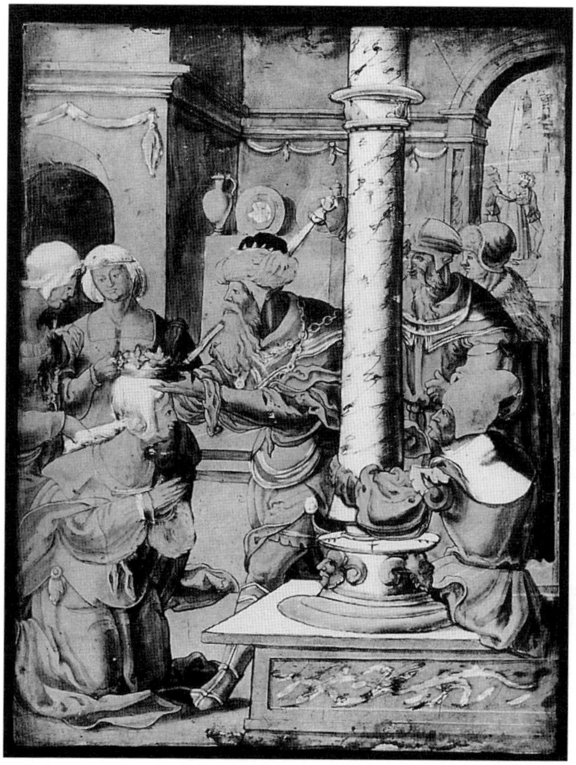

Fig. 62. *Esther being crowned by Ashauerus, upper chantry of Edward IV (William Cole)*

because the whole emphasis is put on the vacant spot soon to be occupied by the returning son. The father is leaning forward in thought, and he, like the other men, is gesticulating. The son is still feeding the swine and has not yet quite 'come to himself'. The paint is rather a dirty black and the drawing is rather weak. The writer has not found either an engraving or another glass panel with a similar representation.

6. *Esther being crowned by Ashauerus*

Rectangle, 28.5 x 21.6 cm. Antwerp School, mid-sixteenth century. Drawn in black paint and yellow stain of two colours, light yellow and orange (Fig. 62).

There are many engravings depicting the story of Esther. It was not, perhaps, as popular as the story of Susannah and the Elders, but its romantic nature gave it an appeal. Two of the King's chamberlains plot against him. The Good Mordechai is rewarded, Hamaan, the villain, is hanged, but overall is the gentle spirit and charm of Esther. She was one of the finalists in a beauty competition organized by the King's officers and she was eventually chosen by him. She 'obtained favour in his sight more than all the virgins; so that he set the royal crown on her head and made her queen instead of Vashti' (Esther II, 7).

She has two maidens behind her and the king has three followers, one of whom is sitting at the base of a column and has his arm around it. Through the arch in the distance is a second scene. The king, with an attendant, is talking to another man, possibly Hamaan. This panel would have been one of a series depicting the complete story. Martin van

Heemskerck, for example, illustrated the story with eight pictures.[18] Although glass-paintings of some of these are to be found in England,[19] the writer has not found any relating to the Windsor panel, nor has he been able to trace the engraving from which the panel was copied. It is similar to many of the Antwerp Mannerist pictures and drawings that were produced in profusion during the sixteenth century. One of the features that point to this origin is the prominence given to the architecture. The central column with its carved base and marbling effect seems to dominate the picture. Who but a Mannerist would give such emphasis to the man's arm round the column? The general delineation of the movement, the flowing drapery and the costume are all in the Mannerist style. Karel Boon has suggested that this is a very late version of a design originally by Swart; there are similar figures to that of Esther in Jan Swart's drawings.

7. *St Cornelius with donor*

Roundel, 19.1 cm in diameter. Probably Netherlandish but showing Rhenish influence in the drawing of the features. Sixteenth century. Drawn in black paint and yellow stain (Fig. 63).

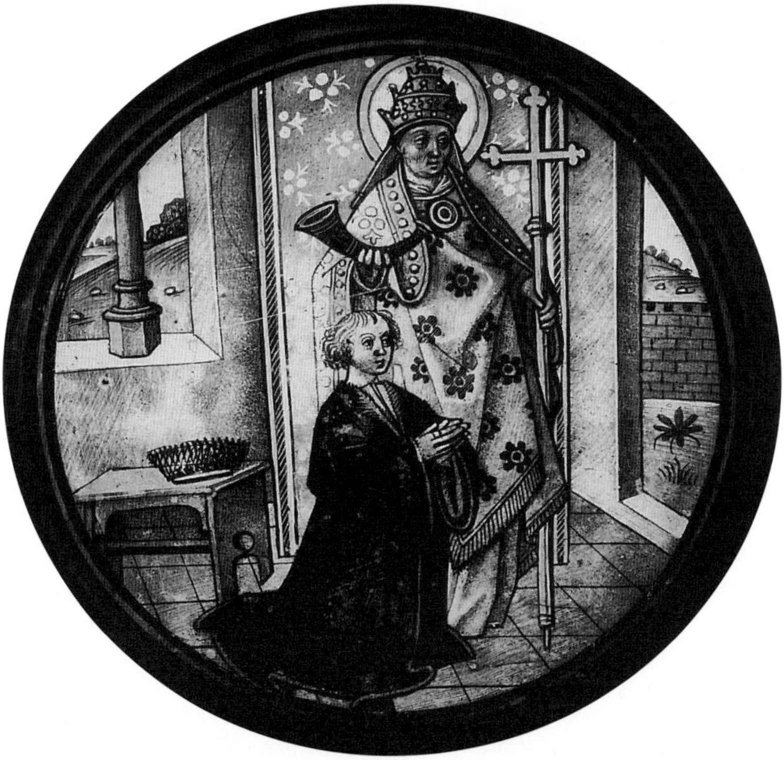

Fig. 63. *St Cornelius with Donor, upper chantry of Edward IV (William Cole)*

18. Kerrich, op. cit., note 5, pp. 29–30.
19. St Mary's, Shrewsbury and the Bodleian Library, Oxford.

A votive panel with the donor kneeling at his patron's side. Pope Cornelius wears his papal tiara and holds his staff in his left hand and his symbol, a horn, in his right. His cope is decorated with septfoils. He stands in front of a tapestry and the landscape is visible on either side through Gothic window openings. The donor is a layman. Behind him is a Gothic stool with his decorated hat on it.

St Cornelius was pope for only a few years, 251–3. His symbol is a play upon his name and his help was beneficial to those with epilepsy or nervous diseases. His principal sanctuaries were at Compiègne and Carnac in France, Cologne and Aachen in Germany and Liège and Niove in Brabant, Belgium.[20]

THE ORIGIN OF THE GLASS

Nothing has been found in either the Chapel or Royal Archives concerning the origin of the glass and the three references to it are so short that they can be quoted in full.

Ordered that Dr Lockman be empowered to agree with Mr Emblin for Wainscotting & fitting up the Queenes Closet according to the plan delivered to the Chapter and with the Glazier for ornamenting the windows with painted glass. [Chapter Acts, 8 April 1782][21]

To Emblin by estimate for work done in the Queen's Closet	70.0.0
For Stained Glass and glaziers Work for Do.	40.2.6
[Audit Book, Michaelmas 1781–2][22]	

in looking into the matter, it appears that we [the Lord Chamberlain's department] have nothing to do with the Fabric. When the chapel was restored and decorated under the superintendence of Mr Willement in 1840/1, the Chapter restored and decorated the windows and the exterior of the Queen's Closets' [Extract from a letter to Sir Thomas Biddulph, Master of the Household, from the Lord Chamberlain, Viscount Sydney, 13 May 1862] [23]

There is therefore no evidence to explain how the Netherlandish glass reached Windsor. It was probably imported in the eighteenth century and there are records of imports in that period. By the turn of the nineteenth century the importation of continental stained glass had developed into a thriving business.[24] In Horace Walpole's *Anecdotes of Painting* appears the following:

About the year 1753 one Asciotti, an Italian, who had married a Flemish woman, bought a parcel of painted glass from Flanders and sold it, for a very few guineas, to the Hon. Mr. Bateman of Old Windsor. Upon that I sent Asciotti again to Flanders, who bought me 450 pieces for which, including expenses of the journey, I paid him 36 guineas. His wife made more journeys for the same purpose and sold her cargoes to one Palmer, a glazier in St Martin's Lane, who immediately raised the price to one, two and five guineas for a single piece, and filled up entire windows with them, and with mosaics of plain glass of different colours. In 1761, Paterson, an auctioneer at Essex-house in the Strand, exhibited the first auctions, imported in like manner from Flanders. All this

20. E. Kirschbaum, *Lexicon der Christlichen Ikonographie*, Freiburg 1968.
21. SGC VI B.8, Chapter Acts 1773–1814.
22. SGC XII B.10.
23. Royal Archives PP Vic. Add. 1324, quoted by gracious permission of H.M. The Queen. I am indebted to Miss Elizabeth Cuthbert for advice and practical help over the records at Windsor and to Mrs Grace Holmes, for much time spent in searching the Chapel records.
24. B. Rackham, 'English importations of Foreign Stained Glass in the Early Nineteenth Century', *JBSMGP*, ii (1927), pp. 86–94, and J. Lafond, 'The Traffic in Old Stained Glass from Abroad during the 18th and 19th centuries in England', *JBSMGP*, xiv (1964), pp. 58–67.

manufacture consisted in rounds of scripture stories in black and yellow, or in small figures of black and white, birds and flowers, in colours and Flemish coats of arms.[25]

This extract reveals that it would have been relatively easy to acquire Flemish glass for the Queen's Closet. The description of the 'rounds of scripture-stories in black and yellow' fits most of the glass. It might even have come through the Hon. Mr Bateman. Doubtless, also, Mr Paterson's auctions were well known in ecclesiastical circles.

In whatever way the glass came to Windsor, the central figure concerning the glass was Dr Lockman. It was he who made arrangements with the glazier. Little is known of him. He was appointed to Windsor in 1758 and was involved in the restoration of the west window (see pp. 3–6). In 1782, the year in which he was overseeing the insertion of the Netherlandish glass, he was advocating the insertion of new glass in the east window. Dr Lockman has not left a list of the glass he installed, but Knight describes it in sufficient detail for the panels to be recognized.[26] One piece he describes has not survived and there have been later additions. He describes numbers 1 to 6 quite recognizably. Despite the rarity of the subject, he gives the correct biblical reference for number 1. He does not mention St Cornelius, while a St Catherine panel is no longer there. He excuses himself from describing every piece by referring to 'other representations, which add to the ornament and decent neatness of the whole'. There have been additions since Knight's day. Undoubtedly, he would have mentioned the portrait of Charles II, had it been there, for it is close to the 'excellent piece in stained glass, of the Wise Men's offering'.

The position of some of the glass has been changed since Knight's time. Numbers 1–5 seem to be in their original places, but Esther was alongside the lost St Catherine in the 'third window' (presumably the most easterly in the north wall). Some rearrangement may have taken place under Willement in 1840–1. This would account for the discrepancies in the accounts of Knight and St John Hope. No information has come to light concerning their arrangement between 1782 and 1840–1; some rearrangement seems likely.

THE GLAZIER

The name of the eighteenth-century glazier of the Queen's Closet is not recorded and there is insufficient evidence to establish his identity with certainty. There were several glaziers at Windsor at the end of the eighteenth century and the simple task of making a surround for the Netherlandish glass could have been given to any of them. William Kimberley repaired the west window in 1767 but is unlikely to have been employed again, as the restoration had not been a success and Kimberley threatened legal action against the Canons, because they had sought comparative estimates and disputed his charges.[27] Nothing is known of the glaziers consulted in connection with Kimberley's bill other than their names, Nathaniel Stephens and William Bigge. It is possible that the Netherlandish

25. Horace Walpole, *Anecdotes of Painting* (1798), iii, p. 159.

26. Knight, op. cit., note 14, pp. 86–7.

27. *Architectural History*, ii, pp. 454 and 471, n. 105. The full story makes interesting reading. Kimberley was a man of standing in Windsor, a JP and twice Mayor. His charge for the west window was £139 10s 0d. The Canons consulted two other glaziers, one of whom would have charged £95 and the other £42 3s 9¼d. After the threat of legal action the Canons paid the full amount.

glass was installed by the artists responsible for some of the new glass, Bristow and West (see p. 103). No reference to the glazier Bristow has been found outside the Windsor archive. Another glazier to be considered is William Webb. Webb appears in a list of *Traders of Windsor* of 1798 as a painter and glazier.[28] He was also recorded by St John Hope as the recipient of £600 through Mr Emblin between 1785 and 1791 for work in the chapel as 'Glazier and Painter'. Although the Chapter Minute concerning the Queen's Closet states that Dr Lockman was to make separate arrangements with Mr Emlyn and the glazier, it seems likely that he delegated much of the supervision to Mr Emlyn.[29]

More research and a detailed examination of the background glass in the Queen's Closet may add to the present meagre evidence and enable the glazier responsible to be satisfactorily identified. We must be grateful that nearly all the glass described by Knight has survived. Would that the stained glass of all our churches had been so well described by an eighteenth-century writer.

28. The writer is indebted to Miss Cuthbert for this information.
29. *Architectural History*, ii, pp. 389, 390, 521.

St George's Chapel, the Eighteenth-Century Windows — and Where Are They Now?

SARAH BAYLIS

INTRODUCTION

By the end of the eighteenth century Windsor Castle was an essential component of any sightseeing tour of England. Many visitors came specifically to survey the progress of a substantial restoration programme initiated by King George III following his decision to make Windsor the chief royal residence. St George's Chapel was particularly in need of renovation by this date: it was described by one visitor as 'a nuisance to the eye and a reproach to the sextons'.[1]

The chapel restoration was begun in the 1780s under the supervision of the chapter carpenter, Henry Emlyn (1729–1815). Emlyn was also an accomplished draughtsman and designer in the latest 'gothick' style.[2] Most of Emlyn's alterations took place in the choir where a new altar-piece, organ and organ-loft were installed and the medieval woodwork of the stalls was repaired and extended. The Royal Pew (Edward IV's Chantry), to the north of the high altar, was also completely refurbished at this time.

Perhaps the most outstanding feature of the new choir was the painted glass *Resurrection* in the east window, the plan for which is said to have originated with the king himself. Benjamin West provided the designs and the east window was executed by the most celebrated glass-painter of the day, Thomas Jervais. Three more windows in the chapel aisles were subsequently filled with glass-paintings of events connected with the birth of Christ. Plans were also broached for a large-scale *Crucifixion* in the great west window.

Little remains today of the late eighteenth-century transformation of St George's Chapel (Pl. IVA). This detailed view of the choir — published in 1819 — chronicles what was effectively the fourth out of five distinct rearrangements of the east end of the chapel: evidence of the many changes in devotional and liturgical emphasis over the centuries.[3] As some critics were quick to point out at the time, this restoration was not without cost to the original fabric. The new organ loft, supported by Emlyn's Coade stone screen, had replaced an early seventeenth-century wooden rood screen which — it was rumoured — Emlyn had destroyed in order to secure an uninterrupted view of the new east window

1. *Gentleman's Magazine* (1786), 1, p. 449.

2. Emlyn was elected a Fellow of the Society of Antiquaries of London in 1795. For his contribution to the early Gothic revival in England see Jane Roberts, 'Henry Emlyn's Restoration of St George's Chapel', *Friends Report*, 5 (1976–7), pp. 331–8, and S.M. Bond, 'Henry Emlyn of Windsor. A craftsman of skill and invention', *Friends Report*, 4 (1962), pp. 99–103. The alterations are also described in 'An Account of all the Great Works which have been executed in St George's Chapel, Windsor from the years 1782 to the end of 1792', in *Architectural History*, ii, pp. 388–94.

3. W. H. Pyne, *History of the Royal Residences*, London 1819, 1, pp. 182–3. The aquatint engraving was by Sutherland after a drawing by Charles Wilde.

and reredos.[4] Emlyn's elaborately carved wooden reredos, replete with heraldry and other motifs, was constructed to the designs of Thomas Sandby: its central feature was a large oil-painting by Benjamin West of *The Last Supper*. It is worth noting here that Emlyn's work had replaced a classical-style reredos by the architect James 'Athenian' Stuart, erected only fourteen years earlier.[5]

Visitors entering the new choir would have been confronted by the eastern window — conceived as a sort of vast, painted glass triptych. The resurrected Christ emerging from the mouth of the tomb dominated the central panel. In the left-hand panel Saints Peter and John were shown running towards the tomb, balanced by the figures of the three Marys approaching slowly from the right-hand side. The new window, with its theatrical use of *chiaroscuro*, billowing clouds and swarming cherubim, must have provided a compelling and dynamic backdrop to the solemn offices performed below. West's highly accomplished figure drawing was never perhaps demonstrated to better effect. It is clear above all that this window was not intended as a mere decorative embellishment to the new choir but as an integral focus of its refashioning — intended to play a continuous and *active* role in the liturgical drama.

In order that nothing should interrupt the narrative in the glass-painting nor weaken the naturalistic effect, the medieval tracery of the window was removed beforehand, leaving behind only scant traces of its original form: this was frequently carried out where the window shape conflicted with the requirements of the glass design. As was the practice in the late eighteenth century, the painted glass was constructed out of large, regular-sized, square panels. Fully vitrifiable enamel colours were applied to the surface of the panels as if on to a canvas. Three thicknesses of glass were involved in the finished product, the fragile painted surface being sandwiched in the middle between one layer of ground glass and one layer of plain glass. The whole was then inserted into a gigantic iron frame within a complex skeleton of supporting crossbars.

The Windsor *Resurrection* exemplified with great boldness the latest taste for religious 'picture windows'. Such works, with their strong emphasis on narrative content and their display of painterly effects, were explicitly reliant upon celebrated Renaissance models. In rejecting the flat, abstract aesthetic of medieval stained glass in favour of a fully pictorial mode of expression, Georgian glass-painters were consciously opening up the possibilities of representation, earning themselves a new popular status. They were fortunate in receiving overt support from Sir Joshua Reynolds and Benjamin West, the first two Presidents of the Royal Academy, who were keen to advertise their own skills as designers of new and fashionable 'picture windows'.[6]

Georgian glass-painters found much support from the general public who expressed a dislike of what they saw as the crudeness of medieval stained glass. The 'Ancient' glass-painters were seen as limited by their need to surround their figures with lead, thereby

4. The rood loft can be seen in Hollar's engraving of the choir in Elias Ashmole's *Order of the Garter*, London 1672.

5. Stuart also produced an alternative design for a 'gothick' screen incorporating a painted-glass rose window. SGC F. 21. D. Watkin, *Athenian Stuart, Pioneer of the Greek Revival*, London 1982, pp. 55–6, pl. 80, describes it as 'a monstrous essay in Georgian Gothick'. No supporting tracery or mullions are indicated.

6. See S. Baylis, 'Glass-Painting in Britain c. 1760–c. 1840: A Revolution in Taste' (unpublished Ph.D. thesis, University of Cambridge, 1989), chap. 2.

destroying the harmony of the outline. As James Dallaway put it, 'Harshness was the unavoidable effect, which they knew not either how to correct, or obviate'.[7]

However, not everyone shared this belief. Any history of St George's Chapel has to confront the somewhat obstreperous — if inspired — personality of John Carter (1748–1817). As an architect, Carter was hostile to the classical tradition of building which he condemned outright as pagan in origin. As a zealous admirer of Gothic architecture, he was highly critical of contemporary methods of restoration.[8] For more than twenty years — largely through the pages of the *Gentleman's Magazine* — John Carter maintained a steadfast protest against what he saw as ignorant and destructive architectural innovations. He was thus moved to condemn Emlyn's Coade stone additions to the choir of St George's Chapel as 'a subterfuge, a fictitious makeshift'.[9] When he came to describe the new east window his scorn knew no bounds. The colossal glass-painting was 'entirely at variance with the contour of the whole interior . . . Here is gained a transparent scenic exhibition and here is lost one of the finest terminations of a religious edifice the land could own . . .'.[10]

Carter's criticism of the new style glass-painting was symptomatic of a changing climate of opinion. He anticipated (and even, to some extent, inspired) the general Victorian condemnation of eighteenth-century glass-painting which would lead eventually to its widespread destruction.

BENJAMIN WEST AND GEORGE III: ARTIST AND PATRON

The personalities of the American-born painter Benjamin West and his patron George III and the vagaries of their personal and professional relationship dominate this episode in the chapel's history.[11] West's meteoric rise to fame can be largely attributed to his unique and privileged position as 'Historical Painter' to the king. In this capacity, between 1768 and 1801, he produced some sixty canvases and received a personal stipend of £1,000 per annum. Nor was this simply a business relationship: after the king's death in 1820 West was said to have declared, 'I have lost the best friend I ever had in my life'. The two men were exact contemporaries and died within six weeks of one another; they were bound together not least by a mutual dedication to the future of the fine arts in Britain and by a desire to promote a national school of historical painters. It was no coincidence that the king's involvement in the formation of the Royal Academy and his patronage of West began simultaneously, for the two events were closely connected.

7. *Observations on English Architecture, Military, Ecclesiastical and Civil Compared with Similar Buildings on the Continent*, London 1806, pp. 283–4.

8. J. Mordaunt Crook, *John Carter and the Mind of the Gothic Revival*, Society of Antiquaries, Occasional papers, London 1995. J.M. Frew, 'Gothic is English: John Carter and the Revival of the Gothic as England's National Style', *Art Bulletin*, 64 (June 1982), pp. 315–19.

9. *Gentleman's Magazine* (1805), 2, pp. 924–6.

10. *Ibid.*

11. After a century and a half of neglect, the career of West has been thoroughly reassessed by A. Staley and H. Von Erffa, *The Paintings of Benjamin West*, New Haven & London 1986, see chaps 3 and 5. Much relevant information is also contained in J.D. Meyer, 'Benjamin West's Window Designs for St George's Chapel, Windsor', *The American Art Journal*, xi (July 1979), pp. 53–65, and N. Pressly, *Revealed Religion, Benjamin West's Commissions for Windsor Castle and Fonthill Abbey*, San Antonio 1983.

The king's interest in the arts had developed at an early age: by the 1760s, with the help of his librarian, Richard Dalton, he was actively involved in collecting and commissioning works of art all over Europe. It soon became clear that he was keen to encourage the resurgence of religious art in England, an idea which still met with substantial resistance from within the Anglican Church. The Reformation injunctions against paintings and sculptures in churches, reinforced by Puritan iconoclasm in the seventeenth century, had left a lingering suspicion of all forms of religious decoration. In 1773 the king approved a plan by the founding members of the Royal Academy to introduce religious paintings into St Paul's Cathedral. Objections were raised on the grounds that they represented a 'popish revival' and the king, tacitly bound as Supreme Governor of the Church of England, had to give way to official pressure. This was not, however, the end of his involvement in the progress of the arts and he remained determined to exercise his own religious convictions in a more private manner at Windsor Castle.

With the king's support, West's standing as an artist went from strength to strength. In 1791 he succeeded Dalton as Surveyor of the King's Pictures, a post he was to retain for almost thirty years. In 1792 he attained the highest and most influential position for an artist when he was elected President of the Royal Academy. West bought a house in Park Street, Windsor; he was also given a room in the castle for his own use where he devoted himself to a wide variety of artistic commissions. The largest and most ambitious was a series of vast biblical paintings illustrating 'the Progress of Revealed Religion' for the walls of a new private royal chapel.[12] George III was clearly attempting to accomplish at Windsor what the Royal Academy had failed to achieve in St Paul's Cathedral a few years earlier. West involved himself totally in the king's plans and worked on these canvases simultaneously with the window designs and altar-painting for St George's Chapel. The two decorative projects were regarded as major steps in the furtherance of Church patronage of the arts in England and the publicity given to them greatly enhanced the king's reputation as an enlightened patron.[13] For complex reasons, the 'Chapel of Revealed Religion' at Windsor was never completed; the canvas-paintings remained in West's studio and the focus of public attention shifted instead to St George's Chapel. However, in 1801 West received instructions to suspend work on all royal commissions. Thus ended his long professional and personal involvement with the king.

The reasons behind Benjamin West's fall from grace are numerous and complex, but a major factor was undoubtedly the gradual deterioration in the king's mental state following his first breakdown in the autumn of 1788. He remained prone to recurrent bouts of 'madness' for the rest of his life and his behaviour was frequently erratic. He developed a suspicion of West's known political loyalties which he increasingly identified as Republican and anti-Royalist. West was also faced with a powerful, outspoken opponent in architect James Wyatt who, after 1796, was employed on extensive alterations to the castle and had become a close confidant of the king. Wyatt had condemned the removal of

12. Pressly, *Revealed Religion*, pp. 15–25. J.D. Meyer, 'Benjamin West's Chapel of Revealed Religion: A Study in 18th Century Protestant Religious Art', *Art Bulletin*, 57, no. 2 (June 1975), pp. 247–65.

13. A letter to the President and Council of the Royal Academy praising the king's devotion to the cause of truth was published in March 1795. 'His majesty has given a noble example of his piety, taste and liberality of sentiment, beyond the narrow fanatical limits of preceding ages, in the manificent decoration of Biblical paintings which he has bestowed on St George's Chapel, Windsor ...'. Signed 'J.F.' (?Joseph Farington), V&A Museum, London, PP. 17. G., vol. 3, p. 786.

the 'beautiful Gothick window work' at the east end of St George's Chapel and considered West personally responsible for this act of philistinism.[14] For once, Wyatt was here in agreement with his arch enemy — John Carter.[15]

It has sometimes been suggested that West's decline from favour is directly attributable to the poor reception of the St George's Chapel windows. There seems little evidence for this belief. It is far more likely that these very public works of art did a great deal to promote West's reputation as an historical and religious artist in the 'grand manner'. It is clear that his relationship with his royal patron had already begun to deteriorate by the time Carter and Wyatt, for their own reasons, were undermining his achievements; West's competence as a designer was not the central issue. By 1796, the king was already failing to keep up his payments to West who had moved permanently back to London and was soon working extensively for William Beckford.[16]

In 1805 West was forced to resign as President of the Royal Academy. His place was taken by James Wyatt. Although he resumed the position the following year, retaining it until his death in 1820, West would never regain his former status and his professional reputation continued its downward path. George IV, who succeeded to the throne in 1820, disliked West intensely and got rid of most of the history paintings which his father had accumulated in bulk. By the mid-nineteenth century West's talents were held in such low esteem as to have earned him the title 'The Monarch of Mediocrity', an artist 'gifted by nature with a dull, careful, tame and feeble mind'.[17] This harsh appraisal persisted well into the present century. Today, it would be fair to say that West's status as a major figure in the developing national school of historical painting has been rightfully re-established.

THE GLASS-PAINTERS: THOMAS JERVAIS AND CHARLES FORREST

Thomas Jervais was the most obvious candidate for the task of executing the new east window. The Dublin-born glass-painter had just completed, to great public acclaim, the work for which he is best remembered today — the west window of the antechapel in

14. K. Garlick and A. Macintyre, eds, *The Dairy of Joseph Farington*, New Haven & London 1979, 3, p. 916, entry for 6 November 1797.
15. These professional animosities are by no means clear-cut. Carter and West collaborated on drawings of the projected east window of St George's Chapel exhibited at the Royal Academy in 1783 and 1785 (West drawing the figures and Carter the architectural setting). *Gentleman's Magazine* (1805), 1, p. 530. See also Crook, *John Carter*, p. 49, pl. 29. Although he is said to have deplored the destruction entailed by the new window at Windsor, Wyatt was not hostile to Georgian painted glass: he personally supervised the introduction of similar glass by Francis Eginton in the east windows of Salisbury and Lichfield Cathedrals; Baylis, 'Glass-Painting in Britain', chap. 2.
16. Beckford commissioned many paintings from West as well as cartoons for painted glass for Fonthill Abbey. Pressly, *Revealed Religion*, pp. 57–67; Baylis, 'Glass-Painting in Britain', pp. 146–8.
17. W. Thornbury, 'West, The Monarch of Mediocrity. West in Newman St.', *Art Journal*, 6 (November 1860), p. 321. The decline in West's artistic reputation was also reflected in the life-span of the east window of Hereford Cathedral, a *Last Supper*, executed by Joseph Backler — a copy of West's altar-painting in St George's. This window, installed in 1823, was removed less than twenty years later.

New College, Oxford, from designs provided by Sir Joshua Reynolds.[18] This window depicts a scene of the *Nativity*, under which are standing symbolic figures of the four Cardinal Virtues and three Christian Graces. As one of the few surviving painted windows of the period, it can be regarded as a real landmark in the development of the medium.

Jervais in fact began work at Windsor before the Oxford window was fully completed. According to the published journals of Mrs Papendiek — a member of the court circle — Jervais took a house in Peascod Street, Windsor, with a garden and outhouses in which he is said to have set up furnaces for burning the glass, and 'having only a wife and no family, the lower rooms . . . were used for the painting'.[19] It seems he was assisted at Windsor by the shadowy figure of his brother John, who had also worked with him at New College. We know almost nothing of John Jervais other than that he was born *c.* 1749 and lived in London until his death in 1804.[20] There are no references to him in the Windsor archives and it can only be speculated what form his assistance took.

Equally little is known of Charles Forrest, pupil and later successor to Thomas Jervais at St George's Chapel: his only other documented involvement in glass-painting was also at New College, Oxford.[21] Like Jervais, Forrest lived in Windsor whilst working on the St George's Chapel glass; he was also married, with a family. Mrs Papendiek records that Forrest was known to be a talented musician who sometimes performed on the flute before the king. From the same source we learn that Forrest's relationship with Jervais had deteriorated by the time of the latter's retirement in 1788, after completion of the east window.[22] Mrs Papendiek hints at a power struggle between the two men: Jervais, despite having no son or obvious successor, was reluctant to pass on the secret of his technical success. Forrest, having an 'honest, upright heart', accepted Jervais's refusal to share his methods but determined he would discover them for himself by experimentation once his contract was ended. In the event, the king had intervened and given the commissions for subsequent windows in the chapel to Forrest alone. It is possible that Jervais's declining health forced him to hand over completely, if reluctantly, at this point — although he did not in fact die until August 1799.

We can only speculate why Forrest, an obscure and, it seems, a relatively inexperienced glass-painter, should have been entrusted with the execution of four large windows in such a prestigious building; how he gained his training as a glass-painter is also something of a mystery. A tentative identification can be made with the artist Charles Forrest, born *c.* 1748, who was admitted to the Royal Dublin Society Schools in 1765. This artist was active as a portrait painter in crayons between 1771 and 1780. He also produced miniatures and exhibited his work with the Society of Artists in London as well as in Dublin.[23]

18. C. Woodforde, *The Stained Glass of New College, Oxford*, London 1950, pp. 39–59; Baylis, 'Glass-Painting in Britain', pp. 59–65. Jervais had recommended Benjamin West but the college selected Reynolds as designer. Jervais's career is summarized in M. Wynne, 'Irish Stained and Painted Glass in the 18th Century', in P. Moore, *Crown in Glory: A Celebration of Craftsmanship Studies in Stained Glass*, Norwich 1982, pp. 58–60.
19. Mrs Papendiek, *Court and Private Life in the Time of Queen Charlotte, The Journals of Mrs Papendiek*, London 1887, I, p. 278.
20. Wynne, 'Irish Glass', p. 60.
21. Papendiek, *Journals*, pp. 2, 39.
22. *Ibid.*, pp. 39–40, 98.
23. W.G. Strickland, *A Dictionary of Irish Artists*, 2 vols, Dublin 1913, I, p. 375; H.L. Mallalieu, *The Dictionary of British Watercolour Artists up to 1920*, 3 vols, Woodbridge 1986, I, p. 132.

Records of this artist's work cease in 1780, which could coincide with his coming to England, having abandoned drawing, and beginning to work for Jervais. He could even have known Jervais beforehand since the latter was a Dubliner by birth and had trained there before coming to England in *c.* 1770. A passing reference to Forrest in the *Gentleman's Magazine* does not throw much light on the matter: he is described here as a 'scholar' who had 'taken up the art at first as an amateur'.[24]

Another name which appears fleetingly in connection with the painted glass of St George's is that of Thomas Phillips (1770–1845) who was born in Dudley and was, for a time, a pupil of the glass-painter Francis Eginton of Birmingham.[25] In *c.* 1790, Phillips moved to London with a letter of introduction to Sir Benjamin West and, after entering the R.A. Schools, briefly became the latter's assistant. Later in his career he became renowned for his fashionable portraits and was made a Royal Academician in 1808. It has been claimed that Phillips assisted West in designing the windows of St George's Chapel,[26] but solid evidence supporting this has not been found. It is more likely that, during his brief apprenticeship to Francis Eginton, Phillips was involved in the production of the heraldic glass for the choir clerestory of St George's Chapel, described below.

THE EAST WINDOW: THE *RESURRECTION*, *c.* 1785

The chapel archives reveal that a considerable driving force behind the project was Dr John Lockman (*c.* 1720–1807), Canon and later Dean, who was ordered by the king early in 1782 to put together a plan for a new east window.[27] In some ways, Lockman was an obvious choice: a few years earlier he had closely supervised the reglazing of the west window; he now suggested to the king that a subscription fund for a new east window be set up amongst the Knights of the Garter, headed by the sovereign himself. The king readily accepted the proposal and inaugurated the subscription with 900 guineas on behalf of himself and his three sons. The whole fund amounted to £4,042 10s, the rest of the money being donated by other members of the royal family, all the Knights of the Garter and the Dean and Canons. The king proved exceptionally generous and donated another £1,000 as further costs were incurred. Although this was a huge project in financial terms, it seems to have been carried through with remarkable swiftness.

Work began immediately on the *Resurrection* window. Benjamin West was commissioned to produce a set of three full-sized cartoons which were squared up and ready for transfer by the glass-painter; he also produced large oil-painted versions of the subjects which were exhibited at the Royal Academy in 1783 as pictures in their own right. Here they provided powerful advertisements for the work underway. The designs for the two outer lights were also engraved as commercial mezzotints in 1784, before the glass was even completed. All the squared-up cartoons for the east window seem at this point to have disappeared without trace. Fortunately, the large oil-painted designs for the

24. 'The Progress &c. of Stained Glass in England', *Gentleman's Magazine* (1817), 1, p. 315. The writer is highly critical of Forrest's aisle windows: 'these performances are evidently inferior in point of distinctness and harmony to the work of Jervais'.
25. See p. 2 of a transcript of an unfinished, undated letter by W.R. Eginton in the Eginton Manuscripts, Birmingham Museums & Art Gallery, Department of Applied Art.
26. J.A. Knowles, 'Glass-painters 1750–1850', *JBSMGP*, 13, no. 3 (1962), p. 516.
27. *Architectural History*, ii, pp. 388–9.

Resurrection (Pl. IVB) and the *Three Marys* (Fig. 64) have survived.[28] The appearance of the left section of the window depicting Saints Peter and John is now known only from Valentine Green's contemporary mezzotint (Fig. 65).[29] There are a number of surviving drawings and rough sketches associated with the east window, now mainly held in various collections in the USA.[30] A sheet of six studies relating to the central *Resurrection* can also be seen in the Royal Collection at Windsor Castle (Fig. 66): these beautifully executed drawings, all displaying a 'characteristic fluency, excitement, and immediacy of inspiration',[31] demonstrate the spontaneity of West's working methods in the preliminary design stages.

It is not difficult to imagine the impact made upon an unsuspecting public by this spectacular new window. Preceded by the glowing figure of an angel, the pale, faintly luminous, semi-naked Christ emerges from the sepulchre, casting off his shroud in triumph. In the foreground Roman soldiers lie sprawled in terror. A host of cherubim and seraphim watch expectantly from above (one of them in fact a posthumous portrait of the king's four-year-old son, Octavius, who had died suddenly in 1783). In the lower right-hand section under a huge sombre sky-scape, the draped, grieving figures of the three Marys approach the tomb with their jars of spices. In the left-hand panel Peter and John race towards the empty sepulchre; Peter overtaken by the eager and more youthful disciple. The central composition, a climax of dramatic visual energy, was thus balanced between the classical restraint and solemnity of the female figures and the sense of urgency and excitement conveyed by the hurrying disciples.

Not surprisingly, the new window roused immediate widespread interest. Fanny Burney, the popular novelist, records in her diary a royal ceremony held on 1 January 1787, to commemorate the re-opening of St George's Chapel.[32] Miss Burney, also a member of the court, describes the vast crowds flocking into the chapel, apparently just as eager to catch a glimpse of the glorious new east window as to see their beloved king in person.

28. Von Erffa and Staley, *Benjamin West*, pp. 363–5, cat. nos 360 and 361, relate to the *Resurrection*, whilst pp. 368–70, cat. nos 367 and 369, deal with the designs for the two outer lights. A squared-up drawing, apparently related to the lost cartoon for the *Resurrection*, is currently in the Delaware Art Museum (*ibid.*, p. 364). The oil design for the *Resurrection*, for which West was paid £525, was sold in 1829 and has been in the Museo del Arte de Ponce, Puerto Rico (fundacion Luis A. Ferre) since 1962. The design for the *Three Maries*, sold in 1829, is currently owned by the National Trust at Tatton Park, Cheshire. Most of West's work relating to the chapel was dispersed at posthumous sale organized by his sons in May 1829. See M. Postle, 'A taste for History: Reynolds, West, George III and George IV', *Apollo* (September 1993), p. 188. West's designs for St George's Chapel could have been claimed as Crown Property but, significantly, neither George III nor George IV attempted to take possession of them.

29. Von Erffa and Staley, *Benjamin West*, p. 369. They also note a related pen-and-ink drawing in the Museum of Fine Arts, Boston, signed by West and dated 1783 (*ibid.*, p. 370). Pressly, *Revealed Religion*, p. 55, no. 31, Fig. 28 illustrates a pen-and-ink sketch, now owned by the Yale Center for British Art, for the *Three Maries*, presumably a *modello* for the larger oil design. The exhibited oil designs for only related to the lower sections of the two outer panels and did not include the groups of angels and cherubs hovering above the figures.

30. Von Erffa & Staley (*Benjamin West*, p. 364) illustrate a pencil drawing clearly related to the cartoon for the *Resurrection*, now in Delaware Art Museum. The authors list all other related drawings.

31. Pressly, *Revealed Religion*, p. 54.

32. Fanny Burney, *Diary and Letters of Madame D'Arblay*, ed. C. Barrett, London 1891, 2, p. 274, 1 January 1787.

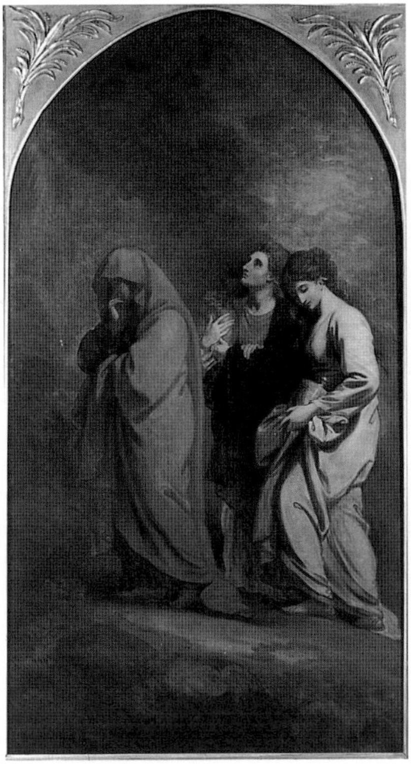

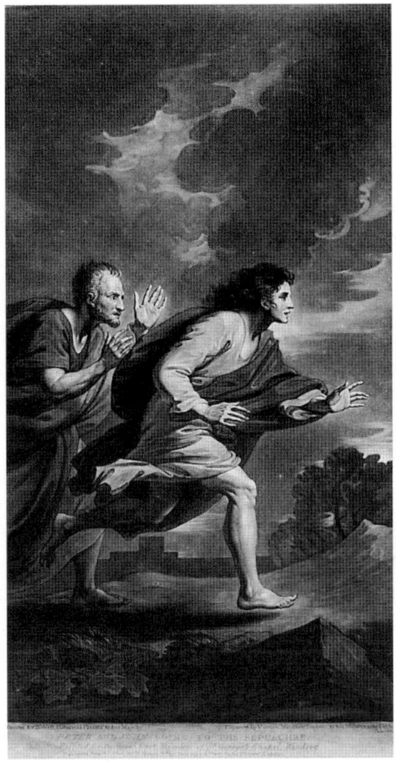

Fig. 64. *Benjamin West, 'The Three Marys going to the Sepulchre', c. 1782. Oil design for the east window of St George's Chapel (Photo reproduced courtesy of The Courtauld Institute of Art. The National Trust, Tatton Park, Cheshire)*

Fig. 65. *Valentine Green, mezzotint engraving after Benjamin West, 'SS Peter and John running to the Sepulchre', 1784 (Photo reproduced courtesy of the British Museum)*

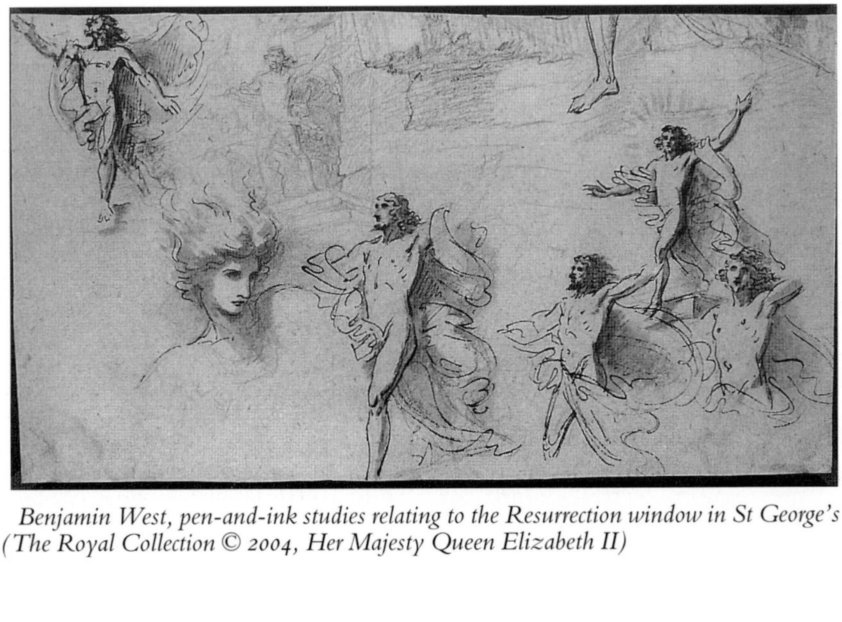

Fig. 66. *Benjamin West, pen-and-ink studies relating to the Resurrection window in St George's Chapel, Windsor (The Royal Collection © 2004, Her Majesty Queen Elizabeth II)*

Mrs Papendiek, the court diarist, suggests that the east window was orginally conceived along less ambitious lines and that initially only the central scene of the *Resurrection* was planned.[33] The king had fallen ill again and Queen Charlotte was reluctant to give permission for the glass to be installed without his presence. As a compromise the window was temporarily fixed *in situ*. The general opinion had been that the glass was too narrow and West was therefore charged to design the two outer wings.

Mrs Papendiek's memory is, however, demonstrably untrustworthy: she records that the window was put up temporarily in 1788 and then permanently after the king's recovery in spring 1789. This is contradicted not only by Burney's diary but also by archival records of payments to workmen relating to the installation of the window which cease altogether in March 1787. Given that West exhibited his painted designs for the two outer scenes, along with the central scene, at the Royal Academy as early as 1783, and that the king's first breakdown occurred in 1788, Mrs Papendiek's account of the window's evolution cannot be considered accurate. It seems likely that the occasion which Mrs Papendiek later misremembered occurred in the autumn of 1786 when West's painted design for the *Resurrection* was exhibited at the east end of the chapel. Fanny Burney, who visited the chapel expressly to see the cartoon, recorded her own reservations.

The Guiding Angel is truly beautiful in it, but our Saviour is somewhat too earthly; He seems athletic as an Hercules, and rather as if he derived His superiority from strength of body than from influence of divinity.[34]

Fanny Burney also met the artist himself on this memorable occasion:

Mr. West . . . was exceeding civil, shewing the cartoon himself and explaining his intentions in it. He spoke of the performance with just such frank praise and open satisfaction as he might have mentioned it, if the work of any artist; pointing out its excellences, and expressing his happiness in the execution — yet all with a simplicity that turned his self-commendation rather into candour than conceit.

The main reason for the display of the cartoon was likely to have been the visit of the archduke and archduchess of Austria in September 1786. The royal guests met Benjamin West as well as Thomas Jervais in the chapel; the glass-painter had even brought along a completed section of the window for their inspection.[35]

In 1791 Horace Walpole paid a visit to Windsor Castle for the first time since the restoration. He highly approved of Emlyn's alterations in the choir.

St George's Chapel, that I always worshipped, though so dark and black that I could see nothing distinctly, is now, being cleaned and decorated, a scene of lightness and grace. There is a new screen prefixed to the choir, so airy and harmonious that I concluded it Wyat's [*sic*]: but it is by a Windsor architect, whose name I forget.[36]

Walpole was not overly impressed by the new east window, however: he found it 'rather too sombre for the Resurrection, though it accords with the tone of the choir'. Like Burney he was critical of what he saw as West's excessive attention to anatomy. 'The

33. Papendiek, *Journals*, 2, pp. 38–9.

34. Burney, *Diaries*, 2, p. 218. A year later she commented on seeing the completed glass, 'this solemn old Chapel is extremely beautified ("a vile phrase!") by this superb window'.

35. J. Galt, *George III, His Court & Family*, London 1820, 2, p. 51.

36. W.S. Lewis, ed., *Horace Walpole's Correspondence*, 12 (i) (1944), pp. 362–3, Walpole to Miss Berry, 9 October 1791.

Christ is a poor figure scrambling to heaven in a fright, as if in dread of being again buried alive; and not ascending calmly in secure dignity . . .', whilst the artist's altar-painting of the *Last Supper* below contained a figure of Judas 'so gigantic', reported Walpole, 'that he seems more likely to burst by his bulk than through guilt . . .'.

During the great storm of 31 May 1796, the new east window was damaged and repaired by the college painter and glazier, Robert Crook. These repairs, coming so soon after completion, were evidently very costly and it was decided to set up a fund to insure against further expenditure.[37] The Dean suggested that recently elected Knights of the Garter and each new knight from now on should provide £50 towards a fund for repairs to the chapel interior and especially to the painted glass. The king agreed to this plan and promptly subscribed £100 for each of his sons. Clearly in these early days the painted glass was very highly valued. Charles Knight — local author and publisher of many guides to Windsor — recalls that on 31 December 1800 he had waited in vain for the usual cannon fire to announce the New Year. The king himself had ordered there should be no discharge of the cannon 'for the new painted window by Mr West', wrote Knight, 'might be broken by the concussion'.[38]

THE AISLE WINDOWS: BENJAMIN WEST AND CHARLES FORREST

The Angel Appearing to the Shepherds, c. 1792

The first of Charles Forrest's windows was installed in the east window of the south aisle (sII). West's preliminary cartoon has not apparently survived, but an oil painting relating to the central portion of this window — now in a private collection — may well have been the 'design' West exhibited at the R.A. in 1790 (Pl. VA).[39]

It is not difficult to imagine this composition transposed to painted glass: the Correggiesque, moonlit apparition of the angel amongst dark, billowing clouds, the swirling, agitated drapery and the flying ringlets creating a heightened sense of drama and excitement. Nor, by the same token, is it difficult to understand the adverse response of those critics who found Forrest's painted glass theatrical in inspiration and antipathetic to the medieval spirit of St George's Chapel.

Further details of this window can be gleaned from a press account of 12 June 1792, which describes the royal family's inspection of the new work.

> The principal Angel in this beautiful group is looking directly down the aisle of the church, and in the act of calling to the spectators, and at the same time pointing up to the Glory on which are the following words, 'Glory to God on high . . .'. The second Angel is looking up to the words — and the heavenly host which attend these Angels have scrols [*sic*] in their hands on which are written as follows — 'For unto you is born this day in the city of David, a Saviour which is Christ the Lord'. The group of angels here described, as announcing glad tidings to men, is composed with taste, and designed with character and expression, and executed in a soft tone of colour which never before appeared on painted glass . . .[40]

37. SGC V.B.8., pp. 35–6, Chapter Acts, 9 January 1797.
38. C. Knight, *Passages from the Life of Charles Knight*, New York 1874, p. 18.
39. Von Erffa and Staley, *Benjamin West*, pp. 329–30, cat. nos 306 and 307. A drawing in the Museum of Fine Arts, Boston, 'The Angel Announcing our Saviour's Birth', differs in some minor respects but is essentially related to the above design: see Pressly, *Revealed Religion*, p. 50, Fig. 26. The oil design was sold in 1990 by Christie's in New York.
40. Quoted by Von Erffa and Staley, *Benjamin West*, p. 329.

The *Windsor Guide* quotes further inscriptions on the scrolls held by the angels and describes shepherds with sheep and a dog visible in the distance. This window, painted in half tints, seems to have been the most striking of Charles Forrest's aisle windows. Even John Carter found this glass tolerable, whilst the *St James's Chronicle* praised West's composition as 'the most graceful we have seen of this artist; he has successfully imitated the style of Correggio, in the colouring, and the execution has great teste'.[41]

In 1847 the Forrest glass was removed to make way for a new window by Thomas Willement of *Christ carrying the Cross*. This was replaced in 1883 by the present window.

The Nativity, c. 1794

The second of Forrest's windows was installed in the west end of the south aisle (sXXXI). A preliminary design by Benjamin West was shown at the Royal Academy in 1793,[42] although the cartoon itself was not exhibited until 1799, five years after installation of the glass. This cartoon, the only one relating to the aisle windows to have survived, is currently at Petworth House in Sussex (Fig. 67).[43] The cartoon, together with the following description by Charles Knight, provide a valuable record of the window.

> The Virgin Mary is seated with the infant Jesus sleeping in her lap, and Joseph, with the most devout attention, is holding a lamp, to give light to her while she performs her maternal offices. The Angel of the Lord, which is a very beautiful figure, accompanied with a group of cherubs, appears with an olive branch . . . In the back and foreground are various objects, either descriptive of the mean situation in which the birth of our Saviour happened, or allusive to the oblation which was to be offered up for the redemption of man.[44]

In 1959, the Dean and Canons of St George's were in correspondence with a Miss Forrest of Australia regarding two pencil drawings believed to relate to the chapel windows: these were the work of her ancestor, Charles Forrest.[45] The archivist, Maurice Bond, had the drawings repaired and remounted but did not pursue the question of their precise relationship with the St George's Chapel glass. The drawings, measuring 21 x 30 in. (53.34 x 76.20 cm) are both very torn and rather faded. They are clearly two halves of a single, vertical design and seem to be closely related, if not identical, to the *Nativity* window as known from the Petworth cartoon. The lower half of the drawing (Fig. 68) is signed and dated in the bottom right-hand corner; it is just possible to discern the name of Charles Forrest; the date is not legible. This half of the drawing, containing Joseph, the Virgin Mary and the infant Christ, is somewhat crudely and hurriedly sketched. The top half (Fig. 69) features a central angel holding aloft an olive branch and surrounded by cherubs.

41. 27–9 April 1790.
42. Von Erffa and Staley, *Benjamin West*, p. 324, cat. no. 299.
43. *Ibid.*, pp. 323–4, cat. no. 298 (illustrated p. 324). Cat. no. 300, illustrated p. 325, is clearly a related composition and was probably exhibited at the R.A. in 1796. It is therefore likely to have been a copy rather than a preliminary design.
44. C. Knight, *The Windsor Guide*, Windsor 1795, p. 64.
45. In her letter, SGC M.29, Miss Forrest claimed that her great-great-grandfather 'Captain [*sic*] Charles Forrest' was the glass-painter responsible for various painted windows in St George's Chapel. (Miss Forrest was also a descendant of the St Leger buried in the Rutland Chantry.) She describes him as an 'an artist at the time of the reign of King George III'. Maurice Bond, having met Miss Forrest, recorded that the drawings had been in Australia since 1839, having been taken there by her grandfather *Captain* Charles Forrest, the grandson of the glass-painter. The drawings are now catalogued as SGC P.347.

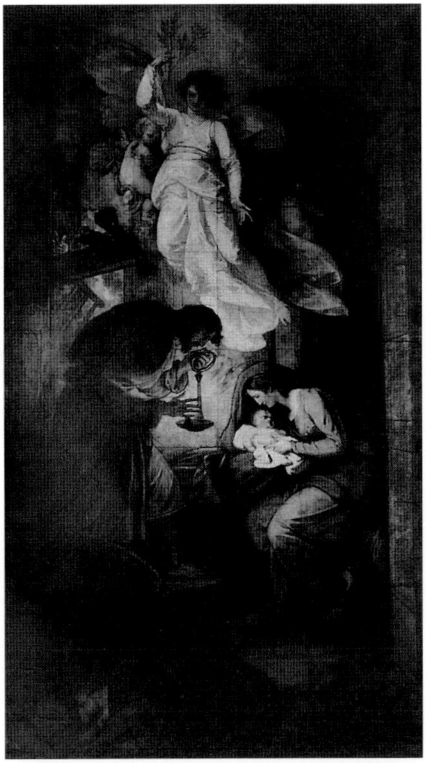

Fig. 67. *Benjamin West, 'The Nativity', cartoon for west window of the south aisle, St George's Chapel,* c. *1792–4 (Photo A.C. Cooper Ltd, The National Trust, Petworth House, Sussex)*

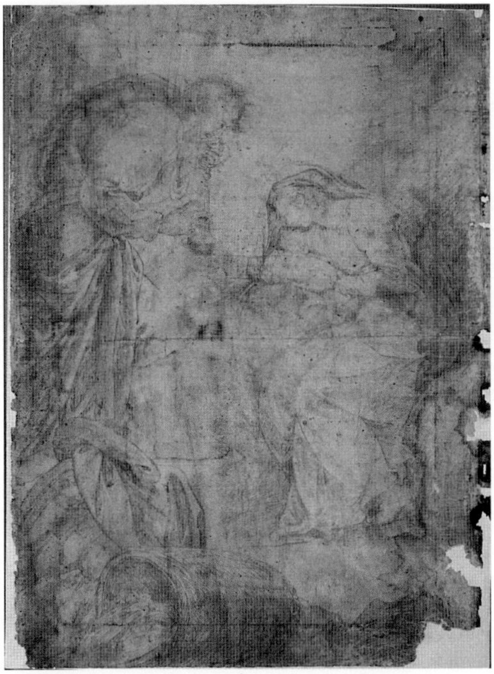

Fig. 68. *Charles Forrest, 'The Nativity', detail of lower portion of drawing related to the south aisle window, St George's Chapel. SGC P.347 (Photo John Crook, © Dean and Canons of Windsor)*

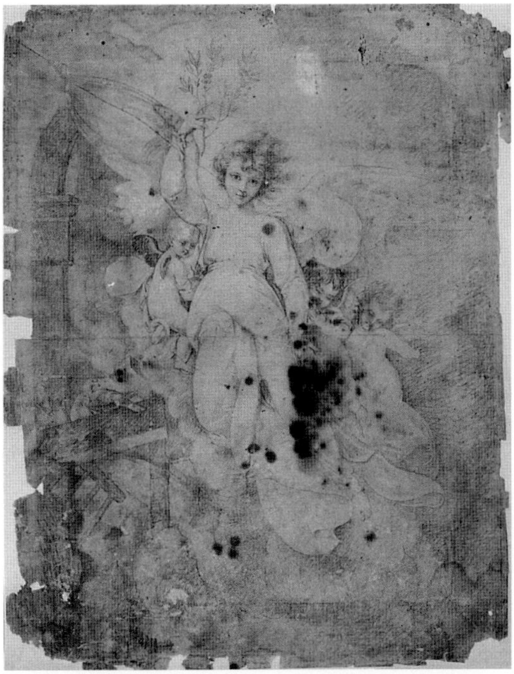

Fig. 69. *Charles Forrest and ?Benjamin West, 'The Nativity', detail of the upper portion of SGC P.347 (Photo John Crook, © Dean and Canons of Windsor)*

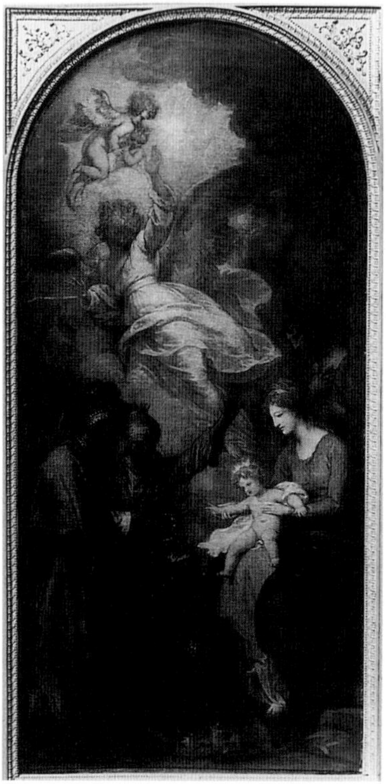

Fig. 70. *Benjamin West, 'The Wisemen's Offering', 1794, oil design for west window of west aisle, St George's Chapel. Location unknown (Photo © The Courtauld Institute of Art)*

Whilst the architectural setting and the cherubs seem to be by the same hand as the lower portion, the main angel has a clarity of outline and overall deftness which would suggest the hand of Benjamin West himself. This figure stands out from the drawing as a whole by virtue of its fluent modelling, particularly of the hair and drapery folds, and the large expressive eyes. The function of this drawing and its place in the design sequence remains a mystery. Possibly Forrest was simply completing for his own pleasure a sketch by Benjamin West which the latter had discarded.

The Adoration of the Magi, c. *1796*

The third of Forrest's windows was installed in the west window of the north aisle (nXXV). A design, or possibly, the actual cartoon for the glass, was exhibited at the Royal Academy in 1797. The only surviving evidence of this window is an oil painting by West, signed and dated 1794, which seems to be a small-scale *modello* for Forrest's glass (Fig. 70).[46] It corresponds with Knight's description in the 1800 *Windsor Guide*:

46. Von Erffa and Staley, *Benjamin West*, pp. 331–2, cat. no. 310. Formerly in the Metropolitan Museum, New York and now in a private collection. This may have been the version exhibited in 1797. A pen-and-ink drawing of the subject, slightly different in composition, was owned by the Bernard Black Gallery in 1968, *ibid.*, p. 331, cat. no. 309.

the infant Jesus, in a reclining posture in the lap of the Virgin Mary, behind whom is Joseph, and in the front are the wise men of the east presenting offerings . . . Over these is a luminous star, and the angel of the Lord.

This glass-painting, like that in the south aisle, was removed *c.* 1869 to make way for two linked Clayton and Bell windows. The history of all four of these eighteenth-century glass-paintings after their removal from the chapel remains as yet an unsolved mystery. The chapel archives are surprisingly silent on the subject and the present essay, written almost 130 years later, would seem to represent the first serious consideration of their fate.

THE WEST WINDOW: THE *CRUCIFIXION*, *c.* 1796 (UNFINISHED)

William Kimberley's 1767 restoration and resetting of the medieval glass in the west window has been fully dealt with elsewhere, but it should be noted here that the idea of redeploying medieval glass in this way was certainly not new, nor unique to Windsor.[47] It is not clear who initiated the proposal to replace Kimberley's arrangement with a brand new *Crucifixion*, but the plan evidently met with mixed reactions. The medieval glass was spared only because the modern window failed to materialize, but it had seemed for a time that this window would also lose its stone mullions and tracery. The intention here, unlike in the east window, was to create one single painted-glass narrative spanning the whole window space. This, it was estimated, would require 1,000 square feet of glass.

The *Crucifixion* was the last historical commission given to West by the king. It was said to have been the largest single composition he ever undertook. The oil design was exhibited at the Royal Academy in 1797 where it was noted by at least two critics to have been painted in West's new experimental manner. This was the so-called 'Venetian secret', a complex process gleaned from Thomas and Ann Jemima Provis, in an attempt to replicate the painting methods of the old masters.[48] West was paid a thousand guineas each for the cartoon and the oil painting, the highest sums he had ever received from the king and for which he attracted considerable criticism.[49] West defended the charges, implying that this was not a high price for such a large composition with some seventy figures in it, 'many of them Colossal in size'. Unfortunately, both the oil design for the *Crucifixion* and the cartoon based on it have since disappeared. The only substantial document of the window's projected appearance is now a squared watercolour drawing of the unfinished painted glass as left by Forrest at his death (Pl. VB).[50]

47. At Ely Cathedral, for instance, a plan to gather together mutilated fragments of medieval glass and arrange them in the eastern window was under discussion from 1758. This plan was eventually discarded in favour of an entirely modern window. S.F. Baylis, 'The most untractable of all Saxon uncouthness: 18th-century painted glass in Ely Cathedral and the removal of the Choir', *The Antiquaries Journal*, 68 (i) (1988), pp. 99–114.
48. Von Erffa and Staley, *Benjamin West*, p. 362, cat. no. 356. The oil design measured 9 ft 3 in. x 7 ft 6 in., including the frame. For further details of West's failed experiments in coloration with the Venetian Secret, see J. Gage, 'Magilphs and Mysteries', *Apollo*, 80 (1964), pp. 38–41.
49. He charged the same total for the whole east window. Interestingly, West was paid more for his full-sized oil designs for glass than for any of his canvas-paintings for the Chapel of Revealed Religion. Von Erffa and Staley, *Benjamin West*, p. 90.
50. SGC XVII.61.18(A). The drawing is watercolour on vellum. Inscribed on the mount is 'Sketch of an unfinished Window painted on Glass by Mr Forrest from a Cartoon by Benj. West Esq. intended for the great West Window of St George's Chapel, Windsor'. An identical drawing is amongst Willement's 'Drawings of Modern stained Glass', BL Add. MS 34873, no. 47, f. 17 dated 1844. No. 49, f. 17 is a drawing inscribed 'from the original sketch by Benjamin West now in the possession of Mr Lodige. Hackney 1845'. It depicts the

Although West had completed the design as early as 1796/7, Forrest does not seem to have begun work on the painted glass until 1799. Joseph Farington, whose diaries give a privileged insight into the private and professional lives of the eminent artists of the day, recorded a visit to the glass-painter's workshops in September 1804. Forrest had by then finished four sections out of a total of nine. Farington describes the laborious process which Forrest employed, using tiny hatching strokes, explaining 'were he to lay the colour upon the glass in broader quantities, it would blister in the burning in. The operation of burning in the colour takes abt. 48 hours'.[51] The painstaking nature of this process could explain why the window remained unfinished at Forrest's death, the exact date of which is unclear: it was certainly no later than October 1807.[52]

After Charles Forrest's death it appears his wife valiantly attempted to complete the window herself, firing the glass which he had left in a sufficiently prepared state.[53] In July 1808, unable to continue any longer with the task of mixing tints and matching colours, Mrs Forrest contacted Benjamin West in the hope that he could suggest someone to help her out. Understandably perhaps after ten years, West's interest in the fate of the *Crucifixion* window was dwindling fast. Not least because his own design had in the end proved something of a failed experiment in coloration. However, West did take it upon himself to try and help poor Mrs Forrest, and in a draft letter to George III, written in the autumn of 1808, he recommends that she should be relieved of her onerous task by one 'Mr Borckhardt'.[54] The mot likely indentification is with Charles Borckhardt (*fl.* 1784–1825) — a miniaturist who also painted portraits in oils and crayons. Why Borckhardt, a relatively obscure artist, should have been selected by West to complete the ill-fated western window for St George's is yet another of the unsolved mysteries haunting the history of this project. It seems probable that Borckhardt knew something of Forrest's painstaking techniques through his own training as a miniaturist. Whatever the case, it was not a successful recommendation. Although a detailed contract dated 3 November 1808 was drawn up for Mr Borckhardt, there is no evidence that any further progress was

right-hand thief in the *Crucifixion*. A sketch by West in the collection of Julius Held, in pen, ink and coloured chalks, probably an early part of the design process, shows a detail of the central *Crucifixion*, illustrated J.D. Meyer, 'Benjamin West's Window Designs for St George's Chapel, Windsor', *The American Art Journal*, xi (July 1979), fig. 9, opp. p. 61. Other related drawings are cited by Von Erffa and Staley, *Benjamin West*, p. 362 nn. 9–11.

51. Garlick and Macintyre, *Farington's Dairy*, 6, p. 2413. Entry for 17 September 1804.

52. A series of letters in the Pennslyvania Historical Society referring to Forrest and the progress of the west window are cited by Meyer, 'West's window designs', p. 62 nn. 35–7. Meyer believes that Forrest could have died earlier in 1806. Samuel Redgrave, *Dictionary of Artists of the English School*, London 1878, p. 157, records that Forrest went to work with Francis Eginton at Soho after completing the aisle windows. No evidence has yet been found to support this — although it could explain the delay both in starting and completing the west window of St George's.

53. It was not unusual to find husband and wife teams in the glass-painting profession. The most celebrated was that of James and Eglington Margaret Pearson who sometimes exhibited in their own London home. They worked independently, as well as in collaboration; the latter's finely detailed work was more highly regarded by some than were her husband's larger religious set-pieces. Mr and Mrs Thomas Hills also exhibited and sold their work in London around the turn of the eighteenth century.

54. Meyer, 'West's window designs', p. 62 n. 36.

made.[55] The king's declining mental and physical health must have further complicated the issue and, despite the conditions laid out in the contract, the necessary funds from the royal coffers were probably not forthcoming.

The underlying reasons for the failure of the west window commission, however, can be sought in changing patterns of taste. Both the aesthetic and the practical drawbacks of the eighteenth-century windows already *in situ* were becoming all too apparent. Meanwhile, as critics began to express a preference for a style of glass-painting more in keeping with its historical surroundings, the medieval stained glass in the west window was beginning to attract more admirers. There can also be no doubt that John Carter's periodic diatribes in the *Gentleman's Magazine* had done much to persuade people that the new style 'picture windows' were both vulgar and inappropriate to their ancient setting. Moreover, well before this time, Benjamin West's artistic reputation had begun to plummet. His work was no longer regarded with respect and he had even become a somewhat laughable figure in the artistic world. Richard Westall, a fellow Royal Academician, who saw West's ambitious design for the *Crucifixion* in 1796, confided to Farington that he thought the crowded composition, 'the strangest thing he ever saw . . . altogether a most absurd jumble. West seemed delighted with the performance, and said he had formed his conception on the Greek model and that a Group of Virgins in one corner serves as the Chorus'.[56]

After Forrest's death and the failure of the plans to complete the commission, the unfinished west window was put into store; the watercolour drawing was probably made as a record to show the extent of completion. In 1846, the window was taken out of store and presented, with the prior approval of Queen Victoria, to the newly built Gothic-style cathedral of St Paul's in Calcutta. It was sold for the sum of £500 but had to be substantially narrowed and altered to fit its new situation. Less than twenty years later this ill-fated glass-painting was totally destroyed by a cyclone.[57]

'VICTORIAN VANDALS'

The unexpected death of Prince Albert in 1861 and the decision to create an appropriate memorial gave the Dean and Canons the ideal opportunity to replace the east window

55. A copy of this contract, drawn up by West on behalf of the king, is in the Pennsylvania Historical Society, *ibid.*, p. 62 n. 37. Borckhardt was to be paid £10 per square foot of completed glass, having first obtained the recipes for the colours from Mrs Forrest. He was to have the same 'painting room with the necessary appendages of frames, stoves, and Cases ... and to which the Dwelling House adjoining, on the same terms on which Mrs Forrest had it ...'. In addition to quarterly payments from £300 a year with which 'he should be able to maintain his station while on that work with respectability', he was to be able to draw on an advance of money as the need arose. I am extremely grateful to Jean Farnsworth of the Preservation Alliance for Greater Philadelphia for her painstaking transcription of this and other documents.

56. Garlick and Macintyre, *Farington's Dairy*, 3, pp. 720–1. Entry 16 December 1796. Two critics who saw the design at the R.A. were equally unconvinced, one described the work as 'an odd mixture of the raw and the gaudy', and the other as having 'a dark and purpurine hue'. Von Erffa & Staley, *Benjamin West*, p. 362.

57. The window is illustrated *in situ* in an anonymous print of the 1840s, see A.N. Mukherjee, ed., *A Short History of St Paul's Cathedral*, Calcutta 1956, p. 5. Stained glass was considered essential in maintaining coolness in the cathedral; further glass was being prepared in London for the eight lancet windows of the Lantern. *Illustrated London News* (18 October 1845), p. 251. The sale of the *Crucifixion* is referred to in SGC XVII.9.4. The Chapter Clerk's Memoranda.

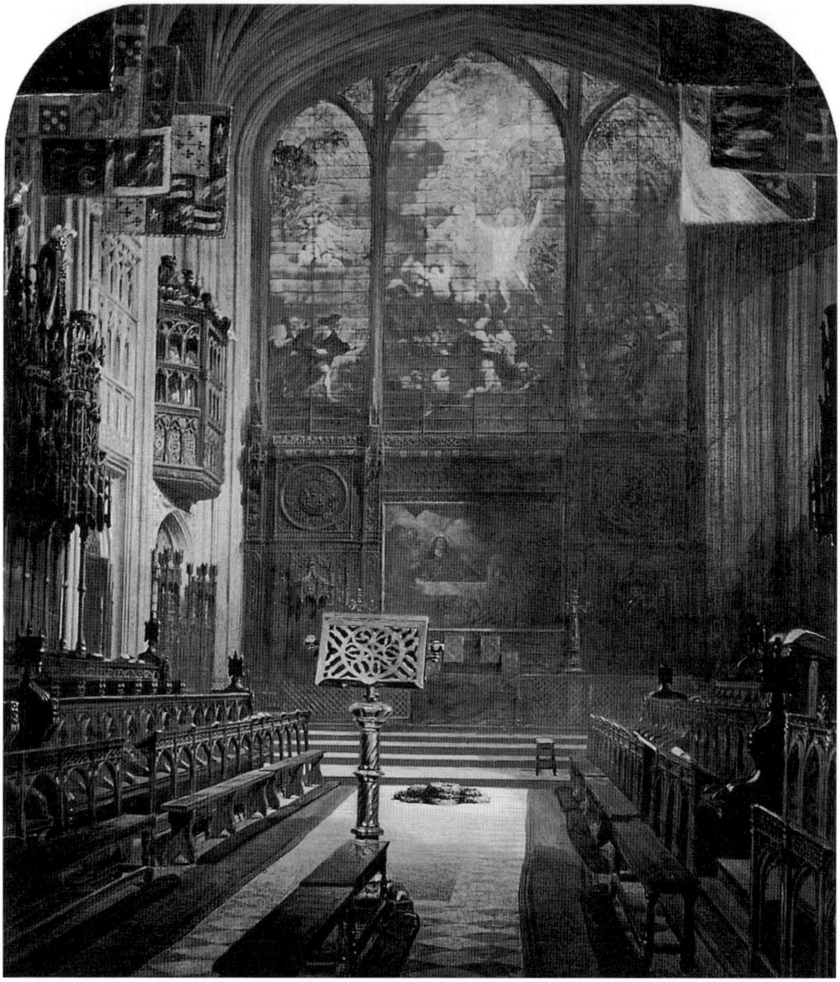

Fig. 71. *J.H. Watson, the east end of St George's Chapel, c. 1860, photograph with some over-painting (The Royal Collection © 2004, Her Majesty Queen Elizabeth II)*

(Fig. 71) with something more suited to contemporary taste. Henry Poole & Sons, a firm of stonemasons based in Great Smith Street, Westminster, who worked extensively for G.G. Scott at Windsor, were employed in August 1862 to dismantle the painted glass from the eastern window and store it in four cases.[58] The only documentation of this event is a plan of the east window, dated 10 August 1862, drawn up by Poole. The drawing is on a

58. See *Poole's Works in Chapel* (1862–9), SGC XVII.61.22. Poole supplied the new black marble altar steps as well as the carved angels around the east window and carried out vital repairs to the stonework. Assisted by Robert Crook, Poole was paid a total of £500 between 1861 and 1862 for removing the glass from the east window. SGC XII.13.25, Audit Book 1857–64. Later, in December 1862, Poole was paid £157 for unspecified work relating to the windows. The Chapter Clerk's Memoranda also refers to the plans to remove the two remaining Benjamin West windows, to replace the stonework and put in new glass.

scale of half an inch to a foot, and each panel of glass is clearly numbered.[59] A copy of this drawing accompained the glass in each of the four packing cases. In 1878 a pencilled note by Mr A.Y. Nutt, the Chapter Surveyor, was made on the plan remaining in the chapel archives. The memo notes baldly that when enquiries were made at that time into the whereabouts of the painted glass — 'no satisfactory reply obtained as to where window went or what become of cases'.

The search for the glass seems to have ceased here. In September 1914, a contributor to *Notes & Queries*, Robert Pierrepoint, raised the question once again; he was an old Etonian who remembered the glass from his schooldays when he had had, he says ironically, 'the bad taste to admire it'. His enquiry led to one interesting response from a Mr W.A. Frost who recalled, mistakenly it seems, that the glass had been taken to South Kensington.[60]

Around the time that the east window was removed, a new alabaster reredos was installed, replacing both Emlyn's gothick altarpiece and Benjamin West's *Last Supper*.[61] Thus — apart from Emlyn's choir screen — nothing now remained of the Georgian arrangement of the east end. A rare mid-century photograph (Pl. VB) is possibly one of the last visual documents of that old arrangement. By August 1869, when Poole removed the 'picture windows' from the west ends of the aisles and prepared the stonework for the new glass, the chapel had begun to take on the appearance it bears today. These aisle windows, like the east windows, were also packed up and put into store. The recent discovery of two squared-up pen and ink drawings of the *Nativity* and the *Adoration of the Magi* suggest that these glass-paintings were dismantled and stored in the same way. The windows are divided up into carefully numbered panels as an aid to future identification.[62] We can only guess what had happened to the *Angel appearing to the Shepherds*, removed some twenty years earlier from the south aisle.

THE JUSTIFICATION

To understand the reasons behind the systematic replacement of the Georgian painted glass, along with other fittings from that period, we have to take into account a number of practical considerations. Right from the start there were certain undeniable problems associated with the enamel-painted glass. Charles Knight felt it necessary to add as a cautionary footnote to his guidebook that the new glass could rarely be appreciated as a whole at any one time of day, except when the sun was obscured by light clouds. Otherwise, he noted, the most favourable time for viewing the east window was from 9 until 11 a.m. and the west, from 3 until 6 p.m. Many visitors who flocked to the chapel, not having the time or patience to wait for the optimum viewing conditions, must have been greatly disappointed by their experience. Moreover, the combined effect of the

59. SGC P.324.

60. *Notes & Queries*, 11 SX (12 September 1914), p. 210. See also 26 September 1914, p. 256. There is no apparent evidence of such a loan or acquisition by the Victoria & Albert Museum, although a loan from H.M. the Queen at Windsor was recorded in January 1863. This glass, a sixteenth-century *Last Supper*, is still in store at the V&A.

61. Von Erffa & Staley, *Benjamin West*, p. 354, cat. no. 346. It was sold by the Dean and Canons in 1978. This, and not the east window, is probably the work which St John Hope refers to as being stored for a while in the ambulatory. *Architectural History*, ii, p. 427.

62. The drawings are SGC P.110/52.

opaque glass in the eastern window and the blackout 'windows' in the clerestory (see below) was to darken the choir substantially, rendering the altar steps distinctly hazardous. It was also reported that Charles Forrest, on more than one occasion, had been required to repaint parts of the new painted glass (including the east window) in order 'to amend the fading tints to which his utmost skill cannot ensure a permanency'.[63] This was not an unusual problem: even the west window of New College, Oxford, once celebrated for its vivid colouring, had by the end of the eighteenth century by all accounts lost much of its original brilliance of tone.

From the moment the new glass-paintings were installed, a lively debate concerning their aesthetic merits and demerits was underway. Everyone, it seemed, had an opinion to voice. John Carter had been the first to raise what were quickly perceived as major issues in the decoration of ancient buildings; his views were soon echoed in print by others.

> However serviceable to the character of the pointed architecture the introduction of the still and subdued light which is admitted through such a medium . . . it must yet remain a subject of much doubt whether it does not suffer on the whole by the insertion of these transparent pictures.[64]

Perhaps the greatest criticism of the eighteenth-century glass-painter was his imputed insensitivity to the architecture he was seeking to embellish in attempting to transfer the naturalistic and illusionistic effects of a canvas painting on to glass. Even when the window structure itself was altered the glass-painter could not escape the limitations of the supporting iron framework — a grid which, no matter how ingenious the attempts to disguise it, always intruded to some extent on the design. It is clear from the following diatribe that the windows in St George's Chapel were no more successful in this respect than others of the period.

> That style of composition may be pronounced obviously wrong which destroys the architecture it pretends to decorate; and that mechanical treatment grossly defective which could find no better contrivance for combining the glass than straight bars, harmonising with none of the lines of the picture, and even bisecting in their inexorable course the faces of some of the principal figures . . . Such as they are, they are a blot upon the unity of the edifice.[65]

As time went by fewer and fewer people could be found to defend the works of eighteenth-century glass-painters. Relegated to the vulgar ranks of a penny peep-show, these Georgian 'transparencies' displaying the 'cold obscurity and vapid colouring of a painted blind' were increasingly regarded as a counterfeit art form. Now considered fundamentally unsuited to the decoration of ecclesiastical buildings, they were, therefore, utterly expendable.

Perhaps the final word should come from Thomas Willement himself, the glass-painter whose own works systematically replaced those of Jervais and Forrest from the 1840s onwards. Willement was by then regarded as representative of a new generation of glass-painters who were working in a revived medieval style, and was widely respected as an academic authority on the subject. 'It has at length been admitted,' he pronounced, 'that oil painting and stained glass for windows are founded on totally different principles and

63. *Gentleman's Magazine* (1805), pp. 2, 926.

64. James Hakewill, *A History of Windsor and its Neighbourhood*, London 1813, pp. 130–7.

65. Ambrose Poynter, *Illustrations of Windsor Castle by the Late Sir Jeffrey Wyattville*, ed. H. Ashton, London 1841, p. 16.

that all attempts to assimilate them have only produced very inferior glass without retaining any of the good effects of an oil-painting.'[66]

Willement's opinions, expressed with such professional conviction, must have helped to persuade the Chapter they were acting for the best in removing these windows, despite their royal and aristocratic connections. However, the fate of this Georgian glass remains one of the most tantalizing and puzzling of all art-historical mysteries. How could painted windows of such scale and status, in a building which has remained constantly under public scrutiny, be permitted simply to disappear? The complete revolution in taste which had occurred since George III commissioned the windows, accompanied by the dramatic decline in popularity of West, the 'Monarch of Mediocrity', are explanations, but hardly justifications for their loss. Ironically perhaps, nothing has done more in recent years to illuminate the need for and facilitate research into Georgian glass-painting than the scholarly reassessment of Victorian stained glass. Only now we are beginning to appreciate the true extent of the vast and often indiscriminate sacrifice of eighteenth-century painted windows at the hands of the zealous, ecclesiologically-inspired Victorians.

SOME UNIDENTIFIED EIGHTEENTH-CENTURY GLASS

Charles Knight's guidebooks to St George's Chapel provide almost the only evidence of three other painted-glass windows installed during the late eighteenth century. Their replacement after only a few years seems to suggest they were not now considered of a high enough quality. They, like the other examples, have disappeared without trace.

The *Windsor Guide* for 1785 records the repair of three windows which had been entirely reglazed with 'elegant stained glass' some two years earlier. In the east window of the south aisle (sII) was a figure of King Edward III under a Gothic canopy; in the lower compartments were King John of France and King David of Scotland with two cardinals. This glass was removed in *c.* 1792 to make way for Forrest's *Angel appearing to the Shepherds*. In the west window of the north aisle (nXXV) a female figure — reputedly Queen Philippa, wife of Edward III —was recorded standing beneath a Gothic canopy; below her were four ecclesiastical figures. This glass was replaced in 1796 by the *Adoration of the Magi*. Likewise, in the arch of the west window of the south aisle (sXXXI) there was formerly a representation of *Christ before Pilate*, replaced in 1794 by Forrest's *Nativity*. The surviving commission books of the York-based glass-painter, William Peckitt (1731–95), record that a large religious glass-painting of 'Our Saviour in the Judgement Hall' after Rubens was sold in London in September 1760 for £10 and apparently installed in St George's Chapel.[67] It seems reasonable to identify this work by Peckitt as one of those 'insignificant paintings' noted by John Carter and which, he seems to suggest, were put up merely as a stop-gap whilst the Forrest glass was under execution.[68] Charles Knight describes the windows in St George's Chapel in the 1780s as composed of old glass selected from scattered remains in various parts of the chapel, together with 'some pieces collected by the Rev. Dr Lockman,

66. *Collegiate Chapel*, pp. 6–7.

67. J.T. Brighton, 'William Peckitt's Commission Book, 1751–95', *The Walpole Society*, 54 (1988), pp. 334–453, no. 68, f. 7, 354. This was apparently Peckitt's first large religious piece.

68. *Gentleman's Magazine* (1805), pp. 2, 820. See also *ibid.* (1805), pp. 1, 530. Carter refers to a visit of *c.* 1783, when he saw the 'two modern paintings' in the western aisle windows 'without the least pretensions to recommend them'.

and others painted by Bristow'. We might assume therefore that the other earlier glass-paintings were poor work by Bristow, a local glazier or glass-painter.[69]

THE CHOIR CLERESTORY WINDOWS: FRANCIS EGINTON, 1782

According to the manuscript account of the restoration of St George's Chapel, the king's original plan had been to incorporate the arms of the knights subscribing to the east window in the new altarpiece, in two circular 'windows' over the stalls of the chancellor and prelate. 'But when this was found not to answer His Majesty signified his pleasure that the Arms should be placed in 2 of the windows, one on the north side and the other on the south side.'[70] The armorial glass was therefore installed in the third window from the east on each side of the choir clerestory: here it remained until the 1840s when it was moved by Willement to its present position in the two windows immediately next to the east end.

These fine examples of Georgian heraldic glass, dated 1782, were executed by Francis Eginton of Birmingham (1737–1805), one of the most highly respected glass-painters of the day (Fig. 72). Eginton may well have been recommended to the king on the strength of a personal acquaintance with Benjamin West, but these pieces have a particular value in being some of the earliest glass Eginton is known to have produced. He had begun his career working for Matthew Boulton in the Soho factory as a general designer and decorator of japanned ware and as a modeller of objects for casting in metal.[71] Eginton entered briefly into partnership with Boulton in the production of silver-plated and ormolu goods and also worked with him on the production of polygraphs, or 'mechanical paintings', but by 1781 he had left Boulton's employ to set up a painted glass manufactory at Prospect Hill House, Soho, and seems to have enjoyed immediate success in this new venture.

Eginton's two windows depict the arms of the Knights of the Garter of 1782 set within a Garter-type Star; above them is the appropriate crown or coronet of rank, helmet mantling and crest, whilst below, on a ribband of garter blue edged with gold, is the name and title. The George is pendant from this ribband. Royal patronage is firmly indicated by 'G.R. 1782' in brilliant yellow in the upper tracery lights. Twelve knights are represented in each of the two windows.

This heraldic programme was, of course, extended in the mid-nineteenth century by Thomas Willement who condemned Eginton's two windows as being of the 'dingiest hue'. It is hard to agree with Willement's criticism. Eginton's work demonstrates the stunning colouristic potential of Georgian heraldic glass. Although its condition has

69. Although Lockman often took the initiative where stained glass was concerned, he seems always to have acted in close consultation with the king. Reference to this glass in the Chapter Acts are confusing. In 1783, Lockman had been given permission to remove the 'square picture' in the east window of the south aisle (SGC XV.B.8, p. 179) whilst an entry for 21 August of the same year informs us that Lockman was 'empowered to remove the square picture in the East end of the north aisle and place it at the other end of the north aisle'. In June 1783, Lockman expressed the royal wish 'that the south windows be ornamented something similar to the window in the other isle'; *ibid.*, p. 176.

70. *Architectural History*, ii, p. 390. The designs for the heraldry were provided by a Mr Livesay.

71. For Eginton's career, see W.C. Aitken, 'Francis Eginton', *Trans. Birmingham & Midland Institute Archaeological Society*, 1872 (1873), pp. 27–43.

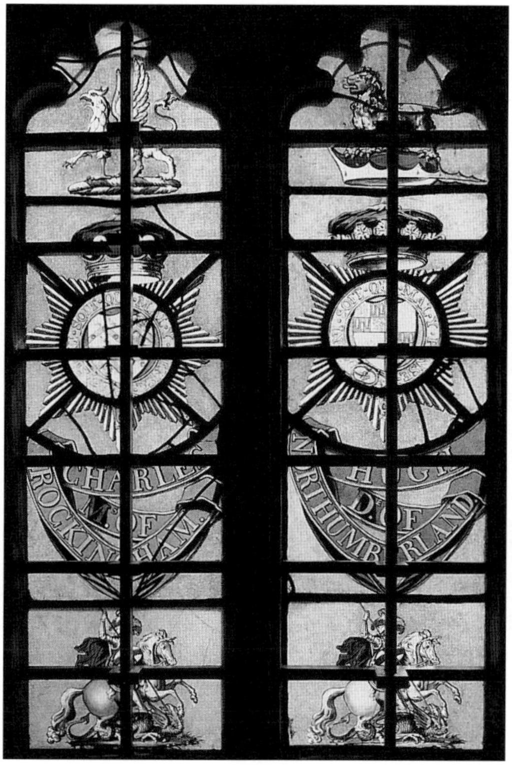

Fig. 72. *Heraldic glass in clerestory window sII by Francis Eginton (© Crown Copyright. NMR)*

deteriorated considerably over two centuries, the enamel painted glass with its greenish-grey background and startling pink and gold coloration stands out vividly against the more sober Victorian windows.[72]

As we have already seen, one of the most common difficulties encountered by Georgian glass-painters was their desire to create a fully three-dimensional and naturalistic image whilst preserving the transparency of the medium. Ambient light fluctuates widely — thus confounding the glass-painter's attempts to fix in advance where the light and shadow should fall. Various measures had therefore to be taken to reduce and control the amount of ambient light. Not long after the *Resurrection* was installed it was decided to close up two of the clerestory windows on each side of the east window with copper plates. These would make the transition from light to dark less glaring and help to throw the painted glass into relief. The copper plates were painted with heraldic insignia and, from the ground at least, were intended to look like painted glass and to harmonize with Eginton's two armorial windows. They contained the arms of the Knights of the Garter during the year in which they were painted. The success of these four fictive copper 'windows', which bore the dates 1799, 1805 and 1812, may be gauged from the fact that they were

72. The Chapter Clerk's Personal Memoranda records that in 1884 he was shown six coloured drawings of the clerestory windows put in at the time of George III. The drawings were 'had Miss Bovingdon's repres'. Miss Bovingdon had been a relative of William Webb, the plumber and glazier. I have been unable to locate these drawings, possibly original designs by F. Eginton.

frequently mistaken for painted glass.[73] As one might expect, Willement regarded these ingenious copper plates as 'ridiculous', and they did not survive his reorganization of the clerestory glazing.[74] Some, if not all, of these fictive window panels were the work of William Webb, plumber and glazier, who worked under the supervision of Henry Emlyn. In 1812 Webb was paid a considerable sum from the window fund — amounting to £117 16s 6d — for work on the clerestory 'windows'. A typical entry among many in the Chapter Bills reads as follows:

15 Iron frames with metal moulding and	94. 10s
Coper Plates in the room of glass-painting	
13 St George's Roses, Stars & Garter	
4 small Crockets of Copper	4s[75]

Webb was evidently required to make frequent, ongoing amendments to the heraldry. Amongst the Artificer's Bills for instance is an entry for 1813 which states that he was paid for various repairs, including taking down the 'copper lite and frame', and 'painting arms coronet & crest of the Marquess of Wellington . . .'.[76]

THE ROYAL PEW (EDWARD IV CHANTRY)

One important element of the king's restoration of St George's Chapel remains largely unchanged to this day. Between 1782 and 1785 Henry Emlyn was involved in the refurbishment of the King's Closet, or Royal Pew, to the north of the Sanctuary. This was a small apartment used regularly by George III as a family pew. In addition to repanelling and refurnishing the interior in a suitably elegant 'gothick' style, Emlyn's brief included the installation of stained glass decoration for the windows. The decorative treatment of the windows in the Royal Pew is entirely typical of this period. The Georgian glazier employed to install older glass in churches, private chapels or domestic windows was often called upon to supply his own ornamental settings and to extend the ancient glass with modern in-filling.

The origins of the continental stained glass in the Royal Pew are something of a mystery but the vogue for importing such glass was well established in England by the 1760s. Emlyn was closely supervised by Dr Lockman in his task and the latter may have been responsible for obtaining the ancient pieces — those sixteenth- and seventeenth-century Flemish panels which were so attractive to collectors at this time. It seems highly likely, as Dr Cole suggests, that Lockman acquired the glass through the Hon. Richard Bateman who lived in Old Windsor. 'Dicky' Bateman, a close friend of Horace Walpole and an equally enthusiastic devotee of the gothick, was certainly acquiring ancient glass in the 1760s whilst transforming The Grove, his own riverside house. The Grove had, amongst other additions, a gothick cloister which was to display much stained-glass decoration.[77]

73. *Windsor Guide* (*c.* 1813), pp. 86–8. Charles Knight, for instance, records all the coats of arms in these six windows, making no distinction between the genuine painted windows and the fakes.

74. *Collegiate Chapel*, p. 7n.

75. SGC XIV, Chapter Bills, bundle for 1812.

76. SGC XIV, Artificers Bills, bundle for 1813.

77. M. McCarthy, *The Origins of the Gothic Revival*, New Haven & London 1987, p. 90. Bateman was responsible for rebuilding the Church of St John the Evangelist in Shobdon, Herefordshire, whose painted glass by Price, completed *c.* 1756, bears many similarities to the decorative glass in the Royal Pew.

Dr Lockman was clearly a collector of ancient glass himself, a common passion amongst members of the clergy. It might seem anomalous that someone with so keen an interest in preserving the medieval glass in the chapel should also have been willing to encourage the installation of modern painted windows with their radically different aesthetic. However, Lockman was not alone in this. Walpole's window decorations at Strawberry Hill — the *locus classicus* for the cult of collecting ancient glass — incorporated numerous contemporary pieces: it is clear that, whilst he was often critical of its technical success, Walpole was by no means opposed to modern painted glass.

The portrait on glass of Charles II, who was known to have worshipped in the Edward IV Chantry, is of late seventeenth-century date and is first recorded in the *Windsor Guide* in 1812. The royal portrait, in vivid enamels and stains, is a copy of an engraving by David Loggan. It is clear from the *Windsor Guide* that some of the original glass in the Royal Pew has since disappeared. One such piece is the royal coat of arms by Bristow recorded in 1785.[78] By 1790 the decorations in the Royal Pew also included 'a rose and a sunflower by West'. The sunflower has disappeared without trace, but the delicately painted pink rose — an oval panel in a simple geometric setting of coloured glass — can still be seen today (Pl. VIA). By 1812 this description had been corrected to 'a sunflower by West and a rose by Jarvis'. Thomas Jervais may well have painted both pieces as it seems doubtful that West would have been involved in any formal way, if at all. Catalogues of sales held in London show that Jervais, in common with all his contemporary glass-painters, frequently exhibited flower pieces such as these. These small-scale, beautifully detailed, enamel-painted panels were highly popular as domestic window ornaments and formed a substantial constituent of the Georgian glass-painter's *œuvre*.

The older panels of stained glass in the Royal Pew still retain their decorative Georgian setting. This type of ornamental glass, which also frames the elaborate carved door to the pew, is typical of the second half of the eighteen century: the combination of simple cross-banding and floral patterns in a somewhat crude but vivid yellow stain, creates a generalized, immediately recognizable 'gothick' effect and was eminently adaptable. Decorative glass like this could be acquired ready-made in large quantities and cut to size by the glazier. In this case the glazier responsible was likely to have been William Webb.

THE URSWICK CHANTRY: CHRIST, ST PETER AND THE FOUR APOSTLES, *c.* 1830

The tragic death in childbirth of Princess Charlotte Augusta — only daughter of the Prince Regent, later George IV — precipitated a profound wave of national mourning combined with the threat of an acute constitutional crisis.

> . . . in the dust
> The fair-hair'd Daughter of the Isles is laid,
> The love of millions! How we did intrust
> Futurity to her![79]

Princess Charlotte was much admired by the British public for her personal beauty as well as her triumph over an unhappy childhood. In 1815, two years before her death, she had

78. SGC XI.B.10, Audit Accounts, 1777–82, 29 July 1782. Bristow was paid the sum of £40 2s 6d.
79. Byron, *Childe Harold*, Canto iv, 169, London 1817.

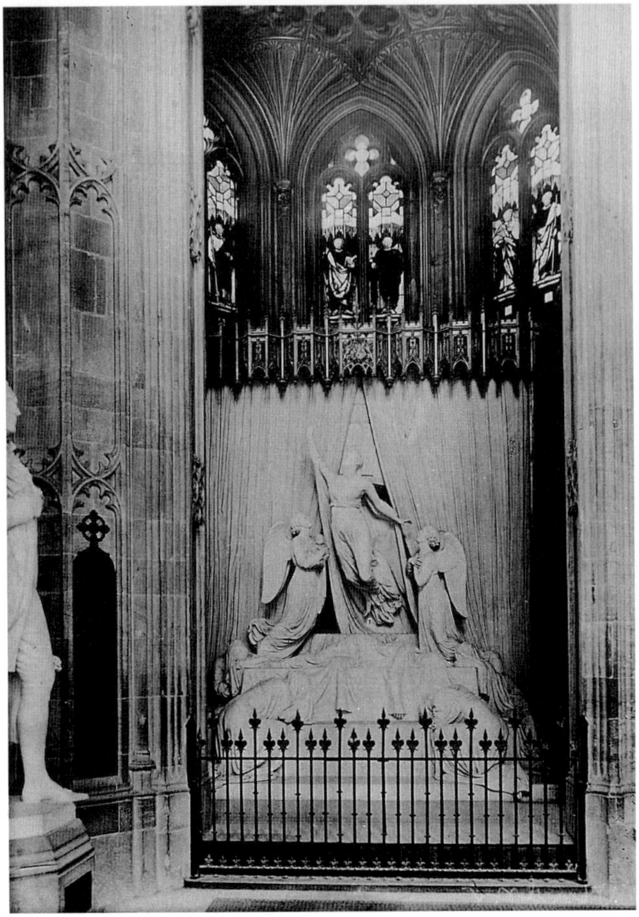

Fig. 73. *The Urswick Chantry and the memorial to Princess Charlotte Augusta (© Crown Copyright, NMR)*

married Prince Leopold of Saxe-Coburg (later king of the Belgians) to great public acclaim. Soon after her death, a subscription fund was established under the patronage of her cousin, the duchess of York, to erect some kind of public memorial. There were many ideas as to what form this should take, but the sixteenth-century Urswick Chantry (or 'Bread Chapel', as it was sometimes called) at the west end of the north aisle of St George's Chapel was finally selected as the ideal site for a commemorative statue by the sculptor Matthew Cotes Wyatt (1777–1862).

The statue depicts the princess's soul ascending to heaven, leaving her lifeless, shrouded body (Fig. 73). Angels accompany the soul of her dead child whilst draped female mourners kneel at her bedside. The statue was installed in the chapel in 1826, having been on public display in the sculptor's studio for some five years. Today, the piece can be regarded as a minor triumph of Romantic spectacle: of classically inspired forms wedded to sensational 'gothick' effects. Contemporaries commented on the 'painful reality of the subject' and in its eerily erotic rendering of the dead mother and the tiny figure of her child, the monument is still a poignant reminder of how precarious women's lives once were. This memorial effectively made Wyatt's career as a sculptor.[80] Despite his overnight success, however, he never achieved a consistent fame and was to remain a somewhat maverick figure in the early Victorian artistic world.[81]

It is important to bear in mind that the memorial was not confined to sculpture alone. The outer stone screen of the chantry was removed and replaced by railings which allowed a better view of the statue and also of the chantry roof now 'embellished with blazonry', and the new painted glass 'executed with great brilliancy by Mr Wyatt'.[82] This was a reference to the orange and purple tinted glass placed in the side windows above the monument, creating a richly colourful effect. According to one press report, 'though perhaps approaching to garishness, these ornaments rather increase by contrast the effect of the pallid marble'.[83] This vivid coloured glass was removed in the 1920s and has not apparently survived.[84]

Tantalizingly little is known about the figural glass now in the three central windows of the Urswick Chantry. The stern-faced St Peter, Christ and the four Apostles stand with their appropriate symbols under elaborate Gothic-style canopies (Pl. VIc). Although the glass is almost certainly late Georgian it cannot yet be attributed with any certainty to a specific glass-painter. Unlike the plain coloured glass there is no reason to assume these windows were an integral part of Wyatt's original conception. However, it seems most likely that they were funded by the same public subscription as the monument itself. This fact would explain the mysterious absence of reference to the windows in the chapel archives. The subscription fund was evidently an enormously successful venture. By 1820, according to a report in *The Times*, over £12,000 had been raised, the bulk of which remained in the bankers' hands, 'to be drawn for as may be required'. The final sum raised was over £15,000. The figural glass was no doubt intended to provide a more solemn and pious counterpoint to Wyatt's theatrical ensemble which was certainly not without its critics. The rich potmetal colours complement the cool smooth sculptural tones and, whilst the paint surface has deteriorated somewhat, the cast light provided by this glass still creates a truly 'gothick' effect.

These three windows are an interesting indication of the way that glass-painting was tending in the later Georgian period. Although the faces of the apostles are still in the pictorial tradition, the figures, their attitudes and architectural settings and the whole compositional format of standing figures under canopies, look forward to the medievalizing glass of Willement and the Victorian glass-stainers, rather than back towards the enamel-painted 'picture windows' of Jervais, Forrest and their contemporaries. One glass-painter known to have had particularly strong associations with the royal family during this period was Joseph Backler (*fl.* 1815–45) who was also, incidentally, well acquainted with

80. For M.C. Wyatt's career, see J.M. Robinson, *The Wyatts. An Architectural Dynasty*, Oxford 1979, pp. 173–88. The third son of James Wyatt, he had started out as a miniaturist, and later worked for his father as a decorative painter in the remodelled State Apartments of Windsor Castle.

81. Robinson casts considerable doubt on Wyatt's skills as a scultpor: he is thought to have executed very little, if any, of his own sculptures, *The Wyatts*, p. 188.

82. *Windsor & Eton Express*, Saturday, 18 March 1826.

83. *Ibid.* Wyatt was to repeat this dramatic lighting effect with equal success a few years later in his mausoleum for the Duchess of Rutland at Belvoir Castle.

84. St John Hoper refers to yellow glass in the western window and purple in the eastern one. *Architectural History*, ii, p. 429, although surprisingly he does not mention the figural glass at all.

Benjamin West.[85] Backler's reputation was at its height in the 1820s. In 1819 he had exhibited some 'Gothic windows' for a mausoleum in the grounds at Claremont, the home of Prince Leopold. The Gothic temple at Claremont was unfinished at the princess's death but she had taken great personal interest in its progress and the prince turned it into a private memorial to his dead wife. Backler's glass was basically heraldic, although there were in the door some small-scale 'monastic figures with rich gothic pinnacles, ornaments, borderings etc. etc.'.[86] This is, however, insufficient evidence to link Backler firmly with the Urswick Chapel windows. In their combination of a painterly style with a scholarly approach to the architectural and ornamental detail, these windows are entirely typical of a new style of glass-painting which was becoming increasingly popular throughout the 1820s and '30s. None of Backler's known windows of this type have survived to allow for close stylistic comparisons. It must also be said that Backler did not by any means have the monopoly of such 'Gothic-style' glass in this period; many other glass-painters in the immediate pre-Victorian era — such as William Collins, John Betton and David Evans — also worked in the newly popularized 'figure-and-canopy' mode. Given their previous connections with Windsor, in addition to close family connections with the Wyatts, the manufactory of William Rapahel Eginton (1778–1834), successor to the Soho works in partnership with Samuel Lowe, might also provide some clue to the provenance of the Urswick Chantry glass. In 1811, W.R. Eginton had been appointed 'Royal Glass-Stainer' to Princess Charlotte of Wales, Prince Leopold of Saxe-Coburg and the duke of Sussex — a title he continued to use after the princess's death.[87] He is also recorded elsewhere as having executed 'many important works for George IV'.[88] Eginton's partner and brother-in-law, Samuel Lowe, died in 1826 after a debilitating illness and soon after this date the firm effectively ceased operations.

85. West was said to have supervised Backler in the execution of a painted window of the *Ascension*. *Magazine of the Fine Arts*, i (1821), p. 187, although West had died in March 1820. Backler produced many copies on glass of paintings by West: in 1818 he exhibited 'The Three Maries at the Sepulchre' and 'King Lear in the Storm' after West. Backler's rendition of West's 'Last Supper' for Hereford Cathedral in *c.* 1823 is probably the most significant example. A small oil and sepia sketch attributed to Benjamin West, entitled 'The Apotheosis of Princess Charlotte', has been identified as a design for a painted-glass window in St George's Chapel. A.P. Oppé, *English Drawings at Windsor Castle, Stuart & Georgian Periods*, London 1950, pl. 94. The dramatic wielding of the highlights and sketchily expressed forms seem closer to the techniques of a transparency. There is no other record of West's involvement in the Urswick Chapel memorial and since he was, by 1817, well out of royal favour, perhaps this sketch was intended as a transparency backdrop to a memorial ceremony commemorating the late princess.

86. *The Literary Gazette* (8 May 1819), p. 316. Claremont is now a privately owned school and none of Backler's glass here has apparently survived the attentions of modern vandals.

87. *A Short Account of the Works Executed by W.R. Eginton, F.A.S.E*, Edinburgh 1818, p. 7. 'For Princess Charlotte of Wales & Saxe-Coburg, a figure of a bishop in ancient costume after Van Dyck'. See also, Anon, *A Century of Birmingham Life, 1741–1841*, Birmingham 1868, pp. 2, 372, press cutting dated 8 July 1816.

88. W.C. Aitken, 'Francis Eginton', *Trans. Birmingham & Midland Institute. Archaeological Section*, 3 (1872), p. 43. W.R. Eginton is believed to have retired from glass-painting and moved to Worcester in *c.* 1826. Some of his last known work is the extensive series of commemorative figures in Brockley Church, Somerset, begun *c.* 1824.

CONCLUSION

In 1978, a piece of eighteenth-century painted glass was given to the Chapter by Mrs E.B. Bowditch who claimed it had come originally from St George's Chapel (Pl. VIB). For many years it had been in a staircase window in the basement of the veterinary surgery in William Street, Windsor — a building demolished in the 1970s redevelopment of Peascod Street.[89] Mrs Bowditch recalls that it was salvaged from a heap of rubbish in the Horseshoe Cloister in St George's Chapel by her husband at some date prior to the Second World War. The piece consists of two square fragments of painted glass leaded together one on top of the other, framed by a border of plain coloured glass. The upper fragment depicts the head of one cherub and the lower, the heads and torsos of two cherubs holding scrolls. It is not possible to identify with absolute certainty which window(s) in St George's Chapel these pieces relate to: groups of cherubs were a stock feature of Benjamin West's religious repertoire. The *Angel appearing to the Shepherds* in particular is recorded as having featured cherubs bearing scrolls and there are certainly great similarities with the figures in the corners of the surviving design.

The possibility that further fragments of this lost programme of painted glass may come to light thus cannot be ruled out. Were these small fragments simply arbitrary casualties in the rather careless removal process? Or were the eighteenth-century windows at some point disposed of discreetly — broken up and sold in small, more manageable sections? At the present moment there are many more questions than answers, but it is hoped that this essay, by putting forward the known facts together with the unknown — not to mention the merely conjectural — will help towards solving the mystery at some point in the future.

ACKNOWLEDGEMENTS

I should like to acknowledge Dr Eileen Scarff, the Archivist of St George's Chapel, for her considerable assistance in the preparation of this article.

89. The gift is recorded in SGC VI.B.19. Chapter Acts, 1 June 1982. I am extremely grateful to Mrs Bowditch for her helpful response to my enquiries and to Dr Eileen Scarff for helping me to trace Mrs Bowditch.

'So Perfectly Satisfactory': The Stained Glass of Thomas Willement in St George's Chapel

SARAH BROWN

INTRODUCTION

In July 1840, the Dean and Canons of Windsor commissioned four heraldic windows (SIII, SIV, NIII, NIV) from stained glass artist Thomas Willement (1786–1871, Fig. 74). These windows for the choir clerestory were to extend the heraldic series commemorating Garter Knights begun by Francis Eginton in 1781.[1] This was the beginning of an association that was to last until 1861, embracing the glazing of the choir clerestory, choir aisles, the ambulatory, the Beaufort, Lincoln and Oliver King chapels and the Chapter Room, and the thorough and sensitive restoration of the great west window. While it was undoubtedly a lucrative commission for Willement, who was to receive a total of nearly £5,000 for his glazing work alone,[2] it is also clear that it was a scheme by which he placed considerable store. In common with many nineteenth-century stained glass artists, Willement was often required to work within the constraints of a tight brief provided by an architect.[3] At Windsor, on the other hand, he dealt directly with his patrons, and was able to influence and direct the development of the glazing scheme. Much of Willement's considerable output of figural stained glass has been lost and many of his schemes of decorative mural painting have been obliterated.[4] His work at St George's, well preserved, well documented and considered by the artist himself to be one of his most important

1. The Eginton windows commemorated those Garter Knights who joined George III in funding Benjamin West's east window. Originally intended to be positioned in the tracery of the window itself, the armorials were eventually installed in the adjoining clerestory windows (*Architectural History*, ii, p. 390). For a full account, see Baylis, pp. 100–2.

2. The Chapter Bills (SGC XIV), contain a list, compiled by Canon Steward Cust, of all disbursements made to Willement in the period 1841–61. There were only four years in which no payments were made at all (1843, 1857, 1858 and 1860) and in most years he received at least £100. The receipts sent from the studio show these sums to have been payments on account.

3. This situation is exemplified by the working relationship between architect William Butterfield and the stained glass artists he employed. Paul Thompson, *William Butterfield*, London 1971, and Michael Kerney, 'The stained glass commissioned by William Butterfield', *JBSMGP*, xx, No. 1 (1996), pp. 1–30.

4. His windows for the Temple Church, made while he was working at Windsor, for example, were destroyed in the Second World War. Other war-time losses include St Dunstan's in the East (1832), St Stephen's, Walbrook (1851) and his very last window, for the Savoy Chapel (1865), all in London. Goodrich Court, Herefordshire, was demolished after the Second World War. Other windows were the victims of changing taste. His St Cuthbert window in Durham Cathedral, for example, was replaced by a Clayton & Bell window of the same subject.

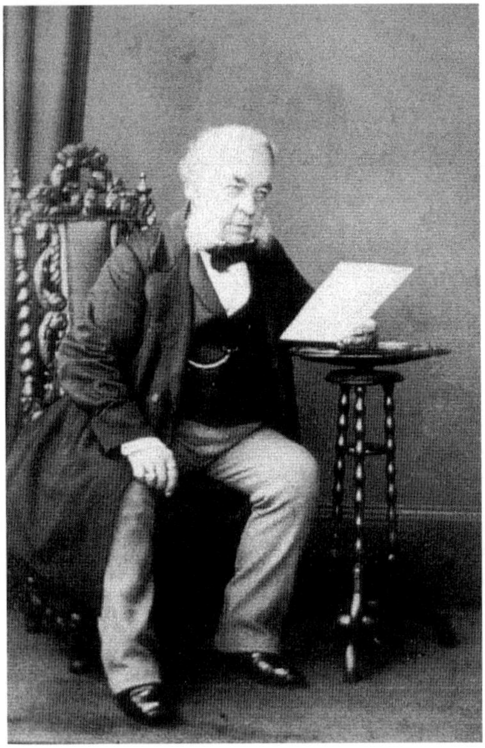

Fig. 74. *Thomas Willement, c. 1860 (Photographer unknown, reproduced courtesy of Dr Arthur Percival, The Faversham Society)*

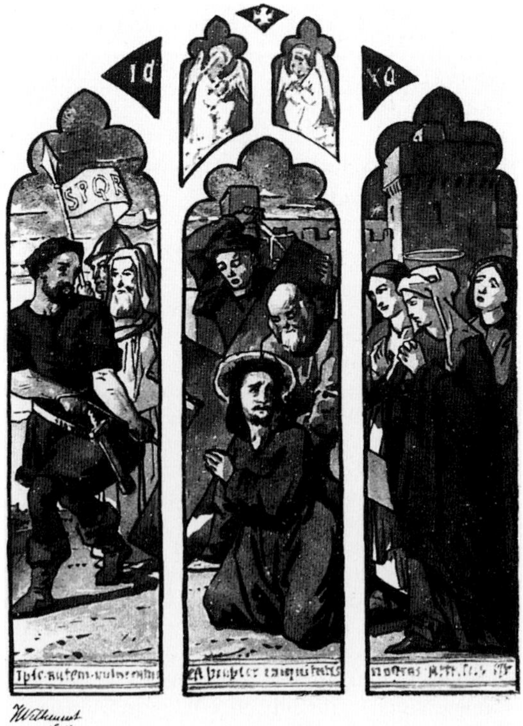

Fig. 75. *'The Carrying of the Cross' installed in window sII in 1847 and removed in 1882, British Library Add. MS 34872 (Reproduced courtesy of the British Library)*

schemes, is invaluable in evaluating the reputation of this prolific but under-rated artist.[5] The east window of the south aisle (sII) installed in 1847, depicting the Carrying of the Cross (Fig. 75), has been removed, the only lacuna in an otherwise complete scheme of choir glazing.[6]

Willement's work at St George's Chapel was by no means confined to stained glass, however; he was also involved in the restoration of heraldic decoration, monuments and furnishings, described in his *Account of the Restorations of the Collegiate Chapel of St George, Windsor with some particulars of the Heraldic Ornaments of that Edifice*, published in 1844 when the glazing work was at an early stage, but providing an insight into the breadth of his interest and the intensity of his personal involvement. The limewash which had coated the chapel interior since the eighteenth century was carefully removed, revealing medieval colour on the roof bosses in the nave and aisles. The medieval heraldic blazons were repainted, mostly accurately, while the armorials of Henry VIII and the contemporary Garter Knights over the crossing were also repainted. The dirt and ingrained varnish disfiguring the choir stalls and canopies were removed and the wooden oriel of the Edward IV chantry was cleaned and gilded. The polychrome decoration on tombs and walls in a number of the chantry chapels was renewed and the armorials on the tomb of Edward IV were emblazoned. Having a realistic grasp of the economics of a major commission, Willement went to considerable lengths to interest and involve descendants of those nobles commemorated by or associated with the chapel's medieval chantries, and was instrumental in persuading the duke of Beaufort, the duke of Rutland and the duke of Newcastle to contribute to the cost of restoration and new glazing.

In choosing Willement to make the new clerestory windows, the Dean and Canons had chosen one of the most successful designers of the nineteenth century. In the same year that he received the Windsor commission, Willement published privately *A Concise Account of the Principal Works in Stained Glass that have been executed by Thomas Willement* (London 1840), in which he listed over two hundred windows made in the period between 1816 and 1840.[7] He had already worked for an impressive range of aristocratic and institutional patrons in both ecclesiastical and domestic settings and had designed for

5. The principal sources for the Willement windows at St George's chapel are: London, BL Add. MS 52413, 'A chronological list of Works Executed in Stained Glass etc by Thomas Willement FSA from the Year 1812 to 1865 inclusive', ff. 26–85 (descriptive lists arranged chronologically, compiled after 1850); BL Add. MS 34872, 'Modern Stained Glass', ff. 2–18 and 47, containing sketches for each window; SGC XVII.9.9, 'St George's Chapel, Windsor. Stained Glass Windows by Thomas Willement', a notebook in Willement's hand, describing the choir aisle windows and their sources, with contemporary annotations, probably by Canon Cust, to whom it belonged. Later notes by Louis Stainton, Chapter Clerk 1922–50. SGC XVIII.61.21 contains bills for many of the windows. SGC XIV contains miscellaneous bills. SGC M.166 is a bundle of letters from Willement to Canon Cust covering the period 1840–61. London, Victoria & Albert Museum, National Art Library, 86.ZZ.169, Willement's studio ledger, ff. 73, 177–81, 468, 475, 502, 520. I am grateful to Mr and Mrs Peter Hawley for allowing me to examine this ledger while it was still in their possession.

6. The Chapter Acts for 10 August 1882 (SGC VI.B.11) record the assent given to the proposal to remove the window. The stone work was altered, turning a three-light window into a five-light one glazed by Ion Pace. See Harrison, p. 163.

7. The earliest window is identified in both BL Add. MS 52413 and the *Concise Account* as the 1812 staircase window for Caerhays Castle in Devon.

many media — stained glass, textiles, ceramics, tiles and architectural painting.[8] By the 1840s he was employing at least six glaziers at his London studio at 25 Green Street, Grosvenor Square.[9] He trained a number of members of the next generation of stained glass artists, notably William Warrington and Michael O'Connor.[10]

EARLY LIFE

The Willements were of Huguenot descent, arriving in England in the late sixteenth century, settling in Norwich. In 1742 and 1743 respectively, two Willement cousins, both named Richard, married sisters Marie and Marguerite Martineau, members of Norwich's leading Huguenot family.[11] Both families were involved in the manufacture and sale of the twilled fabric made of a mixture of worsted, cotton or silk known as bombazine. By the first decade of the nineteenth century the name Willement appears several times in London trade directories in connection with this business.[12]

Thomas Willement's parents had moved from Norwich to London in the 1780s. By *c.* 1786 Thomas Willement senior, 'Coach, Herald and House Painter' and artist to His Royal Highness the Duke of York, was residing at 25 Green Street, Grosvenor Square.[13] Thomas junior was baptized at St Marylebone church on 15 August of the same year. The business may also have occupied number 22 Green Street for some time.[14] However, in 1811 Willement senior claimed to have spent £2,000 on the rebuilding of the greater part of number 25 and trade directories suggest that from *c.* 1805 this was the principal base of the Willement business.[15] A plan of 25 Green Street made in 1811 preserved in the Grosvenor Estate archives shows the premises to have consisted of a substantial house on four storeys, with a covered yard at the side and a three-storey workshop at the rear. The workshop could be entered from passageways from Green Street or North Row.[16] In 1822 this property, described in 1811 as 'Mr Groome's House . . . in the occupation of Mr

8. For a correlated list of Willement's documented works in all media see Michael Archer, Sheila Mole and Clive Wainwright, eds, :Key to Thomas Willement's Papers', unpublished typescript. Copies in the National Art Library (V&A), the National Monuments Record in Swindon and the Society of Antiquaries of London.

9. Their names are scratched on the exterior of the west window: T. Tozer, F. Burrow, G. Lingley, E. Colegate, B. Gilestone, T. Healey. The receipts issued by the studio were signed by Samuel Hubert (in whose hand most of the bills are written), George Longley and a clerk called Russell.

10. Martin Harrison, *Victorian Stained Glass*, London 1980, pp. 17–18.

11. W.J.C. Moens, ed., *The Walloons and their Church at Norwich. Their History and Registers*, Huguenot Society of London, i, Lymington 1887–8, p. 129. I am grateful to Peter and Tanya Hawley for additional information derived from Norwich registers.

12. *Post Office Annual Directory 1804*, p. 254, 'Willement, Tor [*sic*], Norwich Bombazeen Warehouse, Peterborough Court, Fleet Street'. *Post Office Annual Directory 1813*, p. 341, 'Willement & Sons, Bombazeen Warehouse, 6 Gun Street, Old Artillery Ground'. *Kent's Directory 1819*, p. 361, 'Willement, Thos, Bombazeen Manufacturer, 52 Cheapside'.

13. *Survey of London, Volume XL, The Grosvenor Estate in Mayfair, Part II, The Buildings*, London 1980.

14. This address was given on a trade card found by Michael Snodin of the V&A, quoted by Clive Wainwright in Megan Aldrich, ed., *The Craces. Royal Decorators 1768–1899*, London 1990, p. 161. The same address is given in *Holden's Triennial Directory of London 1799*. I am grateful to Martin Harrison for this last reference.

15. *Holden's Triennial Directory 1805*.

16. Grosvenor Estate Archive, drawing. This house no longer survives, but was on the site occupied by the present number 27.

Willement' was leased to Thomas Willement junior, suggesting that Willement senior had retired at this time.[17]

Green Street at the end of the eighteenth century was home to at least twenty tradesmen, at least eight of them serving the building trade. From *c.* 1784 a large stables bounded by Green Street, Park Street and Wood's Mews had been occupied by Murdoch Mackenzie the coach-builder, as a place of manufacture, display and sale of carriages. The coach-building business traditionally employed a wide range of artists, craftsmen and designers, many of them originally clustered around the coach-builders of Covent Garden, many of whom moved westwards to serve the newly fashionable areas such as the developing Grosvenor Estate of which Green Street was a part.[18] It was presumably to tap into this market that Willement senior had first moved to Green Street. It was probably through contacts in the coach-making business that young Thomas met and married (*c.* 1833?) Katherine Griffith (1796–1852), the daughter of Thomas Griffith, Master of the Sadlers' Company. The couple had one son, Arthur Thomas, who died in an accident at Oxford in 1854, in his twenty-first year.[19]

From the 1820s onwards many of the houses in the Green Street area were refurbished and began to attract titled occupants. Even though Willement's developing business was to diversify and become a nationwide practice, he continued to attract work from his near neighbours. As the Green Street premises are unlikely to have been large enough to accommodate every aspect of Willement's enormously varied range of decorative commissions (which included plumbing, wallpapers, textiles and polychrome decoration as well as stained glass), his early associations with others involved in the building and decorating trades no doubt served him well.

Willement's earliest training as an artist was presumably within the orbit of his father's thriving business as a coach and house painter, a business in which a familiarity with heraldic design would have been essential. How he first became involved in stained glass design and manufacture is not known. On the basis of a single sketch of a border design from Canterbury Cathedral, undated, but labelled 'A copy delivered to Mr Eginton for the Great Hall windows, Fonthill Abbey'[20] he would seem to have been employed by William Raphael Eginton (1778–1834), who glazed the Great Western Hall of William Beckford's Gothic fantasy house, Fonthill Abbey.[21] It was perhaps in the employ of Eginton that Willement first gained practical experience of the medium. His sketchbooks, preserved in the British Library, contain many drawings, engravings and cuttings related to the work of the leading enamel glass-painters of the last quarter of the eighteenth century.

17. *Survey of London XL, Part II*, p. 187.

18. A.L. Humphreys, 'Long Acre and the Coach Builders', *Notes and Queries*, clxxxi (1941), pp. 212–15, 228–30. See also Michael Snodin, 'Charles and Edward Crace and Rococo Coach Painting', in *The Craces*, ed. Aldrich, pp. 33–41.

19. I am grateful to Dr Stanley Shepherd for allowing me to read a draft of his entry for the forthcoming *New Dictionary of National Biography*. Katherine and Arthur Thomas are buried, together with Thomas himself, in the vault beneath the sacristy of Davington Priory.

20. BL Add. MS 34783, f. 27.

21. Clive Wainright, *The Romantic Interior. The British Collector at Home 1750–1850*, New Haven & London 1989, p. 116.

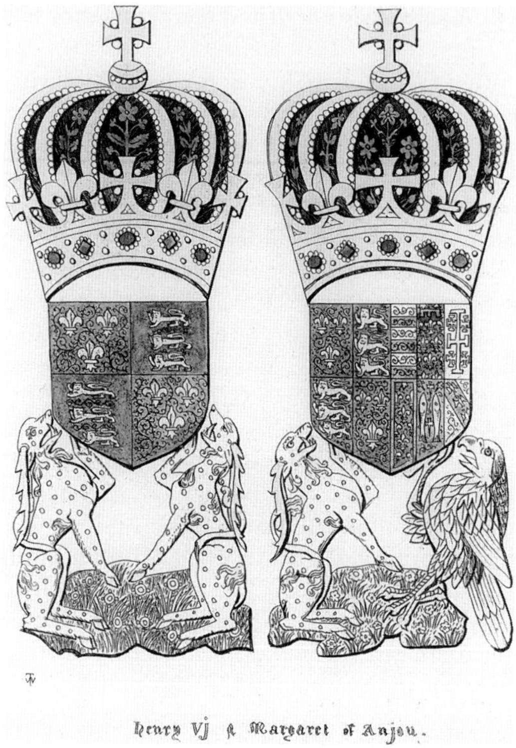

Fig. 76. *Plate IX of Willement's* Regal Heraldry, *London 1821, illustrating fifteenth-century glass from Ockwells in Berkshire (Photo © The Society of Antiquaries of London)*

WILLEMENT BEFORE WINDSOR

Willement's first recorded stained glass commission, in a quasi-seventeenth-century style with small-scale heraldic badges executed in enamels, was made in 1812 for John Trevanion of Caerhays Castle in Cornwall.[22] Indeed, much of his work in the period 1812–40 was heraldic in character.[23] His heraldic researches developed quickly, benefiting from his growing experience of historic buildings and his familiarity with the heraldic manuscripts of the British Museum. Despite the pressures of an increasingly successful business, he found time to publish the results of his work: *Regal Heraldry: The Armorial Insignia of the Kings and Queens of England from Coeval Authorities* (1821) (Fig. 76), *Heraldic Notices of Canterbury Cathedral with Genealogical and Topographical Notes* (1827), *Facsimile of a contemporary roll with the names of the arms of the Sovereign and of the Spiritual and Temporal Peers who sat in Parliament held at Westminster AD 1515* (1829), and in 1834 the first edition of a late fourteenth-century roll of arms, then in the collection of the Revd John Newling of Lichfield, *A Roll of Arms of the Reign of Richard the Second*. The manuscript is now in the

22. Sketches for the Caerhays staircase window are preserved in BL Add. MS 34873, f. 98.

23. Of 290 individual commissions executed in all media in the period 1812–39, over 50% (161 out of 290) involved heraldry. Archer, Mole and Wainwright, *Key to Thomas Willement's Papers*, Section 1.

British Library, where it is known as Willement's Roll (BL Egerton MS 3713).[24] He was appointed Heraldic Artist to George IV and in May 1832 he received the recognition of his academic peers when he was elected a Fellow of the Society of Antiquaries of London.[25]

Willement's career as stained glass artist and decorator evolved in that formative period in which a romantic view of the past gave way to a more accurate, archaeologically based understanding, a period in which a variety of historical styles were to inform and inspire new designs, and in which Gothic was eventually to emerge triumphant. Thomas Rickman's *An Attempt to Discriminate the Styles of English Architecture*, in which the periods of English Gothic were defined and labelled with names that are still recognized today, appeared only in 1817, five years after Willement made his first window. A.W.N. Pugin's influential publications championing the Gothic style only appeared in the late 1830s and 1840s,[26] and a Gothic design for the new Houses of Parliament was chosen only in 1835. The early years of Willement's career thus coincided with a period of historical eclecticism in which Elizabethan and Jacobean domestic architecture was as influential and popular as the various periods and nationalities of Gothic. In the early years of his career Willement himself worked in a variety of pictorial styles based on post-medieval models. In 1824, for example, his window of Christ carrying the Cross at Tyldesley (Lancashire), was based on the seventeenth-century Spanish painting of the same subject above the altar of Magdalen College, Oxford.[27]

Much of his work in the period before the Windsor commission was for the country house or domestic setting. He was employed either directly by a private patron keen to refurbish his home in a historicist style, or through one of the architects that he counted among his friends. His collaborations with architects Anthony Salvin (1799–1881) and Edward Blore (1787–1879) were particularly significant. He worked with Salvin on his first major country house commission, Mamhead in Devon, where he undertook plumber's work (lead rainwater heads) and stained glass. They subsequently worked together at Rufford Abbey, Nottinghamshire, where Willement provided decorative painting, wallpaper and glass, and Scotney Castle in Kent, where he executed the painting and the plumbing work.[28] His work at Harlaxton in Lincolnshire continued after Salvin's departure.

24. C.E. Wright, 'Willement's Roll', *British Museum Quarterly*, xix, No. 3 (1954), p. 49 and pl. XVII, and *English Heraldic Manuscripts in the British Museum*, London 1973, pp. 2, 24 and pl. II. The British Library also preserves a number of unpublished heraldic manuscripts by Willement. See C.E. Wright, 'The Work of Thomas Willement Stained Glass Artist 1812–1865', *British Museum Quarterly*, xxix, Nos 1–2 (1965), pp. 1–5.

25. *Proceedings of the Society of Antiquaries*, 2nd ser. 5 (1870–3), p. 145.

26. Margaret Belcher, 'Pugin Writing', in *Pugin. A Gothic Passion*, ed. Paul Atterbury and Clive Wainwright, London 1994, pp. 105–16.

27. Willement's sketch of the Magdalen painting is in BL Add. MS 34873, f. 12. His design for the Tyldesley window is BL Add. MS 34871, f. 13. The painting was also reproduced in Nathaniel Whittock's *The Decorative Painters and Glaziers Guide*, London 1827, pl. LXXIV. The design was copied by other glaziers, including William Jay Bolton (1816–84) at Tingrith. Jonathan and Ruth Cooke, 'William Jay Bolton at Tingrith', *Journal of Stained Glass*, xxiii (1999), pp. 27–35.

28. See Jill Allibone, *Anthony Salvin, Pioneer of Gothic Revival Architecture*, Columbia 1987. Comparison with the *Key to Thomas Willement's Papers* provides an accurate chronology for their collaboration; Mamhead: painting and glass 1832, glass 1840; Rufford: glass and wallpaper 1839, glass 1846; Scotney: painting and wallpaper 1840, 1842 and 1846.

Willement's country-house work cemented the network of intermingled personal and professional contacts that were a hallmark of his long career. The complexities of the relationships between Willement and his friends, fellow antiquarians and patrons are exemplified by his association with Samuel Rush Meyrick (1783–1848). In 1826 Willement was commissioned by the Board of Ordnance to make heraldic windows for the Horse Armoury at the Tower of London, famed for its display of armoured kings.[29] It was probably this project that first brought him into contact with Meyrick, friend and adviser of Sir Walter Scott, the acknowledged expert on medieval armour, owner of one of the finest private collections, and author of influential books on the subject. Meyrick had supervised the redisplay of the Horse Armoury. He subsequently rearranged the royal armoury at Windsor, for which he was knighted by George IV in 1832.[30] In 1827, having failed to acquire the ruins of medieval Goodrich Castle in Herefordshire, Meyrick began to build Goodrich Court on a site nearby, to designs by Edward Blore.[31] Between 1828 and 1844 Willement made a series of windows for the house (Fig. 77), a mixture of heraldry and depictions of historical personages, a combination to be repeated in the later choir aisle glazing of St George's Chapel, Windsor.[32] Blore became another of Willement's friends and colleagues. They were to work together on a number of occasions — at Lambeth Palace, at Crosby Hall, at Latimers (Buckinghamshire), at Westminster Abbey, at St George's Chapel and at Hampton Court.

Another important friendship within the scholarly community was with architectural draughtsman and illustrator, antiquarian and author Henry Shaw (1800–73). In 1836 Shaw published *Specimens of Ancient Furniture*, followed by *Specimens of the Details of Elizabethan Architecture*, with descriptions by Thomas Moule, for which Willement was to provide some of the plates.[33] Willement had a long-standing interest in decorative plain glazing patterns derived from medieval, sixteenth- and seventeenth-century models; his sketch-books contain numerous examples derived from both ecclesiastical and domestic settings.[34] In 1848 Shaw published a work of particular interest to Willement — his edition of Walter Gidde's 1615 *Booke of Sundry Draughtes principally serving for Glaziers and not impertinent for Plasterers and Gardeners*. His preface acknowledges Willement's assistance: 'I have added to the series a few Designs kindly lent to me by my Friend Mr Willement.' Willement was to use many Elizabethan decorative glazing patterns in his own work; at St George's Chapel the plain glazing in the chapter room owes much to Gidde.

From *c.* 1840 onwards Willement was increasingly associated with a younger generation of architects and designers who adopted a more 'archaeological' approach to the re-creation and restoration of medieval fabric. He was directly involved in a number of

29. Willement, *Concise Account*, p. 14.

30. Wainwright, *The Romantic Interior*, pp. 241–4. After Meyrick's death Sir Richard Wallace acquired part of his collection from the Paris dealer Frederick Spitzer. James Mann, *Wallace Collection Catalogues. European Arms and Armour. I Armour* (London 197?), pp. xv–xvii.

31. Hugh Meller, 'The Architectural History of Goodrich Court, Herefordshire', *Transactions of the Woolhope Naturalists Field Club*, xlii, pt 2 (1977), pp. 175–85. For the interior see Wainwright, *The Romantic Interior*, pp. 241–68.

32. Willement, *Principal Works*, p. 24.

33. In 1825 Willement had made a heraldic window for Thomas Moule's London house in St James's Place, *Concise Account*, p. 15.

34. See BL Add. MS 34866, ff. 96v–9.

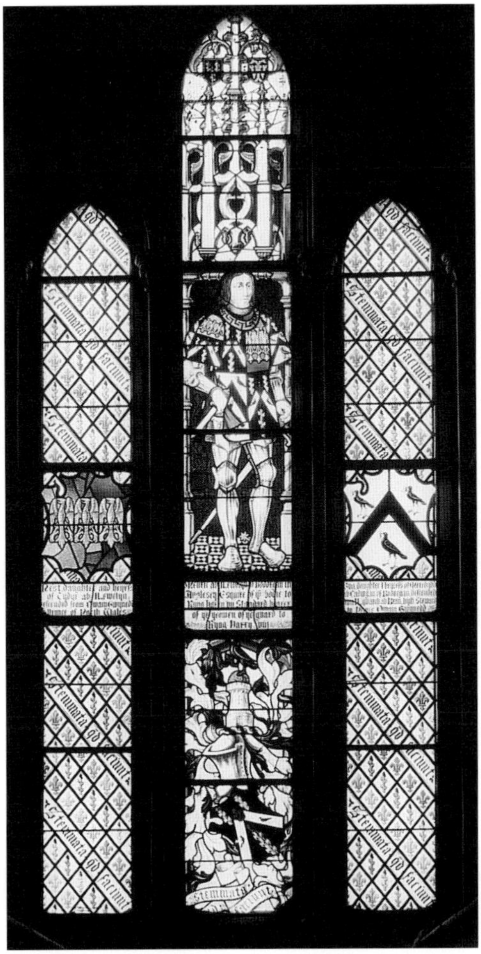

Fig. 77. *Stained glass made in 1828–9 for Samuel Rush Meyrick's new house at Goodrich Court, Hertfordshire (© Crown Copyright. NMR)*

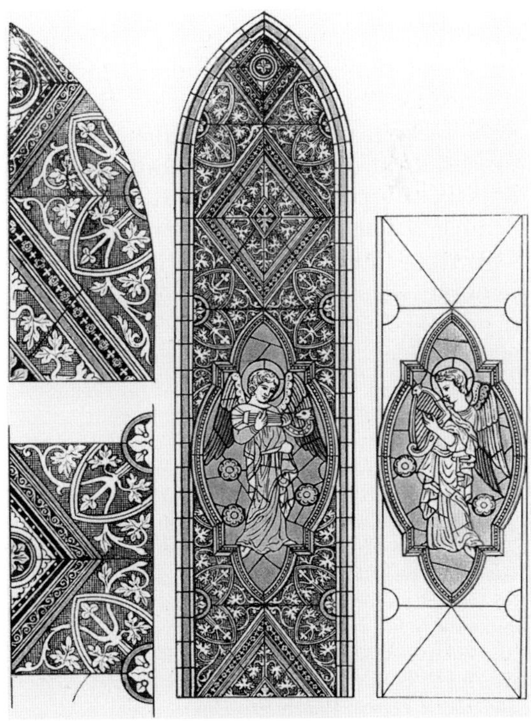

Fig. 78. *Stained glass by Willement for the Temple Church in London. The figures were based on medieval glass in the abbey church of Notre Dame de Bon Port in Normandy, recorded in one of Willement's sketchbooks (British Library Add. MS 34866, f. 33). Lithograph by W.H.R. Essex, 1845 (Photo © The Society of Antiquaries of London)*

church restorations that attracted the favourable notice of the Cambridge Camden Society and its influential publication, *The Ecclesiologist*. As a result, Willement's stained glass made after *c*. 1840 was increasingly influenced by English medieval styles rather than by the more pictorial late medieval and early Renaissance continental art for which he had earlier displayed a preference. One of his most important collaborations was at the Temple church, restored 1840–3 at enormous cost for the Benchers of the Inner and Middle Temple and described as 'an early landmark in the history of the Gothic Revival'.[35] The Restoration Committee 'proceeded to take the opinion of the most eminent architects and artists in London, namely Sir Robert Smirke, Mr Sydney Smirke, Mr Cottingham and Mr Blore, architects, Mr Etty R.A. and Mr Willement F.S.A., artist in stained glass'.[36] The work of the seventeenth century was swept away and the chancel was restored under the direction of Sydney Smirke (1798–1877) and Decimus Burton (1800–81), with woodwork carved from examples supplied by L.N. Cottingham (1787–1847) and polychrome decoration and stained glass executed by Willement.

The scheme was destroyed during the Second World War, but can be recreated from surviving contemporary illustrations, notably W.R.H. Essex's evocative chromolithographs (Fig. 78).[37] Willement's glass is 'archaeologically' Gothic in style and 'mosaic' in execution, derived from specific medieval examples that can be identified in his sketchbooks.[38] The work attracted enormous contemporary interest, although *The Ecclesiologist* compared it unfavourably to Salvin's 1841–3 restoration for the Camden Cambridge Society of the church of the Holy Sepulchre in Cambridge, for which Willement supplied most of the stained glass.[39] In 1845 at Kilndown, in Kent, in a scheme involving Salvin, and A.J.B. Beresford Hope (1820–87) and R.C. Carpenter (1812–55), Willement executed polychrome decoration, although the windows were commissioned from Mayer of Munich.[40] In 1846 he supplied glass for Beresford-Hope's restoration of St Augustine's College, Canterbury, which was acclaimed by *The Ecclesiologist*. The account of the restoration provided by Beresford Hope for the French journal, *Annales Archéologiques,* reveals that Willement's reputation had now achieved an international dimension. In a footnote the eminent editor, Adolphe Didron, described him thus: 'M. Willement est le premier peintre sur verre de L'Angleterre. Ses fenêtres de l'église du Temple à Londres sont réellement remarquables.'[41] At Bodiam church in 1845 and Kemerton church in 1846, Willement worked for R.C. Carpenter, *The Ecclesiologist*'s favourite architect.[42] Also involved at Kemerton and Kilndown, where he had supplied

35. J.M. Crook, 'The Restoration of the Temple Church: Ecclesiology and Recrimination', *Architectural History*, viii (1965), pp. 39–51.

36. *Ibid.*, p. 41.

37. Sydney Smirke and W.H.R. Essex, *Illustrations of the Architectural Ornament and Embellishments, and Painted Glass of the Temple Church, London*, London 1845.

38. The musician angels and Christ in Majesty are especially impressive (BL Add. MS 34871, ff. 40–2). The angels were copied directly from late thirteenth-century originals in the abbey church of Bon Port in Normandy (see BL Add. MS 34866, f. 54).

39. Royal Commission on Historical Monuments of England, *The City of Cambridge*, ii, London 1959, pp. 256–9.

40. Henry Russell Hitchcock, *Early Victorian Architecture in Britain*, London 1954, p. 110.

41. A.J.B. Beresford Hope, 'L'Archéologie en Angleterre', *Annales Archéologiques*, vi (1847), p. 66.

42. *Key to Thomas Willement's Papers*.

designs for metalwork, was the architect William Butterfield (1814–1900) for whom Willement made a small number of windows in the 1840s.[43]

Willement also executed designs for the man now recognized as the most influential Gothic revival architect and designer of the day, A.W.N. Pugin (1812–52). In 1833 Willement was first employed at Alton Towers by Pugin's leading patron, Lord Shrewsbury, providing stained glass and polychrome decoration. In 1840 he executed Pugin's design for the east window of the Convent of our Lady of Mercy, Handsworth, Birmingham, although Pugin was not entirely satisfied with the results. Pugin continued to employ Willement at Alton, in 1841 commissioning him to execute his designs for the east window of St John's Hospital, preferring him over Warrington, whose prices were now just as high.[44] Pugin allowed Willement little leeway in the execution of the design and their association was short-lived. Although there is a record of Willement making some ornamental glass for Oscott in 1840, the principal windows were executed by William Warrington (1786–1869) and a final breach with Pugin came about in 1842. In a letter to Lord Shrewsbury, Pugin accused Willement of being interested only in making money.[45] That Willement was expensive cannot be doubted. That Pugin was a demanding client, having already quarrelled with Warrington, is also demonstrable, and it is not hard to see why their professional relationship should come to grief.

WILLEMENT AS RESTORER AND ANTIQUARIAN

Willement's increasing assurance in his handling of stained glass, decorative painting and textiles in a Gothic idiom from *c.* 1840 onwards was also greatly influenced by his now considerable first-hand experience of the fabric of historic buildings. By 1840 he had worked in many medieval buildings, including Lambeth Palace, Canterbury Cathedral, Hengrave Hall, Stoneleigh Abbey, the halls of a number of City Livery Companies and scores of medieval parish churches. His publication on Canterbury and his sketchbooks in the British Library show the use to which he put his opportunities for study.[46] In addition to creating new glass, textiles and painted decoration for old buildings, Willement was increasingly called upon to restore historic fabric, including old windows. At Charlecote Park in Warwickshire, for example, he was employed by George Lucy between 1831 and 1839 to provide new decorations, fabrics and wallpapers, but was also involved in the restoration of the ancient glass in the Great Hall.[47] Willement went to considerable lengths to preserve as much original glass as possible, taking trouble to match the glass used for any new insertions and employing mending leads to repair any breaks in the old glass at a time

43. Paul Thompson, *William Butterfield*, London 1971, p. 469. Thompson has suggested that in the years 1838 and 1839 Butterfield worked in the office of Worcester architect Harvey Eginton. Willement made stained glass for Eginton's St Michael's church, Worcester (1841), providing an alternative or additional professional link between the two.

44. Stanley A. Shepherd, 'Stained Glass', in *Pugin. A Gothic Passion*, ed. P. Atterbury and C. Wainwright, New Haven and London 1994, pp. 195–6 and fig. 381.

45. Letter of 26 February 1842. A. Wedgwood, *Catalogue of Drawings in the Victoria and Albert Museum. A.W.N. Pugin and the Pugin Family*, London 1985, p. 105, letter 24.

46. BL Add. MSS 34866–34873. The first five of the eight volumes contain drawings and engravings of ancient glass.

47. Wainwright, *The Romantic Interior*, pp. 209–40.

when it was quite common for restorers to discard damaged pieces in favour of their own new insertions.[48] Like many nineteenth-century stained glass artists, Willement was also employed by antiquaries and collectors to install collections of ancient glass acquired on travels abroad or bought from English dealers.[49] In 1827, for example, he installed fragments of English and continental glass from the collection of Alderman W. Fletcher in Begbroke church in Oxfordshire.[50] In the following year he installed late fifteenth-century glass from the abbey of St Bertin in St-Omer in the church at Shiplake in the same county.[51] In 1840 he was employed by Earl Howe to install one of the most important collections of medieval stained glass in the country in Twycross church, Leicestershire, including twelfth-century panels from the abbey of St Denis and thirteenth-century glass from the Sainte-Chapelle.[52] In the following year he was employed to install in St George's church, Hanover Square stained glass of *c.* 1525 from the Carmelite church in Amsterdam by the celebrated Tournai glazier Arnoult de Nijmègue.[53] This project aroused the interest of glass historian Charles Winston, who arranged to draw some of the glass while it was in Willement's hands.[54]

Willement's personal collection of medieval and Renaissance artefacts was to be increasingly important as a source for his own designs. In the preparation of the royal portraits for the James I window at St George's Chapel (sXI) in 1849, for example, he made reference to portraits in his own possession.[55] He took advantage of his own travels abroad to record images on which to base new designs and to acquire objects of interest, including a stained glass border fragment purchased in Rouen.[56] His collection also included an early sixteenth-century design for a stained glass roundel[57] and a superb Renaissance panel from the château of Ecouen, now in the Victoria & Albert Museum.[58]

In 1845, as his work at St George's Chapel gained momentum, he acquired Davington Priory in Kent, a former Benedictine nunnery, which was to be his principal residence until his death in 1871.[59] The church and house underwent extensive restoration and

48. This approach was exemplified by the notorious 1821–5 restoration of the medieval windows of Winchester College Chapel by Betton & Evans, in which most of the medieval glass was copied and replaced. J.D. Le Couteur, *Ancient Glass in Winchester*, Winchester 1928, pp. 69–72.

49. E.A. Kent, 'John Christopher Hampp of Norwich', *JBSMGP*, vi, No. 4 (1937), pp. 191–6; B. Rackham, 'English Importations of Foreign Stained Glass in the early 19th Century', *JBSMGP*, ii, No. 2 (1928), pp. 86–94.

50. P.A. Newton, *The County of Oxford*, Corpus Vitrearum Medii Aevi, Great Britain i, London 1979, pp. 33–5.

51. *Ibid.*, pp. 165–71.

52. H.T. Kirby, 'Ancient Glass at Twycross', *Burlington Magazine*, 82 (1943), pp. 124–7.

53. J. Lafond, 'Arnoult de Nimègue et son Oeuvre', *Amis des Monuments Rouennais. Bulletin Années 1926 & 1927*, Rouen 1930, pp. 137–54.

54. BL Add. MS 33851, f. 42, undated letter from Winston to Willement.

55. SGC M.166, letter from Willement to Canon Cust, 12 January 1849.

56. BL Add. MS 34868, f. 8.

57. Pasted into BL Add. MS 34870, f. 97. Beneath the drawing is an attribution to Jost Ammon.

58. Michael Archer, 'Montmorency's Sword from Ecouen', *Burlington Magazine*, 129 (1987), pp. 298–303. Willement probably bought the panel from the Fonthill sale.

59. He was buried at Davington, bequeathing the manor and advowson of the church in trust to Emma Maria Harrison Bramah and then to her children. I am grateful to Dr Nigel Ramsay for notes on the contents of the will, a copy of which is held in the Canterbury Cathedral Archives (U 307). Miss Bramah is believed to have been TW's illegitimate daughter.

beautification under Willement's direction, providing him with a home appropriate to a prosperous antiquarian gentleman and entrepreneur and the subject of yet another publication, *Historical Sketch of the Parish of Davington in the County of Kent and of the Priory there dedicated to St Mary Magdalene* (London 1862).[60] Much of Willement's decoration of the church has disappeared, removed in the 1930s, but the house preserves more of his work, similar to Charlecote in being a mixture of new work in historical styles and fragments of authentic historic woodwork and stained glass.[61] Early sixteenth-century stained glass roundels, for example, were set into decorative plain glazing strongly reminiscent of the patterns in Walter Gidde's *Booke of Sundry Draughtes*. A figure of St Catherine, on the other hand, is a copy of the late fifteenth-century figure at West Wickham (Kent), where Willement had worked as restorer in 1845.[62] The stained glass in the church at Davington is conceived in a fascinating neo-Romanesque style, inspired by the figures of Christ's ancestors from the clerestory of Canterbury Cathedral of *c.* 1180.[63]

Willement was not the only scholar and designer to benefit from the collections amassed at Davington; his friend Henry Shaw acknowledged Willement's help in two of his publications. Plate forty-one of his *The Decorative Arts Ecclesiastical and Civil of the Middle Ages* (1843) illustrates a sixteenth-century book cover 'in the possession of Mr Willement', while plate fifty-one in volume two of *Dresses and Decoration of the Middle Ages* (1843) illustrates the costume of a Knight of the Garter 'taken from a paper manuscript . . . in the possession of Thomas Willement Esq'. In 1849 architect William Butterfield designed a candlestick for St Mary's Church, Wavendon (Buckinghamshire), based on 'an ancient example in the collection of Mr Willement'.[64] The restoration and refurbishment of Davington turned up many objects of antiquarian interest. At a meeting of the Society of Antiquaries in 1856 Henry Shaw exhibited, with Willement's permission, a fourteenth-century protective 'head-piece' found in the roof space at the Priory and Willement gave a short paper on the same subject to a meeting of the Archaeological Institute.[65]

WINDSOR: THE CHOIR CLERESTORY

Such was the man entrusted with the task of completing the glazing of the choir clerestory of St George's Chapel. His contact with Fonthill in the early years of the century must already have familiarized him with 'modern' depictions of the history and insignia of the Order of the Garter, for Eginton's decoration of the King Edward Gallery there was based

60. See also Clive Wainwright, 'Davington Priory, Kent', in *Country Life* (9 December 1971), pp. 1650–3, and (16 December 1971), pp. 1716–19; and Kenneth Melrose, *Davington Parish and People*, About Faversham 52, Faversham 1996.

61. The polychromy on the walls of the church has been covered under whitewashed and the stained glass of the west wall has been removed. The glazing of the east wall, north aisle and north clerestory survives, although some of the clerestory windows have had their coloured backgrounds removed. The decoration of the organ also remains. I am grateful to Revd Ian Black for showing me round the church.

62. Illustrated in *Country Life* (16 December 1971), p. 1719, fig. 10.

63. Sketch design in BL Add. MS 34871, f. 78 (west window). For the Canterbury glass see M.H. Caviness, *The Windows of Christ Church Cathedral, Canterbury*, Corpus Vitrearum Medii Aevi, Great Britain ii, Oxford 1981, pp. 7–62.

64. Victoria & Albert Museum, *Victorian Church Art*, exhibition catalogue, London 1971, pp. 24–5, item c6.

65. *Proceedings of the Society of Antiquaries*, 3 (1853–6), p. 262; *Archaeological Journal*, xiii (1856), p. 185.

on imagery of Edward III as founder of the Order.[66] The audience chamber of Windsor Castle had been decorated with a series of canvases by Benjamin West (1728–1820) depicting events in the history of the Order. These pictures, painted for George III between 1787 and 1789, have been described as 'the most significant step forward in an accurate representation of the Middle Ages made by any painter in late eighteenth century England' and it is inconceivable that Willement would have been unaware of the cycle.[67] Willement's familiarity with the literature and history of the Order is apparent from his many references to the work of both Elias Ashmole and John Anstis in his *Regal Heraldry* of 1821, which also refers to the decoration of the chapel itself as the source for many of the royal arms illustrated in the book.[68] It can be imagined that the stall plates of the Garter Knights would be irresistible to a heraldic scholar and the arms of the Founder Knights account for the first twenty-six armorials in 'Willement's Roll' published in 1834. It is also possible that the seventeenth-century wooden panels (known as 'the tables') preserved in the deanery depicting the arms of the Knights of the Garter since the Order's inception, designed to be an evolving record, provided a model for the new scheme of choir clerestory windows.[69]

Willement's practical experience of stained glass and his considerable scholarship ideally suited him for the Windsor commission, and yet, although he had been engaged upon the restoration of bosses and monuments for some years, he was not the automatic choice for the new stained glass. Although the Chapter Acts offer no glimpse of the internal debate conducted in the early summer of 1840, it would seem that opinions as to how the glazing should proceed differed. In a private note to Canon Steward Cust accompanying his sketches and estimates, Willement pleaded 'pray use your powerful interest that the Dean's proposition that the new windows should match the old may not be put into practice, as it would totally prevent me from having anything to do with [the] job — which I am *most* anxious for, if it can be done by work which will not hurt my reputation'. This is a revealing document, showing that Willement, perhaps a pupil of Eginton, now regarded himself as an adherent of what might be called a Puginian approach to stained glass.[70] The continuation of the windows in the style of Eginton would have been quite extraordinary at this date. Willement, an admittedly biased observer, described the Eginton windows as being 'of the dingiest tone',[71] while another contemporary commentator described them as being executed in 'a melancholy half-mourning tint of dark slate colour'.[72] By 1840 they certainly would have looked unacceptably old-fashioned. It does not seem very likely

66. Wainwright, *The Romantic Interior*, pp. 115–16.

67. Roy Strong, *'And When Did You Last See Your Father'. The Victorian Painter and British History*, London 1978, pp. 79–85.

68. The catalogue of the 1865 sale of part of Willement's library includes copies of both Ashmole and Anstis. The arms of Edward IV (pl. XII, fig. 1) were 'copied from beneath his portrait opposite the tomb of Oliver King in the Chapel of St George' (Willement, *Regal Heraldry*, p. 46); for the arms of Henry VII he states that 'the same supporters are placed to his achievement which is sculpted on the key stone over the organ screen in St George's Chapel, Windsor, with the date 1528' (*ibid.*, p. 65). The arms in the vault, as the date makes clear, are actually those of Henry VIII.

69. Patrick Mitchell, 'The "Tables" of the Knights of the Garter', in L. Keen and E. Scarff, eds, *Windsor. The Medieval Archaeology, Art and Architecture of the Thames Valley*, Leeds 2002.

70. SGC M.166, letter from Willement to Canon Cust, 17 July 1840.

71. *Collegiate Chapel*, pp. 7–8.

72. *The Gentleman's Magazine*, ns xviii (July to December 1842), p. 516.

that Dean Hobart, whose enthusiasm lay with the breeding of dogs and tortoises, put forward a particularly strenuous case for an alternative artist and Willement's fears proved unfounded.[73] The Canon Steward, the Revd the Hon. Henry Cockayne Cust, on the other hand, was well qualified to champion Willement's cause and Willement's letters to him, preserved in the chapel archive (SGC M.166), reveal that in Cust he had found a patron who shared his own enthusiasms.

Cust and Willement were not strangers. Cust (1780–1861), second son of Baron Brownlow of Belton, had been educated at Trinity College, Cambridge, and was an antiquary and collector in his own right. In addition to his Windsor canonry, he was rector (from 1807) and lord of the manor of Cockayne Hatley in Bedfordshire. He found the church in a parlous state and from the 1820s onwards he instituted a major restoration which involved the reconstruction of the chancel east wall, the construction of a new roof using old bosses from nearby Biggleswade church and the reconstruction of the south aisle.[74] The interior was recoloured and beautified by the introduction of some spectacular seventeenth-century woodwork from Belgium.[75] The choir stalls, from the suppressed Belgian monastery of Oignies, were acquired from a dealer in Charleroi. A set of communion rails was purchased from a church in Malines. The pulpit (now in Carlisle Cathedral), dated 1559, had come from the church of St Andrew in Antwerp. The carved door to the tower came from Louvain and the wooden screen around the family pew in the north aisle came from St Bavon in Ghent. Most of these artefacts were acquired during a series of continental tours made by the Cust family in the summers of 1825–30, centred principally on northern France, Belgium and the upper Rhine.[76] A collection of English fourteenth-century stained glass had been acquired from 'a church in Yorkshire' and was installed by Willement in the east window of the north aisle. He was also commissioned to make four new windows. The first, and most interesting, was the east window installed in 1830, a three-light window in an early sixteenth-century style, copied from ancient models, notably engravings by Dürer. The north and south chancel windows of 1839 commemorate members of Cust's family in armorials of seventeenth-century character, while the tower window, with a figure of St Peter, is in fourteenth-century style, incorporating seventeenth-century enamel-painted fragments. In choosing styles that complemented the imported furnishings, Willement displayed the versatility and sensitivity to historic styles that is such an important characteristic of his work at St George's Chapel. In 1840 Willement installed a window incorporating 'Some old foreign glass of arabesque glass' at Cust's other church, Sywell in Northampstonshire.[77] His association with the family resulted in work for Canon Cust's son, the Revd Robert Needham Cust at Belton church and rectory in 1847 and 1849 and at Manthorpe church in 1848.[78]

73. *Fasti Wyndesoriensis*, p. 53.

74. Chronicled by Robert Needham Cust in *Some Account of the Church of Cockayne Hatley, Bedfordshire* (1851, reprinted 1939). R.N. Cust was Canon H.C. Cust's younger son, who married Dean Hobart's daughter.

75. Charles Tracy, 'The Importation into England of Church Furniture from Continental Europe from the Later Middle Ages to the Present Day', *Journal of the British Archaeological Association*, clii (1999), p. 125.

76. Lincolnshire County Archives, Diaries of Revd the Hon. H.C. Cust, uncatalogued material in the Brownlow Collection. I am grateful to Dr Tracy for additional information supplied in personal communications.

77. Willement, *Principal Works*, p. 72.

78. V&A 86.ZZ.169, ff. 2–3 and 109.

Accompanying his private note begging Cust's help in securing the Windsor choir clerestory commission, Willement submitted a formal letter, an estimate and sketches showing how he proposed to tackle the scheme.[79] The main difference distinguishing the two proposals lay in the number of armorials to be accommodated in each glazed opening. Approval for the less expensive of the two variants was received on 31 July 1840. Work was to begin on four windows, two on either side of the choir, giving priority to the early completion of the two windows on the south side facing the Edward IV chantry (SIII and SIV), by now called the Royal Pew.[80] The two easternmost windows on each side of the choir had been blocked up with sheets of copper painted with heraldry, an expedient intended to enhance the appearance of Benjamin West's Resurrection in the east window by cutting down the amount of surface light falling on it. The heraldic sequence was only taken up in glass in the third window. The first task was thus to remove the copper sheets and move the Eginton windows east, leaving five windows on each side for the new scheme. Willement also proposed the alteration of the Eginton windows by removing the original backgrounds in favour of ornamental quarries.[81] In the event, these alterations did not proceed. In June 1841 Willement was authorized to continue the clerestory series with a further three windows.[82] An eighth (SVI) was installed in October 1842.[83]

Willement's treatment of the clerestory windows was a variation of a formula that he had been evolving and perfecting for some years. His work at Goodrich Court (Fig. 77) and Hampton Court Palace, for example, the latter executed concurrently with the Windsor commission, draw upon English late medieval heraldic models; the armorial glass of Ockwells Manor of *c.* 1460 (Fig. 76), with which Willement was certainly familiar as early as the 1820s, was a particularly influential source.[84] The diagonal banding of the Ockwells backgrounds, for example, is used in the windows of the Oliver King, Lincoln and Beaufort Chapels at Windsor (Pl. VIIA). For the Windsor heraldry, however, Willement also had a continental model in mind, for in a letter to Canon Cust he boasted that 'when finished the windows may compete not unsuccessfully with the heraldic windows of the cathedral of Cologne — every endeavour shall be put into full force'.[85] Willement must have had the early sixteenth-century north nave aisle windows of Cologne cathedral (nXXI–nXXV) in mind.[86] The British Library sketchbooks reveal that Willement had travelled in Germany and had included Cologne in his itinerary. Unfortunately, however, the Cologne drawings are undated and do not include the nave aisle windows.[87] The canopy work in his windows at Goodrich Court are certainly derived

79. SGC M.166, letter from Willement to Canon Cust, 17 July 1840 and BL Add. MS 34872, f. 2. The main difference between the two designs lay in the number of armorials per compartment and the use of ornamental quarries, which had a cost implication; one version was costed at £174 2s and the other at £186 10s.

80. BL Add. MS 34872, f. 2, annotations to sketches.

81. SGC M.166, letter from Willement to Canon Cust, 17 July 1840.

82. SGC Chapter Acts VI.B.10, 24.

83. V&A 86.ZZ.169, f. 73.

84. The arms of Henry VI and Margaret of Anjou in pl. IX of *Regal Heraldry* are attributed to 'Ockwells House', from which he also took the queen's motto. His sketchbooks of ancient glass contain a number of drawings of the Ockwells windows (BL Add. MS 34868, ff. 196–200).

85. SGC M.166, letter from Willement to Canon Cust, 7 August 1840.

86. *Herbert Rode*, Der Mittelalterlichen Glasmalereien des Kölner Domes, *Corpus Vitrearum Medii Aevi*, Deutschland iv, Berlin 1974, pp. 186–207.

87. BL Add. MS 34866, ff. 47–53.

from a late medieval German source, recalling the rather brittle canopy work associated with the workshop of Strasbourg artist Peter Hemel. Second-hand sources cannot be discounted, of course, for by 1820 a great deal of continental stained glass had reached England, and the Cologne windows, greatly admired by nineteenth-century students of stained glass, had featured in a number of publications with which Willement could have been familiar.

Every compartment of the Windsor clerestory windows is bursting with a substantially proportioned coat of arms within a garter, surmounted by a crest and exuberant mantling. Each armorial was labelled on a scroll beneath and the background to each light was filled with diamond quarries bearing the initials S and G for S[anctus] G[eorgius]. The tracery lights contain further shields and double Tudor roses within garters, with the initials 'S' and 'G' in the outer quatrefoils. The scheme is regular, consistent and remarkably legible from the ground. Canon Cust and his colleagues made a sound decision in choosing the design which placed a single armorial in each compartment, one above and one below the transom. The only variation in the basic formula is found in the tracery of the middle window on north and south sides (NV and SV), where the initials S and G give way to those of V[ictoria] R[egina] and the date 1841 (Fig. 79).

Willement's windows may have been stylistically and technically very different from Eginton's, but in their subject matter they complemented them, extending the original scheme, with its finite selection of armorials, turning it into an evolving series commemorating those Knights of the Garter elected in the period from 1781 down to the present. After the installation of the first eight windows (SIII–SVI and NIII–NVI) in the period 1840–2, the pace of glazing at clerestory level slackened. Quarry glazing was installed in the empty clerestory compartments until new Garter Knights were created, enabling the series to be continued into the 'vacant' openings. Ten years was to pass before another window was installed. Ten compartments of NVII were glazed in 1853, at a slightly reduced cost. In some instances, windows remained plain glazed or only partially filled with stained glass for considerable periods, with new panels installed as new knights were created, working from the top down. Window SVII, for example, appears to have been glazed in three phases between 1854 and 1858. In the same year, the heraldry for the upper register of NVIII was ordered. This was to be his last glass for the chapel. The last payment (of £69 18s) was made in 1861 as the upper compartments of NVIII were installed.[88] Willement reminded Canon Cust that there were Garter Knights as yet uncommemorated, but no further windows were ordered. He retired from active practice in 1865.

The clerestory windows were much admired by Willement's contemporaries; 'We know of no example in which the powerful and well-arranged tints of heraldic art have been made to produce an effect so perfectly satisfactory'.[89] His heraldic work at Windsor has also stood the test of time and in many respects is aesthetically the most successful part of his glazing. The windows' rich colour (Pl. VIIB), lively design and clear message read well and complement the theatricality of the heraldic helms and crests surmounting the canopies of the choir stalls and the banners suspended beneath the windows. After

88. SGC M.166, letter of 3 May 1861. In the same letter he reminded Canon Cust that the duke of Newcastle and king of Prussia were new knights yet to be commemorated in glass.

89. *The Gentleman's Magazine*, ns xviii (July to December 1842), p. 517.

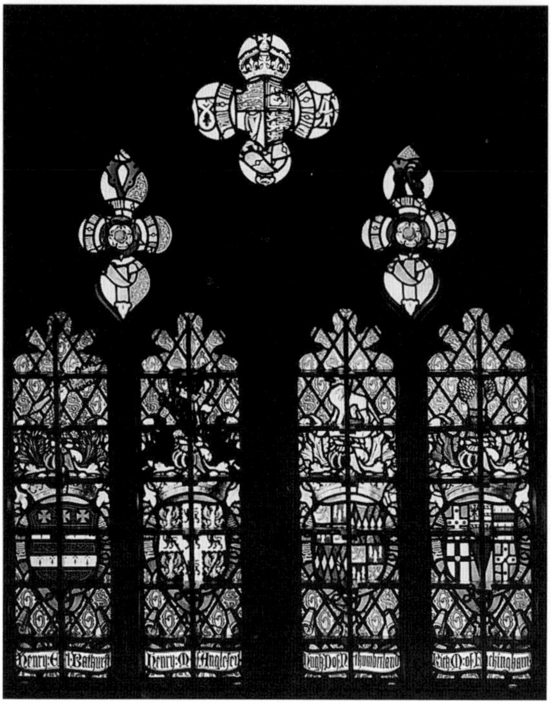

Fig. 79. *Heraldry in window NV, 1841 (© Crown Copyright. NMR)*

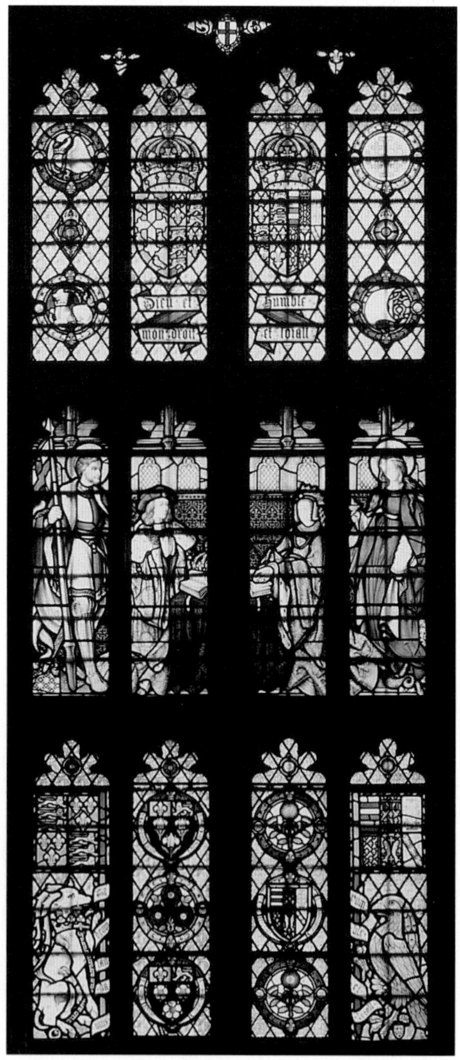

Fig. 80. *Henry VI and Margaret of Anjou in sIX, 1844 (© Crown Copyright. NMR)*

Willement's retirement the Dean and Canons remained committed to the continuation of the scheme, intending that it should entirely fill the nave. In the event Ion Pace's last window was installed in 1899 and the scheme was never completed.

Although the first of the figural windows in the choir aisles (sIX) was not installed until 1844, Willement was contemplating the scheme and how it might be paid for as early as August 1840 — 'I measured the two windows in the north aisle [nII and nIII] and herewith forward a slight sketch for these making one refer to K. Edw[ard] IV and his Queen — the other to Anne sister of the King & her second husband Sir Thos St Leger (Pls VIIA, B, and IXA). If this kind of decoration goes on I think that the Duke of Newcastle and the Marq. of Hastings ought to do something for the windows of their chantries'.[90] At this date he estimated that each north aisle window would cost £70, including carriage and fixing. In the 1850s, when the scheme was drawing to a close, the cost of the aisle windows had escalated to £174 each, excluding the costs of fixing.[91]

THE RESTORATION OF THE WEST WINDOW

It was probably the absence of funds that delayed a decision on the glazing of the choir aisles, for in 1841 the Chapter was distracted by more pressing priorities.[92] In May Willement's friend and colleague, the architect Edward Blore, was commissioned to report on the condition of the chapel and in particular the 'perilous' condition of the west window. He submitted his report in June.[93] Between March and September the medieval stained glass was removed to allow repairs to the stonework to commence.[94] In November a contract was entered into with the masons, requiring that work be complete by July 1842.[95] If Willement was disappointed by the lack of progress with the choir aisle glazing, he was soon to be compensated by the commission to restore the west window, a vast expanse of glass. By October, his ideas as to how to approach the task were well advanced: 'I have already a scheme for the alteration of the glass at present in the west window which I should like to *say* to you when I may have the opportunity.'[96] By April the scheme had developed to the point that a detailed sketch and estimate could be submitted for comment.[97] Willement's restoration involved the introduction into the vacant window openings of ten medieval figures from the chapel's stores, six entirely new figures, canopies, pedestals and quarry backgrounds to all the figures, heraldry for the tracery lights and an inscription at the base. The extent of Willement's restoration of the medieval figures is detailed elsewhere in this volume, but it is clear that his ideas underwent revision as a result of discussion with the canons, in particular with Canons Markham, Canning

90. SGC M.166, letter from Willement to Canon Cust, 7 August 1840. Willement had already worked for the duke of Newcastle at Clumber Castle, Nottinghamshire, in 1824 (BL Add. MS 3471, ff. 4, 48, 72, and Add. MS 34873, ff. 10, 270).

91. He charged only £70 for the Edward IV and Rutland windows. They are significantly smaller than the other north aisle windows and their prices may have been agreed as early as 1840.

92. Since 1797 all new Knights of the Order were required to make a contribution of £50 to the Window Fund (SGC XIII.B.7).

93. *Architectural History*, ii, p. 394; SGC XVII.9.9.

94. SGC XIV, Chapter Bills for 1841.

95. SGC Archives XVII.61.18(e).

96. SGC M.166, letter from Willement to Canon Cust, 8 October 1841.

97. SGC XVII.61.18(c) and SGC M.166, letters from Willement to Cust, 4 and 6 April 1842.

and Cust. Markham, founder of the Essex Antiquarian Society, visited the Green Street studio in May 1842 and supported Willement in the proposal that the six gaps in the main lights should be filled with new figures rather than with heraldry.[98] The other major departure from the first sketch plan lay in the substitution of an inscription for the heraldry originally proposed for the base of the window, and Cust's advice was sought on the wording. Once work began, Willement found the task to be more taxing than envisaged, reporting that problems had arisen because 'the severall parts have been so ridiculously mismatched at the former leading together'.[99]

Willement and his team of glaziers were well qualified for the task of restoring the west window. By 1842 the studio had worked on a number of restorations of glass of a similar period and style of glass-painting, including the Shiplake work of 1828 and the 1841 installation of Antwerp glass at St George's, Hanover Square. In 1837 he had been entrusted with the installation of English late fifteenth-century panels from Holy Trinity, Tattershall in the Great Hall at Burghley House.[100] All of these schemes share a highly modelled painting style and rich late medieval colouring, providing the glaziers with experience useful in dealing with the Windsor west window. Willement's own sketchbooks of examples of ancient glass reveal his long-standing interest in stained glass of the late fifteenth and early sixteenth centuries.

THE CHOIR AISLES

With the clerestory glazing in progress to contemporary approbation, the west window restored to great acclaim and in 1843 the good news that the duke of Beaufort had instructed Willement to proceed with the restoration of the Beaufort chantry, circumstances were auspicious for the choir aisle glazing.[101] Confidence in Willement's talent and professionalism had reached a zenith.

The choir aisle windows, the aspect of Willement's work at Windsor of which he was proudest, cannot be said to be as consistently successful as the clerestory. The aisle windows lack the stylistic homogeneity of the armorials in the clerestory, for Willement made conscious efforts to ensure that each once captured the spirit of the age it represented. Every effort was made to locate contemporary models for the historical portraits and to use appropriate decorative motifs and architectural forms. The most successful windows are undoubtedly those commemorating medieval kings and queens, perhaps because Willement was more familiar with appropriate sources, but also because the two-dimensional decorative nature of medieval images is inherently well suited to the medium of stained glass. Willement was himself very conscious of this and a comparison of the preparatory sketches with the completed windows reveal a number of instances in which the illusionistic backgrounds in the sketches have been substituted for a flat, patterned ground in the executed windows.

98. SGC M.166, letter from Willement to Canon Cust, 6 May 1842.

99. *Ibid.*

100. The glass had been removed from Holy Trinity, Tattershall in 1757. Some was placed in the chapel at Burghley. Richard Marks, *The Stained Glass of Holy Trinity, Tattershall, Lincs.*, New York and London 1984. In 1838 it was reglazed in the Great Hall in an arrangement by Willement. Sketches of the scheme are preserved in BL Add. MS 34871, f. 30.

101. SGC M.166, letter from Willement to Canon Cust, 10 June 1843.

The chapel archives do not shed light on the identity of the originator of this sophisticated glazing scheme. As we have seen, it was contemplated as early as 1840, although Willement's 'slight sketch' of that date for the Edward IV window (nII) does not appear to have survived.[102] In the event, the scheme was begun with the glazing of the south choir aisle, starting with the window commemorating Henry VI and Queen Margaret (sIX, installed in 1844), located opposite the King's tomb, sited between the piers of the arcade (Fig. 80). The window commemorating Edward IV (nII), who initiated the building of the present chapel, was installed in 1845, closely followed by the Henry VII and Henry VIII windows (sVIII and sX).

At its simplest level, the scheme could be said to represent the history of the English monarchy and church from Edward IV (1461–83) in nII, in whose reign the chapel was begun, to the reign of William IV (1830–7) in nVIII. Queen Victoria, only on the throne for three years when Willement's association with Windsor began, was acknowledged in the tracery of the clerestory, the inscription at the base of the west window and a flattering reference accompanying the figure of the duke of Kent in window nVI.[103] The young queen was not especially fond of the Windsor Chapter and its chapel at this date, preferring to attend services in the private chapel of the castle.[104] Into the basic historical framework, themes of ecclesiastical history and events significant to the collegiate church of St George are interwoven; the Henry VIII window (sX), for example, contains the heraldry of the six new bishoprics created in his reign. The Queen Anne window (sXIV) contains the badges of the Society for Promoting Christian Knowledge (founded 1698) and the Society for the Propagation of the Gospel in Foreign Parts (founded 1701).[105] The George III window (nVI) contains a reference to Calcutta diocese, created in 1814[106] and the William IV window (nVIII) contains the armorials of four newly created bishoprics, three of them in the colonies.

The vision of English history presented in the windows is undoubtedly one of Anglican orthodoxy and royal legitimacy. The reign of Richard III is passed over. The Henry VIII window depicts the king, Queen Jane Seymour, the young Prince Edward and the Princess Elizabeth. The king's oldest surviving legitimate child, the Princess Mary, the future Roman Catholic Queen Mary, is noticeably absent and is not the subject of a window of her own. Nor is the reign of James II commemorated, although the young prince as duke of York is included in the Charles I window (sXII, Fig. 81). The ill-fated Charles I is represented as a tragic victim and martyr, with the upper register of the window occupied by angel figures (based on Perugino) bearing symbolic attributes associated with martyrdom. The table on which the king's decapitated body was said to have been laid before its unceremonious burial at Windsor, was one of the Chapter's treasured relics.[107] The Henry VII window (sVIII) conveys a message of relevance to historians of both royalty and the collegiate church; the lower and middle registers contain

102. The surviving sketch (BL Add. MS 34872, f. 10) is dated 1844.
103. In panel 2d are the words 'From him proceeds a Gem to lighten all this Isle'.
104. Olwen Headley, 'Court and Chapel 1760–1873', *Friends Report*, iv, No. 2 (1961), pp. 59–62.
105. In 1836 Willement had made a window for Barbados Cathedral, the gift of the Society.
106. In 1845 the Dean and Canons of Windsor presented the unfinished west window by Benjamin West to Calcutta Cathedral. That Willement assisted in the arrangements can perhaps be inferred from his detailed watercolour of the window, dated 1844 (BL Add. MS 34873, f. 17).
107. The table, with the names of many a curious sightseer carved on it, is now kept in the deanery.

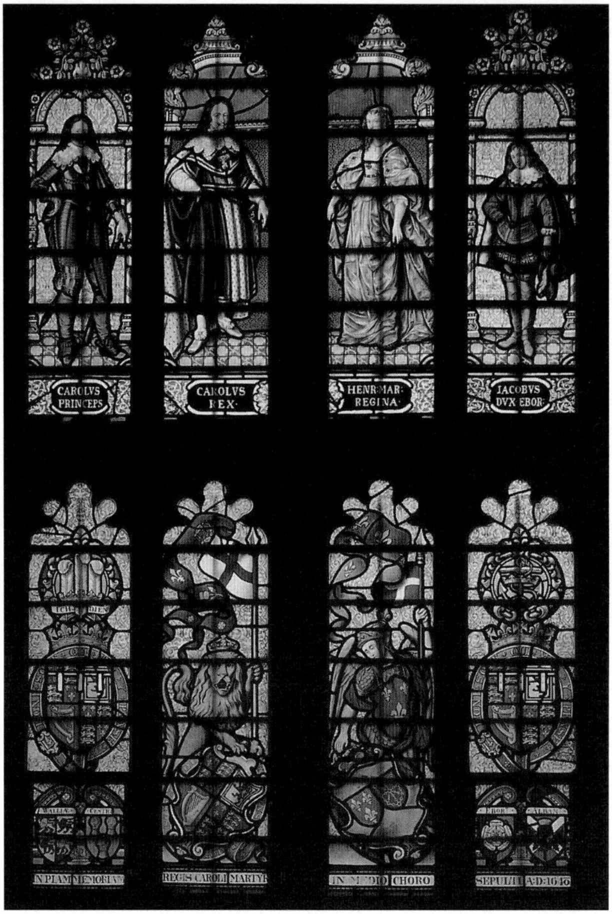

Fig. 81. *Charles I, Henrietta Maria, Prince Charles and the duke of York in sXII, 1849 (© Crown Copyright. NMR)*

figures of Edward III, the founder of the Order, and his sons the dukes of Lancaster and York, the two houses, for so long at odds, united through the marriage of their descendants Henry VII and Elizabeth of York, whose figures occupy the upper register.

It is also notable that a high proportion of the royal figures represented in the choir aisle windows are those sovereigns and their consorts and offspring buried in St George's Chapel.[108] Edward IV and Queen Elizabeth Woodville, Henry VI, Henry VIII, Queen Jane Seymour and Charles I were all buried in the chapel itself, while George III, George IV and William IV were buried in the royal vault beneath what is now the Albert memorial chapel. The windows thus substantiate the chapel's claim to be the royal mausoleum, a role to which Westminster Abbey could also lay claim. St George's status in this regard was threatened in 1861 when Queen Victoria decided to bury the Prince Consort at Frogmore.

108. Shelagh M. Bond, 'The Monuments of St George's Chapel, Windsor Castle', *Historical Monuments relating to St George's Chapel, Windsor Castle*, Windsor 1958.

The late Professor Wainwright's 1972 article on Willement's choir aisle windows established the basic chronology of the scheme and the nature of the documentary sources relating to it.[109] It was this article that first drew attention to the notebook in Willement's hand, formerly the property of Canon Cust, that describes each window and lists the sources for each portrait.[110] The notebook demonstrates the wide-ranging nature of Willement's sources and together with his letters to Canon Cust shed light his scholarly commitment to the search for authentic models. While closer scrutiny of the notebook has revealed a number of anomalies in this account of the scheme, it also shows it to have been indelibly marked by Willement's past career as restorer, heraldic artist and bibliophile. Indeed, the selection of pictorial sources owed as much to the nineteenth-century antiquarian library as to the study of the works of art of the past.

Those windows commemorating medieval kings and queens are among the most successful, reflecting Willement's greater familiarity with appropriate pictorial models. Medieval stained glass provided source material for two of the designs. Window nII of 1845, depicting Edward IV and Elizabeth Woodville (Pl. VIIIB), is an accurate copy of the portraits of the king and queen in the 'Royal Window' in the north-west transept of Canterbury Cathedral (Fig. 82). Willement's sketchbooks are full of Canterbury details. He had been familiar with the window since at least 1827 when his *Heraldic Notices of Canterbury Cathedral* was published, in which its contents were described (but not illustrated). He declared it to be 'an exquisite specimen of that state of the art of the period'.[111] Another ancient window was said to have provided the model for the figures of John of Gaunt, duke of Lancaster and Edmund, duke of York in window sVIII (designed in 1844 and installed 1846, Fig. 83), for the stained glass depicting Edward III and the founder knights of the Order of the Garter in St George's Church, Stamford, is identified as the model. These windows, combining historical figures in the lower register, with narrative scenes of the legend of St George in the upper, had been given by William Bruges, Garter King of Arms, who had paid for the extension of the chancel in the mid-fifteenth century.[112] Bruges and his wife and daughters had also been depicted. In fact, the destruction of these windows was witnessed by the eighteenth-century antiquary William Stukely, who filled the windows of his summer house with medieval glass fragments rescued from the destruction of Stamford's medieval windows.[113] Willement's letter to Canon Cust reveal that it was the plate in Elias Ashmole's history (Fig. 84) that served as the model for the Windsor version, a debt made clear by the fact that the figures in Willement's glass are shown standing, as in Ashmole's plate, whereas Edward III and his companions were kneeling in the Stamford windows.[114] Other slight differences in posture suggest that the model had undergone further adaptation.

109. Clive Wainwright, 'Thomas Willement's windows in the choir aisles', *Friends Report*, v, No. 3 (1971–2), pp. 105–18.

110. SGC XVII.9.9, manuscript notebook entitled 'St George's Chapel, Windsor. Stained Glass by Thomas Willement'.

111. A sketch of the whole window, dated 1844, is pasted into BL Add. MS 34869, f. 41.

112. H.S. London, 'The Garter Windows in St George's Stamford', in *The Life of William Bruges*, Harleian Society, cxi–cxii (1959–60), pp. 57–67.

113. Penny Hebgin-Barnes, *The Medieval Stained Glass of the County of Lincolnshire*, CVMA Great Britain, Summary Catalogue 3, Oxford 1996, pp. 272–6; Stuart Piggott, *William Stukely. An Eighteenth-Century Antiquary*, London 1985, pp. 11, 123.

114. SGC M.166, letter from Willement to Canon Cust, 28 September 1844.

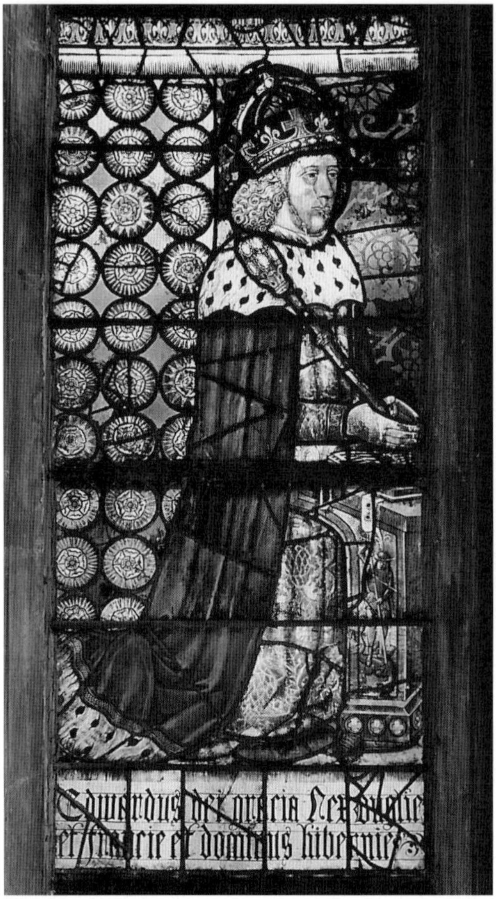

Fig. 82. *King Edward IV from the 'Royal Window' of Canterbury Cathedral,* c. *1482 (© Crown Copyright. NMR)*

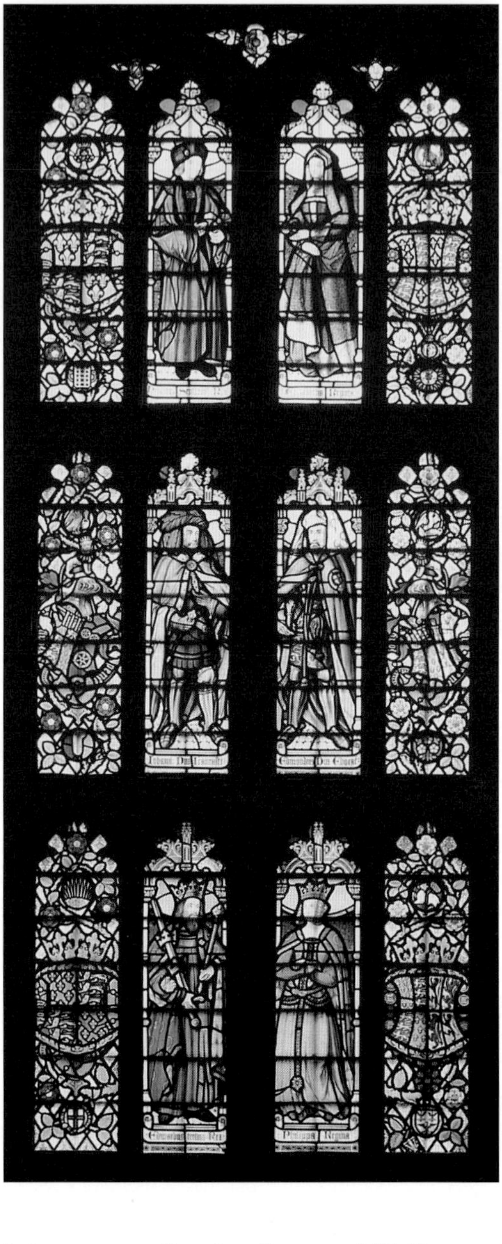

Fig. 83. *Edward III and Philippa of Hainault, the dukes of Lancaster and York and Henry VII and Elizabeth of York in s VIII, 1846 (© Crown Copyright. NMR)*

Willement's library must also have provided a source for the figure of Philippa of Hainault, which is based on the depictions of her in St Stephen's Chapel, Westminster, as stated in the Willement notebook. The chapel was not finally destroyed until the fire of 1834, meaning that Willement would have been familiar with the building. While much of the medieval decoration of the chapel had been preserved beneath Christopher Wren's galleries and panelling, James Wyatt's reconstruction of the chapel interior to accommodate the recently enlarged House of Commons was far more destructive of the medieval

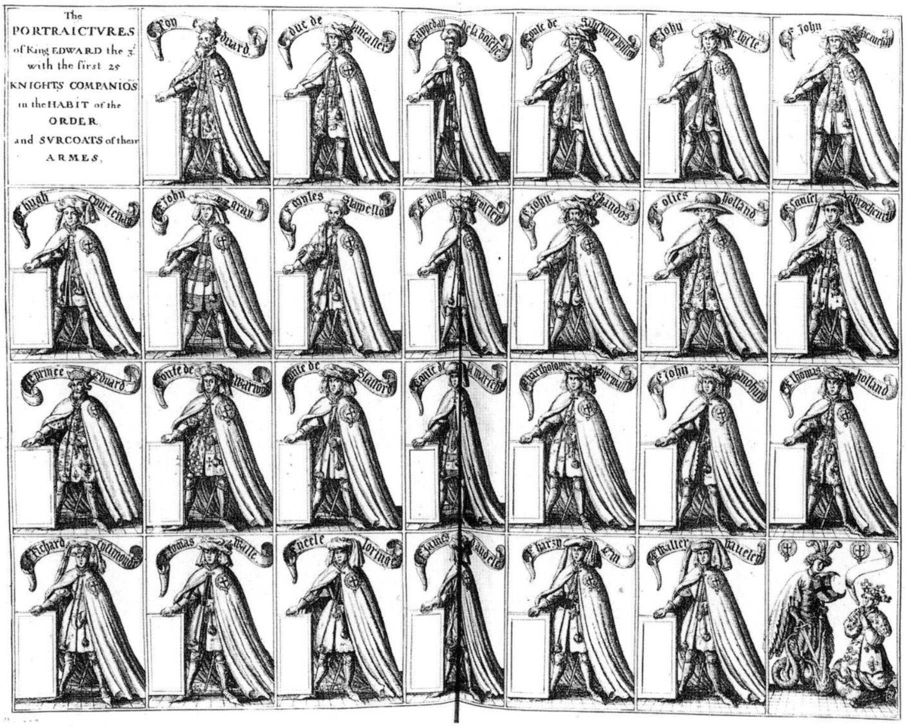

Fig. 84. *Edward III and the founder Garter Knights, illustration between pages 642 and 643 of Elias Ashmole's* Institutions, Laws and Ceremonies of the Most Noble Order of the Garter, *London 1672 (Photo © The Society of Antiquaries of London)*

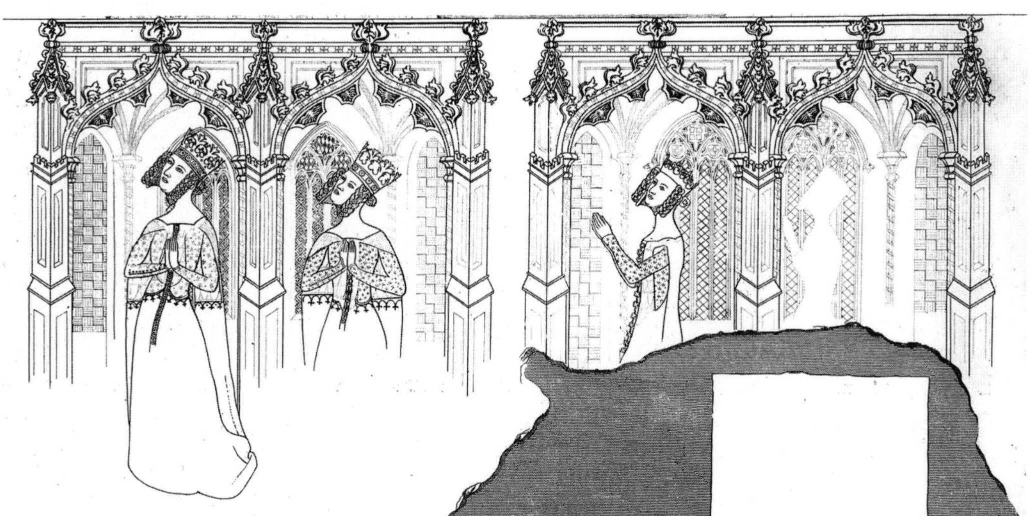

Fig. 85. *Queen Philippa of Hainault represented on the east wall of St Stephen's Chapel, Westminster, illustrated in J. Topham,* Some Account of the Collegiate Chapel of St Stephen, Westminster, *with additional plates, by Robert Smirke, London 1811 (Photo © The Society of Antiquaries of London)*

fabric and by 1800 the image of the queen (Fig. 85), which had been painted on the east wall of the chapel, had been destroyed. Numerous antiquarian draughtsmen strove to record the uncovered decoration before its destruction.[115] Willement certainly had copies of plates from J.T. Smith's *Antiquities of Westminster*, some of which are pasted into his sketchbooks of ancient glass. For the figure of Queen Philippa, however, which had been depicted on the south side of the high altar, the source was probably Richard Smirke's drawings made for the Society of Antiquaries, some of which were published by the Society in 1811.[116]

The source for the figures of Henry VI and Queen Margaret in sIX was given as the tapestry in Coventry town hall. This Tournai work, made for the wall above the dais of the great hall of St Mary's Hall in Bayley Lane, is now thought to have been made *c.* 1500 to commemorate a royal visit by Henry VII and Queen Elizabeth of York, who are depicted in the lower register of the tapestry.[117] The hall, with its famous fifteenth-century window depicting kings of England, had been restored in 1793 and again in 1826, and Willement's various commissions in Warwickshire in the 1830s and early 1840s would have afforded him plenty of opportunity to familiarize himself with one of England's best-preserved medieval cities. He would also, however, have been familiar with the coloured plates of the tapestry reproduced in Henry Shaw's *Dresses and Decoration of the Middle Ages*, where the king and queen are also erroneously identified as Henry VI and Queen Margaret (Fig. 86). The arms of the king and queen and her motto, 'Humble et Loiall', are not attributed in the Windsor notebook, but are those illustrated in *Regal Heraldry* where they are attributed to the stained glass at Ockwells Manor.[118]

The Royal Collections were an obvious source of inspiration for many of the figures in the windows, especially for the Tudor and Stuart monarchs. Willement's letters to Cust describe a number of visits to see the pictures in Windsor Castle, made as a fee-paying member of the public. Hampton Court, a location to which Willement had regular access during the restorations of *c.* 1840–7, was another fruitful source of material.[119] For the portrait of Henry VII (in sVIII) Willement considered a portrait attributed to Mabuse then at Belton in the collection the canon's father, Earl Brownlow. However, comparison of the figures in windows sVIII and sX (Fig. 87) with the painting depicting Henry VII, Elizabeth of York, Henry VIII and Jane Seymour, a 1667 copy by Dutch artist Remigius van Leemput, of the lost Whitehall mural of 1536–7 by Hans Holbein (Fig. 88) reveals

115. John Cherry and Neil Stratford, *Westminster Kings and the Medieval Palace of Westminster*, British Museum Occasional Papers 115, London 1995, pp. 44–9.

116. J. Topham, *Some Account of the Collegiate Chapel of St Stephen, Westminster, with Plans, Elevations, Sections and Specimens of the Architecture and Ornament of the Remaining Parts*, 1st edn, with drawings by John Carter, published by the Society of Antiquaries of London 1795, 2nd edn with additional plates by Richard Smirke, published in 1811.

117. Joan C. Lancaster, *St Mary's Hall, Coventry*, Coventry Papers 3 (1981), pp. 42–4.

118. Thomas Willement, *Regal Heraldry*, p. 39.

119. Simon Thurley, 'Hampton Court Palace in the 19th Century', *Country Life* (1 June 1995), pp. 80–5; H. Colvin and R. Allen Brown, eds, *The History of the King's Works*, vi, 1782–1851, London 1973, p. 334.

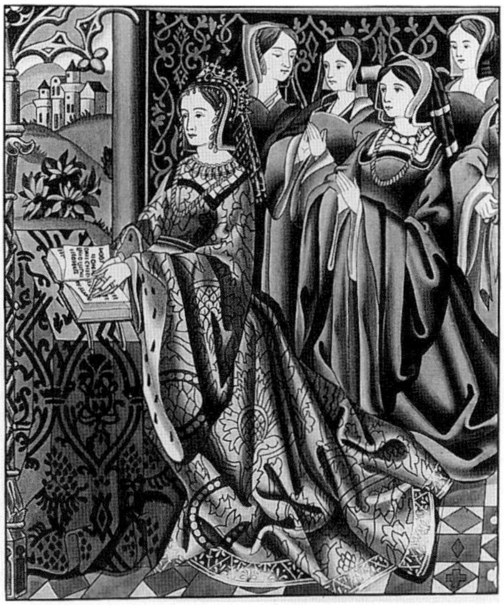

Fig. 86. *'Margaret, Queen of Henry 6th' in the tapestry at St Mary's Hall, Coventry. Illustrated in Henry Shaw's* Dresses and Decoration of the Middle Ages, *London 1843 (Photo © The Society of Antiquaries of London)*

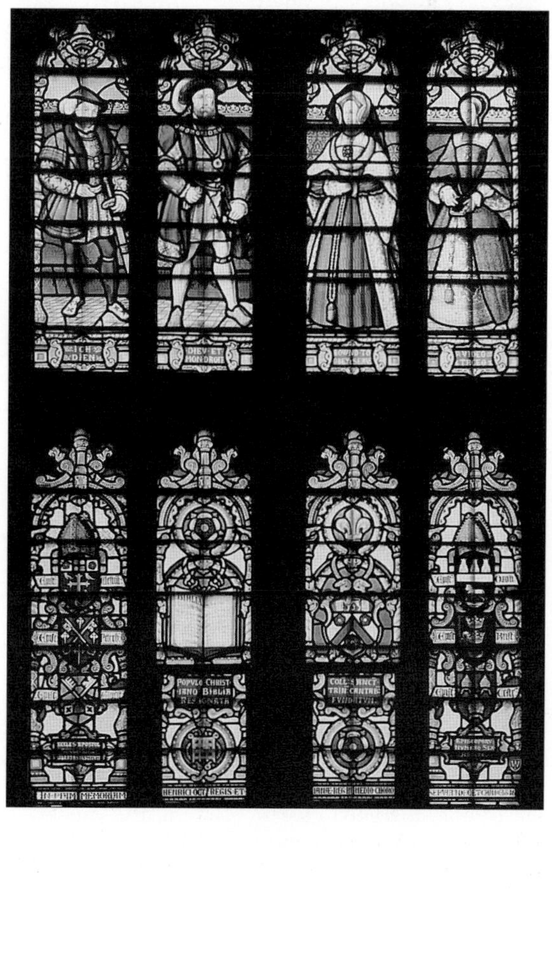

Fig. 87. *Henry VIII, Queen Jane Seymour, Prince Edward and Princess Elizabeth, sX, 1846 (© Crown Copyright. NMR)*

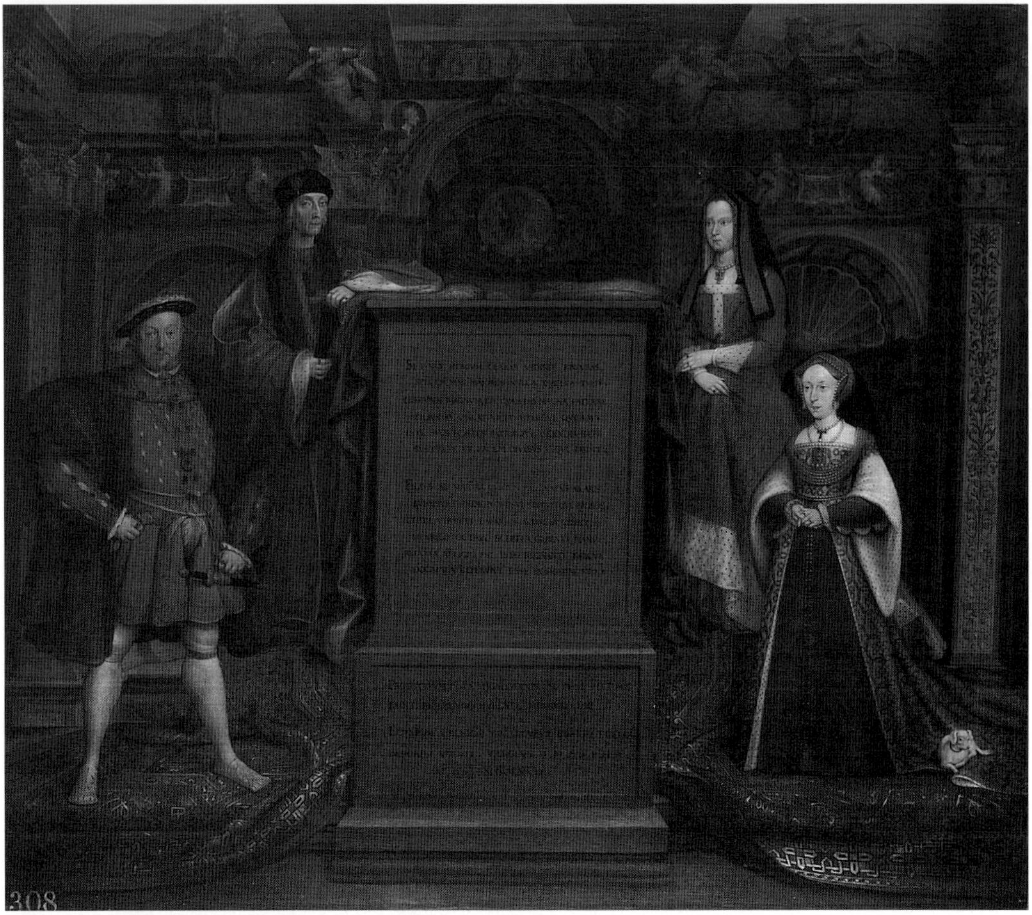

Fig. 88. *Copy of Hans Holbein's Whitehall mural by Remigius van Leemput, 1667 (The Royal Collection © 2005, Her Majesty Queen Elizabeth II)*

this picture to have been his source for all four figures.[120] The figures of Prince Edward and Princess Elizabeth in sX are full-length versions of the three-quarter-length portraits painted in *c.* 1546, with the figure of the prince reversed to face right rather than left.[121]

120. R. Strong, *Holbein and Henry VIII*, London 1967. A fragment of a contemporary version of this subject in stained glass has recently been identified in the east window of St Nicholas, Stanford on Avon (Northamptonshire). Richard Marks, *The Medieval Stained Glass of Northampstonshire*, Corpus Vitrearum Medii Aevi, Great Britain, Summary Catalogue 4, Oxford 1998, pp. 185–6, 190, and *idem.*, 'A Holbeinesque "Royal" Window in England', *Osterreichische Zeitschrift Für Kunst und Denkmalplege*, liv (2000), pp. 385–91. The glass had been installed in Stanford Hall by the 1880s and was transferred to the church in 1932. Although Rushforth suggested a connection with Willement as restorer on stylistic grounds, no documented connection has yet come to light. However, it seems likely that despite the differences between the Holbein original and the version in stained glass at Stanford, the window originated at a royal site, perhaps even Whitehall. Willement worked at a number of royal buildings during his career.

121. The portrait of Princess Elizabeth had been reproduced as a plate in Shaw's *Dresses and Decorations of the Middle Ages*, London 1858.

The image of Charles I is a copy of the Van Dyke portrait of the king in robes of state painted in 1636.[122] The image of Charles's ill-fated older brother, Henry, Prince of Wales (sXI), may have been taken from Isaac Oliver's *c.* 1612 miniature of the prince, also in the Royal Collection, although it is also close to an engraved portrait of the same date by C. Boel.[123]

The later monarchs seem to have presented Willement with more problems and the sketch designs show a greater number of revisions and alterations. In 1853 when he was anxiously seeking models for the George I and George II windows, his researches took him to Windsor Castle, St James's Palace, to the Print Room of the British Museum, whose curator, William Holkham Carpenter (1792–1866) he counted as a friend, and the shops of the commercial print-sellers. Prints are acknowledged in the Windsor notebook as the source of the portraits of Queen Caroline and Princess Augusta (nV, Fig. 89) and a print was also probably the source for the full-length portrait of the Electress Sophia, mother of George I (in nIV), as the original painting was in the palace in Hanover. The notebook records no source for the images of George III and Queen Charlotte (nVI) (Fig. 90), although they can be identified from an examination of the sketch of the first version of the design.[124] In this the king and queen are seated not on straight-backed chairs as in the completed window, but on the medieval coronation chair in Westminster Abbey and this, together with their posture, shows the source to have been Joshua Reynolds' pair of portraits painted for the Royal Academy of Arts, for which the king and queen sat in 1779.[125] These portraits were copied on many occasions, not least by enamel glass-painter James Pearson (*c.* 1740–1838) in a version on glass signed and dated 1793 (Fig. 91). Willement could well have seen Pearson's impressive version of the Reynold's portrait. It remained in Pearson's studio for many years, but passed into the Royal Collection soon after his death and was displayed over the mantelpiece in the king's dining room, until 1925.[126] Willement's appreciation of the pictorial tradition of the stained glass artists of the enamel era is well attested by the numerous engravings of their work pasted into his own sketchbooks, including an engraving of Pearson's clerestory east window at Salisbury Cathedral. Willement would also have been familiar with Pearson's work at Fonthill.

The preparatory sketches for the windows bear many indications of revision.[127] A number of them have paper flaps attached to illustrate variations or amendments to the original design (for example, the upper tier of figures in the Henry VII window, sVIII, Pl. IXB) and in several instances, notably the William and Mary window (sXIII) and the Queen Anne window (sXIV), more than one sketch was made as a result of fairly major revisions. In the north aisle windows, the appearance of some of the kings and queens underwent such significant changes between sketch design and finished window that it

122. Ellis Waterhouse, *Painting in Britain 1530–1790*, Harmondsworth 1969, pl. 42.

123. Roy Strong, *Henry, Prince of Wales and England's Lost Renaissance*, London 1986, pls 33, 50.

124. BL Add. MS 34872, ff. 13, 15.

125. Nicholas Penny, *Joshua Reynolds*, Royal Academy exhibition catalogue, London 1986, pp. 285–6.

126. Sarah Baylis, '"Absolute Magic": A Portrait of George III on Glass by James Pearson', *Journal of Stained Glass*, xxii (1998), pp. 16–30. The panel, fully restored, is now on long-term loan to the Stained Glass Museum in Ely, accession number 92/1.

127. The archive references for all the sketchbook sources are given in the relevant entries of the summary catalogue below.

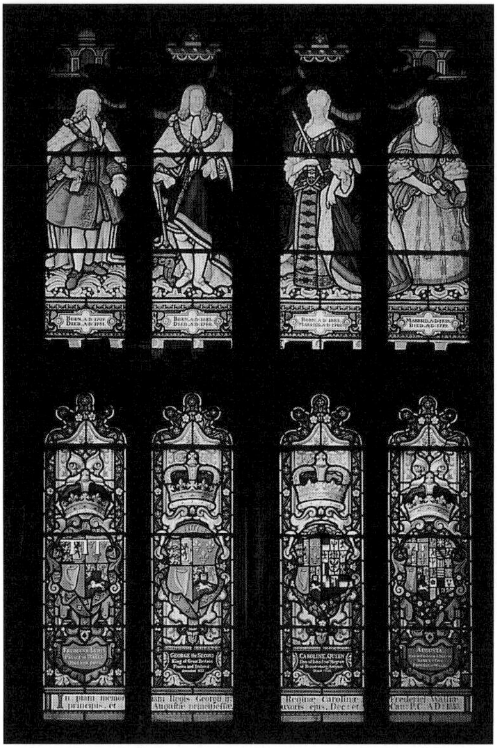

Fig. 89. *George II, Queen Caroline, Frederick, Prince of Wales and Princess Augusta, nV, 1853 (© Crown Copyright. NMR)*

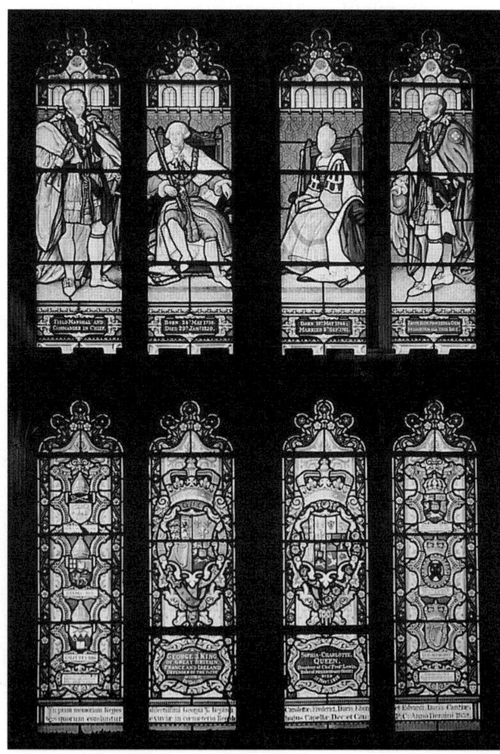

Fig. 90. *George III and Queen Charlotte, nIV, 1852 (© Crown Copyright. NMR)*

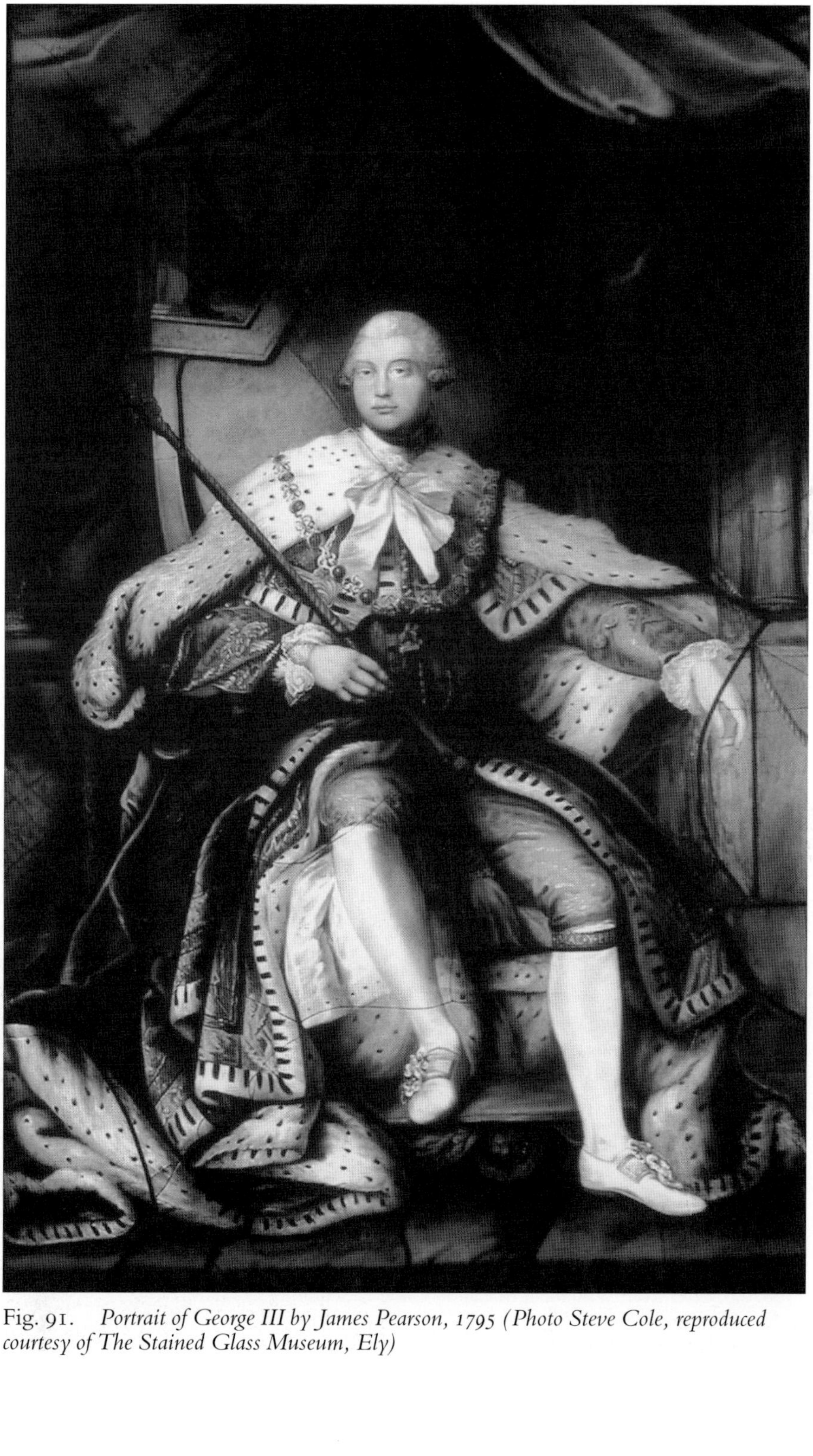

Fig. 91. *Portrait of George III by James Pearson, 1795 (Photo Steve Cole, reproduced courtesy of The Stained Glass Museum, Ely)*

can only be concluded that there had been a complete change of visual model in the interim. That the preliminary ideas were roughed out in advance of the final choice of model is confirmed in a letter concerning the James I window (sXI) of which Willement wrote, 'I have contented myself for present purposes with those portraits which I have in my possession. A more careful selection can be made when we proceed'.[128] This is no doubt the explanation for the very considerable difference in the appearance of the Electress Sophia in the sketch for window nIV when compared to the window itself.[129]

The drawings passed back and forth between Green Street and Windsor and the canons were invited to comment and make suggestions as to alternative motifs. Cust's views were especially valued; 'Be so good as to examine the annexed plans. I have no doubt you will be able to improve them'.[130] The drawings enabled Willement to articulate his own ideas, as in the case of the Charles I window (sXII), for example, designed in September 1848; the letter accompanying the sketch supported his case for a depiction of 'the princes *young*, instead of their being enveloped in awful wigs and the whole would refer to one date — that of his martyrdom'.[131] In a letter written the following day, Willement explains, 'My sketch for the Ch[arles] I window was a mere first idea and wants perfecting in all parts but I thought it might be sufficient for you & the other Canons to talk over'.[132] Willement's ideas on this occasion were approved. In one instance, however, Willement's initial design underwent very considerable revision, presumably at the request of the canons. The sketches for the William and Mary window (sXIII) depict them enthroned and crowned. The finished window (Fig. 92) depicts the seated but uncrowned king and queen at the very moment at which they were offered the crowns of England and Scotland by the marquis of Halifax, representing the two Houses of Parliament.

That the drawings, with comments, were returned so quickly is testament both to the interest and enthusiasm of the canons, especially Canons Cust and Markham, and the efficiency of the postal service. Unfortunately none of Cust's letters to Willement survive, but the sketches themselves are annotated with innumerable faint (and mostly illegible) pencil comments that do not appear to be in Willement's hand. On the drawing of the Henry VIII window (sX), for example, which has a simple heraldic display in the lowest register is the pencilled instruction '6 Bishoprics'.[133] These were duly incorporated in the finished window, rather to its detriment.

The exchange of drawings enabled Willement to involve Cust in the evolution of the designs, and the correspondence gives an insight into the sometimes rather esoteric debates conducted through the post. In 1849 the correct form of the motto of Henry, Prince of Wales was exercising Willement and he sought Cust's views: 'Your son has called here and left Snellings Book of Medals. On the medal of Henry P. of Wales the motto is Pax mentis honest*e* gloria. But in Sandford p.528 both on the engraving and in the letter press it is recorded Pax mentis honest*ae* gloria. Which do you think is right?'[134] Their researches proceeded in tandem; 'have you been able to determine the arrangements on one side of

128. SGC M.166, letter from Willement to Canon Cust, 12 January 1849.
129. BL Add. MS 34872, ff. 9–10.
130. SGC M.166, letter from Willement to Canon Cust, 18 March 1853.
131. SGC M.166, letter from Willement to Canon Cust, 21 September 1848.
132. SGC M.166, letter from Willement to Canon Cust, 22 September 1848.
133. BL Add. MS 34872, f. 4.
134. SGC M.166, letter from Willement to Cust, 2 April 1849.

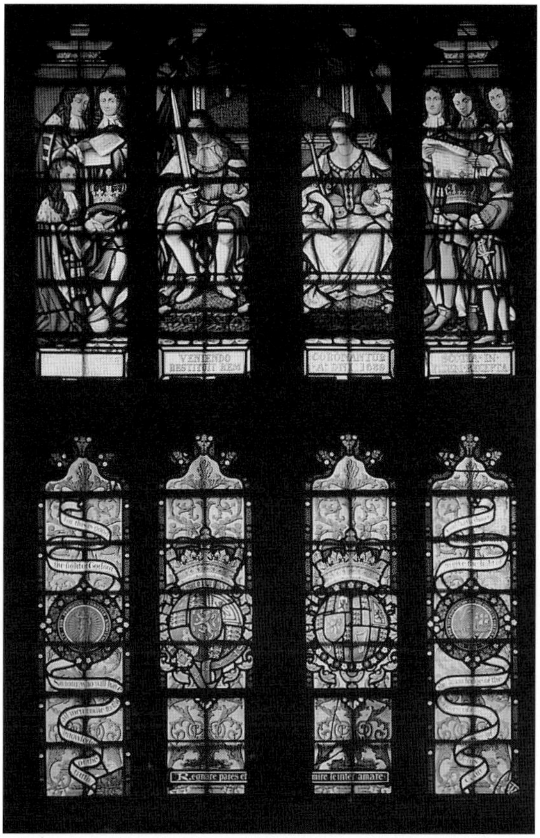

Fig. 92. *William and Mary, sXIII, 1850 (© Crown Copyright. NMR)*

the George I window, ie the line of descent to Sophia the Electress?', asked Willement of Cust in March 1853.[135] The help requested could, on occasion, be of a more practical kind. In 1852 Willement was anxious about the sightlines for the windows in the north aisle and requested Cust to direct 'some person to ascertain how much of the *glass* at the bottom of the lower tier is covered by the *stone battlement* and probably to a spectator on the pavement more may be hidden by it *perspectively* than the *actual* height of the battlement'.[136] For the checking of Windsor sources Cust's son could be called upon for assistance: 'will you ask your son to look at the stall plate of George Lewis Duke of Brunswick and Luxemburg [afterwards King George I]. I want to know what are the quarterings within the shield.'[137] The letters contain several references to Cust family members visiting Green Street.

The drawings could not, of course, give an infallible impression of the quality of the work to be executed in glass, a fact acknowledged by Willement himself when trying to describe the palette for the east window of the south aisle in 1847: 'It is almost impossible

135. SGC M.166, letter from Willement to Canon Cust, 18 March 1853.
136. SGC M.166, letter from Willement to Canon Cust, 27 April 1852.
137. SGC M.166, letter from Willement to Canon Cust, 21 April 1853.

to give the full effect of stained glass.'[138] The exchange of drawings did not, therefore, always result in complete satisfaction. In a letter to Cust written in 1852 in connection with the George III window (n VI), Canon Markham expressed his disquiet about some of the colours used for the background to the thistle, the rose and the shamrock: 'it is a sickly purple or lilac which I do not think suits the rest of the richly coloured armorial bearings.'[139]

The Willement that emerges most frequently from the surviving documentation for the Windsor commission is the antiquarian and entrepreneur. Occasionally, however, we glimpse Willement the draughtsman: 'I have drawn all my portraits but one for the north aisle. On that one I am now engaged. I have then to shade and tint them.'[140] Some of the preparatory sketches, notably the larger-scale details of individual figures (for example those of Queen Anne and the bishops in sXIV and the Prince of Wales in the George II window, nV) are marked with the grid lines necessary to enable them to be enlarged into full-size working drawings. It was at this stage that minor details could be worked out.[141] It is likely that the cartooning was entrusted to a member of the studio. Nothing is yet known of the studio organization, beyond the few names recorded in the west window. Many small adjustments were undoubtedly made at the cartooning stage, usually in the form of a simplification of background detail that might otherwise detract from the impact of the main figures. The architectural background of the Queen Anne scene was simplified, for example, while in the George III window a long curtain suspended on a rail is introduced behind all the figures, linking the lights together and making the scene more two-dimensional. It is impossible to tell to what extent any drawings from life models may have been used in the realization of the full-size cartoons, but it is likely that in two instances the studio acquired 'props' in the form of robes and wigs to ensure that their cartoons were accurate.[142]

Compared to the creative brilliance of A.W.N. Pugin, Willement could not be said to be an artist of genius. His best windows are undoubtedly those that copy most faithfully a specific medieval or Renaissance model. He was, however, a draughtsman of considerable skill, able to adapt a model for a new location with great success. He was an inventive creator of pattern and ornament with an almost encyclopaedic knowledge of works of the past. He was above all a heraldic scholar of distinction. That his windows could sometimes be dull and suffered as a result of the flood of work turned out by the studio cannot be doubted. At Windsor, however, Willement brought to bear all his considerable talents as scholar, designer and craftsman, on what was one of the most important commissions of his career and succeeded in creating what remains one of the most interesting and attractive glazing schemes of the nineteenth century.

138. SGC M.166, letter from Willement to Canon Cust, 18 January 1847.
139. SGC XI.C.66, letter from Canon Markham to Canon Cust, 20 November 1852(?).
140. SGC M.166, letter from Willement to Canon Cust, 3 June 1853.
141. SGC M.166, letter from Willement to Canon Cust, 18 January 1847.
142. Concerning the figure of Queen Adelaide: 'I do not think there will be any problem in supplying robes'. SGC M.166, letter to Canon Cust, 4 January 1853. Concerning the figure of Queen Charlotte: 'her head will be better identified by a wig from the shop of Lawrence'. SGC M.166, letter to Canon Cust, 2 March 1854.

SUMMARY CATALOGUE

A summary catalogue of the stained glass of St George's Chapel, Windsor, by Thomas Willement. For full heraldic details, see Begent and Harrison below.

THE NORTH AND SOUTH CHOIR CLERESTORY

SIII–SIV and NIII–NIV: ARMORIALS OF THE KNIGHTS OF THE GARTER
Ordered: 1840
Installed: 1841 [BL Add. MS 52413, f. 26]
Cost: £174 2s each [V&A 86.ZZ.169, f. 73]
Sketch Design: BL Add. MS 34872, f. 2

SV and NV-NVI: ARMORIALS OF THE KNIGHTS OF THE GARTER
Ordered: June 1841 [SGC Chapter Acts VI.B.10, p. 24]
Installed: November 1841 [V&A 86.ZZ.169, f. 73]
Cost: £174 2s [*ibid.*]

SVI: ARMORIALS OF THE KNIGHTS OF THE GARTER
Installed: October 1842 [V&A 86.ZZ.169, f. 73; BL Add. MS 52413, f. 27]
Cost: £156 2s [V&A 86.ZZ.169, f. 73]

NVII: ARMORIALS OF THE KNIGHTS OF THE GARTER
Installed: (10 compartments), 1851
Cost: £163 2s [V&A 86.ZZ.169, f. 468; SGC Chapter Bills XIV]

SVII: ARMORIALS OF THE KNIGHTS OF THE GARTER
Installed: 1854, 1856, 1858
Cost: £87, £60, £45 [V&A 86.ZZ.169, ff. 502, 520]

NVIII: ARMORIALS OF THE KNIGHTS OF THE GARTER
Installed: (panels 3a–3d and tracery only) May 1861 (ordered 1858, SGC M.166, letter 3 May 1861)
Cost: £69 18s [V&A 86.ZZ.169, f. 502]

THE SOUTH CHOIR AISLE

sII: THE CARRYING OF THE CROSS
Installed: August 1847
Cost: £270 [V&A 86.ZZ.169, f. 179; SGC Bills XVII.61.21]
Sketch Design: BL Add. MS 34872, ff. 4, 47
Removed: 1882 [SGC Chapter Acts VI.B.10]

sVIII: EDWARD III AND HENRY VII
Figures of Henry VII and Queen Elizabeth, the duke of Lancaster and duke of York, Edward III and Queen Philippa, with armorials.
Installed: February 1846
Cost: £174 [V&A 86.ZZ.169, f. 179; SGC Bills XIV]
Sketch Designs: BL Add. MS 34872, f. 3

sIX: HENRY VI
Figures of King Henry VI and Queen Margaret of Anjou, accompanied by St George and St Margaret. Armorials and supporters.
Installed: September 1844
Cost: £164 17s 6d [V&A 86.ZZ.169, f. 178; SGC Bills XIV]
Sketch Design: BL Add. MS 34872, f. 3, SGC Bills XIV

sX: HENRY VIII
Figures of Edward, Prince of Wales (the future Edward VI), Henry VIII, Queen Jane Seymour, Princess Elizabeth (the future Elizabeth I). Armorials and badges of the new bishoprics.
Installed: February 1846
Cost: £174 [V&A 86.ZZ.169, f. 179; SGC Bills XIV]
Sketch Design: BL Add. MS 34872, f. 4

sXI: JAMES I
Figures of Henry, Prince of Wales, James I, Queen Anne, and the Princess Elizabeth (Queen of Bohemia) with armorials.
Installed: June 1849
Cost: £174 [V&A 86.ZZ.169, f. 180]
Sketch Design: BL Add. MS 34872, f. 4

sXII: CHARLES I
Angels bearing cross, crown and palms. Figures of Charles I, the Prince of Wales (the future Charles II), Charles I, Queen Henrietta Maria, James, duke of York (the future James II). Armorials with supporters.
Installed: June 1849
Cost: £174 [V&A 86.ZZ.169, f. 180]
Sketch Design: BL Add. MS 34872, f. 5

sXIII: WILLIAM AND MARY
The crown of England offered to William and Mary by the marquis of Halifax and the crown of Scotland offered by a page, while the earl of Argyll, Sir John Dalrymple and Sir James Montgomery look on.
Installed: June 1850
Cost: £174 [V&A 86.ZZ.169, f. 180; SGC Bills XIV]
Sketch Design: BL Add. MS 34872, ff. 6, 7

sXIV: QUEEN ANNE
The presentation of Queen Anne's Bounty.
Installed: June 1850
Cost: £174 [V&A 86.ZZ.169, f. 180; SGC Bills XIV]
Sketch Design: BL Add. MS 34872, ff. 7, 8

THE LINCOLN CHANTRY: HERALDIC GLASS
Installed: (five windows) 1848 [BL Add. MS 52413, f. 63]
Sketch Design: BL Add. MS 34872, f. 2

OLIVER KING CHANTRY: HERALDIC GLASS
Installed: Old coats of arms restored and provided with new backgrounds, October 1847 [BL Add. MS 52413, f. 58]
Cost: £14 7s 6d [V&A 86.ZZ.169, f. 179]

BEAUFORT CHANTRY: HERALDIC GLASS
Two and a half windows (out of five), glazed at the expense of the duke of Beaufort.
Ordered: 10 June 1843 [SGC M166 letter from Willement to Canon Cust, 10 June 1843]
Installed: 1843 [*Collegiate Chapel*, pp. 19–20, 48–9]

THE NORTH CHOIR AISLE

nII: EDWARD IV
Kneeling figures of Edward IV and Queen Elizabeth Woodville.
Installed: April 1845
Cost: £78 [V&A 86.ZZ.169, f. 178; SCG Bills XIV]
Sketch Design: BL Add. MS 34872, f. 10

nIII: MEMORIAL TO ANNE, DUCHESS OF EXETER — HERALDRY
Glazed at the expense of the duke of Rutland.
Installed: April 1845
Cost: £50 [V&A 86.ZZ.169, f. 181]

nIV: GEORGE I
Figures of Sophia, electress of Hanover and Prince George (afterwards George I).
Installed: June 1853
Cost: £174 [SGC Bills XIV]
Sketch Design: BL Add. MS 34872, ff. 9, 10

nV: GEORGE II
Figures of Frederick, Prince of Wales, George II, Queen Caroline of Brandenburg and Anspach, Princess Augusta of Saxe-Gotha.
Installed: June 1853
Cost: £174 [SGC Bills XIV]
Sketch Design: BL Add. MS 34872, ff. 11, 12

nVI: GEORGE III
Figures of Frederick, duke of York, George III, Queen Charlotte and Edward, duke of Kent, with armorials.
Installed: 1852
Cost: £174 [SGC Bills XIV]
Sketch Design: BL Add. MS 34872, ff. 13, 14, 15 16

nVII: GEORGE IV
Figures of George IV and Princess Charlotte, with armorials.
Installed: 1854
Cost: £174 [V&A 86.ZZ.169, f. 475; SGC Bills XVII.61.21]
Sketch Design: BL Add. MS 34872, f. 17

nVIII: WILLIAM IV
Figures of William IV and Queen Adelaide with armorials.
Installed: 1854
Cost: £174 [SGC Bills XVII.61.21]
Sketch Design: BL Add. MS 34872, f. 18

CHOIR AMBULATORY PASSAGE: ARMS OF EDWARD IV AND QUEEN VICTORIA
Installed: 1854 [BL Add. MS 53413, f. 85]
Cost: £24 10s [V&A 86.ZZ.169, f. 475; SGC Loose Bills XVII.61.21]
Sketch Design: BL Add. MS 34872, f. 9

CHAPTER ROOM: ARMORIALS OF THE DEANS AND CANONS
Six windows in the east wall and one window in the south wall, glazed in the upper parts with fourteen shields of arms, with labels, set into seventeenth-century style ornamental glazing of crown glass. The glazing has since

been reorganized. For present arrangement, see p. 00.
Installed: 1851–2 [SGC M.166, letter of 17 November 1852]
Cost: £62 14s and £11 11s [V&A 86.ZZ.169, f. 468]
Sketch Design: SGC Bills XIV, sketch dated 1851

ACKNOWLEDGEMENTS

The assistance of Dr Eileen Scarff and the late Peter Begent has been invaluable. I would also like to thank Tanya and Peter Hawley for information concerning the Willement family and for allowing me to examine archive material in their possession. Dr Stanley Shepherd very kindly shared with me the text of his entry for the forthcoming *New Dictionary of National Biography*. The advice and suggestions of my fellow authors have also been very much appreciated.

Clayton & Bell and the Stained Glass of St George's Chapel, Windsor

MARTIN HARRISON

This account is concerned with the stained glass windows made by the studios of Clayton & Bell and Ion Pace and placed in St George's Chapel between 1863 and 1949.

THE GREAT EAST WINDOW: THE PRINCE CONSORT MEMORIAL — CLAYTON & BELL, 1862–3 (Pl. XA)

The largest and historically the most important of the new windows placed in the chapel in the latter half of the nineteenth century was the Prince Consort memorial, made by Clayton & Bell for the great east window of the choir in 1862–3. The tendency among stained glass artists to respond to prestigious commissions by producing unusually rich windows may have reflected the generous budget at their disposal, or plain commercial shrewdness. But, for a variety of other reasons, Clayton & Bell's design for the large and complex space at St George's Chapel evinces exceptional care. In confirming, moreover, a fundamental change in approach by one of the busiest and most influential of Victorian firms, the window claims a central place in the chronology of nineteenth-century stained glass.

Prince Albert died on 14 December 1861. The grief of Queen Victoria and of the nation was reflected in a plethora of public and private monuments to the deceased consort.[1] But there was dismay, not least from the dean of Windsor, Gerald Wellesley, at the queen's determination to break with royal tradition and bury Prince Albert in a separate mausoleum at Frogmore, rather than at Windsor. A compromise was reached whereby it was planned to convert the Wolsey Chapel, Henry VII's tomb chapel, into a permanent Albert memorial, and to further commemorate the prince's life in a stained glass window and sculptured reredos at the east end of St George's Chapel (Fig. 93). The architect chosen to supervise all of these works was George Gilbert Scott RA.

Scott had already been appointed architect to St George's Chapel before Prince Albert's death, and had designed the monument to the duchess of Gloucester in the south choir aisle in 1859.[2] His chief task in the chapel was to restore the stonework at the east end of the choir, which had been completely removed in 1786 to accommodate the Sir Benjamin West/Thomas Jervais window. In the summer of 1862, after the removal of the Georgian glass, the task of retrieving the chapel's original fifteenth-century window form was begun. Scott's reconstruction was aided by the view of the chapel in Ashmole's *History of the Order of the Garter*, and by the discovery, while taking out the Georgian glass, of

1. Elizabeth Darby and Nicola Smith, *The Cult of the Prince Consort*, New Haven and London 1983.
2. Scott designed the architectural framework for the memorial; the sculptor was William Theed, a favourite of the Prince Consort.

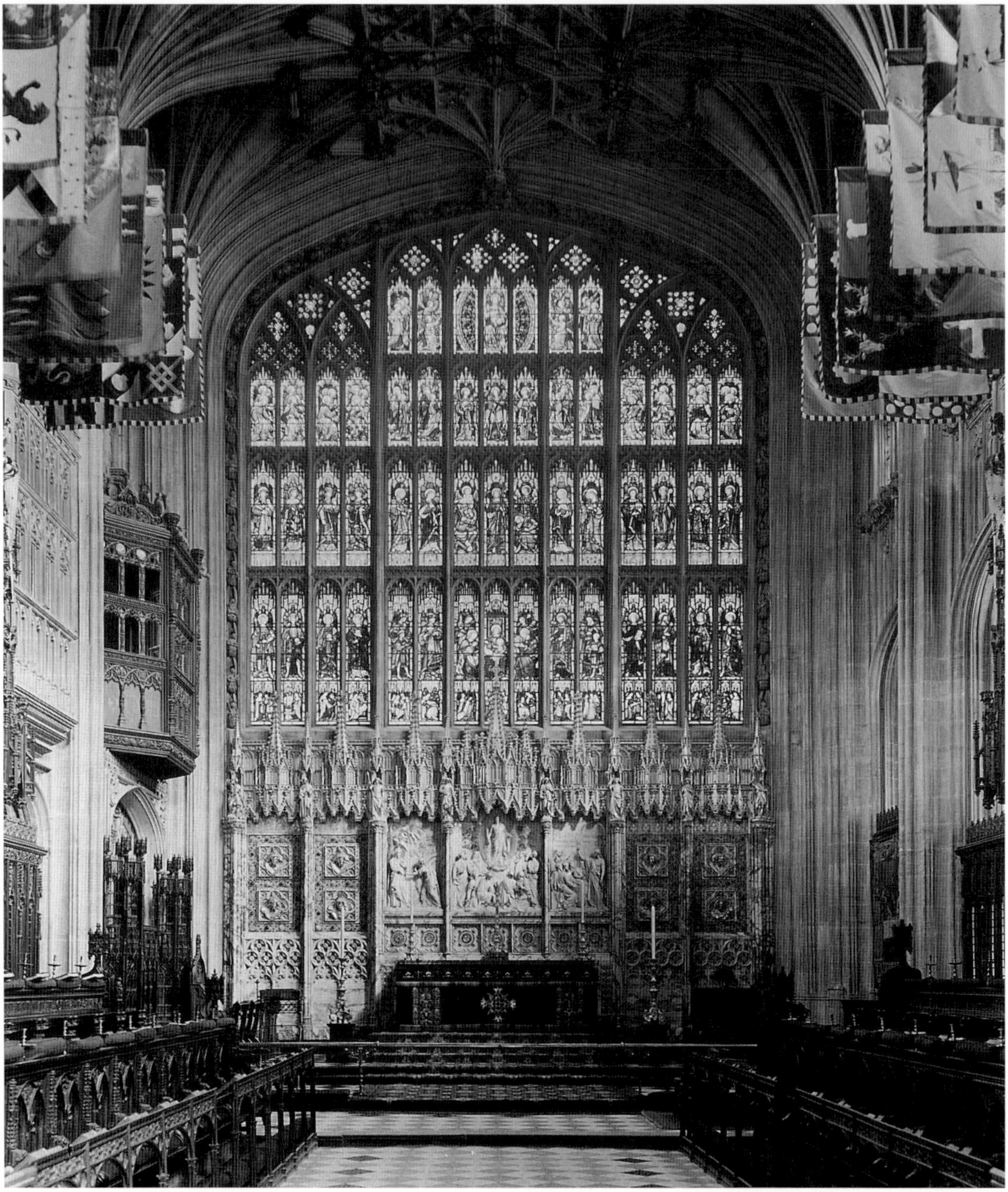

Fig. 93. *The choir looking east (© Crown Copyright. NMR)*

surviving fragments of stonework; the masons employed were the same firm working concurrently for Scott at Westminster Abbey, Henry Poole & Son.

It was at G.G. Scott's instigation that two of his former assistants, John Richard Clayton (1827–1913) and Alfred Bell (1832–95), became partners in 1856. Subsequently, Clayton & Bell were awarded the majority of commissions for stained glass (in addition to decorative works in other media) required by Scott's highly prolific office. Their engagement to make the great east window did not, of course, mark the beginning of the Victorian re-glazing programme in the chapel, for the extensive series of heraldic and figural windows supplied by Thomas Willement had been commenced in 1840. In addition to restoring and augmenting the ancient glass in the great west window, Willement continued to provide new stained glass, principally for the choir aisle windows, until 1861. (As late as 1863 — even further within the period of Scott's involvement at Windsor — Willement executed fifty large windows for the Waterloo Chamber of the Castle.) If Scott, and the Dean and Canons, had wished to maintain continuity in the glazing scheme, they might have considered offering the great east window to Willement. To appreciate why the commission was given instead to Clayton & Bell, it is necessary to consider the evolution of stained glass in the wider context of the Gothic revival.

The course of G.G. Scott's career as an architect is a paradigm for the pervasive influence of the Gothic revival. His father, perpetual curate of Gawcott, Buckinghamshire, was a staunch evangelical. That Scott himself occupied the theological middle ground was acknowledged in his remark, 'Carpenter and Butterfield were the apostles of the high church school — I, of the multitude'.[3] Much of his early career was devoted to designing austere workhouses, but his discovery of the Cambridge Camden Society, and reading Pugin, whose writings, Scott said, 'excited me almost to fury',[4] fired him with a missionary's zeal for the Gothic cause. He subscribed to the Camdenians' journal, *The Ecclesiologist*, and by the early 1840s his designs began to reflect his indefatigable study of ancient Gothic architecture. Formerly a designer of four-square classical buildings, of the kind reviled by Pugin as pagan, Scott became a convert to the archaeologically accurate revival of medieval styles.

The Ecclesiologist, published between 1841 and 1868, promoted the aesthetic and liturgical ideals of the Anglo-Catholic revival in England. Élitist and dogmatic, the journal nevertheless provided detailed and perceptive critical analyses of church building and decoration. During its twenty-seven-year existence, architects and craftsmen were encouraged to become considerably more sophisticated in their application of medieval principles. Stained glass designers were frequently warned against excessive 'modernism' — though the slavish imitation of ancient prototypes was equally condemned. The ecclesiologists equated modernism with pictorialism, with the perspective effects and exaggerated, theatrical, gestures associated with 'decadent' Renaissance styles. They understood the history of medieval Gothic in Hegelian terms as a linear process, whereby after a period of gradual development it reached a peak in the fourteenth century, followed by a steady decline. They believed that a viable nineteenth-century idiom must emerge, but insisted it be founded on fourteenth-century precedent.

The anxious search for originality-within-limits resulted both in stylistic eclecticism and in rapid shifts of taste. Thomas Willement, for all his pioneering efforts in the revival of medieval principles, was one of those artists from an earlier generation who slipped from favour. When he first supplied glass to St George's, he was generally regarded as the leading stained glass artist of his day. Even in 1849 Willement's windows for St Augustine's,

3. Geoffrey Fisher, Gavin Stamp *et al.*, *Catalogue of the RIBA Drawings Collection, The Scott Family*, Amersham 1981, p. 11.
4. *Ibid.*

Canterbury were described in *The Ecclesiologist* as 'the best modern specimens we have seen'.[5] But by 1850, when his pictorial east window for Eton College Chapel was condemned as 'most discreditable',[6] the tide of opinion was evidently turning. The stained glass designed by A.W.N. Pugin and directly inspired by the fourteenth century was now deemed to be 'in a class apart',[7] and soon Willement's windows virtually ceased to attract the journal's notice. The swift fall from grace of early Gothic revival stained glass, a widespread phenomenon, is clearly exemplified at St George's. In 1848 Willement had replaced the West/Jervais *Annunciation to the Shepherds* in the east window of the south choir aisle with his own *Christ Carrying the Cross*; a mere thirty-four years later it, in turn, was no longer deemed appropriate, and was removed to make way for Ion Pace's new window (described below).

Pugin died in 1852, but within a few years the mantle of the Camdenians' *wunderkind* of stained glass had fallen on J.R. Clayton.[8] Pugin, in the three years preceding his untimely death, had collaborated with his friend Richard Cromwell Carpenter on designing stained glass for Carpenter's churches. Having lost Pugin's services, Carpenter immediately undertook to supervise Clayton in the special requirements of designing for stained glass. The enterprise was pronounced a success by *The Ecclesiologist*: Clayton's drawings, they suggested, were 'antique without being distorted' and showed 'thought and talent' in balancing archaeology with innovation.[9] Initially, Clayton's designs were executed by the firm of Ward & Nixon, an arrangement which continued until shortly after Carpenter's own early death in 1855. Then, in order to take direct control over the manufacture of their work, Clayton & Bell set up their own studio in 1856. Shortly after, their south clerestory windows in G.G. Scott's restoration of Westminster Abbey were hailed as 'an epoch in glass painting, from their size, their merit and their locality',[10] the first of many similar encomiums they would receive.

Notwithstanding Clayton & Bell's rapidly enhanced reputation, Scott appears to have harboured reservations about their abilities. Conscious that the Prince Consort memorial was 'a work of such importance', he invited the painter (and fellow Royal Academician) J.R. Herbert to supervise its design.[11] Scott's motive in recruiting Herbert was, he explained to Canon Anson, 'a feeling how uncertain and irregular in their merits the works of our best glass painters are'.[12] He also reasoned that the window it was intended to replace had itself been designed by an eminent painter. Given that West's design was banished from the chapel as 'an acknowledged eye-sore',[13] this seems an odd precedent to cite, but it demonstrates that Georgian artistic élitism was by no means absent in those responsible for the Victorian craft industry.

5. *The Ecclesiologist* (1849), p. 7.
6. *Ibid.* (1850), p. 68.
7. *Ibid.* (1851), pp. 182–4.
8. Clayton began his career as a wood-carver, and in the 1840s (under Theodore Phyffers) modelled carvings for Pugin's and Barry's workmen at the new Palace of Westminster. Thus, from direct experience, as well as indirectly, he may be claimed as a 'Puginian'.
9. *The Ecclesiologist* (1854), p. 178.
10. *Ibid.* (1858), p. 41.
11. SGC, Scott to the Dean, Gerald Wellesley, 20 November 1863. No other instance is recorded of Clayton & Bell acceding to this degree of direct supervision.
12. SGC, Scott to Dean Wellesley, 20 November 1863.
13. SGC XVII.61.20 (d).

John Rogers Herbert (1810–90) had been a painter of popular 'keepsake' subjects who, like his friend A.W.N. Pugin, converted to Roman Catholicism, and painted 'Puginesque visions of Pre-Reformation England'.[14] He had taught alongside the painter William Dyce at the Government School of Design and, like Dyce, had painted frescoes in the palace of Westminster. Both Dyce and Herbert were influenced by the Nazarenes, the group of German religious painters whose work found support in some quarters as an exemplar for the revival of ecclesiastical decoration in England. Dyce's frescoes, painted in the 1850s on the east wall of the ecclesiologists' model town church, All Saints, Margaret Street, London, had met with general approval, but there is little in Herbert's more derivative Overbeck-ian paintings to explain why Scott placed such faith in their author's advice. It is certainly difficult to adduce from the rather weak composition and pictorial rendering of space in his painting *Labore est orare*, exhibited at the Academy in 1862, an aptitude for the two-dimensional medium of stained glass. In short, the decision to enlist Herbert — who had never designed stained glass — is puzzling, especially in view of the high reputation gained by Clayton & Bell's previous achievements. It is possible that Scott initially approached William Dyce, who had advised him on the decoration of Lichfield and Salisbury Cathedrals, and was referred instead to Herbert. Herbert does, moreover, appear to have gained some sort of reputation in stained glass matters, since he (together, paradoxically, with Clayton) was among the five-man jury for the stained glass section of the 1862 International Exhibition at South Kensington.

Since Clayton & Bell had provided windows for several of the cathedrals Scott was restoring, it is unlikely that he was apprehensive about their ability to work on a large scale. But Scott's single-mindedness and commercial acumen barely concealed a sense of doubt on questions of style, manifest in his ambivalence concerning the efforts of his craftsmen-collaborators. In his autobiography, some of Scott's sternest judgments were reserved for stained glass, which he characterized as 'this most unhappy art'.[15] Clayton & Bell's work specifically suffered, he suggested, because 'No real art can stand against a constant high pressure and working against time',[16] a remark which, considering Scott's own prodigious but uneven output, carries an unintended irony.

For their part, Clayton & Bell were deeply offended by Scott's proposal, which they felt would undermine their authority. In June 1862 Scott was obliged to write to Canon Anson excusing the delay in sending Clayton & Bell's preliminary sketch design for the window, saying, 'They have, in fact, been wasting this time by a very needless objection to the arrangement as to Mr Herbert, — very much to my annoyance'.[17] There appears to have been no liaison with the Dean and Canons concerning the terms of Herbert's employment, for when he presented a bill for his services the Dean was obliged to write to both Scott and Clayton & Bell seeking clarification. Scott related how 'Mr Clayton at first kicked violently against it as thinking it seemed to place him in a subordinate position', adding, 'I dare say Mr Clayton thinks that the window owes but little to Mr

14. William Vaughan, *German Romanticism and English Art*, New Haven & London 1979, p. 230.

15. G.G. Scott jnr, ed., *Personal and Professional Recollections*, London 1879, p. 222.

16. *Ibid.*

17. SGC, Scott to Canon Anson, 6 June 1862. Six years later, Clayton became embroiled in the controversy over Pugin's authorship of certain designs for the Palace of Westminster. At one point in the lengthy saga he contested the views of J.R. Herbert, which might suggest a lingering resentment stemming from the Windsor episode. See *The Building News* (1868), pp. 143, 202, 217, 233.

Herbert, this may be owing to the delicate manner in which Mr Herbert brought his advice to bear, knowing the jealousy which had been felt of anything tending to reduce the credit due to the actual glass painters'.[18] Clayton & Bell played down the artist's role: 'Mr Herbert's influence in no way touched the authorship of the work, but was confined to a few suggestions as to points of . . . detail . . . principally relating to costumes. We may add that Mr Herbert expressed throughout the heartiest approval of our work.'[19] Notwithstanding their vested interest in minimizing Herbert's contribution, Clayton & Bell's finished window exhibits no firm evidence of his influence on the essentials of its design.

The ramifications of this fractious episode extend beyond the specifics of the Prince Consort memorial, and illuminate the wider issue of the status of Victorian stained glass artists and craftsmen in general. There is abundant evidence for the dissatisfaction felt by many architects, from Pugin onwards, with their glaziers, and as early as the 1840s, the influential author and antiquary Charles Winston was advocating the introduction of 'real artists'[20] as the most effective way to raise standards in the design of stained glass. The distinction made by G.G. Scott between an 'artist' (J.R. Herbert) and a 'glass painter' (J.R. Clayton) will already have been noted. If William Dyce declined to become involved at Windsor, his apprehension may be explained by his disappointing encounters with stained glass makers, of whom he wrote: 'The truth is our glass painters are mere money making glaziers who dread the introduction of a kind of art which would require better workmen and so diminish their profits.'[21]

When William Morris founded his decorative arts business in 1861 he was able to call on artists of the calibre of Rossetti, Burne-Jones, and Madox Brown, as its chief figure designers. His promotion of this new venture as 'the only really artistic firm of the kind, the others being only glass painters in point of fact (like Clayton & Bell)',[22] echoes the pejorative connotation Scott attached to the term 'glass-painter'. Scott, though, contradicted himself on this point when he also hailed Clayton & Bell as 'the first in this country who became glass-painters because they were artists'.[23] Advocating in 1852 that stained glass wanted 'a little pre-Raphaelitism', the architect G.E. Street (who himself became an important patron of Clayton & Bell in 1860) voiced what would remain the abiding concern of most architects when he warned against confusing the aims of fresco painting or easel art and stained glass, which 'ought to be simply an architectural decoration . . . high art in the ordinary sense, cannot co-exist with the proper use of the materials at our disposal'.[24]

While Scott agonized over the Windsor window the artist/craftsman issue was brought into sharp focus at the 1862 International Exhibition, an event which included the first public display of William Morris's products. The architect William Burges had earlier

18. SGC, Scott to Dean Wellesley, 20 November 1863.

19. SGC, Scott to Dean Wellesley, 23 November 1863.

20. Charles Winston, *An Inquiry into the Differences of Style Observable in Ancient Glass Paintings especially in England; with Hints on Glass Painting*, Oxford & London 1847, p. 287.

21. Dyce to J.R. Hope-Scott, 25 January 1849. Dyce Papers XXVIII, Aberdeen Art Gallery.

22. Charles Harvey and Jon Press, *William Morris: Design and Enterprise in Victorian Britain*, Manchester 1991, pp. 50–1. Letter from Morris to Revd F.B. Guy, 19 April 1861.

23. G.G. Scott jnr, *op. cit.*, n. 15.

24. G.E. Street, 'On Glass Painting', *The Ecclesiologist* (1852), pp. 237–47.

identified as one of the principal 'defects in modern glass . . . [the] . . . lack of an adequately coloured cartoon from the *artist* to guide the *workman*' [my italics].[25] In reviewing the exhibits for the *Gentleman's Magazine*, Burges praised some of Morris's glass, pronouncing the *Parable of the Vineyard* window (designed by Rossetti) 'very beautiful'. But he did not totally reject the claims of the 'glass painters', stating that 'it is very true that one or two of the exhibitors represented in the gallery are artists, for example Mr Clayton, and Mr Powell of the firm of Hardman & Co.', though his qualification, 'but what can one man possibly do in a large firm where he has to direct all the work as well as do the more important drawings?', recalls Scott's similar cautionary note.[26]

The art-or-craft debate may not be one on which concensus is ever reached, but following recent re-evaluations of nineteenth-century decorative arts Clayton & Bell's finest stained glass is now widely appreciated. By 1861, immediately prior to the Windsor commission, they had reached a peak in the development of their 'High Victorian' manner. Clayton in particular had, to a considerable degree, transcended his Puginian origins. The intrinsic medievalism of his designs was modified by numerous external influences — his admiration for Italian *quattrocento* art, his acquaintance with Rossetti and others of the Pre-Raphaelite circle, his wide experience as both a sculptor and a book illustrator, and by neo-classicism (he amassed important collections of the work of John Flaxman and Alfred Stevens). Clayton was an eclectic, yet he was able deftly to integrate diverse sources into an effective, architectonic synthesis. Having achieved a style of considerable vigour and tension, Clayton & Bell promptly turned away from it in favour of greater restraint, a change which indicates not so much a decline as a response to different stimuli. The Prince Consort memorial window was a pivotal commission in this respect, ushering in the next phase of the firm's development.

At St George's Chapel, which John Harvey described as 'the last great building of the Perpendicular style',[27] the stonework that Scott was restoring in the east window dated from the late fifteenth century. It would be some twenty years before the Perpendicular style gained wider acceptance among Victorian architects, and Scott, a convinced adherent of Decorated or 'Middle-Pointed', died in 1878 without being reconciled to it. Thus, both for Scott, and to some extent for Clayton & Bell, whose preference lay with earlier medieval styles, the design for the stained glass necessitated some flexibility of their principles if it were to harmonize with its architectural setting. Its general conception, in fact, approximates to that of the late Gothic great west window at the opposite end of the Chapel. G.E. Street included the great west window in a list of 'some of the finest figure and canopy windows in England . . . late glass, but still very fine and good in principle'. Since Street would doubtless have concurred with his contemporary William Burges, who called St George's 'a most miserable specimen of architecture',[28] it suggests that where stained glass was concerned greater latitude was tolerated on issues of style.

While Scott probably put forward Clayton & Bell as makers of the east window, it should be noted that Canon C.L. Courtenay also strongly supported their selection.

25. *The Builder* (1861), p. 529.
26. *The Gentleman's Magazine* (1862), p. 7.
27. John Harvey, *The Perpendicular Style*, London 1978, p. 213.
28. *Vide* Street in *The Ecclesiologist* (1852), p. 244; Burges, *The Building News* (1865), p. 605.

Charles Leslie Courtenay, brother of the earl of Devon, had been domestic chaplain to Queen Victoria from 1843 to 1849. In 1849 he married one of the queen's maids of honour, Lady Caroline Summers, and in the same year was appointed vicar of Bovey Tracey, Devon. Shortly after his arrival there he determined to build a chapel of ease to the old parish church, and St John the Evangelist, Bovey Tracey, was duly consecrated in 1853. His architect was R.C. Carpenter. The stained glass for the east window of St John's was designed by J.R. Clayton — the earliest recorded example of his work in the medium. Thus Courtenay, who was made a canon of Windsor in 1857, had already been the patron of one of Clayton's and Carpenter's first collaborations.[29] Not only was Courtenay involved at the beginning of Clayton's career, he continued to follow it with interest. In a letter to Dean Wellesley he referred to Clayton & Bell's windows for the abbeys of Westminster and Sherborne, and noted that their work had the approval of the architect William Slater. (In 1858 Courtenay had commissioned Slater, R.C. Carpenter's pupil and successor, to add a north aisle to the old parish church at Bovey Tracey.) It was Courtenay who resisted Thomas Gambier Parry's alternative suggestion to try the Birmingham stained glass firm John Hardman & Co. at Windsor, on the grounds that though they produced 'sometimes very beautiful things [they were] sometimes the very contrary'.[30]

Canon Courtenay's reintroduction of ceremony and ritual at Bovey Tracey was not achieved without opposition, and his Anglo-Catholicism had also, presumably, to be moderated in his dealings with the royal household, in view of the queen's antipathy to ritualism. A distinguished antiquary, Courtenay was largely responsible for the iconographical scheme of the east window. He ingeniously avoided any potential difficulty over 'how best . . . to combine the two elements, the purely memorial and the purely religious'[31] by taking as the central theme 'the Incarnation of the Son of God, and the consequent glorification of human nature, by union with Divinity in the One Person of Jesus Christ',[32] and linking this with passages from the life of Christ which subtly alluded to the public and private virtues of Prince Albert. The fifteen subsidiary panels in the lowest tier of the window refer more directly to the consort's good works, but both he and Queen Victoria are represented in idealized form, rather than as life-like portraits. Reading from the bottom of the window, the seven main lights between the two principal mullions illustrate four leading themes; they are, in ascending order, *The Adoration of the Magi* (Pl. XB), *The Resurrection*, *Archangels*, and *Christ in Glory*; the side lights depict angels and elders. Canon Courtenay had originally intended a *Transfiguration* in the second tier, but Clayton & Bell 'found this impossible and have adopted *The Resurrection*, which I like better'.[33] Considering the conflict that the design of the window provoked, the autonomy that Courtenay seems to have been granted concerning its design is, perhaps, surprising.

Clayton & Bell's design for the window conforms quite faithfully to the dictates of the architecture. All fifty-two lights have borders of architectural canopy-work, more varied and elaborate than those in the west window, and of an early to mid, rather than late, fifteenth-century character. Both canopies and flesh are painted on white glass, facilitating

29. My grateful thanks are due to Revd J.A. Pease, vicar of St John's since 1981, for his kind assistance with information concerning C.L. Courtenay at Bovey Tracey.

30. SGC XVII.5.20.

31. *The Memorial Window in St George's Chapel* (1863), p. 4.

32. *Op. cit.*, p. 5.

33. SGC, Canon Courtenay to Canon Anson, 20 August 1862.

ample light transmission. Only in the *Adoration of the Magi* (Pl. XB), *Resurrection*, and *Christ in Glory* passages are the subjects carried across the two supporting mullions, though there is no spatial recession and any tendency towards perspective effects is carefully avoided. In comparison with the west window the main point of departure is in the greater animation of the poses in some of the figures and, appropriately in what is basically a *Te Deum* design, the implied movement across and upwards through the composition.

That this is a transitional window in the firm's development is illustrated in the painting of draperies. The drapery folds in Clayton & Bell's windows around 1860 were painted in firm, sweeping lines recalling the thirteenth-century 'pothook' style of drawing (a facsimile of Villard de Honnecourt's famous sketchbook had been published in 1859, and may have been a source). But at Windsor the figures are broken up into smaller leaded sections, which precludes the flowing linearity which typifies the firm's work of the period immediately prior to 1862; there is greater emphasis on pattern and texture in the draperies and their folds are rendered in a more mannered, somewhat agitated style which became even more prevalent in the firm's later work. The facial types, however, conform in general to Clayton's highly effective early idiom, redolent of low-relief sculpture, painted on white glass with minimal shading and with stylized wavy hair.

The same width as the great west window, 29 feet, the great east window is 30, as opposed to 36 feet in height. It is intersected by three transoms and fourteen mullions to comprise the total of fifty-two lights. One of Clayton & Bell's most substantial achievements was, as Maurice Bond observed, that the window 'avoids being a gallery of figures which could be arranged in almost any order, and has quite a complex unifying scheme'.[34] The colour palette, which, in the firm's subsequent work, was often more restricted (the primaries predominating), is augmented here by a wide range of secondary hues — eau-de-nil, violet, olive, ochre and steely blue. The colours are though, predominantly reticent in tone, especially when compared to the vivid polychromy of earlier Clayton & Bell productions.

The task of filling an important late Gothic window may have been a factor in directing Clayton & Bell towards later medieval sources. It was reported that their cartoons for the window were presented for the inspection of the Ecclesiological Society 'by the hand of Mr Grylls'.[35] None of Clayton & Bell's nineteenth-century record books survive, but in the absence of documentary proof it could be inferred from this that the Mr Grylls in question — Thomas J. Grylls — had possibly assisted Clayton with the Windsor cartoons. Certainly when Grylls, and another Clayton & Bell pupil, John Burlison, founded their own studio in 1868, they pioneered what might be termed the 'Perpendicular Revival' in stained glass. The east window might, therefore, be claimed as a catalyst in the wider inspiration from later medieval styles.

The evolution of Clayton & Bell's design can also be placed in the context of another, and to some extent parallel, event which occurred in 1862 — the revision by the architect G.F. Bodley of his initial design for the church of All Saints, Cambridge. His rejection of the 'boyish, antagonistic'[36] Franco/Italian Gothic he had originally planned, in favour of a

34. Maurice Bond, *Stained Glass at St George's Chapel*, n.d., unpaginated.
35. *The Ecclesiologist* (1863), p. 59.
36. Bodley was referring to his slightly earlier church of St Michael and All Angels, Brighton: *RIBA Journal* (11 January 1908), p. 146.

more refined English idiom, was an early indication of a re-alignment that would become prominent in the later stages of the Gothic revival. Bodley, who took the deepest interest in the decoration of his churches, had previously gone to Clayton & Bell for much of his stained glass (e.g. at Bicknor, Kent; Canon Frome, Herefordshire; St Michael & All Angels, Brighton), but in 1861 became the first patron of William Morris's new firm. Probably the single most influential aspect of Morris's earliest stained glass was its subtle and subdued colouring; it would hardly have gone unnoticed by Clayton & Bell, any more than would have the loss of Bodley's custom. Morris himself definitely claimed responsibility for having effected such a modification of their work, for he later declared that 'Clayton & Bell . . . do very fair glass now since we have taught them how to colour'.[37]

The qualified praise accorded to Clayton & Bell's window by Maurice Bond is an accurate reflection of recent opinion. Describing it as 'one of their greatest achievements', he nevertheless compared it unfavourably to the great west window, to which it 'does not fully compete in size, age or quality', and felt that 'The colouring and quality of the glass are inferior in brilliance and originality'.[38] Sir Nikolaus Pevsner dismissed it in one word — 'dull'.[39] Contemporary reaction had been more favourable: Queen Victoria thought the window 'really magnificent',[40] and *The Ecclesiologist* called it 'one of the best windows . . . which has been placed in any English church since the revival'.[41]

The great east window was completed in time for the marriage of the Prince of Wales in March 1863. Scott had recently been selected by Queen Victoria to design the national Albert memorial, in Kensington Gardens. Clayton was an important collaborator in the scheme, designing the mosaics (made by Salviati) in the gables of the memorial, and having trained one of its team of sculptors, J.F. Redfern. It was specifically his work on this project that, on its completion in 1872, earned Scott his knighthood. Clayton & Bell themselves were appointed glass-painters to the queen in 1883. In addition to the St George's windows, their complete set of stained glass for the Albert memorial chapel was probably a contributory factor in gaining them the royal warrant.

In an estimate which specified their intention to use 'the very best materials'[42] Clayton & Bell were to receive £1,135 for the great east window; the sculptor John Birnie Philip received £1,200 for the Derbyshire alabaster reredos.[43] The window of 1786 which they replaced had cost £4,900, a total which included Sir Benjamin West's charge of £1,500 for the use of his cartoons. Canon Courtenay's description of the iconography confirms that the scheme was intended to unify the window and the reredos below, although of the latter only the central compartments had been completed by March 1863.

Among the many Prince Consort memorials erected throughout Britain, both in sculpture and stained glass, Clayton & Bell were responsible for at least one further example. Dating from 1864 it survives in the east window of the north chancel aisle of

37. William Morris to Emma Oldham (his sister); undated letter (*c.* 1870), William Morris Gallery, Walthamstow, ref. J.556. I wish to thank Peter Cormack for bringing this to my attention.

38. Bond, *op. cit.*

39. N. Pevsner, *Buildings of England. Berkshire*, Harmondsworth 1966, p. 272.

40. Royal Archives, Windsor Castle, RAY 109/20. By gracious permission of H.M. The Queen.

41. *The Ecclesiologist* (1863), p. 107.

42. SGC XVII.61.20.(d).

43. SGC XVII.9.4.

Great Malvern Priory, another building restored by G.G. Scott. Much smaller in scale than the St George's Chapel window, it is interesting in that it develops some of the later medieval tendencies introduced at Windsor, and which would themselves be carried further in Clayton & Bell's other windows in St George's.

NORTH AISLE WEST WINDOW (nXXV): PATRIARCHS AND PROPHETS — CLAYTON & BELL, 1870 (Pl. XIA)

Upper row (l. to r.): Adam; Joel; Seth; Enoch.
Middle row: Enoch; Methuselah; Noah; Melchizedek.
Lower row: Lot; Abraham; Isaac; Jacob.

SOUTH AISLE WEST WINDOW (sXXXI): APOSTLES — CLAYTON & BELL, 1870 (Fig. 94)

Upper row (l. to r.): St Peter; St John the Evangelist; St James Major; St Andrew.
Middle row: St Philip; St Bartholomew; St Simon; St Jude.
Lower row: St Matthew; St Mathias; St James Minor; St Thomas.

The systematic banishing of the eighteenth-century stained glass from St George's Chapel continued with the removal, in the summer of 1869, of Sir Benjamin West's *Adoration of the Magi* and *Nativity* windows from the west end of the north and south aisles respectively. The windows which replaced them will be discussed together, since they were installed at the same time and were conceived as a pair, Old Testament figures to the north, New Testament to the south. Though less prominent, they are scarcely less interesting than the Prince Consort memorial, and afford an ideal opportunity to measure Clayton & Bell's evolution during the eight years that had elapsed since their first window for the chapel. They are, unfortunately, much less comprehensively documented. By 1870 the Gothic revival was no longer a topic of urgent discourse, and architectural journals were becoming increasingly preoccupied with the secular sphere. The cessation of *The Ecclesiologist*, in 1868, was further confirmation of this, and incidentally eliminated, for the present-day historian, an important source of contemporary comment. Its demise coincided with a decrease in church building, which in turn was exacerbated by the economic depression of the early 1870s. None of these factors was propitious for the stained glass trade, which appears to have contracted in 1870, and steadily declined thereafter (though the largest firms, such as Clayton & Bell, seem to have been cushioned from serious repercussions). Stained glass, in common with ecclesiastical architecture, no longer attracted such regular or fervent debate, and consequently important developments in the medium passed by without notice.

The *Patriarchs* and *Apostles* windows are of the 'figure and canopy' mode, established by the great west window and followed in the Prince Consort memorial. The design of the canopies is again of an earlier style than the architecture, and in this instance was based specifically on the late fourteenth-century tabernacles framing the *Patriarchs* and *Saints* in the side windows of New College Chapel, Oxford (the pedestals in the original are omitted at Windsor). Clayton & Bell placed new heraldic stained glass in the hall of New

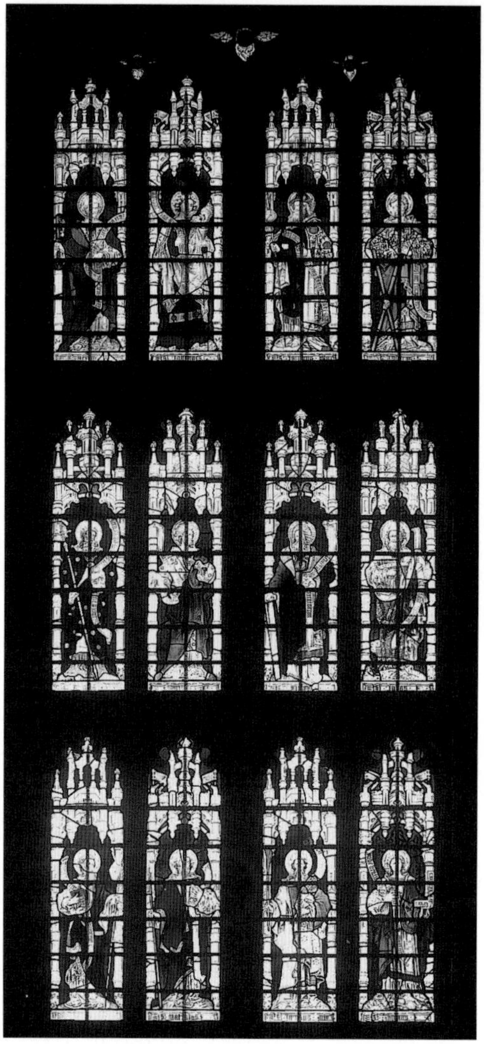

Fig. 94. *Apostles in sXXXI, Clayton & Bell, 1870 (Photo J. Crook, © Dean and Canons of Windsor)*

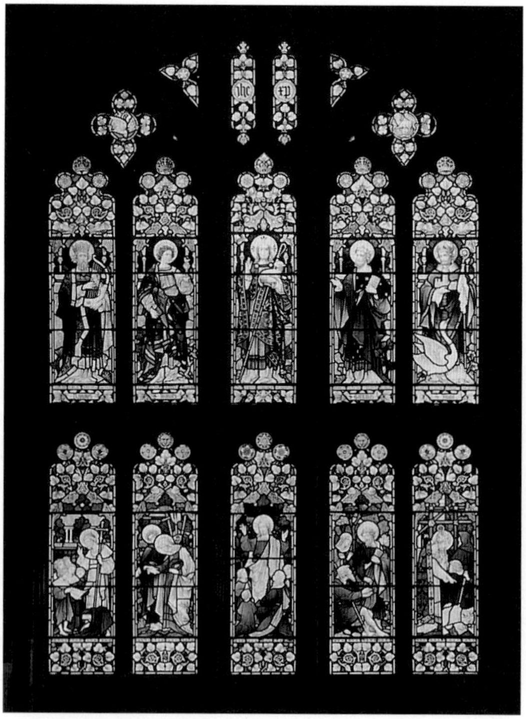

Fig. 95. *East window of the south aisle (sII) by Ion Pace, 1882–3 (© Crown Copyright. NMR)*

College as part of G.G. Scott's restoration in 1865, and may have familiarized themselves with the windows of the chapel at the same time.[44]

It is, however, the figure drawing of the *Patriarchs* and *Apostles* which indicates the greatest transformation since Clayton & Bell's east window of 1862–3. But, in attempting to assess specifics of design, the problem of how to interpret the hierarchical and systematized organizational structures of the larger nineteenth-century studios is encountered. The devolution of the work-force involved a sharp distinction between the designers and the fabricators of stained glass, and even at the design stage separate sketch artists and cartoonists were employed, with the latter group further divided between figure and canopy draughtsmen. The eminent designer and author Lewis F. Day spent two years in the 1860s as 'Keeper of Cartoons' to Clayton & Bell; the existence of such a post is a reminder of the repercussions of streamlined production methods, since Day's function must have been primarily to facilitate the efficient adaptation and re-use of existing cartoons. Given the volume of work which the larger studios produced, such expedients were perhaps inevitable; the practice was widespread in the nineteenth century, though neither, it should be remembered, was it unknown in the Middle Ages.

After about 1885 it is possible to recognize the hand of at least one designer, George Daniels, in the figures of what are nominally Clayton & Bell windows. Daniels, who had been apprenticed to the firm from 1870 to 1876, became one of the most sought-after freelance cartoonists in London.[45] That his individual figure drawing style is discernible in the windows of at least ten different London studios is a phenomenon which awaits further investigation. In 1870, however, Clayton & Bell's stained glass adhered closely to their established 'house style', and it is doubtful if the principals had abdicated control over the more important design decisions at this date. In view of the limited documentation of their complex operating procedures, attributions to specific designers can only be tentative; nevertheless, there are grounds for suggesting that the figures of *Patriarchs*, *Prophets*, and *Apostles* are the work of J.R. Clayton. First, if lacking the illustrious connotations of the Prince Consort memorial, the assignment remained an important one, and is unlikely to have been delegated to the staff designers and cartoonists; a personal visit by Clayton to Windsor to discuss the commission confirms this.[46] Next there is what can be deduced from the evidence in the windows themselves. The figures in the east window were drawn in a relatively conventionalized medievalist manner, which could feasibly have been scaled up from Clayton's sketches by an assistant well versed in his requirements. The figures in the westerly windows are more naturalistic, in a freer personal idiom which would have been difficult for a separate cartoonist to reproduce faithfully. The figures are quite monumental by comparison with those in the east window, conceived in the round and with increased emphasis on modelling and voluminous folds of drapery. Spatially and in their massing the principal debt their drawing owes is not to the Middle Ages but to the High Renaissance.

44. Christopher Woodforde, *The Stained Glass of New College, Oxford*, London 1951, p. 62.
45. Although Clayton and Bell remained responsible for the broad treatment of their windows, within them Daniels' figures are readily identifiable. Among other studios to which Daniels supplied figure cartoons are A. Hemming & Co., Mayer & Co. (of Munich), Horace Wilkinson, and (after 1920) F.C. Eden.
46. SGC XVII.61.19. Clayton visited the chapel on 14 January 1870.

Alfred Bell's figure draughtsmanship was limited, as G.G. Scott observed, by his having 'neglected a regular drilling in the elements of art'.[47] J.R. Clayton, on the other hand, had received formal training at Leigh's Art School, the Clipstone Street Life School, and the Royal Academy. Assuming that the design was not turned over to one of the office juniors, then of the two partners Clayton seems the more likely candidate as author of these windows. The contemporary references cited in the discussion of the east window clearly imply that it was J.R. Clayton who was the dominant force in control of their figure design. His obituary in *The Times* affirms that 'Much of the work came from Clayton's pencil',[48] and J.W. Knowles, while not a completely reliable source, stated that Clayton was primarily responsible for the figures and Bell for canopies and ornament.[49] The division of responsibilities may not have been quite as clear-cut as Knowles suggested, since Alfred Bell is recorded as having designed numerous figure subjects for other firms at the beginning of his career in the 1850s,[50] but a body of work exists in which the figure design can be fairly confidently assigned, on stylistic grounds, to J.R. Clayton.

A renewed interest in post-medieval models was becoming a significant characteristic of English stained glass by 1870, partly in reaction to the increasing commercialism which encouraged the repetitious and unimaginative exploitation of Gothic motifs. In stained glass designs by artists of the stature of Burne-Jones and Henry Holiday, Italian Renaissance influences were integrated into their own idiom and reinterpreted with power and originality, rather than merely imitated. If less innovative than Burne-Jones or Holiday, some of the more commercial designers pursued similar paths; Clayton & Bell were no exception, though in the largest studios the sources of inspiration were generally more diffused, subsumed, as has been remarked, into the 'house style'. In Clayton & Bell's *œuvre* the figures in the *Patriarchs* and *Apostles* windows are atypical in some respects, for nowhere in their work is the attempt to break with Gothic more overt.

The broad, painterly conception of the figures has forced Clayton & Bell into using glass of irregular sizes. A common constructional problem with windows of this character — William Morris had to cope with similarly 'difficult' designs by Burne-Jones and Madox Brown — it was not one with which Clayton & Bell can have been familiar. Consequently, several passages are disrupted by arbitrary leadlines, which tend to interfere with, rather than accentuate, the design. The external ferrimenta exacerbates this fault, bisecting many of the figures' heads. In spite of this, the heads of the *Apostles*, in particular, have a quite powerful, Dürer-esque quality, only partly diluted by the slight paint loss which is evident in parts of both windows. The reposeful, statuesque figures are mostly rendered in fairly cool tones, though there are spots of richer colour, for example in *Jacob*'s red and yellow brocaded robe (*Patriarchs* window), achieved by silver staining over acid-etched flashed ruby glass.

Clayton & Bell's exactly contemporary windows in the north choir clerestory of Gloucester Cathedral provide, in their breadth of treatment, a parallel with the *Patriarchs* and *Apostles*; but while the massive New Testament figures at Gloucester are certainly an appropriate response to their lofty position, they lack the variety and richness of treatment

47. Scott, *Recollections*, p. 221.
48. *The Times*, 7 July 1913.
49. J.W. Knowles (manuscript notes on glass-painters), Victoria & Albert Museum.
50. Bell designed for James Powell & Sons, Lavers & Barraud, and Pilkington's, from 1854–7.

evident at Windsor. When the later work of Clayton & Bell is eventually given the detailed consideration it warrants, it seems likely that these enigmatic windows will also be accorded a key position in their *œuvre*.

RUTLAND CHAPEL: NORTH BAY WINDOW (nXI) — CLAYTON & BELL, 1865 and 1894 (Pl. XIb)

Lower tier: Jubal; Miriam; Deborah; King David, 1865.
Middle tier: Angels with labels and musical instruments, 1894.

In comparison with the great east window, and the west windows of the aisles, Clayton & Bell's conception for filling the much simpler Rutland Chapel window in 1865 followed a more conventional figure-and-quarry mode, a type common in English glazing at the time St George's was built.

By the time the middle tier was added, in 1894, Ion Pace had replaced Clayton & Bell as the chapel's stained glass artist, and the decision to revert temporarily to Clayton & Bell in this instance was presumably taken in the interests of unifying the two tiers. Ironically, this was only partly achieved; though they correspond closely enough in overall design, the twenty-nine years separating the two tiers had witnessed a marked change in Clayton & Bell's technique, which had evolved from the softer modelling of the flesh and drapery painting in 1865 to the crisper, harder style of 1894. The disparity is further accentuated by a small amount of paint loss in the earlier panels. The two levels provide a clear demonstration of the changes in Clayton & Bell's work in the latter part of the nineteenth century.

The design of the angel figures in the middle tier (for which Clayton & Bell's preparatory sketch survives in the chapel's archives) can be attributed, on grounds of style, to George Daniels. Typical of his manner are the rounded heads of the angels, and the tight 'corkscrew' curls of their hair. The reasonably complete record of Daniels' freelance design commissions which survives is not, unfortunately, specific with regard to his work for Clayton & Bell after 1887; this attribution cannot, therefore, be confirmed by documentary sources.[51]

The four Old Testament figures playing musical instruments commemorate the death in 1863 of Isabella Georgina, wife of Sir George Elvey, organist to St George's Chapel. The biblical phrases in the inscriptions are adapted from Revelation 14, verse 13: 'And I heard a voice from Heaven saying unto me, write Blessed are the dead which die in the Lord from henceforth: Yea, saith the Spirit, that they may rest from labours; and their works do follow them.' Sir George himself is commemorated by the musician and label-bearing angels in the middle tier.

BRAY CHAPEL: PRINCE IMPERIAL MEMORIAL WINDOWS (sXV–sXIX) — ION PACE, 1882

In 1882 the Dean and Canons transferred their patronage from Clayton & Bell to another artist, Ion Pace (1846–1928). The reasons for this remain unclear. No correspondence has

51. My thanks are due to Mrs Muriel Simpson, the artist's grand-daughter, who kindly checked her files for references to George Daniels.

come to light which suggests dissatisfaction with Clayton & Bell who, paradoxically, were appointed Glass Painters to Queen Victoria in the following year. Pace, on the other hand, was only just beginning to establish his business. He first exhibited at the Royal Academy in 1880 and the earliest entry of his firm in the Post Office London Directory of 1881. It may be significant that Pace appears to have had the backing of Alfred Young Nutt, Clerk of Works at Windsor Castle and Surveyor to the Dean and Canons of St George's. Nutt later raised an important (and often ignored) factor which may have had a bearing on Pace's original employment, when he reminded the Keeper of the Privy Purse of the economical advantages of employing Pace, who 'has done such beautiful work already . . . and I am also quite sure his charges are little more than half what the big firms would ask . . . .'[52]

Pace's work throughout the chapel is technically competent rather than artistically inspired. His heraldic glass is quite boldly conceived and accomplished in execution — Maurice Bond described the Bray Chapel windows as 'elaborate, if inaccurate'.[53] Heraldic stained glass does not appear to have been a specialization of Pace's, and no other extensive series is documented. A further explanation for Pace's introduction may be that he was a former pupil of Clayton & Bell, which, if a less costly alternative was being sought, might have been supposed to ensure stylistic continuity. One authority states that prior to setting up his own studio he had been Clayton & Bell's chief designer; an early Ion Pace window at Irthington, Cumberland, certainly bears many similarities to contemporary work by Clayton & Bell.[54]

Notwithstanding Pace's lengthy career — he continued until at least 1923 — he was never prolific. Operating a small studio must have been a precarious venture, whereby the loss of a few commissions might place the business in jeopardy. About 1888 Pace vacated his original premises at 2 Duke Street, Adelphi, for a less central location in Fulham Road. He remained here until 1901, when he removed even farther afield to Hounslow; this final move was no doubt precipitated by the unfortunate circumstance briefly recorded in the notebook of the Chapter Clerk: 'Ion Pace 252 Fulham Rd. Goods seized and sold 1901.'[55] Although he apparently recovered from this setback, it is fair to say that Pace never received wide recognition for his stained glass.

Pace's most substantial claim to be remembered will probably rest on his windows in St George's Chapel and three subsequent commissions connected with the royal family. He made several windows for the Osborne estate church at Whippingham, Isle of Wight, commencing with a new east window in 1900. In 1902 he supplied a memorial window to Queen Victoria for the private chapel at Windsor Castle, and from 1905 provided a series of windows in the royal mausoleum at Frogmore.[56] Pace's son donated a small panel of his father's work depicting *The Annunciation* to the Victoria & Albert Museum in 1932, which

52. Letter from A.Y. Nutt to Sir Dighton Probyn, accompanying memorandum dated 7 August 1909. Royal Archives, Windsor Castle. Quoted by gracious permission of H.M. The Queen.

53. Bond, *op. cit.*

54. It is not certain, however, to what extent Pace was a designer in his own right; the ubiquitous George Daniels, for example, occasionally provided Pace with figure cartoons.

55. SGC XVII.29.2.

56. My thanks are due to Mrs Diana Biles, of Cowes, and Miss Pamela Clark, Registrar of the Royal Archives, for confirming details of Pace's work.

is on permanent display in the Museum.[57] No Pace archive has been discovered, and the chronicle of his eclipse concludes with a letter written by his daughter-in-law in 1945, explaining that all but one of his designs were given for salvage in the Second World War.[58]

CHOIR SOUTH AISLE, EAST WINDOW (sII) — ION PACE, 1882–3 (Fig. 95)

Upper tier (l. to r.): King David; St John the Evangelist; Christ the Good Shepherd; St Barnabas, St Hugh of Lincoln.
Lower tier (l. to r.): St Gregory the Great teaching plainsong; St John comforting the Virgin Mary; Christ blessing children; St Barnabas distributing gifts to the poor; St Hugh supervising the building of Lincoln Cathedral.

In August 1882 the Chapter approved the removal of Willement's *Christ Carrying the Cross* and its replacement 'with tracery more appropriate and new stained glass as a memorial to the late Revd Hugh Pearson'.[59]

Fixed in June 1883, this is Ion Pace's only figurative window in St George's. Pace's limitations as a designer, less evident within the conventions of heraldic glass, are here more manifest. Technically proficient — the glass painting itself is quite skilful — it is somewhat pedestrian in conception and uninspired - even coarse - in colour, a pale greenish-yellow predominating. The stylized plant forms in the canopies fail to resolve the problem of relating the ten principal figure subjects to the architectural whole; by the end of the decade, Christopher Whall, pioneer of Arts & Crafts movement stained glass, was, in comparison, much more effectively integrating foliate surrounds into his designs. Here their awkward relationship with the rest of the window is possibly explained by the fact that the backgrounds are recorded as having been designed not by Pace but by A.Y. Nutt, whose contribution appears to have been detrimental to the homogeneity of the two main elements.

Pace's sketch for this window, dated 1882 and bequeathed by Nutt's descendants in 1978, survives in the Windsor Borough Collection.

CHOIR CLERESTORY, TWO WESTERNMOST BAYS (NVIII and SVIII) AND NAVE CLERESTORY WINDOWS: FIRST AND SECOND FROM EAST, SOUTH AND NORTH SIDES (NXVI, NXVII, SXVI, SXVII) — ION PACE, 1886–99 (Fig. 96)

In 1885 it was resolved that Ion Pace should be engaged to complete the series of heraldic windows in the choir clerestory, following the plan established by Willement. The Chapter decided in 1886 to continue the sequence by gradually filling the corresponding

57. The panel is said to have been a copy of one made for the bishop of Winchester's library; if this is so, the original is no longer *in situ*.
58. Letter from Rose Mabel Pace to Fr Francis Nolan, 29 November 1945, kindly communicated to me by Mr Peter Howell.
59. SGC XV.61.19.

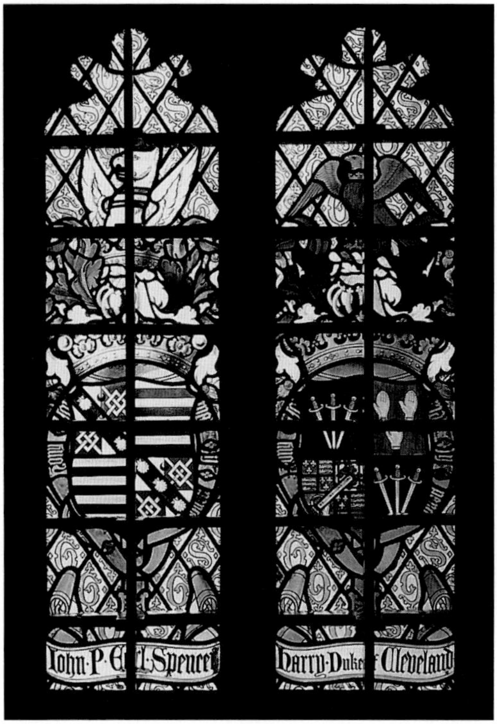

Fig. 96. *Choir clerestory, heraldry by Ion Pace in SVIII, 1886 (© Crown Copyright. NMR)*

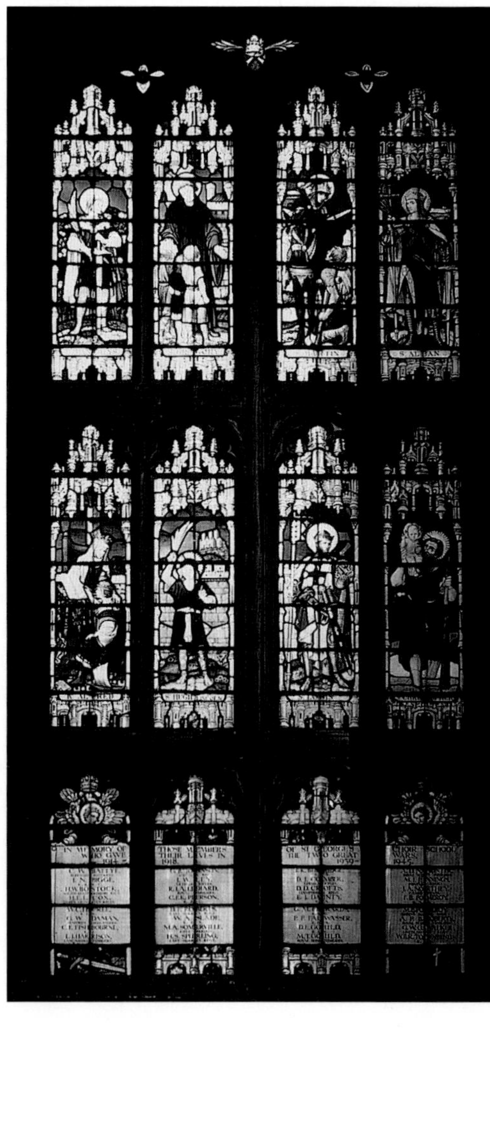

Fig. 97. *The War Memorial Window (nXIV), Clayton & Bell, 1920–1 and 1949 (Photo J. Crook, © Dean and Canons of Windsor)*

windows in the nave. Three windows of the nave clerestory series were completed by Pace between 1886 and 1888; with the addition of the window placed to commemorate Victor, prince of Naples, in the south nave clerestory in 1899, the series came to a halt, ending Pace's connection with the chapel. The more westerly nave clerestory windows have retained their plain glazing up to the present day.

WAR MEMORIAL WINDOW, NORTH NAVE AISLE (nXIV) — CLAYTON & BELL, 1920–1 and 1949 (Fig. 97)

Top row (l. to r.): St Pancras; St Gregory the Great; St Martin of Tours; St Alban.
Middle row: King Alfred with his mother; Little St Hugh; St Louis, king of France; St Christopher.
Bottom row: Names of past members of the Choir School of St George's Chapel who were killed in the two World Wars.

By the time that this, the last of Clayton & Bell's windows to be placed in the chapel, was commissioned, the structure of the firm had undergone major changes. Alfred Bell had died in 1895, and when J.R. Clayton retired in 1907 he was succeeded as head of Clayton & Bell by one of Alfred Bell's sons, John Clement Bell (1860–1944). J.C. Bell was in turn joined in partnership by his son Reginald Otto Bell (1886–1950) in 1908. The sole surviving account book of the firm confirms that this window was ordered on 17 July 1920 by H.J.W. Deane, chapter clerk, at an estimated cost of £350.

The demand for stained glass, in steady decline since about 1865, was only briefly arrested by the brisk trade in First World War memorials. The larger studios — and Clayton & Bell were not excepted — had already contracted considerably by 1920. Fluctuations in trade rendered it less feasible to maintain a large permanent staff, and more use was made of freelance workers. One such craftsman, Horace Wilkinson, was dismissed when Clayton & Bell suffered 'a drop in orders from America'.[60] Commercial considerations, however, were not the only factors in the scaling-down of Clayton & Bell's operations. Reginald Bell, in particular, was uncomfortable with the streamlining of production methods and the consequent loss of the principal's artistic autonomy inherent in the systems operated by large stained glass firms.

All of the correspondence in the chapel's archives suggests that the design of the window should be credited to John Clement Bell. Stylistically, however, it is closer in appearance to the somewhat freer style of Reginald Bell. It may be significant that at the Royal Academy exhibition of 1920 Reginald Bell exhibited two designs for an (unspecified) war memorial window. It should also be noted that certain passages in the designs (the head of *St Christopher*, for example) retain affinities with the work of George Daniels. This may indicate the pervasiveness of his draughtsmanship within the firm, that he was responsible for Bell's early guidance in the medium, or that he executed the full-sized cartoons for this window from Bell's original sketch.

60. *Journal of the British Society of Master Glass Painters*, xii, no. 3 (1958), pp. 222–4.

The window commemorates former members of the St George's Choir School who died in the two World Wars (the inscription panel in the lowest tier having been modified in 1949 to include the names of those who died in the Second World War). Appropriately, the iconography depicts soldier saints and themes of boyhood.

John Piper and the Stained Glass of the King George VI Memorial Chapel, 1967–9

MICHAEL ARCHER

After the death of King George in 1952, his body was placed in the royal tomb-house at Windsor. It was not until the mid-1960s that it was decided that a permanent resting place should be found within St George's Chapel. In consultation with the royal family, the Chapter decided to build a memorial chapel 'in the angle between the east wall of the Rutland Chapel and the north wall of the north quire aisle and this to occupy on the north side of St George's Chapel a position similar to the Oliver King Chantry on the south side'.[1] The chapel was designed by George Pace in association with Paul Paget of Seely and Paget, surveyors to St George's Chapel, and the interior was constructed of Clipsham ashlar stonework with a floor of polished Purbeck freestone. The intention was that the 'plan shape, windows, mullions, buttresses, parapet and window glazing are all conceived as a mixture of the architectural aesthetics of the late medieval ages and modern architecture'.[2] As constructed, the building consists of two small interlinked chapels entered from the north choir aisle down a short flight of steps. These lead into a mortuary chapel with a ledger stone of black marble and opening out beyond it a liturgical chapel with altar, lit by five windows designed by John Piper and executed by Patrick Reyntiens in 1969 (Pl. XII). All the windows have entirely abstract compositions. The two flanking the altar have the strongest colours, emphasizing the main focus of the chapel. In both windows the lights nearest the area directly above the altar have a modulated dark blue ground broken by red and yellow flame-like forms, shading off at the left-hand edge of the left window and the right outer edge of its counterpart into pale turquoise blue and cloudy white textured glass. The two windows further to the east are much paler, consisting of textured misty white glass with a fine skein of lead lines relieved by clusters and larger accents of turquoise blue and yellow. At a higher clerestory level there are four panels which have a strong orange-yellow ground with darker brown areas relieved by scattered spots of sharp turquoise.

It would appear that the original intention was to have 'plain glass of the very highest quality and perhaps slightly tinted'.[3] This idea was superseded by George Pace's proposal that a 'flower expert' should be called in to do the windows and the specifications produced in June 1968 include a statement that they should 'contain a flower motif'.[4] Further discussions between Paget and Pace led to a decision that Piper should be approached by Paget in August and in a memorandum of that month 'It was unanimously agreed that good coloured glass in the windows will be a real enhancement of the chapel: John Piper's suggestion is awaited. It is hoped that there will be a motif of colour rather

1. P.G. Pace, *The Architecture of George Pace*, London 1990, p. 217.
2. *Ibid.*, p. 219.
3. SGC CL 22/1, letter of 26 July 1968 from Paul Paget to the Dean.
4. SGC M.110(c).

than the depicting of any objects running through the windows'. On 7 October George Pace wrote to the dean:

I have received from John Piper the first sketch of the stained glass. In my opinion this is excellent and it is a solution based on what Paul Paget and I outlined as being the desirable approach so as to make sure of the total impact of the chapel. You will note that the windows which are symmetrical about the stone altar have the most colour and this grows in intensity towards the centre line, thus concentrating the eye about the centre portion of the corona-like tower. The three windows to the east are, of course, not in the same plane as those in the wall behind the altar and cannot be seen by the public when looking into the chapel from the north choir aisle. These windows are generally grey-ish in colour and their main function is to send a flood of light across the chapel. The clerestory windows in the corona are basically golden in colour which should send a very interesting light into the corona from a source hidden from those looking into the chapel from the north choir aisle . . . John Piper would like to do a full-size cartoon of one of the windows when he comes back from France, and if, in the meantime, Paul Paget is able to arrange for a model of the chapel to be made, he would then prepare better transparencies to place in the window openings.[5]

In the event the designs met with full approval and no further cartoons or transparencies were thought necessary. From the start Queen Elizabeth, the Queen Mother had been consulted and since she greatly admired Piper's work, she had been happy to give him complete freedom of action.[6] When the designs were shown both to her and to the queen,

they were awfully pleased with them. They particularly liked the light blue variations towards the outside of the principal windows. They were also very glad to think that the windows not visible from the aisle would let in a good deal of daylight.[7]

By the end of October Piper and Reyntiens were formally authorized to proceed. Full-size cartoons were made and by 12 December Paget was able to report that 'I paid a visit last week to Mr Patrick Reyntiens' studio where the stained glass to the designs of John Piper is making good progress'.[8] A few days later Pace wrote to Paget:

I had a good look at the glass last Saturday. The result is exactly what I had in mind except for the bright red pieces. I have advised that these should be matted down near the edges and that considerably more lead cames should be inserted to bring down the scale.[9]

The leading was duly modified, even though some of the lines subsequently appeared rather arbitrary. The glass itself was French and German, much of it left over from the Coventry Cathedral commission.[10] The yellowish-brown clerestory windows in the 'corona' are unusual in Piper's work since they are largely carried out in brown enamel and yellow stain. The design and execution of the windows had to carried out in a very short space of time and they were completed in the following year. The dedication took place on 31 March 1969. The cost was met by the Knights of the Garter who especially wished to make a presentation to the Memorial Chapel, in view of George VI's particular interest in the Order.

Queen Elizabeth, the Queen Mother had known John Piper since 1942, when he had painted two sets of twelve paintings of Windsor Castle for her. He had been recommended

5. SGC CL 22/1.
6. Communication from Sir Alistair Aird, Comptroller to H.M. Queen Elizabeth, the Queen Mother.
7. The Dean to John Piper, 30 October 1968.
8. SGC CL 22/1.
9. SGC CL 22/1.
10. Communication from Patrick Reyntiens.

to the then queen by Kenneth Clark, Surveyor of the King's Pictures at that time, who had recruited Piper for his War Artists scheme. She had subsequently been present at the dedication in May 1956 of the windows Piper had designed for Oundle School Chapel, his first stained glass commission. Since 1953 she had been an Honorary Freeman of the Grocers' Company, who were patrons of the school and financed these windows through one of their trust funds. The antecedents of the Windsor design went back to an abortive commission in the early 1960s for three windows in the apse of Pershore Abbey.[11] In 1963 Piper was able to develop his ideas further when he was asked by Pace to design a west window for St Mark's, Broomhill, Sheffield. Since the church had been largely destroyed by fire during the war, Piper thought it appropriate to produce an abstract design based on the general idea of 'Flames'. In 1961 Pace had commissioned Piper to do a window for Llandaff Cathedral, and they were to share an exhibition, *Two Modern Christian Artists*, held at the University of York in 1967. Given their close association at the time, it is not surprising that Pace should have turned to Piper for the Windsor commission.

The windows of the George VI Memorial Chapel are some of the last entirely abstract glass John Piper was to design. As a young man in the 1930s he had participated wholeheartedly in the avant-garde exploration of the possibilities of abstraction in his constructions and oils. He had exhibited with the '7 & 5 Society' and contributed articles and illustrations of this work to *Axis*, a 'quarterly review of contemporary "Abstract" painting and sculpture' edited and produced by Myfanwy Evans. During and after the war his style moved increasingly towards representation, although his awareness of abstract forms in landscape and architecture was always present and continued to find expression in a number of his stained glass compositions between the mid-1950s and about 1970. Martin Harrison has pointed out 'that the religious context in which the windows would be seen gave him a greater freedom to abstract his subject'.[12] In 1938 Piper had written that

> The early Christian sculptors, wall-painters and glass-painters had a sensible attitude towards abstraction. However hard one tries, one cannot catch them out indulging in pure abstraction. Their abstraction, such as it is, is always subservient to an end — the Christian end, as it happened.[13]

In the windows he designed for Windsor, Piper was well aware that, particularly when the medium is coloured glass, the expression of spiritual concepts can be just as, if not more, effectively realized through the symbolic use of colour and abstract forms as it can through more obviously representational means.

BIBLIOGRAPHICAL NOTE

Much of the information in this essay has been drawn from the archives of St George's Chapel and correspondence in the possession of the late John and Myfanwy Piper. Besides the works cited in the notes, the following articles are of relevance.

Anon., 'King George VI Chapel', *Building* (29 March 1968), p. 85.
Anon., 'King George VI Memorial Chapel, Windsor', *Building* (12 September 1969), p. 102.

11. Information supplied by John Piper.
12. Martin Harrison in his introduction to *John Piper. Painting in Coloured Light*, the catalogue of an exhibition held at Kettle's Yard Gallery, Cambridge, 3 December–9 January 1983.
13. 'Abstraction on the Beach', *Vingtième Siècle*, 1 July 1938, p. 41.

Anon. ('Miscellany'), 'New Windsor Chapel', *Architectural Review* (February 1970), pp. 153–4.
June Osborne, *John Piper and Stained Glass*, Stroud 1997, p. 96.
George G. Pace, 'The King George VI Memorial Chapel, St George's Chapel, Windsor Castle', *Friends Report*, 4 (1968–9), pp. 421–5.

The Heraldic Windows of St George's Chapel

PETER BEGENT with the assistance of HUBERT CHESSHYRE and ROBERT HARRISON[1]

THE SOUTH CHOIR CLERESTORY

SII

In common with the other clerestory windows of the choir, this consists of twelve lights (see prefatory window plans). The apex is composed of three quatrefoils. The interspaces between and below the quatrefoils are filled with coloured glass.

The window, together with its northern neighbour (window NII), was glazed in 1782 by Francis Eginton and contains the arms of Knights of the Garter of that year. Each coat of arms is displayed within the Garter at the centre of an eight-pointed star resembling the Garter Star. The star is ensigned by the appropriate crown or coronet of rank and is set within a background of plain grey quarries. Beneath the star is a partially folded ribbon of blue edged with gold, like the Garter, but bearing in gold letters the name of each knight. Pendant from the ribbon is the figure of St George in armour facing to the sinister, mounted on a white horse and wearing a red cloak, his lance striking the mouth of the dragon at his feet.

1a

This and the remaining eleven lights display the arms in the manner detailed above.
Crest: On a wreath argent and gules, a sagittary passant, the body proper the hind part argent. Below: The coronet of an earl. *Arms*: Quarterly, 1 & 4 Ermine on a bend azure a magnetic needle pointing to the polar star or PETTY, 2 & 3 Argent a saltire gules and a chief ermine, a crescent gules for difference FITZMAURICE. *Legend*: WILLIAM E^L. OF SHELBURNE

1b

Crest: On a wreath or and sable, a reindeer statant or. Below: The coronet of a viscount. *Arms*: Quarterly, 1 & 4 Barry of ten or and sable BOTTEVILLE, 2 & 3 Argent a lion rampant, tail nowed and erect gules THYNNE. *Legend*: THOMAS VISC^T. WEYMOUTH

1c

Crest: On a wreath argent and gules, a wolf passant argent collared and chained, the chain reflexed over the back or. Below: The coronet of an earl. *Arms*: Quarterly, 1 & 4 Barry of eight argent and gules a cross flory sable GOWER, 2 & 3 Azure three laurel leaves or LEVESON. *Legend*: GRANVILLE EARL GOWER

1. Final revision of this heraldic schedule remained incomplete at the time of Peter Begent's untimely death. Robert Harrison kindly took up the task of final revision and checking of the text and his generous assistance is warmly acknowledged by the editor.

1d

Crest: Out of a ducal coronet or a griffin's head gorged with a collar gemel gules between two wings elevated argent. Below: The coronet of a duke. *Arms*: Quarterly, 1 & 4 Quarterly argent and gules, in the second and third quarters a fret or, overall on a bend sable three escallops argent SPENCER, 2 & 3 Sable a lion rampant argent, on a canton argent a cross gules CHURCHILL. *Legend*: GEORGE D^{E}. OF MARLBOROUGH.

2a

Crest: On a wreath or and sable, a griffin passant wings elevated argent. Below: The coronet of a marquess. *Arms*: Quarterly, 1 & 4 Argent on a chevron engrailed azure between three martlets sable three crescents or WATSON, 2 & 3 Sable a chevron between three leopard's faces or WENTWORTH. *Legend*: CHARLES M^{S}. OF ROCKINGHAM

2b

Crest: On a chapeau gules turned up ermine, a lion statant, tail extended azure, langued gules. Below: The coronet of a duke. *Arms*: Quarterly, 1 & 4 Quarterly (i & iv) Or a lion rampant azure armed and langued gules PERCY, (ii & iii) Gules three lucies haurient argent LUCY, 2 & 3 Azure five fusils conjoined in fess or PERCY (ANCIENT). *Legend*: HUGH D^{E}. OF NORTHUMBERLAND

2c

Crest: Out of a ducal coronet gules, a plume of five ostrich feathers argent, banded with a line the visible length in the form of a chevron azure. Below: The coronet of a duke. *Arms*: Quarterly of six; 1 Argent six cross-crosslets fitchy sable three, two and one, on a chief azure two mullets or pierced gules CLINTON, 2 Argent a fess and in dexter chief a mullet gules ODYNGESELES, 3 Gules three eagles displayed or LIMSEY, 4 Quarterly or and gules SAY for CLINTON, 5 Gules a cross within a bordure conjoined or EUDO, 6 Quarterly or and gules an escarbuncle sable MANDEVILLE. *Legend*: HENRY D^{E}. OF NEWCASTLE.

2d

Crest: On a coronet composed alternately of crosses formy and fleurs de lis or the cap gules turned up ermine, a lion statant guardant crowned or, gorged with a label of three points argent, the centre point charged with a cross gules and the outer points with an anchor azure. Below: A coronet as in the crest. *Arms*: The Royal Arms of King George III with a label of three points as in the crest. *Legend*: P^{R}. W^{M}. HENRY OF BRUNS^{K}. LUNEN^{G}.

Note: Later Duke of Clarence and subsequently King William IV.

3a

Crest: On a coronet composed alternately of crosses formy and fleurs de lis or the cap gules turned up ermine, a lion statant guardant crowned or, gorged with a label of five points argent, the centre point charged with a cross gules and the others with fleurs de lis azure. Below: A coronet as in the crest. *Arms*: The Royal Arms of King George III as above without the crown of Charlemagne in the fourth quarter, differenced by a label as in the crest. *Legend*: HENRY FRED^{K}. D^{E}. OF CUMBERLAND.

3b

Above: On a coronet composed alternately of crosses formy and fleurs de lis or a cap gules turned up ermine, a lion statant guardant crowned or, gorged with a label of five points argent, the centre point charged with a fleur de lis azure and the others with a cross gules. Below: A coronet as in the crest. *Arms*: The Royal Arms of King George III as above differenced by a label as in the crest. *Legend*: WILL^{M}. HENRY D^{E}. OF GLOUCESTER.

3c

Crest: Out of a ducal coronet or, a horse courant argent in front of a column gules ensigned by a coronet or from which issues a peacock's tail proper charged with a mullet of six points or, all between two sickles argent handled gules with peacocks feathers proper attached to the outer edges. Below: The coronet of a duke. *Arms*: Quarterly of twelve, 1 Or semy of hearts gules a lion rampant azure LUNE(N)BURG, 2 Gules two lions passant guardant or BRUNSWICK, 3 Azure a lion rampant argent crowned or EBERSTEIN, 4 Gules a lion rampant or within a bordure company argent and azure HOMBURG, 5 Or a lion rampant gules DIEPHOLZ LION, 6 Gules a lion rampant or LAUTERBURG LION, 7 Per fess: in chief, Or two bear's paws erect sable HOYA; in base, Gyronny argent and azure OLD BRUCKHAUSEN, 8 Azure an eagle displayed argent, langued, beaked and membered gules DIEPHOLZ EAGLE, 9 Per fess: in chief, Checky argent and gules HOHNSTEIN; in base, Barry of six or and gules NEW BRUCKHAUSEN, 10 Argent a stag's attire in bend gules REGENSTEIN, 11 Argent a stag trippant sable KLETTENBURG, 12 Argent a stag's attire in bend sinister sable BLANKENBURG. *Legend*: CHARLES P^{R}. & D^{E} OF BRUNSWICK.

3d

The crest, coronet and arms as 3c. *Legend*: FERDINAND D^{E}. OF BRUNSWICK.

Tracery Quatrefoils

A: A lion couchant to the sinister and reguardant crowned or. Above, in gold against a blue field, the letter 'G' and below the figures '17'.

B: Within the Garter and ensigned by an imperial arched crown, the Royal Arms of King George III (before 1801) viz.: Quarterly, 1 Gules three lions passant guardant or ENGLAND, impaling Or within a double tressure flory counter flory (omitted from the dexter side) a lion rampant gules langued azure SCOTLAND, 2 Azure three fleurs de lis or FRANCE, 3 Azure a harp with a female bust or, stringed argent IRELAND, 4 Tierced in pairle reversed, (i) Gules two lions passant guardant in pale or BRUNSWICK, (ii) Or semy of hearts gules a lion rampant azure LUNEBERG, (iii) Gules a horse courant argent WESTPHALIA (HANOVER); overall an inescutcheon Gules the crown of Charlemagne or (the badge of the Arch Treasurer of the Holy Roman Empire). In the lower part of the quatrefoil is the upper part of a figure of St George in armour, wearing a red cloak.

C: A unicorn couchant to the dexter and regardant argent, armed, crined and unguled or gorged and with a chain reflexed over the back or. Above in gold against a blue field the letter 'R' and below the figures '82'.

SIII

All the lights have a background of quarries bearing alternately the letters S and G in gold. Unless otherwise stated, the helmets are of silver with gold bars and are turned to the dexter. All arms are within the Garter.
Above each shield is, where applicable, a coronet of rank.

1a

Crest: On a wreath argent and sable, an elephant's head erased argent tusked or. *Mantling*: Gules doubled argent. The coronet of an earl. *Arms*: Quarterly, 1 & 4 Sable on a fess argent, between three elephant's heads erased argent tusked or, three mullets sable PRATT, 2 & 3 Sable a chevron between three spear heads argent JEFFRYS. *Legend*: John Earl Camden.

1b

Crest: On a wreath argent and sable, a unicorn's head erased argent, armed and crined or. *Mantling*: Vert doubled argent. The coronet of a duke. *Arms*: Quarterly, 1 & 4 Vert on a chevron between three unicorn's heads erased argent, armed and crined or, three mullets sable KER, 2 & 3 Gules three mascles or WEAPONT. *Legend*: John D. of Roxburgh.

1c

Crest: On a chapeau gules turned up ermine, a peacock in its pride proper. *Mantling*: Azure doubled or. The coronet of a duke. *Arms*: Or two bars azure a chief quarterly 1 & 4 azure two fleurs de lis or, 2 & 3 gules a lion passant guardant or MANNERS, being the Augmentation granted by King Henry VIII in 1525 to commemorate descent from a sister of King Edward IV. *Legend*: John Hen: D: of Rutland.

1d

Crest: On a wreath argent and azure, a lion's head erased proper, langued and collared gules, upon the collar a bezant. *Mantling*: Azure doubled argent. The coronet of an earl. *Arms*: Argent on a saltire azure a bezant YORKE. *Legend*: Philip Yorke E: of Hardwicke.

2a

Crest: On a wreath or and gules, a stag trippant proper, attired and unguled or. *Mantling*: Gules doubled or. The coronet of a duke. *Arms*: Quarterly, 1 & 4 Quarterly France Modern and England , 2 Scotland, 3 Ireland; overall a baton sinister argent SCOTT, Duke of Monmouth. *Legend*: Henry D: of Buccleugh [*sic*].

2b

Crest: Out of a ducal coronet or two arms counter embowed vested gules gauntlets or, each holding an ostrich feather argent. *Mantling*: Azure doubled argent. The coronet of a duke. *Arms*: Azure a cross moline argent BENTINCK. *Legend*: W: Hen^{y}: D: of Portland.

2c

Crest: Out of a ducal coronet or a panache of five ostrich feathers azure. *Mantling*: Sable doubled or. The coronet of an earl. *Arms*: Or a fess between three wolve's heads couped sable HOWE. *Legend*: Richard Earl Howe.

2d

Crest: Out of a ducal coronet or a griffin's head argent, beaked or and gorged with a collar gemel gules between two wings elevated and displayed argent. *Mantling*: Gules doubled argent. The coronet of an earl. *Arms*: Quarterly argent and gules, in the second and third quarters a fret or, overall on a bend sable three escallops argent SPENCER. *Legend*: Geo. John E: Spencer.

3a

Crest: On a wreath argent and azure, a stork proper resting its dexter claw upon an anchor or. *Mantling*: Azure doubled argent. The coronet of an earl. *Arms*: Sable a fess checky argent and azure between three bezants PITT. *Legend*: John E: of Chatham.

3b

Crest: On a wreath argent and azure, eight arrows in saltire or, heads in base, barbed and flighted argent, banded gules, buckled and garnished or and ensigned by a morion proper. *Mantling*: Azure doubled argent. The coronet of a marquess. *Arms*: Barry of ten argent and azure overall six escutcheons three, two and one sable, each charged with a lion rampant argent. A crescent sable for difference CECIL. *Legend*: James M: of Salisbury.

3c

Crest: Out of a ducal coronet or a bull's head argent armed or charged with a rose gules. *Mantling*: Azure doubled or. The coronet of an earl. *Arms*: Azure three dexter gauntlets or FANE. *Legend*: John E: of Westmoreland [*sic*].

3d

Crest: On a chapeau gules turned up ermine, a lion statant guardant or gorged with a ducal coronet argent. *Mantling*: Gules doubled argent. The coronet of an earl. *Arms*: Gules on a bend between six cross-crosslets fitchy argent an escutcheon or charged with a demi lion rampant pierced through the mouth with an arrow within a double tressure flory counter flory gules, above the escutcheon a mullet sable for difference HOWARD, with the Augmentation for the battle of Flodden, 1513. *Legend*: Fred^{k}: E: of Carlisle.

Tracery Quatrefoils

A: A gold background, within the Garter, a Tudor rose proper. In the upper leaf the letter 'S' in red.
B: Against a background of gold rays a shield within the Garter bearing Argent a cross gules.
C: As left but with the letter 'G'.

SIV

Quatrefoils, quarries, helmets and Garters as window SIII.

1a

Crest: On a wreath or and gules, a dragon statant or. *Mantling*: Gules doubled or. The coronet of a viscount. *Arms*: Quarterly, 1 & 4 Or a bend checky argent and azure between two lions rampant gules STEWART, 2 & 3 Gules a saltire argent NEVILL. The first quarter is differenced with a label of three points sable. *Legend*: Robt: Visc: Castlereagh.

1b

A gold helmet affronty ensigned by an arched gold crown with white and silver pearls and a red cap. *Mantling*: Gules doubled or. *Arms*: Quarterly, 1 & 4 Gules a castle or CASTILE, 2 & 3 Argent a lion rampant purpure LEON. In base Argent a pomegranate proper GRANADA. Overall, on a circular cartouche Azure three fleurs de lis or ROYAL ARMS of the BOURBON Kings of France. *Legend*: Ferd: King of Spain.

1c

A gold helmet affronty ensigned by an arched gold crown with white pearls. *Mantling*: Azure doubled or. *Arms*: Quarterly, 1 & 4 Gules a lion rampant or holding in its dexter paw a Roman sword, the hilt or, the blade argent and in its sinister paw a bundle of arrows also argent, 2 & 3 Quarterly, (i & iv) Gules a bend or CHALONS, (ii & iii) Argent a bugle horn stringed azure ORANGE; overall an escutcheon checky of nine pieces or and azure GENEVA. Overall an escutcheon, Azure billetty a lion rampant or NASSAU. *Legend*: W^{m}: P^{r}: of the Netherlands.

Note: In the nave (clerestory window NXVII, 2c) the same arms are displayed, albeit incorrectly, for William III, King of the Netherlands where the lion in the first quarter is crowned. The first quarter displays the arms used by Louis Bonaparte, King of Holland, which were adopted and later adapted by future Orange Kings of the Netherlands.

1d

A gold helmet affronty ensigned by the crest of Saxe Cobourg, viz. Out of a coronet or a pyramidal chapeau barry of ten or and sable a crown of rue bendwise vert ensigned by a coronet or, from which arises a panache of peacocks' feathers proper. *Mantling*: Sable doubled or. *Arms*: Quarterly, 1 & 4 the Hanoverian Royal Arms, (i & iv) England, (ii) Scotland, (iii) Ireland, an inescutcheon tierced in pairle reversed, Gules two lions passant guardant or BRUNSWICK, Or semy of hearts gules a lion rampant azure LUNEBURG, Gules a horse courant argent WESTPHALIA (HANOVER), overall a label of five points argent, the centre point charged with a rose gules seeded or, 2 & 3 Quarterly of seventeen, (i) Azure a lion rampant barry argent and gules LANDGRAVE OF THURINGIA, (ii) Gules an escarbuncle or having at the centre an escutcheon argent CLEVES, (iii) Or a lion rampant sable MEISSEN, (iv) Or a lion rampant sable JULICH, (v) Argent a lion rampant gules crowned azure BERG, (vi) Argent an eagle displayed gules PALATINATE OF SAXONY, (vii) Sable an eagle displayed argent PALATINATE OF THURINGIA, (viii) Or semy of hearts gules a lion rampant crowned sable ORLAMUNDE, (ix) Argent three bars azure EISENBURG, (x) Azure a lion rampant per fess or and argent TONNA GLEICHEN, (xi) Argent a rose gules ALTENBURG, (xii) Gules plain SOVEREIGN RIGHTS, (xiii) Argent three beetle's pincers gules ENGERN, (xiv) Or a fess checky gules and argent MARCK, (xv) Gules a pillar argent crowned or ROENHILD, (xvi) Or on a mount vert a cock sable HENNENBERG, (xvii) Argent three chevrons gules RAVENSBERG. Overall an escutcheon Barry of ten or and sable a crown of rue bendwise vert SAXONY. *Legend*: F. Leop^{d}: P. of Saxe Cobourg.

Note: The husband of Princess Charlotte, daughter of the Prince Regent (afterwards King George IV), and later King of the Belgians. The arms were assigned in 1818 after the death of his wife, who bore a similar label but of three points.

2a

A gold helmet affronty ensigned by a gold arched crown with a blue cap. *Mantling*: Azure doubled or. *Arms*: Azure three fleurs de lis or. *Legend*: Louis XVIII King of France.

2b

A gold helmet affronty ensigned by a gold arched crown. *Mantling*: Sable doubled argent. *Arms*: Argent an eagle displayed sable crowned or, langued gules, beaked and membered or, on each wing a kleestengel or, holding in the dexter claw a sceptre and in the sinister an orb, both or. On the breast of the eagle the cypher F R ensigned by a crown or PRUSSIA. *Legend*: Fred[k]: W[m]: K. of Prussia.

Note: The charge and term kleestengel is unknown in British heraldry. The literal translation is 'clover stalk' and they are usually shown as the stylized version of the breast and wing bone of an eagle.

2c

A gold helmet affronty ensigned by a mitre (or house crown) in gold and red studded with pearls. *Mantling*: Sable doubled or. *Arms*: Or a double headed eagle displayed sable, crowned and armed or, beaked and langued gules, holding in the dexter claw a sword and a sceptre, the sword blade argent, the hilt and sceptre or and in the dexter claw an orb or. The eagle is charged upon the breast with an escutcheon, Gules a fess argent AUSTRIA. *Legend*: Francis Emp: of Austria.

2d

Crest: On a wreath argent and azure, a seahorse assurgent or crined azure supporting with the dexter foot a cross formy gules. *Mantling*: Azure doubled argent. The coronet of an earl. *Arms*: Azure on a fess wavy argent a cross formy gules, in chief two estoiles or on a chief wavy argent a cormorant sable holding in its beak a branch of seaweed inverted vert JENKINSON. *Legend*: Robert E: of Liverpool.

3a

Crest: Out of a ducal coronet or, a bull's head erased sable, armed and langued or. *Mantling*: Sable doubled argent. The coronet of an earl. *Arms*: Quarterly, 1 & 4 Argent a maunch sable HASTINGS, 2 & 3 Argent a fess between three pheons sable RAWDON. *Legend*: Francis Earl Moira.

Note: Later Marquess of Hastings.

3b

Crest: Out of a ducal coronet gules a plume of five ostrich feathers argent banded with a line the visible length in the form of a chevron azure. *Mantling*: Azure doubled argent. The coronet of a duke. *Arms*: Quarterly, 1 & 4 Argent six cross-crosslets fitchy sable three, two and one, on a chief azure two mullets or pierced gules CLINTON, 2 & 3 Quarterly (i & iv) Azure three pelicans vulning themselves argent PELHAM, (ii & iii) Gules two demi belts in pale argent buckles in chief or. *Legend*: Hen: P: D: of Newcastle.

Note: The demi belts were assumed by the Pelham family in the 17th century to commemorate the alleged capture of King John of France at the Battle of Poitiers. Unfortunately there is no firm authority for this legend but there is a suggestion that the buckle, which had been used as a badge by the Pelhams for many years, may have been assumed following the privilege of carrying a sword before King Henry IV granted to

Sir John Pelham in 1399 (Pat. 1 Hen IV p2 m37) (CPR 1399–1401, p. 45). See generally L.F. Salzman, 'Early History of Pelham', *Sussex Arch. Coll.*, LXIX, 53–70.

3c

Crest: Out of a ducal coronet or, a demi lion rampant gules holding a spear erect proper and thereon flowing a swallow tailed pennon argent, charged in the hoist with a cross gules. *Mantling*: Gules doubled argent. The coronet of a marquess. *Arms*: Quarterly, 1 & 4 Gules a cross argent between twenty plates, five in each quarter in saltire WELLESLEY, 2 & 3 Or a lion rampant gules, gorged with a ducal coronet or COWLEY. In chief an escutcheon charged with the crosses of St George, St Andrew and St Patrick being the union badge of the United Kingdom. (Augmentation granted to Arthur Wellesley, later created Duke of Wellington after the victories in Spain in 1812). *Legend*: Arthr: M: of Wellington.

3d

A gold helmet affronty ensigned by a mitre crown of red, blue and gold studded with pearls. *Mantling*: Sable doubled or. *Arms*: Or a double headed eagle displayed sable, crowned, beaked and membered or, holding in the dexter claw a sceptre and in the sinister claw an orb, both or, charged upon the breast with an escutcheon bearing the arms of Moscow, viz. Gules the mounted figure of St George slaying the dragon all proper. *Legend*: Alexr: Emp: of Russia.

SV

Quarries, helmets and Garters as window SIII.

1a

Crest: On a wreath argent and gules, a scaling ladder in bend sinister or, points and hooks sable. *Mantling*: Gules doubled argent. The coronet of an earl. *Arms*: Quarterly, 1 & 4 Gules a lion rampant within a bordure engrailed argent, in dexter chief a mullet or for difference GREY, 2 & 3 Barry of six argent and azure a bend gules, charged in chief with a bezant GREY of NORTON. *Legend*: Charles: Earl Grey.

1b

A gold helmet affronty ensigned by an arched crown with a blue cap. *Mantling*: Sable doubled or. *Arms*: Quarterly of twelve; 1 Or semy of hearts gules, a lion rampant azure LUNEBURG, 2 Gules two lions passant guardant or BRUNSWICK, 3 Azure a lion rampant argent crowned or EBERSTEIN, 4 Gules a lion rampant or within a bordure company argent and azure HOMBURG, 5 Or a lion rampant gules crowned azure DIEPHOLZ LION, 6 Per fess; in chief Gules a lion rampant or LAUTERBURG LION, in base Barry or and gules LAUTERBURG, 7 Per fess; in chief Or two bear's paws erect sable HOYA, in base, Gyronny argent and azure OLD BRUCKHAUSEN, 8 Azure an eagle displayed argent DIEPHOLZ EAGLE, 9 Checky argent and gules HOHNSTEIN, 10 Argent a stag's attire in bend gules REGENSTEIN, 11 Argent a stag trippant sable KLETTENBURG, 12 Argent a stag's attire in bend sinister sable BLANKENBURG. *Legend*: Aug: D. of Brunswick. Wolf.

1c

Crest: On a chapeau gules turned up ermine, a lion statant guardant or gorged with a ducal coronet argent. *Mantling*: Gules doubled argent. The coronet of a duke. *Arms*: Gules on a bend between six cross-crosslets fitchy argent an escutcheon or charged with a demi lion pierced through the mouth with an arrow within a double tressure flory counter flory gules HOWARD, with the Augmentation for the battle of Flodden 1513. *Legend*: Bernard D. of Norfolk.

1d

Crest: On a chapeau gules turned up ermine, a lion statant guardant or ducally crowned azure and gorged with a collar counter-compony ermine and azure. The coronet of a duke. *Arms*: The Royal Arms of King Charles II, viz. Quarterly, 1 & 4 Quarterly France Modern and England, 2 Scotland, 3 Ireland, overall a baton sinister compony of six pieces azure and ermine. *Legend*: George D. of Grafton.

Note: The baton sinister is erroneous. The Grafton arms granted to Henry Fitzroy, second illegitimate son of King Charles II by Barbara Villiers, were debruised by a baton sinister compony azure and argent and are so depicted on the stall plate of this duke. The arms depicted in the window are those of George Fitzroy, Duke of Northumberland, Barbara Villiers' third son who died without issue in 1716.

2a

Crest: Out of a ducal coronet or an ash tree proper. *Mantling*: Gules doubled argent. The coronet of an earl. *Arms*: Gules a fess between six mullets argent ASHBURNHAM. *Legend*: Geo: E. of Ashburnham.

2b

A gold helmet affronty ensigned by the crest of SAXONY, viz. Out of a coronet or a pyramidal chapeau barry of ten or and sable a crown of rue bendwise vert, ensigned by a gold coronet from which arises a panache of peacocks' feathers proper. *Mantling*: Sable doubled or. *Arms*: Quarterly of seventeen; 1 Azure a lion rampant barry argent and gules crowned argent LANDGRAVE OF THURINGIA, 2 Gules an escarbuncle or charged at the centre with an escutcheon argent CLEVES, 3 Or a lion rampant sable MEISSEN, 4 Or a lion rampant sable JULICH, 5 Argent a lion rampant gules crowned azure BERG, 6 Sable an eagle displayed or PALATINATE OF THURINGIA, 7 Argent an eagle displayed gules BRANDENBURG, 8 Or semy of hearts gules a lion rampant sable crowned gules ORLAMUNDE, 9 Argent three bars azure EISENBERG, 10 Azure a lion rampant per fess or and argent TONNA IN GLEICHEN, 11 Argent a rose gules ALTENBURG, 12 Gules plain SOVEREIGN RIGHTS, 13 Argent three beetle's pincers gules ENGERN, 14 Or a fess checky argent and gules MARCK, 15 Gules a pillar argent crowned or ROENHILD, 16 Or on a mount vert a cock sable HENNENBERG, 17 Argent three chevrons gules RAVENSBERG. Overall an escutcheon, Barry of ten or and sable a crown of rue bendwise vert SAXONY. *Legend*: Bern[d]: D. of Saxe Meinengen [*sic*].

2c

A gold helmet affronty ensigned by an arched crown without a cap. *Mantling*: Sable doubled or. Arms: Or three stag's attires fesswise in pale, points to the sinister sable WÜRTTEMBERG, impaling Or three lions passant in pale sable, the dexter forepaws gules SWABIA. *Legend*: Will: K. of Wirtemberg [*sic*].

2d

Crest: On a wreath argent and gules, a goat statant argent, armed, crined and unguled or. *Mantling*: Gules doubled argent. The coronet of a duke. *Arms*: Argent a lion rampant gules on a chief sable three escallops argent RUSSELL. *Legend*: John: D. of Bedford.

3a

Crest: On a wreath or and azure, an heraldic tyger statant or, crined sable langued gules. *Mantling*: Azure doubled or. The coronet of a duke. *Arms*: Quarterly ermine and azure a cross or OSBORNE. *Legend*: Geo: Wm: D. of Leeds.

3b

Crest: On a wreath argent and sable, a serpent nowed proper. *Mantling*: Sable doubled argent. The coronet of a duke. *Arms*: Sable three buck's heads caboshed argent CAVENDISH. *Legend*: Wm: D. of Devonshire.

3c

Crest: On a wreath argent and azure, a garb or supported by two lions rampant, the dexter argent, the sinister azure. *Mantling*: Azure doubled argent. The coronet of a marquess. *Arms*: Barry of ten argent and azure, six escutcheons sable three, two and one each charged with a lion rampant argent CECIL. *Legend*: Brownlow M. of Exeter.

3d

Crest: On a chapeau gules turned up ermine, a lion statant guardant or crowned gules gorged with a collar company argent and gules each piece argent charged with a rose gules seeded or barbed vert. *Mantling*: Gules doubled argent. The coronet of a duke. *Arms*: Quarterly, 1 & 4 Quarterly France Modern and England, 2 Scotland, 3 Ireland, overall an escutcheon gules three buckles or DUKEDOM OF AUBIGNY, all within a bordure company argent and gules each piece argent charged with a rose gules barbed and seeded proper. *Legend*: Chas: D: of Richmond.

Tracery Quatrefoils

A: Against a gold background within the Garter and ensigned by the letter V in red, a Tudor rose barbed and seeded proper
B: Against a green background within the Garter and ensigned by an imperial arched crown with a red cap, the Royal Arms post 1837, viz. Quarterly, 1 & 4 England, 2 Scotland, 3 Ireland. To the dexter the figures in silver 18 and to the sinister 41.
C: As A but ensigned by the letter R.

SVI

Quarries, helmets and Garters as window SIII.

1a

Crest: On a chapeau gules turned up ermine a lion passant guardant or gorged with a collar company ermine and azure. *Mantling*: Azure doubled or. *Arms*: Quarterly, 1 & 4 Azure three sinister gauntlets or VANE, 2 & 3 the Royal Arms of King Charles II, viz. Quarterly, (i & iv) Quarterly France Modern and England, (ii) Scotland, (iii) Ireland, overall a baton sinister ermine FITZROY. (See SVIII, 2d). *Legend*: Wm Duke of Cleveland.

1b

A gold helmet affronty ensigned by a gold arched crown. *Mantling*: Azure doubled or. *Arms*: Azure three fleurs de lis or. *Legend*: L: Philippe K. of the French.

1c

A gold helmet affronty ensigned by a gold crown. *Mantling*: Sable doubled or. *Arms*: Quarterly of twenty three; 1 Or a lion rampant sable JULICH, 2 Gules an escarbuncle or charged in the centre with an escutcheon argent CLEVES, 3 Argent a lion rampant gules crowned azure BERG, 4 Gules three hearts or BREHNA, 5 Gules a horse forcene argent WESTPHALIA, 6 Sable a lion rampant or COBURG, 7 Azure a lion rampant barry argent and gules crowned argent LANDGRAVE of THURINGIA, 8 Or a lion rampant sable MEISSEN, 9 Per pale: Dexter; Azure a column argent crowned or ROENHILD, Sinister; Or on a mount vert a cock sable or HENNENBURG, 10 Azure a lion rampant crowned or LICHTEMBERG, 11 Azure an eagle displayed crowned or PALATINATE of SAXONY, 12 Sable an eagle displayed or PALATINATE of THURINGIA, 13 Or two pales azure LANDSBERG, 14 Argent three beetle's pincers gules ENGERN, 15 Or semy of hearts gules, a lion rampant azure crowned gules ORLAMUNDE, 16 Azure a lion rampant per fess or and argent PLEISSEN, 17 Argent a rose gules ALTENBURG, 18 Argent three bars azure EISENBERG, 19 Or a fess checky argent and gules MARCK, 20 Argent three chevrons gules RAVENSBERG, 21 Gules plain SOVEREIGN RIGHTS, 22 Azure a lion rampant argent TONNA, 23 Or a bend argent, in chief a raven proper holding in its beak a ring or RAVENSTEIN. Overall an escutcheon, Barry of ten or and sable a crown of rue bendwise vert SAXONY. *Legend*: Ernest Duke of Saxe Coburg Gotha.

Note: The field of Roenhild is usually gules.

1d

Crest: On a chapeau gules turned up ermine, a wyvern or. *Mantling*: Azure doubled argent. The coronet of an earl. *Arms*: Barry of six argent and azure GREY. *Legend*: Philip Earl de Grey.

Note: Earl de Grey was born Thomas Robinson, son of Thomas Robinson, Baron Grantham. He first took the name of Weddell by Royal Licence 7 May 1803. In 1833 he succeeded his aunt as Earl de Grey of Wrest and changed his name to de Grey by Royal Licence 23 June 1833.

2a

A gold helmet affronty ensigned by a gold arched crown. *Mantling*: Sable doubled or. *Arms*: Barry of ten or and sable a crown of rue bendwise vert SAXONY. *Legend*: Fred^{k}: K: of Saxony.

2b

Crest: On a wreath argent and azure, a portcullis chained or. *Mantling*: Azure doubled argent. The coronet of a duke. *Arms*: Quarterly France Modern and England all within a bordure company argent and azure. BEAUFORT for SOMERSET. *Legend*: Henry D: of Beaufort.

2c

Crest: On a wreath argent and vert, a garb vert. *Mantling*: Vert doubled argent. The coronet of a duke. *Arms*: Quarterly of six; 1 & 6 Vert on a cross argent five torteaux GRENVILLE, 2 Quarterly, (i & iv) Or an eagle displayed sable LEOFRIC, (ii & iii) Argent two bars sable each charged with three martlets or TEMPLE, 3 Ermine two bars gules NUGENT, 4 Argent on a cross sable a leopard's face or BRYDGES, 5 Argent a pile gules CHANDOS. *Legend*: Rich[d]. D. of Buckingham.

Note: The arms of Chandos are usually Or a pile gules.

2d

Crest: On a wreath argent and azure, eight arrows in saltire or, heads in base barbed and flighted argent, banded gules buckled and garnished or and ensigned by a morion proper. *Mantling*: Azure doubled argent. The coronet of a marquess. *Arms*: Barry of ten argent and azure overall six escutcheons three, two and one sable each charged with a lion rampant argent, a crescent sable for difference, CECIL. *Legend*: James M. of Salisbury.

3a

Crest: On a wreath argent and sable, a wolf passant argent collared and chained or. *Mantling*: Gules doubled argent. The coronet of a duke. *Arms*: Quarterly, 1 & 4 Barry of eight argent and gules a cross flory sable GOWER, 2 Azure three laurel leaves or LEVESON, 3 Gules three mullets or within a bordure also or charged with a double tressure flory counter flory gules SUTHERLAND. *Legend*: Geo: D: of Sutherland.

3b

Crest: On a wreath or and azure, a talbot statant or. *Mantling*: Azure doubled or. The coronet of a marquess. *Arms*: Quarterly, 1 & 4 Azure a portcullis chained or, on a chief also or between two Tudor roses proper a pale azure charged with a cross flory between five martlets or (Augmentation of the Marquess of Westminster by Royal Licence 5 December 1831), 2 & 3 Azure a garb or GROSVENOR. *Legend*: Rob[t]: M: of Westminster.

3c

Crest: The Royal Crest differenced by a label of three points argent, between two ostrich feathers argent each with a scroll in base one bearing the word "ich" the other bearing the word "dien". A gold helmet affronty ensigned by a single arched coronet of crosses formy and fleurs de lis. *Mantling*: Gules doubled or. *Arms*: The Royal Arms post 1837, viz. Quarterly, 1 & 4 England, 2 Scotland, 3 Ireland, overall an escutcheon Barry of ten or and sable a crown of rue bendwise vert SAXONY, the whole differenced by a label of three points argent. *Legend*: Albert Pr: of Wales [later King Edward VII].

3d

A gold helmet affronty ensigned by a gold arched crown. *Mantling*: Sable doubled argent. *Arms*: Argent an eagle displayed sable, crowned, beaked and membered or, on each wing a kleestengel or, holding in the dexter claw a sceptre and in the sinister an orb, both or. On the breast of the eagle the cypher FR ensigned by a crown, all gold PRUSSIA. *Legend*: Fred[k]: W[m]: K: of Prussia.

Note: For kleestengel see SIV 2b.

Tracery Quatrefoils

A: Against a gold background within the Garter a Tudor rose barbed and seeded proper ensigned by the letter 'S' in red.
B: Within the Garter and surrounded by gold rays, the coat Argent a cross gules.
C: As A but ensigned by the letter 'G'.

SVII

Quarries, helmets and Garters as window SIII. Quatrefoils as window SVI.

1a

A plume of feathers argent and or, banded purpure and vert arising from a red jewel surmounted by a crescent and a star in silver surrounded by silver rays. *Arms*: Within a wreath of gold leaves, Gules the Tughra argent. The whole within ribbons vert fringed or. *Legend*: Abdul Medjeh Khan.

Note: For details of the Tughra see notes to NXVI, 1b.

1b

Crest: On a wreath argent and gules, a wolf passant argent collared and lined or. *Mantling*: Gules doubled argent. The coronet of an earl. *Arms*: Quarterly, 1 & 4 Barry of eight argent and gules a cross flory sable GOWER, 2 Azure three laurel leaves or LEVESON, 3 Gules three clarions or GRANVILLE, at fess point a crescent or. *Legend*: Granville Earl Granville.

1c

Crest: On a wreath or and azure, a talbot statant or. *Mantling*: Azure doubled or. The coronet of a marquess. *Arms*: Quarterly, 1 & 4 Azure a portcullis chained or on a chief also or between two Tudor roses proper a pale azure charged with a cross flory between five martlets or (Augmentation of the Marquess of Westminster by Royal Licence 5 December 1831), 2 & 3 Azure a garb or GROSVENOR. *Legend*: Ric^{d}. M. of Westminster.

1d

A gold helmet affronty, out of a gold coronet an eagle displayed sable crowned or, on each wing a kleestengel or, charged on the breast with the cypher FR or. *Mantling*: Sable doubled argent. *Arms*: Argent an eagle as in the crest, holding in the dexter claw a sceptre and in the sinister claw an orb both or, all within a bordure company argent and sable PRUSSIA. *Legend*: Fre^{d}. W^{m}. Pr. of Prussia.

Note: The Crown Prince of Prussia, who married the Princess Royal, succeeded to the Imperial Crown of Germany as Kaiser Frederick III. He was the father of Kaiser Wilhelm II. For kleestengel see SIV 2b.

2a

A gold helmet affronty ensigned by an arched crown decorated with imperial eagles or. *Mantling*: Dexter: Azure doubled argent; Sinister: Gules doubled argent. *Arms*: Azure a Roman eagle displayed, head to the sinister, the talons grasping a thunderbolt fesswise or NAPOLEONIC FRANCE. *Legend*: Napoleon III Emperor.

Note: The crown depicted is that especially made for Emperor Napoleon III who was, however, never crowned. It was broken up by order of the Chamber of Deputies in 1886.

2b

A gold helmet affronty ensigned by an arched crown or. *Mantling*: Dexter: Vert doubled argent; Sinister: Gules doubled argent. *Arms*: Gules a cross argent SAVOY. *Legend*: V.E: K^{g} .of Sardinia.

2c

Crest: On a wreath argent and azure, an heraldic tyger statant argent, langued gules, armed crined and tufted or. *Mantling*: Azure doubled argent. The coronet of an earl. *Arms*: Azure a bend engrailed argent plain cotised or FORTESCUE. *Legend*: Hugh E: Fortescue.

2d

Crest: On a wreath or and sable, a talbot sejant sable collared or. *Mantling*: Sable doubled or. The coronet of a viscount. *Arms*: Quarterly, 1 & 4 Or an eagle displayed sable for LEOFRIC, EARL OF MERCIA, 2 & 3 Argent two bars sable each charged with three martlets or TEMPLE. *Legend*: H.I: V^{t} Palmerston.

Note: The first quarter is fictitious. It has been suggested that the second is alluding to the 'temple haunting martlets' of Psalm 84, 3 & 4. The eagle is usually gules.

3a

Crest: On a wreath or and azure, a dexter cubit arm in armour holding a sword bend sinisterwise proper hilt and pommel or. *Mantling*: Azure doubled or. The coronet of a marquess. *Arms*: Quarterly, 1 & 4 Azure three sinister gauntlets or in chief a trefoil slipped or VANE, 2 & 3 Or a bend company counter company argent and azure between two lions rampant gules STEWART. *Legend*: Ch: W^{m}. M: of Londonderry.

3b

Crest: On a chapeau gules turned up ermine, a lion rampant gules supporting an arrow, head downwards or, tipped and flighted argent. *Mantling*: Gules doubled argent. The coronet of an earl. *Arms*: Argent a lion rampant gules between three pheons sable EGERTON. *Legend*: Francis E: of Ellesmere.

3c

Crest: On a chapeau gules turned up ermine a lion statant guardant or gorged with a ducal coronet argent. *Mantling*: Gules doubled argent. The coronet of an earl. *Arms*: Gules on a bend between six cross-crosslets fitchy argent an escutcheon or charged with a demi lion rampant pierced through the mouth with an arrow within a double tressure flory counter flory gules; above the escutcheon a mullet sable for difference HOWARD with the augmentation for the battle of Flodden, 1513. *Legend*: Geo: W^{m}: Fk: E: of Carlisle.

3d

Crest: On a wreath or and azure, two naked arms drawing a bow with an arrow proper. *Mantling*: Azure doubled or. The coronet of an earl. *Arms*: Quarterly, 1 & 4 Azure three boar's heads couped or, armed argent within a double tressure flory on the outer edge or GORDON, 2 & 3 Quarterly, (i & iv) Gules three cinquefoils ermine pierced of the field HAMILTON, (ii & iii) Argent a lymphad sails furled sable EARLS of ARRAN. *Legend*: G^eo^: Ham^ton^: Go^n^: E: of Aberdeen.

Note: The tressure in the first and fourth quarters should be charged alternately with thistles, roses, and fleurs de lis or. The second and third quarters (themselves quartered) should be surrounded by a bordure sable.

SVIII

Quarries, helmets and Garters as window SIII.

1a

A gold helmet affronty ensigned by an arched crown with a red cap. *Mantling*: Gules doubled argent. *Arms*: Argent five escutcheons in cross azure each charged with five plates in saltire, all within a bordure gules charged with seven castles or PORTUGAL. *Legend*: Louis King of Portugal.

1b

A gold helmet affronty ensigned by an arched crown with a red cap. *Mantling*: Gules doubled argent. *Arms*: A cross formy throughout argent fimbriated gules DANNEBORG, between, 1 Or semy of hearts gules three lions passant in pale azure crowned or DENMARK, 2 Or two lions passant in pale azure SCHLESWIG, 3 Per fess: in chief, Azure three crowns or SWEDEN; in base, per pale, dexter, Gules a stock fish erect argent crowned or ICELAND, sinister, per fess, in chief, Azure a ram argent FAROES, in base, Azure a polar bear sejant rampant argent GREENLAND, 4 Per fess: in chief, Or ten hearts gules 4, 4 and 2 in chief a lion passant azure KINGDOM of the GOTHS; in base, Gules a wyvern or KINGDOM of the VANDALS. On an escutcheon, Quarterly, 1 Gules an escutcheon per fess argent and gules between three demi-nettle leaves and as many passion nails in pairle argent HOLSTEIN, 2 Gules a swan argent, beaked, membered and ducally gorged or STORMARN, 3 Gules a knight in armour mounted upon a horse and holding a sword argent and a shield or DITMARSKEN, 4 Gules a horse's head couped or LAUENBURG. Overall an escutcheon per pale, dexter, Or two bars gules OLDENBURG, sinister, Azure a cross formy or DELMENHORST. *Legend*: Christian King of Denmark.

1c

A gold helmet affronty ensigned by an arched crown or coronet with a red cap. *Mantling*: Azure doubled argent. *Arms*: Azure a lion rampant queue fourchy barry argent and gules crowned or holding in the dexter paw a sword erect argent HESSE. *Legend*: Louis III Duke of Hesse.

1d

Crest: On a wreath argent and gules, a lion's jamb erect and erased or, holding a cherry branch fructed proper. *Mantling*: Gules doubled argent. The coronet of an earl. *Arms*: Quarterly, 1 Argent three martlets gules, on a chief engrailed also gules three annulets or COWPER, 2 Quarterly or and gules a bend argent, a crescent argent for difference CLAVERING, 3 Quarterly, (i) Azure billety a lion rampant or NASSAU, (ii) Or a lion rampant gules crowned or KATZ-ENELNBOGEN, (iii) Gules a fess argent VIANDEN, (iv) Gules two lions passant or DIETZ, overall on an escutcheon Argent a lion rampant sable LORDSHIP OF LECK, 4 Gules a fess between three cross-crosslets fitchy or, a crescent or for difference GORE. *Legend*: Francis Earl Cowper.

Note: The bend in the second quarter should be sable and is so depicted on Earl Cowper's stall plate. The arms depicted in quarter 3 are those of Louis de Nassau Lord of Auverquerque, illegitimate son of Maurice, Prince of Nassau whose descendant was created Earl of Grantham. The earl's daughter and co-heiress Henrietta married the second Earl Cowper.

2a

Crests: 1 On a wreath argent and gules, a lion statant azure, 2 On a wreath argent and gules, a seahorse naiant proper. *Mantling*: Gules doubled argent. The coronet of a marquess. *Arms*: Quarterly, 1 & 4 Or a saltire and a chief gules, on a canton argent a lion rampant azure BRUCE, 2 & 3 Argent a chevron gules between three chapeaux tails to the dexter azure BRUDENELL. *Legend*: George Marq: of Ailesby.

2b

Crests: 1 On a wreath argent and azure, a beehive beset with bees volant proper, 2 On a wreath argent and azure, a sagittary passant, the body proper the hindpart argent. *Mantling*: Dexter, Azure doubled ermine; Sinister, Gules doubled ermine. The coronet of a marquess. *Arms*: Quarterly, 1 & 4 Ermine on a bend azure a magnetic needle pointing to the polar star or PETTY, 2 & 3 Argent a saltire gules a chief ermine FITZMAURICE. *Legend*: Henry Marqu: of Lansdne.

2c

Crest: Out of a ducal coronet or, a griffin's head argent beaked or gorged with a collar gemel gules between two wings elevated and displayed argent. *Mantling*: Gules doubled argent. The coronet of an earl. *Arms*: Quarterly, 1 & 4 Quarterly argent and gules, in the second and third quarters a fret or overall on a bend sable three escallops argent, a crescent sable for difference SPENCER, 2 & 3 Barry of eight or and gules POYNTZ. *Legend*: John P. Earl Spencer.

2d

Crest: On a wreath argent and sable, a falcon rising belled or, ducally gorged gules. *Mantling*: Sable doubled argent. The coronet of a duke. *Arms*: Quarterly, 1 & 4 Sable three swords in pile, points in base argent, hilts or PAULET, 2 Azure three sinister gauntlets or VANE, 3 the Royal Arms of King Charles II, viz. Quarterly, (i & iv) France Modern and England quarterly, (ii) Scotland, (iii) Ireland, overall a baton sinister ermine FITZROY. *Legend*: Harry Duke of Cleveland.

Note: Arms granted to Charles Duke of Southampton, eldest illegitimate child by Barbara Villiers. He succeeded his mother to the duchy of Cleveland. His daughter Grace married Henry Vane.

3a

A gold helmet affronty ensigned by a gold arched crown with a red cap. *Mantling*: Gules doubled argent. *Arms*: Quarterly of six, 1 Or a buffalo's head caboshed sable, armed and ringed argent, crowned and langued gules MECKLENBURG, 2 Azure a griffin segreant or PRINCIPALITY of WENDEN, 3 Per fess: in chief, Azure a griffin segreant or, in base, Vert a bordure argent PRINCIPALITY OF SCHWERIN, 4 Gules a cross formy argent crowned or RATZEBURG, 5 Gules a dexter arm argent issuant from clouds in sinister flank and holding a finger ring or COUNTY of SCHWERIN, 6 Or a buffalo's head sable armed argent, crowned and langued gules

LORDSHIP of ROSTOCK. Overall an escutcheon, Per fess gules and or STARGARD. *Legend*: Fred[k] Duke of Mecklenbg.

3b

On a gold helmet affronty the Royal Crest, the lion charged with a label of three points argent, the centre point charged with a cross gules, the two outer points with an anchor azure. *Mantling*: Gules doubled argent. *Arms*: The Royal Arms post 1837, charged with an escutcheon for Saxony and differenced by a label of three points argent, the centre point charged with a cross gules, the two outer points with an anchor azure. *Legend*: Prince Alfred E: Albert [later Duke of Edinburgh].

3c

Crest: On a wreath argent and gules, a scaling ladder in bend sinister or, points and hooks sable. *Mantling*: Gules doubled argent. The coronet of an earl. *Arms*: Quarterly, 1 & 4 Gules a lion rampant within a bordure engrailed argent, in dexter chief a mullet or for difference GREY, 2 & 3 Barry of six argent and azure a bend gules charged in chief with a bezant GREY of NORTON. *Legend*: Henry Earl Grey.

3d

Crests: 1 On a wreath azure and or, a goat's head erased erminois, 2 On a wreath argent and gules, a wolf passant argent, collared and chained or, 3 On a wreath argent and azure, a cat-a-mountain sejeant proper. *Mantling*: Azure and gules doubled or. The coronet of a duke. *Arms*: Quarterly, 1 & 4 Barry of eight argent and gules a cross flory sable GOWER, 2 Azure three laurel leaves or LEVESON, 3 Gules three mullets or, within a bordure also or charged with a double tressure flory counter flory gules SUTHERLAND. *Legend*: George Duke of Sutherl[d].

Tracery Quatrefoils

A & C: Lower Quatrefoils. Against a gold background, a Tudor rose barbed, seeded and slipped proper.
B: Against a green background and within the Garter which is surrounded by gold rays, Argent a cross gules.

THE SOUTH NAVE CLERESTORY

SXV

A medieval gold hempbrake appears in lights 1b and 1c.

Windows **SXVI** to **SXXI** are composed of twelve lights, at the head of which are three quatrefoils. The quatrefoils of SXVI and SXVII contain; *Upper*: Against a red background within a circlet composed of a formal pattern in gold, a sun in splendour, surrounded by silver leaves pendant from gold stalks. *Lower*: Against a red background within a circlet and surrounded by leaves as above, a white rose seeded gold. At the apex of each light is a gold leopard's face. Each light has a border of a formal pattern of silver and gold and has a background of quarries bearing a white rose barbed, seeded, slipped and leaved gold. The helmets, save where otherwise indicated, are of silver with visors of gold bars and are turned to the dexter. All the arms are within the Garter.

SXVI

1a

A gold helmet affronty ensigned by a gold coronet, from which arises an eagle displayed sable crowned or, on each wing a kleestengel or and having upon the breast the letters F R also or. *Mantling*: Sable doubled argent. *Arms*: Argent an eagle displayed as the crest but having in the dexter claw a sceptre or and in the sinister an orb azure banded and with a cross or, all within a bordure company argent and sable PRUSSIA. *Legend*: William Prince of Prussia 1877 [later Kaiser Wilhelm II].

Note: For kleestengel see SIV 2b.

1b

A gold helmet affronty ensigned by an gold arched crown with a red cap. *Mantling*: Gules doubled argent. *Arms*: Gules a cross argent SAVOY. *Legend*: Humbert, King of Italy 1878.

1c

A gold helmet affronty. *Crest*: On a coronet composed alternately of crosses formy and strawberry leaves a lion statant guardant crowned or charged with a label of three points argent the centre point charged with a fleur de lis azure and the outer two points each with a cross gules. *Arms*: Quarterly, 1 & 4 England, 2 Scotland, 3 Ireland, overall an escutcheon charged with the arms of Brunswick, Luneberg and Westphalia (Hanover), charged with a label of three points gules the centre point charged with a horse courant argent. Overall a label of three points argent, the centre point charged with a fleur de lis azure and the outer two points each with a cross gules. *Legend*: George Fred[k] Duke of Cumberland 1878.

Note: The duke's names were Ernest Augustus William Adolphus George Frederick and so appear upon his stall plate. Why only the last two appear here is uncertain.

1d

Crest: On a wreath argent and gules, issuant from a wreath of oak leaves proper, a tower triple turreted argent. *Mantling*: Gules doubled argent. *Arms*: Per saltire in chief gules, a triple turreted tower argent in fess argent two lions rampant sable, in base gules an eagle displayed or. *Legend*: Benjamin Earl of Beaconsfield 1878.

2a

Crest: On a wreath argent and gules, a lion's face gules crowned or encircled by an oak bush proper. *Mantling*: Gules doubled argent. *Arms*: Argent a lion rampant within a double tressure flory counter flory gules, all within a bordure azure. *Legend*: Thomas Earl of Zetland 1872.

2b

On a gold helmet affronty a Kaianian crown or studded with pearls and ensigned by three feathers argent. *Mantling*: Azure doubled argent. *Arms*: Per fess azure and vert a lion couchant guardant argent, in front of a sun in splendour or. *Legend*: Nasir-Ed Deen Shah of Persia 1873.

2c

Crest: On a chapeau azure turned up ermine, an ostrich argent holding in its beak a horseshoe or. *Mantling*: Gules doubled argent. *Arms*: Per pale gules and azure three eagles displayed argent COKE. *Legend*: Thomas W. Earl of Leicester 1873.

2d

A gold helmet affronty ensigned by a gold arched crown with a red cap. *Mantling*: Azure doubled argent. *Arms*: Azure a cross couped argent GREECE. An escutcheon, Quarterly, 1 Or semy of hearts gules three lions passant in pale azure crowned or DENMARK, 2 Or two lions passant in pale azure SCHLESWIG, 3 Gules an escutcheon per fess argent and gules between three demi nettle leaves or and as many passion nails in pairle argent HOLSTEIN, 4 Gules a horse's head couped argent LAUENBURG. Overall an inescutcheon Or two bars gules OLDENBURG, impaling Azure a cross formy or DELMENHURST. *Legend*: George 2, King of Greece 1876.

Note: The demi nettle leaves in the Holstein coat should be argent and the horse's head in the Lauenburg arms should be or.

3a

Crest: On a wreath argent and sable, a demi lion rampant argent charged with three trefoils slipped vert grasping in its dexter paw an arrow pheoned and flighted proper, the shaft or. *Mantling*: Sable doubled argent. *Arms*: Quarterly, 1 & 4 Argent three Moor's heads couped at the neck in profile sable, wreathed azure and argent CANNING, 2 Gules three spear heads palewise in fess argent SALMON, 3 Sable a goat salient or MARSHALL. *Legend*: Stratford Viscount Stratford de Redcliffe 1869.

3b

Crest: Out of a ducal coronet composed of fleurs de lis, on a mount vert a stag at gaze or. *Mantling*: Vert doubled or. *Arms*: Vert a chevron between three stags at gaze or ROBINSON. *Legend*: George Fred: Earl de Grey and Ripon.

3c

Crest: On a wreath or and azure, a talbot statant or. *Mantling*: Azure doubled or. Arms: Quarterly, 1 & 4 Azure a portcullis chained or on a chief also or between two Tudor roses proper a pale azure charged with a cross flory between five martlets or. Augmentation of the Marquess of Westminster by Royal Licence 5 December 1831. 2 & 3 Azure a garb or GROSVENOR. *Legend*: Hugh Marquess of Westminster 1870.

3d

A gold helmet affronty ensigned by a gold arched crown with a red cap. *Mantling*: Vert doubled or. *Arms*: Vert an armilliary sphere or placed upon the Cross of the Order of Christ (Gules fimbriated or charged with a cross argent) encircled by an annulet azure fimbriated on both sides argent and charged with nineteen mullets argent. *Legend*: Pedro 2 Emperor of Brazil 1871.

SXVII

Quatrefoils, heads and borders as window SXVI. All arms within the Garter as previously. Helmets as window SXVI.

1a

Crest: On a wreath or and azure, a dragon statant or. *Mantling*: Azure doubled or. *Arms*: Quarterly, 1 & 4 Or a bend company argent and azure between two lions rampant gules STEWART, 2 Argent a bend engrailed between six martlets sable TEMPEST, 3 Azure three sinister gauntlets apaumy or VANE. *Legend*: Chas. Marq: of Londonderry 1888.

1b

A gold helmet affronty ensigned by a gold coronet, from which arises an eagle displayed sable crowned or, on each wing a kleestengel or and having upon the breast the letters F R also or. *Mantling*: Sable doubled argent. *Arms*: Argent an eagle displayed as the crest but having in the dexter claw a sceptre or and in the sinister an orb azure banded and with a cross or, all within a bordure company argent and sable PRUSSIA. *Legend*: Henry Prince of Prussia 1889.

Note: For kleestengel see SIV 2b.

1c

A gold helmet affronty ensigned by an gold arched crown with a red cap. *Mantling*: Purpure doubled or. *Arms*: Per pale: Dexter: Or three stag's attires fesswise in pale points to the sinister sable WURTEMBURG; Sinister: Or three lions passant guardant in pale sable SWABIA. *Legend*: Charles King of Würtemburg 1890.

1d

A gold helmet affronty ensigned by a gold arched coronet with a red cap. *Mantling*: Gules doubled argent. *Arms*: Gules a cross argent SAVOY. *Legend*: Victor Prince of Naples 1891.

2a

Crest: On a chapeau gules turned up ermine, a lion statant tail extended azure langued gules. *Mantling*: Gules doubled argent. *Arms*: Quarterly, 1 & 4 Quarterly (i & iv) Or a lion rampant azure armed and langued gules PERCY, (ii & iii) Gules three lucies haurient argent LUCY, 2 & 3 Azure five fusils conjoined in fess argent PERCY (ANCIENT). *Legend*: Alg: Geo: Duke of Northumberland 1886.

Note: The fusils should be or.

2b

Crest: On a wreath gules and argent, a bull argent pied sable collared or. *Mantling*: Gules doubled argent. *Arms*: Gules on a saltire argent a rose gules barbed and seeded proper NEVILL OF ABERGAVENNY. *Legend*: William Marq: of Abergavenny 1886.

2c

Crest: On a chapeau gules turned up ermine, a lion statant guardant or gorged with a ducal coronet argent. *Mantling*: Gules doubled argent. *Arms*: Quarterly, 1 Gules on a bend between six cross-crosslets fitchy argent an escutcheon or, charged with a demi lion rampant pierced through the mouth with an arrow within a double tressure flory counter flory gules HOWARD with the augmentation for the battle of Flodden 1513, 2 Gules three lions passant guardant in pale or, a label of three points argent BROTHERTON, 3 Checky or and azure WARRENNE, 4 Gules a lion rampant or FITZALAN. *Legend*: Henry Duke of Norfolk 1886.

2d

A gold helmet affronty ensigned by a gold arched coronet with a red cap. *Mantling*: Gules doubled or. *Arms*: Tierced in pale, 1 Or a lion rampant gules crowned azure HAPSBURG, 2 Gules a fess argent AUSTRIA, 3 Or on a bend gules three allerions displayed argent LORRAINE. *Legend*: Rudolph Prince of Austria 1887.

3a

Crest: On a wreath or and sable, a dexter arm couped below the elbow vested argent grasping a club or, ensigned by the motto: FRAPPE FORT. *Mantling*: Sable doubled or. *Arms*: Sable a chevron or goutty de sang between three cinquefoils ermine WODEHOUSE. *Legend*: John Earl of Kimberley 1885.

3b

Crest: On a wreath or and sable, on a mount a beacon fired proper, behind it a ribbon bearing the words NISI DOMINUS. *Mantling*: Sable doubled or. *Arms*: Sable a lion passant guardant or between three closed helmets argent COMPTON. *Legend*: William Marq: of Northampton 1885.

3c

Crest: A chapeau gules turned up ermine, bearing a plume of peacock's feathers proper. *Mantling*: Azure doubled or. *Arms*: Azure a cross moline or MOLYNEAUX. *Legend*: William Philip Earl of Sefton 1885.

3d

A gold helmet affronty ensigned by a gold arched coronet with a red cap. *Mantling*: Gules doubled argent. *Arms*: Quarterly, 1 & 4 Azure a lion queue fourchy barry of ten argent and gules crowned or, armed and langued gules, within a bordure compony gules and argent HESSE, 2 & 3 Argent two pallets sable BATTENBURG. *Legend*: Henry Prince of Battenburg 1885.

Windows SXVIII to SXXII are of plain glass, save that a medieval gold hempbrake appears in the following panels: SXVIII, 3b, 2b and 2c, SXX, 3c, 2b and 1b, SXXII (composed of fifteen lights), 3c.

THE NORTH CHOIR CLERESTORY

NII

The window is of similar design to SII (see p. 00).

1a

Crest: On a chapeau gules turned up ermine, a lion statant guardant or ducally crowned azure and gorged with a collar counter-compony argent and azure. Below: The coronet of a duke. *Arms*: The Royal Arms of King Charles II, viz. Quarterly, 1 & 4 France Modern and England quarterly, 2 Scotland, 3 Ireland, overall a baton sinister company of six pieces argent and azure. Arms: granted to Henry Duke of Grafton, second son of King Charles II by Barbara Villiers. *Legend*: AUGUSTUS D. OF GRAFTON.

1b

Crest: On a wreath or and azure, a dragon's head erased sable, ducally gorged and chained or NORTH. *Arms*: Azure a lion passant or between three fleurs de lis argent. *Legend*: Sr. FREDERICK NORTH [commonly known as Lord North before succeeding his father as Earl of Guilford].

1c

Crest: On a wreath argent and sable, a serpent nowed proper. Below: The coronet of a duke. *Arms*: Quarterly, 1 & 4 Sable three buck's heads caboshed argent CAVENDISH, 2 & 3 Per bend embattled argent and gules BOYLE. *Legend*: WILLIAM D. OF DEVONSHIRE.

1d

Crest: On a chapeau gules turned up ermine, a peacock in its pride proper. Below: The coronet of a duke. *Arms*: Or two bars azure, a chief quarterly 1 & 4 Azure two fleurs de lis or, 2 & 3 Gules a lion passant guardant or MANNERS. *Legend*: CHARLES D. OF RUTLAND.

2a

Crest: On a wreath or and argent, an heraldic tyger statant or tufted sable, langued gules. Below: The coronet of a duke. *Arms*: Quarterly of six, 1 & 6 Quarterly ermine and azure a cross or OSBORNE, 2 Argent two bars gules, a canton gules charged with a cross argent, a crescent or for difference BROUGHTON, 3 Argent a chevron vert between three annulets gules (coat unidentified), 4 Azure on a fess or between three lions passant argent, three lapwings proper HEWETT, 5 Or a chevron between three lozenges azure, on a chief gules an eagle displayed or HYDE. *Legend*: THOMAS D^{E}. OF LEEDS.

Note: Extensive research has failed to identify the third quarter, which was brought in by Broughton.

2b

Crest: On a wreath argent and sable, a griffin's head couped or, wings elevated, beaked sable. Below: The coronet of a duke. *Arms*: Quarterly, 1 & 4 Quarterly (i & iv) Argent three lozenges conjoined in fess gules within a bordure sable MONTAGU, (ii & iii) Or an eagle displayed vert, beaked and membered gules MONTHERMER, 2 & 3 Sable a lion rampant argent, on a canton argent a cross gules CHURCHILL, with the Augmentation granted to Sir Winston Churchill in 1661/2. *Legend*: GEORGE D^{E}. OF MONTAGU.

2c

Crest: On a wreath argent and sable, the bust of a Moor couped at the shoulders in profile proper wreathed about the temples argent and azure. Below: The coronet of an earl. *Arms*: Quarterly, 1 & 4 Sable on a bend cotised argent a rose gules barbed and seeded proper between two annulets sable CONWAY, 2 & 3 Quarterly (i & iv) Or on a pile gules between six fleurs de lis azure, three lions passant guardant in pale or SEYMOUR AUGMENTATION, (ii & iii) Gules two wings conjoined in lure or SEYMOUR. *Legend*: FRANCIS E^{L}. OF HERTFORD.

Note: See NIV, 2d.

2d

Crest: On a wreath or and azure, a demi lion rampant gules armed and langued azure. Over, the motto *Nobilis:Ira*. Below: The coronet of an earl. *Arms*: Or a fess checky argent and azure, within a double tressure flory counter flory gules STUART. *Legend*: JOHN E[L] OF BUTE.

3a

See notes to window SII. *Crest*: Out of a coronet or two buffalo's horns argent, issuing from the extremeties and fesswise from the outer edges linden branches leaved vert. Below: An arched crown with a red cap. *Arms*: Quarterly of seven, 1 Argent a patriarchal cross gules HERSFELD, 2 Per fess sable and or, in chief a mullet of six points argent ZIEGENHEIM, 3 Or a lion rampant guardant gules, crowned azure KATZENELNBOGEN, 4 Gules two lions passant in pale or DIETZ, 5 Per fess sable and or, in chief two mullets of eight points argent NIDDA, 6 Quarterly (i & iv) Or three chevrons gules HANAU, (ii & iii) Barry gules and or RISNEE, 7 Gules an escutcheon per fess argent and gules between three demi nettle leaves and as many passion nails in pairle argent HOLSTEIN. Overall on an escutcheon, Azure a lion rampant, queue fourchy barry argent and gules crowned or HESSE. *Legend*: FREDERICK P[R] OF HESSE CASSEL.

Note: The mullet in the Ziegenheim arms is normally Or.

3b

Crest: Out of a ducal coronet a pair of stag's attires or. Below: A crown or of several arches with a red cap. *Arms*: Quarterly, 1 Azure billetty a lion rampant or NASSAU, 2 Or a lion rampant gules crowned azure KATSENELNBOGEN, 3 Gules a fess argent VIANDEN, 4 Gules two lions passant guardant or DIETZ. Overall an escutcheon Quarterly, 1 & 4 Gules a bend or CHALONS, 2 & 3 Or a bugle horn azure stringed or ORANGE. An inescutcheon, Checky of nine pieces or and azure GENEVA. *Legend*: WILLIAM P[R] OF ORANGE.

3c

Above: On a coronet composed alternately of crosses formy and fleurs de lis or, a lion statant guardant crowned or, gorged with a label of three points argent, on the centre point a cross gules. Below: A similar coronet without the crest. *Arms*: The Royal Arms of King George III differenced with a label as in the crest. In the fourth quarter on an escutcheon Argent a wheel of six spokes gules BISHOPRIC OF OSNABRUCK. *Legend*: FRED: AUG. B[P] OF OSNABRUCK [Frederick, second son of King George III, afterwards Duke of York].

3d

Crest: Out of a coronet or, a panache of peacock's feathers proper charged with a buffalo's head caboshed sable, armed and ringed argent, crowned and langued gules, rising from a closed palisado crown alternately azure, or, gules, argent and sable. Below: A crown of several arches with a red cap. *Arms*: Quarterly of six, 1 Or a buffalo's head caboshed sable armed and ringed argent crowned and langued gules MECKLENBURG, 2 Azure a griffin segreant or PRINCIPALITY OF WENDEN, 3 Per fess, in chief azure a griffin segreant or; in base vert PRINCIPALITY OF SCHWERIN, 4 Gules a cross formy argent crowned or RATZEBURG, 5 Gules a dexter arm issuant from clouds argent in sinister flank and holding a finger ring or COUNTY OF SCHWERIN, 6 Or a buffalo's head sable armed argent crowned and langued gules LORDSHIP

OF ROSTOCK. Overall an escutcheon, Per fess gules and or STARGARD. *Legend*: ADOLPHUS D^{E}. OF MECKLENBURG.

Note: The base in the arms of the Principality of Schwerin is sometimes bordured Argent.

Tracery Quatrefoils

A: As SII save that the lion is charged with a label of three points argent.
B: As window SII save that the inescutcheon in the fourth quarter is plain gules and the whole is differenced by a label of three points argent.
C: As SII.

NIII

Quarries, helmets and Garters as South Side.

1a

Crest: Out of a coronet composed of eight fleurs de lis or, an estoile argent. *Mantling*: Gules doubled or. The coronet of a duke. *Arms*: Quarterly or and gules, overall a bend vair SACKVILLE. *Legend*: JOHN FRED: D. OF DORSET.

1b

Crest: On a chapeau gules turned up ermine, a lion statant azure, langued gules. *Mantling*: Azure doubled or. The coronet of a duke. *Arms*: Quarterly, 1 & 4 Quarterly (i & iv) Or a lion rampant azure, armed and langued gules PERCY, (ii & iii) Gules three lucies haurient argent LUCY, 2 & 3 Azure five fusils conjoined in fess or PERCY (ANCIENT). *Legend*: HEN: D: OF NORTHUMBERLAND.

1c

A gold helmet affronty surmounted by an arched crown or coronet. *Mantling*: Sable doubled or. *Arms*: Quarterly of twenty three; 1 Or a lion rampant sable JULICH, 2 Gules an escarbuncle or charged in the centre with an escutcheon argent CLEVES, 3 Argent a lion rampant gules crowned azure BERG, 4 Gules three hearts or BREHNA, 5 Gules a horse forcene argent WESTPHALIA, 6 Sable a lion rampant or COBURG, 7 Azure a lion rampant barry argent and gules, crowned argent LANDGRAVE of THURINGIA, 8 Or a lion rampant sable MEISSEN, 9 Per pale; Dexter: Gules a column argent crowned or ROENHILD, Sinister: Or on a mount vert a cock sable HENNENBERG, 10 Per fess argent and azure a lion rampant counterchanged crowned or LICHTEMBERG, 11 Azure an eagle displayed crowned or PALATINATE of SAXONY, 12 Sable an eagle displayed or PALATINATE of THURINGIA, 13 Or two pales azure LANDSBERG, 14 Argent three beetle's pincers gules ENGERN, 15 Or semy of hearts gules a lion rampant sable crowned gules ORLAMUNDE, 16 Azure a lion passant per fess or and argent PLEISSEN, 17 Argent a rose gules ALTENBURG, 18 Argent three bars azure EISENBERG, 19 Or a fess checky argent and gules MARCK, 20 Argent three chevrons gules RAVENSBERG, 21 Gules plain SOVEREIGN RIGHTS, 22 Azure a lion rampant argent TONNA, 23 Or a bend argent, in chief a raven proper holding in its beak a ring or RAVENSTEIN. Overall an escutcheon Barry of ten or and sable a crown of rue bendwise vert SAXONY. *Legend*: ERNEST D. OF SAXE C. GOTHA.

1d

Crest: On a wreath argent and azure, an heraldic tyger statant or crined sable langued gules. *Mantling*: Azure doubled argent. The coronet of a duke. *Arms*: Quarterly ermine and azure a cross or OSBORNE. *Legend*: FRANCIS D: OF LEEDS.

2a

Crest: As light 3a but differenced with a label of three points argent, the centre point charged with a cross gules and the outer points each with two hearts in pale gules. *Legend*: PRINCE ADOLPHUS [later Duke of Cambridge].

2b

Crest: On a wreath argent and azure, a portcullis chained or. *Mantling*: Azure doubled argent. The coronet of a duke. *Arms*: Quarterly France Modern and England all within a bordure company argent and azure BEAUFORT for SOMERSET. *Legend*: HENRY D: of BEAUFORT.

2c

Crest: On a wreath argent and vert, a garb vert. *Mantling*: Vert doubled argent. The coronet of a marquess. *Arms*: Quarterly of six; 1 & 6 Vert on a cross argent five torteaux GRENVILLE, 2 Quarterly, (i & iv) Or an eagle displayed sable LEOFRIC, (ii & iii) Argent two bars sable each charged with three martlets or TEMPLE, 3 Ermine two bars gules NUGENT, 4 Argent on a cross sable a leopard's face or BRYDGES, 5 Or a pile gules CHANDOS. *Legend*: GEO. M: OF BUCKINGHAM.

2d

Crest: On a wreath argent and sable, a mount vert a stag lodged reguardant argent, attired and unguled or, gorged with a chaplet of laurel vert, vulned on the shoulder gules. *Mantling*: Sable doubled argent. The coronet of a marquess. Arms: Sable goutty d'eau, on a fess argent three Cornish choughs proper CORNWALLIS. *Legend*: CHA: M: CORNWALLIS.

3a

A gold helmet affronty ensigned by a coronet composed alternately of crosses formy and fleur de lis or thereon a lion statant guardant crowned or, gorged with a label of three points argent, on the centre point a cross gules and on each of the two outer points an anchor azure. *Mantling*: Gules doubled or. *Arms*: The Hanoverian Royal Arms before 1801 viz. Quarterly, 1 England impaling Scotland, 2 France Modern, 3 Ireland, 4 Tierced in pairle reversed Brunswick, Luneburg, Westphalia (Hanover). Overall a label as in the crest. *Legend*: PRINCE WILLIAM HENRY [later King William IV].

3b

As light 3a but differenced with a label of three points argent, on the centre point a cross gules and on each of the two outer points a fleur de lis azure. *Legend*: PRINCE EDWARD [later Duke of Kent and father of Queen Victoria].

3c

As light 3a, but differenced with a label of three points argent, on the centre point a fleur de lis azure and on the two outer points a cross gules. *Legend*: PRINCE ERNEST [later King of Hanover].

3d

As light 3a but differenced with a label of three points argent, on the centre point two hearts in pale gules and on the two outer points a cross gules. *Legend*: PRINCE AUGUSTUS [later Duke of Sussex].

Tracery Quatrefoils

A: Against a gold background and with the Garter, a Tudor rose proper ensigned by the letter 'S' in red.
B: Against a background of golden rays and within the Garter, Argent a cross gules.
C: As *A* but with the letter 'G'.

NIV

Quatrefoils, quarries, helmets and Garters as window NIII.

1a

Crest: On a wreath or and sable, a dragon passant argent. *Mantling*: Sable doubled or. The coronet of an earl. *Arms*: Or six annulets three, two and one sable LOWTHER. *Legend*: Wm E: OF LONSDALE.

1b

Crest: Out of a ducal coronet or, a demi lion rampant gules holding a spear erect proper and thereon flowing a forked pennon argent charged in the hoist with a cross gules. Below, on the same staff the Augmentation as in the arms. *Mantling*: Gules doubled argent. The coronet of a marquess. *Arms*: Quarterly, 1 & 4 Gules a cross argent between twenty plates, five in each quarter in saltire WELLESLEY, 2 & 3 Or a lion rampant gules ducally gorged or COWLEY. Overall an escutcheon purpure charged with an estoile between eight spots of the royal tiger in pairs saltirewise or, representing the standard of the Sultan of Mysore AUGMENTATION (Sign Manual Dec. 1790) granted in recognition of his success as Commander in Chief in the destruction of Mysore. *Legend*: RICHARD M:OF WELLESLEY.

Note: The estoile upon the augmentation as depicted in the window is of a different pattern to that on the stall plate, where it is shown as argent.

1c

Crest: On a chapeau gules turned up ermine, a lion statant guardant or ducally crowned gules gorged, with a collar company argent and gules, on each piece argent a rose gules barbed and seeded proper. *Mantling*: Gules doubled or. The coronet of a duke. *Arms*: Quarterly, 1 & 4 France Modern quartering England, 2 Scotland, 3 Ireland. Overall an escutcheon, Gules three buckles or DUKEDOM of AUBIGNY. All within a bordure company argent and gules, on each piece argent a rose gules barbed and seeded proper. *Legend*: CHAS D: OF RICHMOND.

1d

Crest: On a wreath or and sable, a falcon proper preying on a stork argent. *Mantling*: Sable doubled or. The coronet of a duke. *Arms*: Quarterly, 1 & 4 Or on a chief sable three escallops or GRAHAM, 2 & 3 Argent three roses gules barbed and seeded proper MONTROSE. *Legend*: JAMES D: OF MONTROSE.

2a

Crest: On a wreath argent and gules, a tower azure, issuant from the battlements thereof a demi lion rampant or, ducally crowned gules holding in its paws a grenade fired proper. *Mantling*: Gules doubled argent. The coronet of an earl. *Arms*: Quarterly ermine and gules STANHOPE. *Legend*: PHILIP E: OF CHESTERFIELD.

2b

Crest: Out of a ducal coronet or, a panache of six ostrich feathers alternately argent and azure. *Mantling*: Azure doubled argent. The coronet of an earl. *Arms*: Azure a buck's head caboshed argent. LEGGE. *Legend*: GEORGE E: OF DARTMOUTH.

Note: The panache usually consists of five feathers.

2c

Crest: On a wreath argent and gules, a wolf passant argent collared and chained or. *Mantling*: Gules doubled argent. The coronet of a marquess. *Arms*: Quarterly, 1 & 4 Barry of eight argent and gules a cross flory sable GOWER, 2 & 3 Azure three laurel leaves or LEVESON. *Legend*: George M: of Stafford.

2d

Crest: On a wreath argent and sable, the bust of a Moor in profile couped at the shoulders proper, wreathed about the temples argent and azure. *Mantling*: Sable doubled argent. The coronet of a marquess. *Arms*: Quarterly, 1 & 4 Sable on a bend cotised argent, a rose gules barbed and seeded or between two annulets sable CONWAY, 2 & 3 Quarterly, (i & iv) Or on a pile gules between six fleurs de lis azure three lions passant guardant in pale or AUGMENTATION granted to Edward Seymour in 1547 in memory of his sister's marriage to King Henry VIII, (ii & iii) Gules two wings conjoined in lure or SEYMOUR. *Legend*: Francis M: of Hertford.

Note: The augmentation, often said to have been that granted to Queen Jane, is recorded in J.R. Dasent, ed., *Acts of the Privy Council*, NS, ii (1547–50), pp. 530–3. The annulets in the Conway coat are usually gules.

3a

Crest: On a wreath argent and azure, a portcullis chained or. *Mantling*: Azure doubled argent. The coronet of a duke. *Arms*: Quarterly France Modern and England all within a bordure company argent and azure BEAUFORT for SOMERSET. *Legend*: HEN: CHA: D: OF BEAUFORT.

3b

Crest: Out of a ducal coronet or, an oak tree proper, fructed and penetrated transversely in the main stem by a frame saw proper, the blade inscribed with the word 'Through', the frame or. *Mantling*: Gules doubled argent. The coronet of a marquess. *Arms*: Quarterly, 1 & 4 Gules three pierced cinquefoils ermine HAMILTON, 2 & 3 Argent a lymphad sails furled and oars sable EARLS of ARRAN. *Legend*: JOHN JAS: M: OF ABERCORN.

3c

Crest: On a wreath argent and azure, a wyvern wings elevated vert holding in its mouth a sinister hand proper couped at the wrist gules. *Mantling*: Dexter: Azure doubled argent. Sinister: Gules doubled argent. The coronet of an earl. *Arms*: Per pale azure and gules three lions rampant argent HERBERT. *Legend*: GEORGE E: OF PEMBROKE.

3d

Crest: On a wreath argent and sable, a pegasus courant argent winged and unguled or. *Mantling*: Sable doubled argent. The coronet of an earl. *Arms*: Argent a chevron between three griffins passant sable FINCH. *Legend*: GEO: E: OF WINCHILSEA.

Note: The pegasus is usually ducally gorged or.

NV

Quarries, helmets and Garters as window NIII.

1a

Crest: On a wreath or and sable, a reindeer statant or collared sable. *Mantling*: Sable doubled or. The coronet of a marquess. *Arms*: Quarterly, 1 & 4 Barry of ten or and sable BOTEVILLE, 2 & 3 Argent a lion rampant tail nowed and erect gules THYNNE. *Legend*: THO: M: OF BATH.

1b

A gold helmet affronty ensigned by a gold arched crown with a blue cap. *Mantling*: Azure doubled or. *Arms*: Azure three fleurs de lis or FRANCE. *Legend*: CHARLES X K: OF FRANCE.

1c

Crest: Out of a coronet composed of eight fleurs de lis or, an estoile argent. *Mantling*: Gules doubled or. The coronet of a duke. *Arms*: Quarterly or and gules overall a bend vair SACKVILLE. *Legend*: CHARLES D: OF DORSET.

1d

A gold helmet affronty ensigned by a mitre crown, the rim gold, the mitre blue, green and red. *Mantling*: Sable doubled or. *Arms*: A doubled headed eagle displayed sable, crowned, armed, langued and membered or, holding in the dexter claw a sceptre and in the sinister an orb all gold, charged on the breast with the arms of Moscow, viz. Gules the mounted figure of St. George slaying the dragon all proper. *Legend*: NICHOLAS E: OF RUSSIA.

Note: The legends in panels 1a–1d cannot be seen as they are totally obscured by the stone crenellations. They were provided by the Archivist from an earlier survey.

2a

A gold helmet affronty ensigned by a gold arched crown with a red cap. *Mantling*: Azure doubled or. *Arms*: A cross formy throughout argent fimbriated gules DANNEBORG, between, 1 Or semy of hearts gules three lions passant in pale azure crowned or DENMARK, 2 Or two lions passant in pale azure SCHLESWIG, 3 Per fess; in chief, Azure three crowns or SWEDEN, in base, per pale, dexter, Gules a stock fish erect argent crowned or ICELAND; sinister, per fess in chief Azure a ram argent FAROES; in base Azure a polar bear sejant rampant argent GREENLAND, 4 Per fess; in chief Or ten hearts gules 4, 4 and 2, in chief a lion passant azure KINGDOM of the GOTHS; in base Gules a wyvern or KINGDOM of the VANDALS. On an escutcheon, Quarterly, 1 Gules an escutcheon per fess argent and gules between three demi nettle leaves and as many passion nails in pairle argent HOLSTEIN, 2 Gules a swan argent beaked, membered and ducally gorged or STORMARN, 3 Gules a knight in armour mounted upon a horse and holding a sword argent and a shield or DITMARSKEN, 4 Gules a horses head couped or LAUNBERG. Overall an escutcheon, per pale, dexter, Or two bars gules OLDENBURG; sinister, Azure a cross formy or DELMENHORST. *Legend*: FRED: VI. K OF DENMARK.

2b

A gold helmet affronty ensigned by a gold arched crown with a red cap. *Mantling*: Azure doubled argent. *Arms*: Argent five escutcheons in cross azure each charged with five plates in saltire all within a bordure gules charged with seven castles or PORTUGAL. *Legend*: JOHN :VI: K. of Portugal.

2c

Crest: On a wreath or and gules, a demi griffin segreant sable beaked winged and membered or, holding an esquire's helmet in profile argent. *Mantling*: Gules doubled or. The coronet of a marquess. *Arms*: Gules in chief two esquire's helmets in profile argent and in base a garb or CHOLMONDELEY. *Legend*: GEO: J: M: OF:CHOLMONDELEY.

2d

Crest: On a wreath argent and sable, the bust of a Moor in profile couped at the shoulders proper, wreathed about the temples argent and azure. *Mantling*: Sable doubled argent. The coronet of a marquess. *Arms*: Quarterly, 1 & 4 Sable on a bend cotised argent a rose gules barbed and seeded or between two annulets sable CONWAY, 2 & 3 Quarterly, (i & iv) Or on a pile gules between six fleurs de lis azure three lions passant guardant in pale or SEYMOUR AUGMENTATION, (ii & iii) Gules two wings conjoined in lure or SEYMOUR. *Legend*: FRANCIS M: OF HERTFORD.

Note: See notes to NIV, 2d.

3a

Crest: On a wreath argent and sable, a dexter arm in chain mail embowed, the hand proper grasping a spiked club the handle or the head proper. *Mantling*: Sable doubled argent. The coronet of an earl. *Arms*: Sable two bars ermine, in chief three crosses formy or BATHURST. *Legend*: HENRY: EARL BATHURST.

3b

Crest: On a wreath argent and sable, a demi heraldic tyger sable ducally gorged, tufted and maned argent. *Mantling*: Sable doubled argent. The coronet of a marquess. *Arms*: Sable on a cross engrailed between four eagles displayed argent, five lions passant guardant sable PAGET. *Legend*: HENRY: M OF ANGELSEY.

3c

Crest: On a chapeau gules turned up ermine, a lion statant tail extended azure langued gules. *Mantling*: Azure doubled or. The coronet of a duke. *Arms*: Quarterly, 1 & 4 Quarterly (i & iv) Or a lion rampant azure armed and langued gules PERCY, (ii & iii) Gules three lucies haurient argent LUCY, 2 & 3 Azure five fusils conjoined in fess or PERCY (ANCIENT). *Legend*: HUGH: D OF NORTHUMBERLAND.

3d

Crest: On a wreath argent and vert, a garb vert. *Mantling*: Vert doubled argent. The coronet of a marquess. *Arms*: Quarterly of six; 1 & 6 Vert on a cross argent five torteaux GRENVILLE, 2 Quarterly (i & iv) Or an eagle displayed sable LEOFRIC, (ii & iii) Argent two bars sable each charged with three martlets or TEMPLE, 3 Ermine two bars gules NUGENT, 4 Argent on a cross sable a leopard's face or BRYDGES, 5 Or a pile gules CHANDOS. *Legend*: RICH: M: OF BUCKINGHAM.

Tracery Quatrefoils

A and *C*: as NIII but ensigned by the letters V and R.
B: Against a green background and within the Garter, the Royal Arms post 1837, viz. Quarterly 1 & 4 England, 2 Scotland, 3 Ireland, the whole ensigned by an imperial arched crown or. On the dexter side appear the figures 18 and on the sinister 41.

NVI

Quatrefoils, quarries, helmets and Garters as window NIII.

1a

A gold helmet affronty ensigned by a gold arched crown. *Mantling*: Sable doubled or. *Arms*: Quarterly of twenty three; 1 Or a lion rampant sable JULICH, 2 Gules an escarbuncle having at the centre an escutcheon argent CLEVES, 3 Argent a lion rampant gules crowned azure BERG, 4 Gules three hearts or BREHNA, 5 Gules a horse forcene argent WESTPHALIA, 6 Sable a lion rampant or COBURG, 7 Azure a lion rampant barry argent and gules crowned argent LANDGRAVE of THURINGIA, 8 Or a lion rampant sable MEISSEN, 9 Per pale; dexter, Gules a column argent crowned or ROENHILD, sinister, Or on a mount vert a cock sable HENNENBERG, 10 Per fess argent and azure a lion rampant counterchanged crowned or LICHTEMBERG, 11 Azure an eagle displayed or PALATINATE of SAXONY, 12 Sable an eagle displayed or PALATINATE of THURINGIA, 13 Or two pales azure LANDSBERG, 14 Argent three beetle's pincers gules ENGERN, 15 Or semy of hearts gules a lion rampant sable crowned gules ORLAMUNDE, 16 Azure a lion rampant per fess or and argent PLEISSEN, 17 Argent a rose gules ALTENBURG, 18 Argent three bars azure EISENBERG, 19 Or a fess checky gules and argent MARCK, 20 Argent three chevrons gules RAVENSBERG, 21 Gules plain SOVEREIGN RIGHTS, 22 Azure a lion rampant argent TONNA, 23 Or a bend argent in chief a raven proper holding in its beak a ring or RAVENSTEIN. Overall an escutcheon, Barry of ten or and sable a crown of rue bendwise vert SAXONY. *Legend*: ERNEST D: OF COBURG GOTHA.

1b

Crest: On a chapeau gules turned up ermine, an eagle wings addorsed or preying upon a child proper swaddled gules, in a cradle laced or. *Mantling*: Azure doubled argent. The coronet of an earl. *Arms*: Argent on a bend azure three stag's heads caboshed or STANLEY. *Legend*: EDWARD E. OF DERBY.

1c

Crest: On a chapeau gules turned up ermine, a lion statant guardant or gorged with a collar company ermine and azure. *Mantling*: Azure doubled or. The coronet of a duke. *Arms*: Quarterly, 1 & 4 Azure three sinister gauntlets or VANE, 2 & 3 The Royal Arms of King Charles II viz. Quarterly (i & iv) France Modern and England quarterly, (ii) Scotland, (iii) Ireland. Overall a baton sinister ermine FITZROY. *Legend*: WM DUKE OF CLEVELAND.

1d

On a gold helmet affronty the crest of Saxony, viz. Out of a coronet or a pyramidal chapeau barry of ten or and sable a crown of rue bendwise vert, ensigned by a plume of peacock's feathers proper out of a coronet or. *Mantling*: Dexter: Sable doubled or; Sinister: Gules doubled or. *Arms*: Quarterly 1 & 4 The Royal Arms post 1837, viz. Quarterly (i & iv) England, (ii) Scotland, (iii) Ireland, differenced by a label of three points argent on the centre point a cross gules, 2 & 3 Barry of ten or and sable a crown of rue bendwise vert SAXONY. (Arms granted to Prince Albert upon his marriage to Queen Victoria in 1840). *Legend*: PRINCE ALBERT.

Note: The legends on panels 1a–1d were supplied by the Archivist from an earlier survey.

2a

Crest: On a wreath argent and azure, a beehive beset with bees volant proper. *Mantling*: Azure doubled argent. The coronet of a marquess. *Arms*: Quarterly, 1 & 4 Ermine on a bend azure a magnetic needle pointing to the polar star or PETTY, 2 & 3 Argent a saltire gules a chief ermine FITZMAURICE. *Legend*: HEN: M: OF LANSDOWNE.

2b

Crest: On a chapeau gules turned up ermine, a lion statant guardant or gorged with a ducal coronet argent. *Mantling*: Gules doubled argent. The coronet of an earl. *Arms*: Gules on a bend between six cross-crosslets fitchy argent an escutcheon or charged with a demi lion rampant, pierced through the mouth with an arrow within a double tressure flory counter flory gules; above the escutcheon a mullet sable for difference HOWARD with the augmentation for the battle of Flodden 1513. *Legend*: GEO: E: OF CARLISLE.

2c

Crest: Out of a ducal coronet or a phoenix, the body azure, the head and wings vert, the wing feathers alternately azure and gules. *Mantling*: Gules doubled or. The coronet of a duke. *Arms*: Quarterly, 1 & 4 Or on a pile gules between six fleurs de lis azure, three lions passant guardant or SEYMOUR AUGMENTATION (see NIV, 2d), 2 & 3 Gules two wings conjoined in lure or SEYMOUR. *Legend*: EDW^{D}. D: OF SOMERSET.

Note: The crest is usually out of a ducal coronet a phoenix or.

2d

A gold helmet affronty. *Crest*: Out of a ducal coronet or, an apple tree proper between two eagle's wings sable, each semy of hearts argent. *Mantling*: Azure doubled argent. *Arms*: Azure three eagles displayed argent LEININGEN. *Legend*: CHA: P: OF LEININGEN.

Note: The tree in the crest presents some difficulty. A number of armorials refer to it as an apple tree but most, save for a fifteenth-century edition, state that it is 'fructed' with hearts, or in some instances cinquefoils argent. The Prince's stall plate appears to show the tree fructed with gold objects.

3a

Crest: On a wreath or and gules, a stag trippant proper attired and unguled or. *Mantling*: Gules doubled or. The coronet of a duke. *Arms*: Quarterly, 1 & 4 The Stuart Royal Arms, viz. Quarterly (i & iv) France Modern and England quarterly, (ii) Scotland, (iii) Ireland, overall a baton sinister argent, (arms granted in 1667 to JAMES CROFTS (later SCOTT), Duke of Monmouth, eldest illegitimate son of King Charles II), 2 & 3 Or on a bend azure an estoile between two crescents or SCOTT. *Legend*: WALTER D: OF BUCCLEUGH.

3b

A gold helmet affronty ensigned by an open gold coronet thereon crowned a lion statant guardant or gorged with a label of three points argent, on the centre point a fleur de lis azure and the outer two points each with a cross gules. Immediately below the label is a further label of three points gules, the centre point being charged with a horse courant argent. *Mantling*: Gules doubled or. *Arms*: The Royal Arms of Hanover after 1801 without the Electoral Bonnet or insignia of the Arch Treasurer of the Empire, viz. Quarterly, 1 & 4 England, 2 Scotland, 3 Ireland. Overall an escutcheon tierced in paire, 1 Brunswick, 2 Lunenburg, 3 Westphalia (Hanover) differenced with labels as in the crest. *Legend*: PR: GEO: OF CUMBERLAND [later King of Hanover].

3c

As light 3b, but arms and crest differenced with a label of three points argent, on the centre point a cross gules and upon the outer two each with two hearts in pale gules. Immediately below the label is a further label of three points argent. *Legend*: PR: GEO. OF CAMBRIDGE.

3d

Crest: Out of a ducal coronet or, an oak tree proper fructed and penetrated transversely in the main stem by a frame-saw proper, the blade inscribed with the word 'Through' the frame or. *Mantling*: Gules doubled argent. The coronet of a duke. *Arms*: Quarterly, 1 & 4 Quarterly (i & iv) Gules three pierced cinquefoils ermine HAMILTON, (ii & iii) Argent a lymphad sails furled and oars sable EARLS of ARRAN, 2 & 3 Argent a heart gules ensigned by an imperial crown proper, on a chief azure three mullets argent DOUGLAS. *Legend*: ALEX: D. OF HAMILTON.

NVII

Quatrefoils, quarries, helmets and Garters as window NIII.

1a

Crest: Out of a ducal coronet or, a griffin's head argent beaked or gorged with a collar gemel gules between two wings elevated and displayed argent. *Mantling*: Gules doubled argent. The coronet of an earl. *Arms*: Quarterly argent and gules, on the second and third quarters a fret or overall on a bend sable three escallops argent. SPENCER. *Legend*: FREDERICK E: SPENCER.

1b

Crest: On a wreath argent and sable, a lion's gamb erased sable holding a trefoil slipped argent. *Mantling*: Sable doubled argent. The coronet of a marquess. *Arms*: Quarterly, 1 & 4 Sable a trefoil slipped within an orle of eight mullets argent PHIPPS, 2 Paly of six argent and azure a bend gules ANNESLEY, 3 The Stuart Royal Arms, viz. Quarterly (i & iv) France Modern and England quarterly, (ii) Scotland, (iii) Ireland, within a bordure company ermine and azure. Arms Granted by King James II to Lady Catherine Darnley, his illegitimate daughter by Catherine Sedley. *Legend*: C.H. M: OF NORMANBY.

Note: The azure pieces in the bordure of the third quarter should be charged with fleurs de lis or.

1c

Crest: Out of a ducal coronet or, a triple plume of ostrich feathers argent. *Mantling*: Gules doubled argent. The coronet of an earl. *Arms*: Quarterly, 1 & 4 Lozengy argent and gules FITZWILLIAM, 2 & 3 Sable a chevron between three leopard's faces or WENTWORTH. *Legend*: CH. W. E: FITWILLIAM.

1d

Crest: On a chapeau gules turned up ermine, a lion statant azure langued gules. *Mantling*: Azure doubled or. The coronet of a duke. *Arms*: Quarterly, 1 & 4 Quarterly (i & iv) Or a lion rampant azure PERCY, (ii & iii) Gules three lucies haurient argent LUCY, 2 & 3 Azure five fusils conjoined in fess or PERCY (ANCIENT). *Legend*: A: D: OF NORTHUMBERLAND.

2a

Crest: On a wreath argent and sable, the bust of a Moor in profile couped at the shoulders proper, wreathed about the temples argent and azure. *Mantling*: Sable doubled argent. The coronet of a marquess. *Arms*: Quarterly, 1 & 4 Sable on a bend cotised argent a rose gules barbed and seeded or between two annulets sable CONWAY, 2 & 3 Quarterly (i & iv) Or on a pile gules between six fleurs de lis azure, three lions passant guardant in pale or SEYMOUR AUGMENTATION, (ii & iii) Gules two wings conjoined in lure or SEYMOUR. *Legend*: RICHARD M: OF HERTFORD [see notes to NIV, 2d].

2b

Crest: On a wreath argent and gules, a goat statant argent armed and unguled or. *Mantling*: Gules doubled argent. The coronet of a duke. *Arms*: Argent a lion rampant gules, on a chief sable three escallops argent RUSSELL. *Legend*: FRANCIS D: OF BEDFORD.

2c

Crest: On a chapeau gules turned up ermine, a lion statant guardant or ducally gorged argent. *Mantling*:Gules doubled argent. The coronet of a duke. *Arms*: Gules on a bend between six cross-crosslets fitchy argent, an escutcheon or charged with a demi lion rampant pierced through the mouth with an arrow within a double tressure flory counter flory gules HOWARD with the augmentation for the battle of Flodden 1513. *Legend*: HEN. CHA: D: OF NORFOLK.

2d

Crest: On a wreath argent and gules, a lion rampant argent ducally crowned or. *Mantling*: Gules doubled argent. The coronet of an earl. *Arms*: Argent on a cross gules five escallops or VILLIERS. *Legend*: GEO: FR: E: OF CLARENDON.

3a

Crest: Out of a ducal coronet or, an oak tree proper, fructed and penetrated transversely in the main stem by a frame-saw proper the blade inscribed with the word 'Through', the frame or. *Mantling*: Gules doubled argent. The coronet of a marquess. *Arms*: Quarterly, 1 & 4 Gules three pierced cinquefoils ermine HAMILTON, 2 & 3 Argent a lymphad sails furled and oars sable EARLS of ARRAN. *Legend*: JAMES M: OF ABERCORN.

3b

Crest: On a chapeau gules turned up ermine, a lion statant tail extended or. *Mantling*: Gules doubled or. The coronet of an earl. *Arms*: Quarterly, 1 & 4 Gules a lion rampant within a bordure engrailed or TALBOT, 2 & 3 Azure a chevron between three mullets or CHETWYND. *Legend*: CHA: CHETWY: E: TALBOT.

3c

Crest: On a wreath argent and azure, a wyvern wings elevated vert holding in the mouth a sinister hand couped at the wrist gules. *Mantling*: Dexter: Gules doubled argent; Sinister: Azure doubled argent. The coronet of an earl. *Arms*: Per pale azure and gules three lions rampant argent HERBERT. *Legend*: EDWARD EARL OF POWIS.

3d

Crest: On a wreath argent and sable, an elephant's head erased argent, tusked or. *Mantling*: Sable doubled argent. The coronet of a marquess. *Arms*: Quarterly, 1 & 4 Sable on a fess argent between three elephant's heads erased argent tusked or, three mullets sable PRATT, 2 & 3 Sable a chevron between three spear heads argent JEFFRYS. *Legend*: GEORGE CHA. M: OF CAMDEN.

NVIII

Quatrefoils, quarries, helmets and Garters as window NIII.

1a

Crest: On a wreath argent and gules, a goat statant argent armed and unguled or. *Mantling*: Gules doubled argent. The coronet of an earl. *Arms*: Argent a lion rampant gules, on a chief sable three escallops argent, above the centre escallop a mullet argent for difference RUSSELL. *Legend*: JOHN EARL RUSSELL.

1b

Crest: On a chapeau gules turned up ermine, a bull statant sable armed, unguled and ducally gorged or. *Mantling*: Sable doubled argent. The coronet of an earl. *Arms*: Quarterly, 1 & 4 Argent three bulls passant sable ASHLEY, 2 & 3 Gules a bend engrailed between six lions rampant or COOPER. *Legend*: ANTHONY E: OF SHAFTESBURY.

1c

Crests: 1 Out of a ducal coronet or, a triple plume of ostrich feathers argent, 2 On a wreath or and sable, a griffin passant argent. *Mantling*: Dexter: Gules doubled argent, Sinister: Sable doubled or. The coronet of an earl. *Arms*: Quarterly, 1 & 4 Lozengy argent and gules FITZWILLIAM, 2 & 3 Sable a chevron between three leopard's faces or WENTWORTH. *Legend*: W. SPENCER E: FITZWILLIAM.

1d

A gold helmet affronty ensigned by a gold arched crown with a red cap. *Mantling*: Azure doubled argent. *Arms*: Azure a lion rampant queue fourchy barry argent and gules crowned or, holding in the dexter paw a sword erect argent, hilt and pommel or HESSE. *Legend*: FREDK LOUIS PRINCE OF HESSE.

2a

Crest: Out of a mural coronet or, a dragon's head argent charged with an ermine spot. *Mantling*: Azure doubled or. The coronet of an earl. *Arms*: Quarterly, 1 & 4 Azure three crescents or RYDER, 2 & 3 Gules three lapwings or a bordure argent TERRICK. *Legend*: DUDLEY E: OF HARROWBY.

Note: The crescents are usually differenced with an ermine spot.

2b

Crests: 1 Out of a ducal coronet gules, a plume of five ostrich feathers argent banded with a line the visible length in the form of a chevron azure, 2 On a wreath argent and azure, a peacock in his pride proper. *Mantling*: Dexter: Azure doubled or. Sinister: Azure doubled argent. The coronet of a duke. *Arms*: Quarterly, 1 & 4 Argent six cross-crosslets fitchy sable three, two and one, on a chief azure two mullets or pierced gules CLINTON, 2 & 3 Quarterly (i & iv) Azure three pelicans argent vulning themselves proper PELHAM, (ii & iii) Gules two demi belts in pale argent the buckles in chief or (see note to SIV, 3b). *Legend*: HENRY DUKE OF NEWCASTLE.

2c

Crest: On a wreath argent and sable, a demi lion rampant argent charged with three trefoils slipped vert, holding in its dexter paw an arrow pheoned and flighted proper, the shaft or. *Mantling*: Sable doubled argent. The coronet of an earl. *Arms*: Quarterly, 1 & 4 Argent three Moor's heads couped in profile proper, wreathed about the temples argent and azure CANNING, 2 & 3 Or on a bend azure a mullet between two crescents or, all within a bordure engrailed gules SCOTT. *Legend*: CHARLES EARL: CANNING.

2d

Crest: Out of a ducal coronet or, a phoenix rising or. *Mantling*: Gules doubled or. The coronet of a duke. *Arms*: Quarterly, 1 & 4 Or on a pile gules between six fleurs de lis azure, three lions passant guardant or SEYMOUR AUGMENTATION (see NIV, 2d), 2 & 3 Gules two wings conjoined in lure or SEYMOUR. *Legend*: EDW^{D} A. DUKE: OF SOMERSET.

3a

Crest: Out of a ducal coronet or, a demi lion rampant gules holding a spear erect proper and thereon flowing a fork tailed pennon argent charged in the hoist with a cross gules. *Mantling*: Gules doubled argent. The coronet of a duke. *Arms*: Quarterly, 1 & 4 Gules a cross argent between twenty plates, five in each quarter in saltire WELLESLEY, 2 & 3 Or a lion rampant gules gorged with a ducal coronet or COWLEY. In chief an escutcheon charged with the cross of St. George, St Andrew and St. Patrick being the Union badge of the United Kingdom (WELLINGTON AUGMENTATION. See SIV, 3c). *Legend*: ARTHUR D: OF WELLINGTON.

Note: This panel is for the second duke.

3b

Crest: On a wreath argent and sable, a serpent nowed proper. *Mantling*: Sable doubled argent. The coronet of a duke. *Arms*: Sable three buck's heads caboshed argent CAVENDISH. *Legend*: WM: D. OF DEVONSHIRE.

3c

A gold helmet affronty ensigned by a gold arched crown with a red cap. *Mantling*: Gules doubled argent. *Arms*: Argent, five escutcheons in cross azure, each charged with five plates in saltire, all within a bordure gules charged with seven castles or PORTUGAL. *Legend*: PEDRO V. K: OF PORTUGAL.

3d

Crest: On a chapeau gules turned up ermine, an eagle, wings addorsed or preying on a child proper, swaddled gules in a cradle laced or. *Mantling*: Azure doubled argent. The coronet of an earl. *Arms*: Argent on a bend azure three stag's heads caboshed or STANLEY. *Legend*: EDW: G. E: OF DERBY.

THE NORTH NAVE CLERESTORY

The structure, helmets, Garters, quarries, heads and borders, are all as in the windows on the south side of the nave clerestory.

NXVI

1a

A gold helmet affronty ensigned by a gold and silver Mitre Crown (the Imperial Crown of Russia). *Mantling*: Sable doubled or. *Arms*: Or a double headed eagle displayed sable, beaked and armed gules, crowned with a mitre crown infulae or, holding upright in the dexter claw a sceptre and in the sinister claw an orb azure decorated or. The eagle is charged upon the breast with an escutcheon bearing, Gules the mounted effigy of St George slaying the dragon, all proper, MOSCOW, around which hangs the collar and badge of the Order of St Andrew. The eagle's wings are charged with eight escutcheons: Dexter: 1 Argent a dragon sable winged gules crowned or KAZAN, 2 Gules an eagle displayed argent crowned or POLAND, 3 Or a double headed eagle displayed sable, charged upon the breast with a shield azure bearing a cross triple traversed argent, all within a bordure or TAURIA, 4 Tierced in pairle reversed (i) Azure an angel argent, holding in the dexter hand a sword or and in the sinister hand a buckler argent KIEV, (ii) Gules a lion or holding in his paw a latin cross argent VLADIMIR, (iii) Or a throne gules supported by two bears affronty sable, each bear holding a sceptre or, crossed in saltire NOVGOROD. Sinister: 1 Azure a royal crown surmounting a scimitar fesswise proper ASTRAKHAN, 2 Ermine two martins counter rampant supporting a royal crown, behind them two arrows in saltire and a bow in fess gules SIBERIA, 3 Or St George proper mounted upon a horse sable slaying a dragon sable winged vert GEORGIA, 4 Gules semy of nine roses argent overall a lion rampant crowned or, brandishing with a vambraced dexter paw a sword argent hilt and pommel or holding in its sinister paw and standing upon a scimitar argent, hilt and pommel or FINLAND. *Legend*: Alexander 2 Emp. of Russia 1867.

1b

A gold helmet affronty ensigned by a red fez having a white plume. *Mantling*: Gules doubled argent. *Arms*: Gules the Tughra argent. *Legend*: Sultan Abdul Aziz Khan 1867.

Note: The origin of the Tughra is said to lie in the action of the Sultan Murad I, who not being a 'man of scholarly parts', signed a treaty by wetting his open hand with ink and drawing it across the document, leaving a trail of smears within which the scribes wrote his name, the title of Khan and the epithet *el-Muzaffor-Diama* 'the ever victorious'. The characters within the Tughra changed with each sovereign.

1c

Crest: On a wreath or and sable, a lion couchant guardant argent supporting with the dexter paw a banner gules charged with a dexter hand apaumé couped argent, the staff or. *Mantling*: Sable doubled argent. *Arms*: Quarterly, 1 & 4 Sable a lion rampant argent, on a canton argent a cross gules CHURCHILL, with the augmentation granted to Sir Winston Churchill in 1661/2, 2 & 3 Quarterly Argent and gules in the second and third quarters a fret or, overall on a bend sable three escallops argent SPENCER. In chief an escutcheon, Argent a cross gules upon which is another escutcheon Azure three fleurs de lis or. Augmentation granted to George (Spencer), 5th Duke of Marlborough in 1817, indicating his descent from John, 1st Duke of Marlborough. *Legend*: John Duke of Marlborough 1868.

1d

As light 2c, but the crest and arms differenced by a label of three points argent, on the centre point a cross gules and on each of the two outer points a heart gules. *Legend*: Prince Leopold Geo: Duncan Albert 1869.

2a

Crest: On a chapeau gules turned up ermine, a lion statant guardant or crowned gules gorged with a collar company argent and gules, each piece argent charged with a rose gules barbed and seeded proper. *Mantling*: Azure doubled or. *Arms*: Quarterly, 1 & 4 France Modern quartering England, 2

Scotland, 3 Ireland. Overall an escutcheon, Gules three buckles or DUKEDOM OF AUBIGNY. The whole within a bordure compony argent and gules, each piece argent charged with a rose gules barbed and seeded proper. *Legend*: Charles Duke of Richmond 1867.

2b

Crest: On a wreath argent and azure, a portcullis chained or. *Mantling*: Azure doubled or. *Arms*: Quarterly France Modern and England all within a bordure compony argent and azure. SOMERSET. *Legend*: Henry Duke of Beaufort 1867.

2c

Crest: On a gold helmet affronty a coronet composed alternatively of crosses formy and fleur de lis or, having thereon a lion statant guardant crowned or, charged with a label of three points argent, on the centre point a cross gules and on each of the two outer points a fleur de lis azure. *Mantling*: Gules doubled ermine. The Royal Arms, viz. Quarterly, 1 & 4 England, 2 Scotland, 3 Ireland. An escutcheon Barry or and sable a crown of rue bendwise vert SAXONY. Overall a label as in the crest. *Legend*: Prince Arthur W. Albert 1867.

2d

A gold helmet affronty ensigned by a gold and silver mitre or house crown. *Mantling*: Sable doubled or. *Arms*: Or a double headed eagle displayed sable, crowned with a mitre crown with infulae or, armed gules, holding upright in the dexter claw a sceptre or and a sword, the blade argent, the hilt or and in the sinister claw an orb azure decorated or. The eagle is charged upon the breast with an escutcheon bearing tierced in pale 1 Or a lion rampant gules crowned or HAPSBURG, 2 Gules a fess argent AUSTRIA, 3 Or on a bend gules three allerions displayed argent LORRAINE. Above and between the eagles' heads is an additional mitre crown with infulae or. *Legend*: Francis Joseph Emp: of Austria 1867.

3a

Crest: Out of a ducal coronet or, a demi lion rampant gules holding a spear erect proper and thereon flowing a fork-tailed pennon, the hoist argent charged with a cross gules, the fly gules. *Mantling*: Gules doubled argent. *Arms*: Quarterly, 1 & 4 Gules a cross argent between twenty plates five in each quarter in saltire WELLESLEY, 2 & 3 Or a lion rampant gules COWLEY. The whole differenced at fess point with an annulet argent. *Legend*: Henry Richd Earl Cowley 1866.

3b

A gold helmet affronty ensigned by a gold arched crown with a red cap. *Mantling*: Sable doubled or. *Arms*: Sable a lion rampant or, armed and langued gules BELGIUM (DUKE OF BRABANT). *Legend*: Leopold 2 King of the Belgians 1866.

3c

A gold helmet affronty. *Crest*: Out of a ducal coronet or, a lion rampant crowned or holding a long handled axe, the blade argent, the haft or. *Mantling*: Gules doubled or. *Arms*: Quarterly, 1 Gules a lion rampant crowned or, holding a long handled axe, the blade argent, the haft or NORWAY, 2 Or two lions passant in pale azure SCHLESWIG, 3 Gules an escutcheon per fess argent and gules between three demi nettle leaves and as many passion nails in pairle argent HOLSTEIN, 4 Gules a swan argent, beaked, membered and ducally gorged or STORMARN. In base, Gules a knight in armour mounted upon a horse and holding a sword argent and a shield, trappings or DITZMERS. Overall an escutcheon, Quarterly, 1 & 4 Or two bars gules OLDENBURG, 2 & 3 Azure a cross formy or DELMENHORST. *Legend*: Fred. C.C. Duke of Schleswig Holstein 1866.

Note: Known as Prince Christian, he married Queen Victoria's third daughter, Princess Helena.

3d

Crest: On a chapeau gules turned up ermine, a peacock in its pride proper. *Mantling*: Azure doubled or. *Arms*: Or two bars azure, a chief quarterly, 1 & 4 Azure two fleurs de lis or, 2 & 3 Gules a lion passant guardant or MANNERS. *Legend*: Charles Duke of Rutland 1867.

NXVII

1a

As NXVI, 2c, except that the crest and arms are differenced by a label of three points argent, on the centre point a cross gules. *Legend*: Prince Albert Victor 1883.

1b

Crest: On a wreath or and sable, a boar's head fesswise couped close or armed argent, langued gules. *Mantling*: Sable doubled or. *Arms*: Quarterly, 1 & 4 Gyronny of eight or and sable CAMPBELL, 2 & 3 Argent a lymphad sails furled oars sable pennons and flags gules LORNE. *Legend*: George Duke of Argyle 1884.

Note: The boar's head is usually erased.

1c

Crest: On a chapeau gules turned up ermine, an eagle, wings addorsed or, preying on a child proper, swaddled gules in a cradle laced or. *Mantling*: Azure doubled argent. *Arms*: Argent on a bend azure, three stag's heads cabossed or STANLEY. *Legend*: Edward Earl of Derby 1884.

1d

As SXVII, 2c, except that the crest and arms are differenced by a label of five points argent, on the centre point an anchor azure. *Legend*: Prince George Frederick 1884 [later King George V].

2a

A gold helmet affronty ensigned by an gold arched crown. *Mantling*: Gules doubled argent. *Arms*: Quarterly of ten, 1 Or four pallets gules ARAGON, 2 Per saltire in chief and base Or four pallets gules and in the dexter and sinister Argent an eagle displayed sable SICILY, 3 Gules a fess argent AUSTRIA, 4 Azure semy de lis or within a bordure compony argent and gules BURGUNDY (MODERN), 5 Or semy de lis azure FARNESE, 6 Or five torteaux two, two and one and in chief a hurt charged with three fleurs de lis or MEDICI, 7 Bendy or and azure, a bordure gules BURGUNDY (ANCIENT), 8 Or a lion rampant sable FLANDERS, 9 Argent an eagle displayed gules TYROL, 10 Sable a lion rampant or BRABANT. Overall a cartouche Quarterly, 1 & 4

Gules a castle or CASTILE, 2 & 3 Argent a lion rampant purpure LEON, in base Argent a pomegranate proper GRANADA. The cartouche has overall another cartouche bearing Azure three fleurs de lis or ROYAL ARMS of the BOURBON Kings of France. *Legend*: Alphonso 12 King of Spain 1881.

2b

A gold helmet affronty ensigned by an gold arched crown with a red cap. *Mantling*: Sable doubled or. *Arms*: Barry of ten or and sable a crown of rue bendwise vert. SAXONY. *Legend*: Albert King of Saxony 1882.

2c

A gold helmet affronty ensigned by an gold arched crown with a red cap. *Mantling*: Gules doubled argent. *Arms*: Quarterly, 1 & 4 Gules a lion rampant crowned or holding in its dexter paw a Roman sword, the hilt or, the blade argent and in the sinister paw a bundle of arrows, 2 & 3 Quarterly, (i & iv) Gules a bend or CHALONS, (ii & iii) Or a horn stringed azure ORANGE, overall an escutcheon, Checky of nine pieces or and azure GENEVA. Overall an escutcheon, Azure billety a lion rampant or NASSAU. *Legend*: William 3 King of Netherlands 1882.

Note: These arms are incorrect and were only in use until 1815 since when the Nassau coat with some additions has been used.

2d

Crest: On a chapeau gules turned up ermine, a lion statant guardant or, ducally crowned azure and gorged with a collar counter-company argent and azure. *Mantling*: Azure doubled or. *Arms*: The Royal Arms of King Charles II, viz. Quarterly, 1 & 4 France Modern and England quarterly, 2 Scotland, 3 Ireland, overall a baton sinister company of six pieces argent and azure. *Legend*: Augustus Cha: Duke of Grafton 1884.

3a

Crest: On a wreath argent and azure, six arrows in saltire or heads in base barbed and flighted argent, banded gules, buckled and garnished or and ensigned by a morion proper. *Mantling*: Azure doubled argent. *Arms*: Quarterly, 1 & 4 Barry of ten argent and azure, overall six escutcheons three, two and one sable, each charged with a lion rampant argent CECIL, 2 & 3 Argent on a pale sable, a conger's head erased and erect or charged with an ermine spot GASCOYNE. *Legend*: Robert Marquess of Salisbury 1878.

3b

Crest: On a wreath argent and gules, a goat statant argent, armed and unguled or. *Mantling*: Gules doubled argent. *Arms*: Quarterly of twelve, 1 & 12 Argent a lion rampant gules, on a chief sable three escallops argent RUSSELL, 2 Azure a tower argent LA TOUR, 3 Barry of six gules and or MUSTIAN, 4 Gules three herrings haurient argent HERRING, 5 Sable three chevrons ermine WISE, 6 Sable three dovecots argent SAPCOTES, 7 Sable crusily a lion rampant argent LONG, 8 Argent on a cross sable a leopard's face or BRYDGES, 9 Gules on a chevron argent three mullets or, in dexter chief a lion passant guardant or CARR, 10 Azure a cross or between four falcons close argent WRIOTHESLEY, 11 Argent two bars and in chief three lions rampant sable HOWLAND. *Legend*: Francis C. Duke of Bedford 1880.

Note: Mustian, Wise and Sapcotes usually bear differences and the mullets in Carr should be sable.

3c

As NXVI, 1a. *Legend*: Alexander 3 Emp: of Russia 1881.

3d

A gold helmet affronty ensigned by a gold arched crown. *Mantling*: Gules doubled argent. *Arms*: Dexter; per fess, in chief: Azure three crowns or SWEDEN, in base: Azure three bends sinister wavy argent, a lion rampant crowned or FOLKUNGA, impaling, Sinister; Gules a lion rampant crowned or, holding a long handled axe, the blade argent, the haft or NORWAY. Overall a cross formy of three arms or. At fess point an escutcheon, per pale; dexter: Per bend azure and gules a bend argent, overall a vase or VASA, impaling, sinister: Azure an eagle displayed sable, in chief seven stars argent and in base a bridge with two towers over water argent PONTECORVO (BERNADOTTE). *Legend*: Oscar 2 King of Sweden 1881.

Windows NXVIII to NXXII are of plain glass save that a medieval gold hempbrake appears in the following: NXX, quatrefoil A; NXXI, 2c; NXXII, 2b and 2d.

THE SOUTH CHOIR AISLE AND AMBULATORY

The Choir Ambulatory

Between 1785 and 1787 two hexagonal skylights were inserted into the ceiling vault. These were later glazed by Thomas Willement.

North

A border of blue interspersed with a floral decoration in white and gold. With the Garter ensigned by a gold arched crown with a red cap, Quarterly France Modern and England. Above the Garter and on either side of the crown are the letters E IV and R. in gold.

South

Border as north. Within the Garter ensigned by a crown as north, Quarterly, 1 & 4 England, 2 Scotland, 3 Ireland. Above on either side of the crown the letters in gold V and R.

The Lincoln Chapel

The chapel opens from the south-east corner of the south choir aisle and contains the tomb of Edward Clinton, Earl of Lincoln (1512–85) and his third wife Elizabeth Fitzgerald (1528–90). There are five windows, each of four lights and with a quatrefoil at the apex. The upper two lights in each window contain a coat of arms, below which is an inscription.

sIII

1a

Apex, border, and background as 2a. The motto (see below) is repeated in all three bends.

1b

As 1a.

2a

A red border and at the apex a blue and gold floral decoration. The background is composed of three quarries, each charged with a mullet or pierced argent, interspersed with three bends, the upper bearing the motto LOYAULTE N'A HONTE, the two lower bends having a formal floral decoration in black. Within the Garter and ensigned by the coronet of an earl and having on each side a red quatrefoil: Argent six cross-crosslets fitchy sable on a chief azure two mullets or pierced gules CLINTON, impaling, in chief, Barry nebuly of six or and sable BLOUNT; centre, Sable a bend or between six fountains STOURTON; in base, Argent a saltire gules FITZGERALD. *Inscription*: Edward Earl of Lincoln K.G. High Admiral of England mar^{d}. 1. Elizabeth Blount 2^{ly} Ursula Stourton 3^{ly} Elizabeth Fitzgerald.

Note: Elizabeth Blount had been the mistress of King Henry VIII and was the mother of his illegitimate son Henry Fitzroy, Duke of Richmond and Somerset.

2b

Apex, border, background and motto as 2a. Within a circlet sable bearing a formal foliage pattern in gold, ensigned by the coronet of an earl and having on each side a quatrefoil azure: CLINTON impaling, in chief Argent a maunch sable HASTINGS; in base Or on a chief gules three chaplets or MORRISON. *Inscription*: Henry, Earl of Lincoln married 1st Katherine Hastings 2^{ly} Elizabeth Morrison.

Tracery Quatrefoil

Against a red background and within the Garter, an anchor argent the stock cabled with a rope or.

sIV

1a

As sIII, 1a but with a blue border and apex as sIV, 2a.

1b

As 1a.

2a

Background and motto as sIII, 2a, but with a blue border and having at the apex a floral decoration in red and gold. Within a circlet as sIII, 2b and having on each side a quatrefoil azure CLINTON with a crescent argent for difference, impaling Argent a lion passant between three cross-crosslets fitchy gules DIGHTON. *Inscription*: Sir Edward Clinton Knight; second son, married Mary daughter of Thomas Dighton, Esquire.

2b

Apex, background and border as 2d. Within a circlet as sIII, 2b, having on each side a quatrefoil azure CLINTON with a mullet argent for difference. An escutcheon of pretence, Ermine on a fess sable a castle triple towered argent HILL. *Inscription*: Francis Clinton Esquire; third son, married Priscilla daughter and (heir) of Iohn Hill Esquire.

Note: These inscriptions are misleading. Edward Clinton was the second son of Henry Earl of Lincoln. Francis Clinton was Edward's third son.

Tracery Quatrefoil

Against a red background, within a circlet sable edged argent containing a formal pattern of gold quatrefoils, enfiled by a ducal coronet gules, six feathers sable ribbed or penned sable, arched and interlaced.

sV

1a

As sIII, 1a.

1b

As 1a.

2a

Apex, background and border as sIII, 2a. Within a circlet as in sIII, 2b, ensigned by an earl's coronet and having on each side a quatrefoil azure CLINTON impaling, in chief Argent a double headed eagle displayed sable within a bordure sable bezanty KILLIGREW; in base Argent three choughs sable PENYSTON. *Inscription*: Francis, Earl of Lincoln married, first Elizabeth Killigrew, secondly Susan Peniston.

2b

Apex, background and border as 2a. Within a circlet with coronet and quatrefoils as 2a CLINTON impaling Quarterly, 1 & 4 Azure three pelicans vulning themselves argent, 2 & 3 gules two demi belts in pale buckles in chief argent PELHAM. *Inscription*: Henry, Earl of Lincoln, married Lucy, daughter of Thomas, Lord Pelham.

Tracery Quatrefoil

Background and within a circlet as quatrefoil sIV. Azure a mullet or pierced gules.

sVI

1a

Apex, border and background as 2a, but with a motto on each bend: 1. LOYAULTE N'A HONTE; 2. VINCIT AMOR PATRIA; 3. LOYAULTE N'A HONTE.

1b

As 1a, but bends 1. VINCIT AMOR PATRIA; 2. LOYAULTE N'A HONTE; 3. VINCIT AMOR PATRIA.

2a

A blue border and having at the apex a formal floral decoration in red and gold. The background is composed of quarries bearing alternately a mullet pierced argent and a buckle argent, the inside of the latter being or. The quarries are interspersed with three bends, the upper bearing the motto VINCIT AMOR PATRIA, the two lower having formal floral decorations. Within the Garter ensigned by the coronet of a duke and having on each side a quatrefoil gules CLINTON with an escutcheon of pretence for PELHAM. *Inscription*: Henry Fiennes Duke of Newcastle K.G. married Katharine daughter and co-heir of the Rt. Hon. Henry Pelham.

2b

Within a circlet ensigned by the coronet of a duke and having on each side a quatrefoil azure, Quarterly, 1 and 4 CLINTON, 2 and 3 PELHAM, impaling Quarterly ermine and gules, the first quarter bearing a crescent argent for difference STANHOPE. *Inscription*: Thomas Duke of Newcastle: married Anna-Maria daughter of William Earl of Harrington.

Tracery Quatrefoil

Against a red background and within the Garter, a buckle, point in chief argent.

sVII

1a

As sVI, 1a, but with blue and gold floral decorations at the apex and with a red border.

1b

As sVI, 1b but with apex and bordure as 1a.

2a

Background and motto as sVI, 2a, but with a red border and a formal floral decoration in blue and gold. Within the Garter ensigned by the coronet of a duke and having on each side a red quatrefoil, Quarterly, 1 and 4 CLINTON, 2 and 3 PELHAM; an escutcheon of pretence, Quarterly, 1 and 4 Per pale gules and sable on a cross engrailed argent five lozenges purpure on a chief argent three eagles' legs erased à la quise sable MUNDY, 2 and 3 Gules within a bordure of martlets an escutcheon argent CHADWICK. *Inscription*: Henry Pelham Duke of Newcastle K.G. married Georgiana dau: of Edward Miller Mundy M.P. for the Co. of Derby by Georg: Chadwick.

2b

Apex, background, motto and border as sVI, 2b, with the Garter and ensigned by the coronet of a duke: Enfiled by a ducal coronet gules five ostrich feathers argent banded with a line the visible length in the form of a chevron azure. *Inscription*: Henry Pelham Duke of Newcastle K.G. Repaired the Monument of his Ancestor and decorated these Windows AD 1848.

Tracery Quatrefoil

As sV but mullet is within the Garter.

The South Choir Aisle (s VIII–sXIV)

sVIII

This window depicts the descent of the crown from King Edward III, through his two sons John of Gaunt and Edmund of Langley, to King Henry VII and the subsequent union of the Houses of Lancaster and York. The continuity of the theme is shown by the pattern of roses, red for Lancaster and white for York, which form a background on either side of the window.

1a

Background of quarries, each bearing formal foliage and a gold rose. *In chief*: Upon a blue circle, a sunburst having a bleu celeste base with a nebuly design from which issues golden rays. *Centre*: Surrounded by the Garter, fringed purpure and ensigned by an open gold crown, Quarterly France Ancient and England. *In base*: The shield of St George within the Garter. On either side of the shield are the letters E and R.

1b

Canopy and background as 3b. King Edward III wearing an open crown and clad in a blue robe over which is a cloak of red powdered with Garters and edged in gold, lined with brown fur. He bears in his right hand a two-handed sword upon which are impaled two open crowns, and in his left hand a gold sceptre. Below upon a scroll is the legend: *Edwardus tertius Rex.*

1c

Canopy and background as 3b. Queen Philippa wearing a headdress of the 14th century upon which is placed an open crown. She is clad in a blue bodice edged with gold and red and a purple skirt edged with gold, over which is a cloak. Beneath, upon a scroll is the legend: *Philippa Regina.*

1d

Quarries and roses as 1a. *In chief*: Upon a circle of red and green a white hind lodged, sheltering under a bush. *Centre*: A shield fringed as in 1 and ensigned by an open gold crown, Quarterly France Ancient and England impaling Quarterly, 1 & 4 Or a lion rampant sable FLANDERS, 2 & 3 Or a lion rampant gules HOLLAND (Arms of HAINAULT). Surrounding the shield is a collar composed of red roundels bearing gold letters making up the words MYN BID DEN YE. Pendant from the collar is a red cross patonce having between each arm a gold fleur de lis. Upon the centre of the cross is a roundel bearing the letters i h c. *In base*: A shield bearing Or three eagles displayed gules. Above the shield is the date 1340 and on either side the letters P and R. At the base of this light is the monogram TW 1846 [for Thomas Willement].

Note: The letters upon the collar and perhaps allusively on the cross refer to two mottoes used by Queen Philippa MYN BIDDENYE and ICH WURDE MUCH (see *Archaeologia*, xxx (1846), p. 372). They may be translated as 'My Prayer' and 'I Was Glad'. The shield in base is intended to represent the arms of Robert de Eglesfield, confessor to Queen Philippa, the founder in 1340 of the Queen's College, Oxford, which uses the arms Argent three eagles displayed gules.

2a

Quarries and roses as 1a. *In chief*: Upon a circle of blue and green, a gold falcon holding in its beak and a claw a silver padlock. *Centre*: A barred gold helm facing to the sinister bearing for the crest;

On a chapeau gules turned up ermine, a lion statant crowned or gorged with a label of three points ermine. Mantling: Gules doubled ermine. Within the Garter, Quarterly France Ancient and England overall a label of three points ermine, impaling Gules three Catherine wheels or ROLET. *In base*: Upon a circle of red and blue an ostrich feather ermine.

Note: The shield is for the marriage of John of Gaunt, Duke of Lancaster with Catherine Swynford née Rolet. She was his third wife and had been his mistress for some years during which a number of children surnamed Beaufort were born. King Henry VII's mother was descended from the eldest of these children.

2b

Under a canopy, John of Gaunt wearing a red headdress and the mantle of the Garter over a red surcoat (jupon), holding in the right hand a black baton surmounted by a silver fleur de lis, the legs being encased in gold armour. He wears the Garter below the left knee. Below and upon a scroll the legend: *Iohann: Dux Lancastr:*.

2c

Under a canopy, Edmund, Duke of York, as light 2b save that he wears a headdress of white powdered with Garters and a surcoat of Quarterly France Ancient and England with a label of three points argent each point charged with three torteaux. He bears in his right hand a gold mace. Beneath, on a scroll is the legend: *Edmondus Dux Eborac:*.

2d

Quarries and roses as 1a. *In chief*: Upon a red circle, a silver falcon within a closed gold fetterlock. *Centre*: On a barred gold helmet facing to the dexter, for the crest; On a chapeau gules turned up ermine, a lion statant crowned or gorged with a label of three points argent, on each point three torteaux. Mantling: Gules doubled ermine. Within the Garter, Quarterly France Ancient and England impaling Quarterly 1 & 4 Gules a castle or CASTILE, 2 & 3 Argent a lion rampant purpure LEON. *In base*: On a red circle three roses argent seeded or surmounted by green foliage.

Note: The shield denotes the marriage of Edmund of Langley with Isabel of Castile from which the Yorkist claimants to the throne descended.

3a

A background of quarries as in 1a. *In chief*: a circle with a blue background having thereon a hawthorn bush proper ensigned by a gold arched crown. *Centre*: Within the Garter a shield framed at the upper and lower edges by a purple floral fringe and ensigned by an arched gold crown, bearing Quarterly France Modern and England. *In base*: A circle having a blue background bearing a portcullis chained or. The whole of the decorations are surrounded by a rose branch proper bearing roses gules barbed vert and seeded or.

3b

Under a canopy against a background blue in chief and green in base, King Henry VII wearing a red robe trimmed with brown and a brown fur cap with a red jewel surrounded by pearls. Beneath the figure upon a scroll is the legend: *Henricus Septimus Rex*.

3c

Within a canopy and background as 3b. Queen Elizabeth wearing a brown gown trimmed with ermine over a red underskirt and having a headdress of the 15th century edged with gold and with pearls. Beneath on a scroll is the legend: *Elizabetha Regina.*

3d

Quarries as 1a. *In chief*: Within a red circlet against a background of gold, a bull sable horned and unguled or. *Centre*: A shield fringed and surmounted, having on each side a white rose between two red roses bearing Quarterly France Modern and England impaling Quarterly France Modern and England. Pendant from the shield is a gold cord supporting a medallion the centre of which is red and bears the monogram HE. *In base*: A red circle bearing thereon a white rose surrounded by gold rays. The decorations are surrounded by a rose branch as in 1 but bearing white roses.

Tracery Quatrefoils

At the apex of the window are three quatrefoils, the remainder being twelve lights grouped in three ranges each of four lights.
B: Against a gold background with green leaves, a rose per pale gules and argent seeded or.
A: Same background but with a red rose.
C: Same background but with a white rose.

sIX

This window is a memorial to King Henry VI.

1a

A background of quarries bearing a formal floral decoration. An heraldic antelope sejant argent facing sinister, attired and unguled or, chained and gorged as light 3a, bearing a blue staff from which is a banner of Quarterly England and France Modern. A legend appears on a scroll wrapped about the staff: *Te Deum Laudamus.*

1b

Quarries as 1a. Upper circle with rose as 3a. Within a circle, the upper part of which consists of a formal floral decoration interspersed with gold fleurs de lis, the lower part bearing the legend: *Collegium beatae maria de Etona*, a shield bearing Sable three lilies argent slipped vert seeded or, on a chief per pale azure and gules, to the dexter a fleur de lis or and to the sinister a lion passant guardant or ETON COLLEGE. *Centre*: Within a formal floral decoration in blue interspersed as before, against a silver background three roses gules slipped vert seeded or. *In base*: Within a circle as above but with the motto: *Colleg: Regale Cantabridgiae* a shield bearing Sable three roses argent seeded or barbed vert, on a chief per pale azure and gules to the dexter a fleur de lis or, to the sinister a lion passant guardant or KING'S COLLEGE, CAMBRIDGE.

Note: King Henry VI founded both Eton College and King's College, Cambridge.

1c

Quarries as light 1a, but with a letter M. Within a formal floral decoration of red interspersed as previously, against a silver background three daisies proper slipped or. *Centre*: Within a circlet the upper part of which is of a formal floral decoration in blue interspersed with a gold fleur de lis, the bottom part bearing the legend: *Coll: Reginale Cantabridgiae*, a shield bearing Quarterly of six, 1 Barry of six argent and gules HUNGARY, 2 Azure semy de lis or a label of three points gules NAPLES, 3 Argent a cross potent between four crosses or JERUSALEM, 4 Azure semy de lis or a bordure gules ANJOU, 5 Azure semy of cross-crosslets fitchy two barbels haurient addorsed or BAR, 6 Or on a bend gules three alerions displayed argent LORRAINE, all within a bordure vert QUEENS' COLLEGE CAMBRIDGE. *In base*: Within a red circle three daisies slipped all proper.

Note: Queen Margaret founded Queens' College, Cambridge.

1d

Quarries as light 1c. *In chief*: a daisy within a circlet. An eagle facing dexter supporting in its dexter claw a red staff from which flies a banner having upon it the arms of ANJOU (see 3c). A legend appears upon a scroll wrapped about the staff, *Humble et loiall.* At the base of this light is a small shield bearing the monogram TW [for Thomas Willement].

2a–2d

The figures contained in this and the following three lights form a continuous picture. Within a room or hall, the lower part of the walls of which are green, above being stonework and windows leading to a timbered roof. To the left is the figure of St George in gold armour over which he wears a surcoat of Argent a cross gules and a cloak of red lined pink. In his left hand he bears a jousting spear from which hangs a pennon, Argent a cross gules. His right hand rests on the shoulder of the kneeling figure of King Henry VI, who wears a blue cloak lined with red and trimmed with ermine and has about his neck a gold chain. On his head is a red hat in which is a blue jewel against a gold background. The hands are raised in prayer. He kneels at a table covered with a red cloth upon which lies a half open book with green fastenings. Adjacent to the book is a gold arched and jewelled crown. Queen Margaret has in front of her an open book with green fastenings upon which her hands rest. She is dressed in a gold cloak lined with blue and trimmed with ermine and has about her neck a gold rope and a necklace of gold pieces. She wears a headdress of red and gold edged with gold drops and has upon her head an open coronet. Behind her stands the figure of St Margaret dressed in a red robe with white sleeves edged in gold, over which is a purple cloak edged in green. In her right hand she bears a gold cross ornamented with pearls and around her hair is a silver band having at the centre of the forehead a gold quatrefoil.

3a

Background of quarries as 1a. *In chief*: Within a green circle a rose gules seeded or. *Centre*: Within a formal floral decoration in red interspersed by two fleurs de lis and two leopard's faces in gold, against a blue background, a swan rising argent beaked and legged gules, gorged with a coronet and chained or. Below, in the centre of the window is a rose gules, barbed and seeded or, ensigned by a gold arched crown. *In base*: Within a circle of formal floral decorations in blue interspersed with two fleurs de lis and two leopard's faces or, against a red background an heraldic antelope lodged argent bezanty attired and unguled or gorged with a coronet and chained or.

Note: Queen Margaret bore a daisy as a badge in allusion to her name in French (Marguerite), and it is said that it was worn as a favour by the people on her arrival in England.

3b

Quarries as light 3a. *In chief*: A rose as light 3a. *Centre*: Upon a shield ensigned by an arched gold and jewelled crown having within a red cap, Azure a cross patonce between five martlets or EDWARD THE CONFESSOR impaling Quarterly France Modern and England HENRY VI. *In base*: the motto: *Dieu et mon droit.*

3c

Quarries as light 3a but with the letter M. *In chief*: Within a green circle a daisy proper. *Centre*: Upon a shield ensigned as 3b, Quarterly France Modern and England impaling Quarterly of six, 1 Barry of six (usually eight) argent and gules HUNGARY, 2 Azure semy de lis or a label of three points gules NAPLES, 3 Argent a cross potent between four crosses or JERUSALEM, 4 Azure semy de lis a bordure gules ANJOU, 5 Azure semy of cross-crosslets fitchy two barbels haurient and addorsed or BARR, 6 Or on a bend gules three alerions displayed argent LORRAINE. (The coat is ANJOU for Queen Margaret, wife of King Henry VI.) Below is the motto: *Humble et loiall.*

3d

Quarries as 3c. *In chief*: a daisy as 3c. *Centre*: Within a circlet of formal floral decorations in blue as 1, the arms of Jerusalem (see above 3c). Below the circlet a daisy proper slipped or surmounted by a gold arched crown. *In base*: Within a circlet of formal floral decoration in red. On a blue background a ship with a single square rigged sail having masts and tackle of gold. Upon the sail is the motto EN DIEU, repeated twice.

Tracery Quatrefoils

A: A shield bearing the arms of St George within the Garter having on either side on a silver background the letters S and G
B and C: On a blue background a gold fleur de lis.

sX

This window is a memorial to King Henry VIII and the early years of the Reformation.

1a

Under a canopy, three shields. *Upper*: Ensigned by a gold mitre with infulae of purple fringed with gold, Azure a cross patonce between five martlets or, on a chief or a pale quarterly of France Modern and England between two roses gules seeded or. On either side is the legend EPISC: WESTM: (SEE of WESTMINSTER suppressed 1550). *Centre*: Gules, two keys addorsed in saltire, wards outwards and in chief or between four cross-crosslets fitchy argent. On either side the legend *EPISC: PETERB*: (SEE of PETERBOROUGH). *In base*: Azure two keys in saltire, wards inward and in chief argent. On either side is the legend *EPISC: GLOCST*: (SEE of GLOUCESTER).

At the base of the window, upon a red background bordered with gold, the following in silver: *ECCLES: APOSTOL: ANGLICANÆ LIBERTAS RESTITUTA.*

1b

Within a circle of white and gold, against a blue background, a Tudor rose barbed and seeded proper. Below this is an inner canopy within which, against a blue background, is displayed an open book having a red cover, the leaves edged with gold. In it is written on the left-hand page: *BIBLIA. The Bible, that is the holy Scripture of the Olde and New Testament, faithfully and truly translated out of Douche and Latin in to Englishe MDXXXV.* On the right-hand page is: *S. Paul II Tessa: III praie for us that the worde of God maie have fre passage, and be glorified even as it is with you.* Underneath the book is the legend in silver letters: *POPULO CHRISTIANO BIBLIA RESIGNATA.* At the base of the window, within a circle as in chief, against a blue background a gold chained portcullis.

Note: The left-hand page of the book contains the title of the Coverdale Bible of 1535.

1c

Within a circle as light 1b, against a blue background a gold fleur de lis. *Centre*: Within an inner canopy and background as light 1b, a shield bearing Argent a chevron between three roses gules seeded or and on a chief gules a lion passant guardant between two books, with fastenings to the dexter or. Below is the legend in silver letters on red: *COLL: SANCT. TRIN: CANTAB: FVNDATVM* (TRINITY COLLEGE CAMBRIDGE). *In base*: Within a circle as light 1b, a Tudor rose barbed and seeded proper.

1d

Three shields. *Upper*: Ensigned by a mitre, Sable a fess argent, in chief three demi ladies couped at the waist, heads affronty proper, crowned, arrayed and veiled or, in base an ox argent horned and unguled or, passing a ford, barry wavy of four azure and argent. On either side the legend: EPISC: OXON: (SEE OF OXFORD). *Centre*: Sable three open crowns or. On either side *EPISC: BRIST.* (SEE of BRISTOL). *In base*: Gules three mitres with infulæ or. On either side EPISC: CESTR: (SEE of CHESTER). In the base of this light in silver letters upon a red background is the legend: EPISCOPORV: NVMERO. SEX. ADDITI. In the bottom right-hand corner of the light is a small shield bearing the monogram T.W. [Thomas Willement]. Along the base of the four lower lights is the following:

IN PIAM MEMORIAM HENRICI OCT: REGIS ET IANÆ REG: IN MEDIO CHORO SEPVLTI DEC ET CAN P.C. 1846.

Note: These three episcopal shields and those in light 1a represent the six new bishoprics established by King Henry VIII.

2a

Under a canopy, at the apex a demi wreath of green and gold leaves, against a background of a tiled chequered pavement and green walls, surmounted by a gold frieze and having at the top blue sky, King Edward VI dressed in the costume of the mid-16th century. He wears a red hat with a plume of ostrich feathers, a tunic of cloth of gold decorated upon the sleeves with red four-petalled devices and has around his neck a blue cord from which is pendant a gold and pearl decoration and a red rose seeded gold. Over the tunic is a short cloak of purple fringed at the collar with fur and at the sleeves and skirt with gold. The hose is red and he wears the Garter below the left knee. His shoes are white with the four leafed pattern in red as upon the tunic. His left hand grasps the quillon of a sword, the scabbard of which is blue, the quillons and grip gold. Below the figure upon a red background is a motto in silver: ICH DIEN.

2b

Canopy and background as light 2a. King Henry VIII dressed in the costume of the mid-sixteenth century, a cloth of gold tunic and a brown jewelled hat with a plume of ostrich feathers. Around his neck is a jewelled collar and a gold cord from which is pendant a red jewel surrounded by pearls. He wears a red cloak trimmed at the neck and lined with fur, trimmed at the sleeves and skirt with a white and gold border. His hose is white and he wears the Garter below the left knee. His shoes are gold with a silver floral decoration. In his right hand he grasps a glove and in his left he holds a dagger, the latter being black with silver and gold decoration. Below, as light 2a, is the motto: *DIEU ET MON DROIT.*

2c

Background as previously. Queen Jane Seymour, wearing a close headdress of gold edged with pearls. Her brown hair lies loose upon her back. She wears a bodice of white embroidered with gold with red sleeves, and a red skirt over which is a cloak or mantle of white embroidered with gold, the sleeves being of ermine. Around her neck, close under the chin, is a gold cross below which is a rope of pearls. At the breast is a multi coloured jewel. A cord of gold pieces interspersed with pearls and terminating in a gold tassel hangs from the waist. Below is the legend: *BOWND TO OBEY & SERVE.*

2d

Canopy and background as previously. Princess Elizabeth wearing a headdress of black edged with gold and pearls. Around her neck is a rope of pearls. At her breast is a silver cross surrounded by a gold oval having pendant there from three pearls. She is clad in a white under skirt embroidered in gold, over which is a dress of red lined with white, embroidered with gold. From her waist hangs a white and gold cord ending in a gold tassel. She holds a black book edged with gold. Below, as previously, is the motto: *VIDEO TACEO.*

3a

Under a canopy, *In chief*: the letters E.P. in gold. *Centre*: within the Garter having above and below a border purpure and ensigned by three ostrich feathers enfiled by a gold and jewelled coronet a shield bearing Quarterly France Modern and England, a label of three points argent (PRINCE EDWARD, later EDWARD VI). Pendant from the Garter within an oval surrounded by a formal floral decoration of gold green and blue against a background of red and green, a gold cannon with a silver carriage having a gold chain affixed to the breech. Above the cannon is a gold linstock and below a sponge holder of silver with a gold sponge and ladle.

Note: The so-called Prince of Wales feathers is a badge used by the Heir Apparent. King Edward VI was never created Prince of Wales.

3b

Canopy as previously. In chief: the letters H.R. in gold. *Centre*: within the Garter with a border as previously, ensigned by a gold arched crown adorned with jewels and pearls and having a red cap, a shield bearing Quarterly France Modern and England (HENRY VIII). Pendant from the Garter an oval as previously but with a red background having thereon a rose and slipped gold, about which is the legend: *FIDEI DEFENSOR.*

3c

Canopy as previously. In chief: the letters in gold J.R. *Centre*: within a wreath formed of green leaves adorned with blue flowers and gold embellishments, ensigned by a crown as light 2, Quarterly France Modern and England impaling quarterly of six: 1 Or on a pile gules between six fleurs de lis azure, three lions passant guardant or, 2 Gules two wings conjoined in lure or SEYMOUR, 3 Vair BEAUCHAMP OF HACHE, 4 Argent three demi lions rampant couped gules STURMY, 5 Per bend argent and gules, three roses in bend countercharged MACWILLIAM, 6 Argent on a bend gules three leopard's faces or COKER. (The shield is for Queen Jane Seymour, the third wife of King Henry VIII, who granted the first quarter to her as an augmentation). Pendant from the wreath on an oval as light 2, a round tower with a gateway argent, having within a mound or from which rises another tower also argent. Issuant from the inner part of the second tower are four roses, two on each side, each or and argent slipped or. From above the gateway rises a tree or adorned with flowers or and argent and surmounted by an arched crown or. Above the crown a phoenix affronty displayed crowned or membered argent arising from its flames or.

3d

Canopy as before. *In chief*: the letters in gold E.P. *Centre*: within a wreath as in 3c ensigned by a gold and jewelled coronet under which is the motto *Semper Eadem*, on a lozenge Quarterly France Modern and England (PRINCESS later QUEEN ELIZABETH I). Below, on an oval pendant from the wreath as light 3b a silver falcon standing upon a gold stock, having upon its head a gold crown and in its dexter claw a gold sceptre, having arising from the stock two flowers upon each side, one each of gold and silver (a badge used by her mother, Queen Anne Boleyn).

Tracery Quatrefoils

A, B and C as sIX.

sXI

The window is a memorial to King James I.

1a

Background of quarries decorated alternately the letters H and P. In the apex, within a blue convoluted circle against a white background the letters H.P. in gold. *In chief*: within a formal floral decoration of red and green, upon a star of gold, three ostrich feathers enfiled by a gold coronet, below which is the motto: ICH DIEN. *Centre*: within the Garter ensigned by a gold coronet with a red cap, Quarterly, 1 & 4 Quarterly France Modern and England, 2 Scotland, 3 Ireland, overall a label of three points argent (THE ROYAL ARMS OF THE STUARTS differenced for HENRY PRINCE OF WALES). *In base*: Within a formal floral decoration as in chief against a silver background upon a gold coronet a lion statant guardant crowned or gorged with a label of three points argent.

1b

Background of quarries bearing the letters R and J. At the apex a shield bearing Ireland. *In chief*: Within a formal floral decoration of blue and purple a Tudor rose impaling a thistle all proper ensigned by a gold arched crown. *Centre*: Within the Garter the royal arms of the Stuarts ensigned by a gold arched crown with a red cap. *In base*: Within a circle as in chief two flags in saltire the dexter bearing Argent a cross gules, the sinister Azure a saltire argent. The base of the flag staffs which are of gold, pass through a gold arched crown under which is the legend: *FIRMANTUR BINA SUB UNO.*

1c

Background of quarries bearing the letters R and A. At the apex, Gules a wyvern couchant tail nowed or. *In chief*: Within a circlet the letters in green A.R. entwined with a red cord. *Centre*: Within a wreath of red and white roses and thistles all proper, Quarterly of five, a cross paty throughout Argent fimbriated gules; 1 Or semy of hearts gules, three lions passant in pale azure crowned or DENMARK, 2 Gules a lion rampant crowned or, holding upright in the fore paws an axe argent NORWAY, 3 Azure three open crowns or SWEDEN, 4 Or ten hearts gules and in chief a lion passant azure KINGDOM OF THE GOTHS, 5 Gules a wyvern passant tail nowed or KINGDOM OF THE VANDALS; overall an escutcheon Quarterly, 1 Or two lions passant in pale azure SCHLESWIG, 2 Gules an escutcheon between three nettle leaves and three nails in pairle argent HOLSTEIN, 3 Gules a swan argent beaked sable, gorged with a gold coronet STORMARN, 4 Azure a chevalier armed at all points brandishing his sword, his charger argent, trappings or DITMARSKEN. In the centre of the escutcheon, an inescutcheon bearing Or two bars gules OLDENBURG, impaling Azure a cross or DALMENHURST. *In base*: Within a circle as in chief upon a label of Azure doubled or: *LA MIA GRANDEZZA DA EXCELSO.*

1d

In the apex within a blue circle the letters in gold E.R. *In chief*: Within a wreath out of a gold coronet a vulture's wing sable powdered with nenuphar leaves. *Centre*: Within a wreath of green leaves and gold roses bound in blue and ensigned by an open gold crown, Quarterly 1 & 4 PALATINATE, 2 & 3 BAVARIA (see 3d); overall an inner escutcheon of the Arch Steward of the Empire impaling the Stuart Royal Arms. *In base*: Within a wreath as 1a, upon a mount vert between two buffalo horns lozengy argent and azure, a lion sejant affronty crowned or. In the bottom right-hand corner of this light is a small shield with the monogram T.W. [Thomas Willement]. Along the base of lights is the legend: *HENRICVS ROSAS REGNA JACOBVS.*

2a

Within a canopy consisting of a semi-circular arch raised upon two pillars standing upon a tiled floor and against a background of gold, the upper part being blue, Henry, Prince of Wales, dressed in the costume of the early seventeenth century. He wears a lace ruff and has a doublet and breeches of cloth of gold over which is a short red cloak edged with gold. Pendant from a blue ribbon about the neck is the Lesser George. His left hand rests upon the pommel of a sword, the hilt of which is gold. His hose is white with red garters and the shoes are the same colour each bearing a red rose with gold seeds. Below his left knee he wears the Garter. Below is the legend in gold letters upon a blue background: HENRICUS PRINC: WALL:.

2b

Under a canopy, King James I in the costume of the early 16th century, wearing a brown hat trimmed with gold and with two ostrich feathers held in place by a brooch shaped as a fleur de lis composed of gold and pearls. His doublet is brown with gold embroidery and has a collar of white lace. Over the doublet he wears a violet cloak lined in green. Around his neck he wears the collar of the Order of the Garter pendant from which is the George within the Garter. His breeches are brown striped with gold, his hose brown and his shoes white. About his left knee is buckled the Garter. In his hand is white glove trimmed with gold. Below is the legend in gold letters upon a red background: JACOBVS ANG: SCOT: FRAN: ET HIB: REX.

2c

Canopy and background as light 2a. Queen Anne, wife of King James I, wears a low cut gown of the early seventeenth century. Upon her head are two ropes of pearls and a jewel of gold, with three pearls pendant from it. She wears a high lace collar. Her dress is brown embroidered with gold and with pink roses, the sleeves are white embroidered and with gold. In her left hand she carries a white embroidered handkerchief. Below is the legend in gold letters against a red background: ANNA REGINA.

2d

Elizabeth, Queen of Bohemia, daughter of King James I, wearing a gown of the early seventeenth century. Her hair is powdered with gold ornaments. Upon her forehead is a gold jewel. She wears a stand-up white lace collar and a brown dress embroidered with gold, over which is a brown cloak edged with gold and lined with red. In her right hand she bears a gold-handled fan of peacocks' feathers and in her left hand is a white embroidered handkerchief. Below is the legend in gold letters against a blue background: ELIZABETHA: REG BOHEM:.

3a

Background of quarries bearing alternately the letters in gold H and P. Within a wreath of thistles proper a shield, ensigned by a gold coronet with a violet cap, bearing Or a lion rampant within a double tressure flory counter-flory gules, a label of three points azure. Upon each point is an escutcheon bearing: on the dexter Argent a rose gules seeded or, centre: Argent two chevrons gules, sinister: Or a fess checky argent and azure STEWART; (the arms of PRINCE HENRY, eldest son of King James I, as PRINCE OF SCOTLAND). Pendant from the wreath is a badge of gold bearing Azure a saltire argent ST ANDREW. Above the wreath, upon a label argent doubled gules is the legend: ME JVVAT IRE PER ALTVM and below the wreath upon a similar label: FAX MENTIS HONESTÆ GLORIA.

Note: It is suggested that the arms upon the centre of the label are wrong and that it should be Argent a chevron gules for the Earldom of CARRICK, which since 1469 has been vested in the heir to the Scottish throne.

3b

Background of quarries as before but bearing the letters R and J. *In chief*: Within a wreath purpure interspersed with four gold quatrefoils and four red with blue and gold bindings, upon a mount vert a lion sejant affronty gules crowned or, bearing in the dexter paw a sword, the blade argent, the hilt or, and in the sinister paw a sceptre or both erect and palewise. Below the wreath upon a label argent doubled azure is the motto: IN MY DEFENS, GOD ME DEFEND. *In base*: Within a wreath of thistles proper ensigned by a gold crown with a red cap, a shield bearing the arms of SCOTLAND.

3c

Background of quarries as before but bearing the letters R and A. *In chief*: Within a wreath purpure, arising from a gold coronet a demi lion rampant guardant, queue fourchy azure crowned or. Below: upon a label is the motto: REGNA FIRMAT PIETAS. *In base*: Within a formal floral decoration of green leaves bearing blue and gold flowers and ensigned by a crown a shield bearing SCOTLAND, impaling Or semy of hearts gules, three lions passant guardant azure crowned or DENMARK.

3d

Background of quarries as before but bearing the letters E and R. Within the Garter ensigned by an Electors bonnet gules turned up ermine tierced in pairle reversed, 1 Sable a lion rampant or facing sinister crowned gules THE PALATINATE, 2 Lozengy bendy argent and azure BAVARIA, 3 Gules an orb or ARCH STEWARD OF THE HOLY ROMAN EMPIRE. Above the shield upon a label as in 1: FREDERICVS COMES PALATINVS and below: SUPERATA TELLVS SYDERA DONAT.

Note: The lion in the Palatinate coat usually faces dexter.

Tracery Quatrefoils

A, B and C as sIX.

sXII

The window is a memorial to King Charles II.

1a

Against a formal floral background of gold upon a white field, within a circle of a formal decoration of purple gold green and red with an inner background of blue, three ostrich feathers enfiled by an open gold coronet which has below it the motto *ICH DIEN*. Below the circle within the Garter and ensigned by a gold arched crown, the Stuart Royal Arms with a label of three points argent CHARLES, PRINCE OF WALES. In the base of the window against a formal classical background of gold and purple two shields. To the dexter: Quarterly, 1 & 4 Gules a lion passant guardant or, 2 & 3 Or a lion passant guardant gules PRINCES OF GWYNEDD (later used for the PRINCIPALITY OF WALES). Above is the legend *WALLIÆ* . To the sinister: Azure three garbs or EARLDOM OF CHESTER. Above is the legend: *CESTRIE*.

Note: The arms of the Princes of Gwynedd are usually reversed i.e. Quarterly, 1 & 4 Or a lion passant guardant gules, 2 & 3 Gules a lion passant guardant or.

1b

Against a background as 1a. A lion rampant guardant crowned or, facing sinister holding in its sinister paw a spear, the point argent the haft or from which floats a split tailed standard. In the hoist are the arms of St George, Argent a cross gules, the fly being gules powdered with the rose, fleur de lis and thistle in gold. The dexter paw is placed upon a shield which bears the Stuart Royal Arms within the Garter and is tilted to the sinister.

1c

Background as in 1a. An angel dressed in Roman armour, its head and shoulders turned and tilted to the dexter having wings of gold doubled purple. Around the shoulders and waist is draped a red scarf. Across the breast plate of the armour is a surcoat of Azure three fleurs de lis or. In its left hand the figure holds a spear, the point argent, the haft or, from which floats a split-tailed standard. In the hoist Gules a cross argent, the fly being azure powdered with gold fleurs de lis. The right hand rests upon a wreath of green leaves and purple and white bandings. The centre of the wreath is gold and upon it are two shields. To the dexter: Azure three fleurs de lis or FRANCE; to the sinister: Gules a cross, saltire and double orle of chains, linked or NAVARRE. Below the shields, engraved in the gold field is the monogram HMR [for Henrietta Maria Regina].

1d

Background as 1a. Within a circle as 1a. Against a blue background an anchor cabled or enfiled by a gold open coronet. Beneath the circle within the Garter ensigned by an open gold coronet, the Stuart Royal Arms with a label of three points ermine JAMES, DUKE OF YORK AND ALBANY. In the base against a similar background to the base of 1a, two shields. To the dexter: Per pale murrey and azure a rose argent seeded or slipped vert, above which is the legend: EBOR: To the sinister: Azure a saltire argent, overall a thistle proper, above which is the legend: ALBAN. Across the base of lights 1a–1d is the legend: IN PIAM MEMORIAM REGIS CAROLI MARTYR IN MEDIO CHORO SEPULTI A: D: 1648. In the bottom right-hand corner is a shield bearing the monogram T.W. [Thomas Willement].

2a

A canopy of gold and silver pillars arched in green and gold, against a white background bearing a formal floral decoration in gold. Above the canopy are seven Tudor roses upon gold stalks and leaves. Charles, Prince of Wales, later King Charles II, wears armour of the mid-seventeenth century with a white lace collar. Around his neck, upon a blue ribbon, is the Lesser George. His leg armour is worn over red breeches which end in gold hose and he wears gold shoes with red flaps. His left hand rests upon a black stick, the top of which is gold. At the base of the window upon a black background is the legend in gold: CAROLVS PRINCEPS.

2b

This and light 2c form one picture. Within a canopy of gold and white pillars and a gold and white arch, King Charles I stands upon a chequered floor against a background of green with a gold frieze, having above it a background of a blue sky. He is dressed in robes of the mid-seventeenth century. He has long brown hair, a moustache and beard. He wears a white lace collar and a robe of scarlet and ermine. Around his neck is the collar of the Garter, pendant from which is the George. His left hand rests upon a sword, the belt and hilt of which are gold. He wears white hose and white satin shoes with white decoration. Underneath is the motto in gold upon a black background in gold letters: CAROLVS REX.

2c

Queen Henrietta Maria, wife of King Charles I, in a dress of the mid-seventeenth century. Her dress is of gold from which protrudes white lace sleeves and is decorated about the bodice with pearls and with red jewels. Around her neck is a single string of pearls with a pendant pearl drop. Underneath is the legend: HENR: MAR: REGINA.

2d

Under a canopy and with roses above as in light 2a, James Duke of York, dressed in a costume of the mid-seventeenth century. He has long brown hair and a lace collar. Around his neck is pendant from a blue ribbon the Lesser George. Both his doublet and breeches are of scarlet embroidered in gold. He wears thigh length brown boots and a cloak of green edged with gold and lined with blue. In his left hand he holds a brown hat with a white and red feather. Underneath upon black in gold lettering is the legend JACOBVS DVX EBOR:.

3a

Under a canopy, an angel dressed in robes of blue, gold and white, with wings of purple and blue. The angel has a halo of gold and white and holds in its right hand a cross. Above the canopy is a blue sky with gold stars.

3b

Within a similar canopy, an angel holding an open silver crown.

3c

As 3b, the angel holding in its right hand a silver chalice.

3d

As 3b, the angel holding in its left hand a green palm branch.

Tracery Quatrefoils

A, B and C as sIX.

sXIII

The window is a memorial to King William III and Queen Mary II.

1a

Background of formal classical floral design in gold against a white background, the border of the windows having a formal pattern in red interspersed with green and white flowers. Within a wreath composed of green leaves interspersed with blue and white flowers, a seal or medallion consisting of a fluted gold background against which stands a female figure in robes of gold, holding in her left hand a gold cross, her right hand being up-lifted. Around the border, which is of black is the following in gold: SOCIETY FOR PROMOTING CHRISTIAN KNOWLEDGE 1698. On a white scroll which extends from the top to the bottom of the light, in black letters: FOR THIS IS GOOD AND ACCEPTABLE IN THE SIGHT OF GOD OUR SAVIOUR WHO WILL HAVE ALL MEN COME TO THE KNOWLEDGE OF THE TRUTH.

1b

Background and border as 3a. Within a formal floral decoration of purple and green surrounded by the Garter and ensigned by gold arched crown decorated with jewels and pearls and having a red cap, the Stuart Royal Arms having an escutcheon Azure billety a lion rampant or (arms of William of Orange as King William III).

1c

Within a floral decoration as 3a, surrounded by a border of red and white flowers and ensigned by a crown, an impaled coat, to the dexter the Stuart Royal Arms with the escutcheon as 1b, impaling the Stuart Royal Arms undifferenced (arms of King William III and Queen Mary II as Joint Sovereigns).

1d

Background and border as 1a. Within a wreath, a gold medallion having a three-masted ship under sail having at the prow a flag bearing a cross. Upon the fore peak is a male figure holding an open book in his right hand. To the left arise cliffs upon which are five native figures, at the back of which are trees. At the top left is depicted the sun sending forth rays, below which, upon a scroll is the legend: TRANSLENS. ADIUVA. NOS. Around the medallion upon a black border in gold letters is: SOCIETY FOR THE PROPOGATION OF THE GOSPEL IN FOREIGN PARTS 1701. On a scroll which extends from the top to the bottom of the light, in black letters on white: GOD HATH SHINED INTO OUR HEARTS TO GIVE LIGHT OF THE KNOWLEDGE OF THE GLORY OF GOD IN THE FACE OF JESUS CHRIST.

Across the base of the lights, against a red background with a gold border, the legend in gold letters: REGNARE PARES ET MIRE SE INTER AMARE. At the bottom right-hand corner of this light is a small shield bearing the monogram T.W. [Thomas Willement].

2a–2d

The background is of a room with stone walls with a gold frieze. The floor is of blue tiles interspersed with gold. At the centre of the picture is a canopy of red with gold tassels with a background of green edged with gold. Under the canopy is a double throne the steps to which are covered with a carpet of red with a gold pattern. On the left is the seated figure of King William III, wearing a full wig, having a lace ruff and a gold doublet with a belt of blue. Around his neck is the collar of the Garter from which is pendant the George. His hose is of white and his shoes are white trimmed with gold. Around his left leg is the Garter. His feet rest upon a green cushion with gold tassels. Overall he wears a red robe with collar and trimmings of ermine. In his right hand a sword is held upright. In his left hand is a gold orb. On the right side of the double throne is seated Queen Mary II. Around her neck is a string of pearls. She wears a bodice of purple edged in silver with green and gold decorations. The skirt is of white with a gold pattern. Her feet rest upon a cushion of green with gold tassels. Overall she wears a robe. Pendant from each shoulder are strings of pearls. In her left hand she bears a gold sceptre and in her right hand a gold orb. To the left of the throne are two standing male figures clad in purple robes with ermine collars and wearing full wigs. They are holding and apparently reading a folded paper which is headed: 'Declaration of the Two Houses of Convention'. In front kneels the Marquess of Halifax, dressed in the coronation robe of a peer, worn over a green doublet fringed in white and gold, having white hose. He holds in uplifted hands a red cushion with tassels of gold upon which rests an arched gold crown with a red cap (the English crown). To the right of the throne stand the Earl of Argyll, Sir John Dalrymple and Sir James Montgomery, wearing peers' coronation robes, the centre figure holding a folded paper which is headed: 'Scotland' (the Scottish Coronation oath). Before these figures stands a page clad in green doublet which has a gold belt from which hangs a sword, the grip of which is gold, the guard and quillons silver and the scabbard purple. His hose is of yellow and his shoes buff. In his uplifted hand he bears a purple cushion upon which rests an arched gold crown with a purple cap (the Scottish crown). Across the base of these panels within a blue border is the following legend in gold letters upon white: TIBI CURA ANGLIÆ FATIS DATA VENIENDO RESTITUIT REM CORONANTUR A°. DMI: 1689 SCOTIA IN FIDEM RECEPTA.

Note: King William and Queen Mary sit upon the throne whilst, to the left, officials of the House of Lords read the Declaration of the two Houses of Convention (Declaration of Rights). The Houses of Parliament were styled Houses of Convention in the interregnum between the flight of King James II and the acceptance of the throne by William and Mary.

3a

Background of formal classical floral design in gold against a white background, the border of the windows having a formal pattern in red interspersed with green and white flowers terminating at the apex in white flowers and green leaves. Within a circlet of white and gold against a red background, out of a coronet formed alternately of crosses formy, strawberry leaves and silver balls, two gold stags' antlers.

3b

Background and borders as 3a. Within the Garter ensigned by a coronet as 3a but with a red cap, within an inner circle of gold; Quarterly, 1 Azure billety a lion rampant or NASSAU, 2 Or a lion rampant guardant gules crowned argent KATZENELNBOGEN, 3 Gules a fess argent VIANDEN, 4 Gules two lions passant guardant or DIETZ. An escutcheon; Quarterly, 1 & 4 Gules a bend or CHALONS, 2 & 3 Or a bugle horn azure stringed gules ORANGE. An inescutcheon; Checky of nine or and azure GENEVA. In chief: an escutcheon, Or a fess gules MOERS. In base: an escutcheon, Gules a fess embattled counter embattled argent BUREN.

Note: The coat is NASSAU for William of Orange (King William III).

3c

Background and border as 3a. With a wreath of green leaves interspersed with red and white flowers and tied with a blue ribbon, ensigned by a coronet and cap, Nassau impaling the Stuart Royal Arms with a label of three points ermine. (Marriage of William of Orange with Mary, d. of King James II.)

3d

Background and border as 3a. Within a circle as 3a, against a red background, a gold open coronet ensigned by a lion statant guardant crowned or.

Tracery Quatrefoils

A, B and C as sIX.

sXIV

This window depicts the presentation of the Deed of Gift (Queen Anne's Bounty) which placed the first fruits and tenths, which had been confiscated by King Henry VIII, in a trust for the augmentation of the stipends of poor clergy.

1a

Background and border as sXIII. Within the Garter ensigned by an arched crown with a red cap, a shield bearing, to the dexter a gold rose and to the sinister a gold thistle, both slipped and entwined. In chief: in black letters upon a silver label doubled gold the word *CONCORDES*. Below in gold letters upon red: *TUEATUR UNITA DEUS*.

1b

Background and border as 1a. Within the Garter ensigned by an arched and jewelled crown, Quarterly, 1 & 4 England impaling Scotland, 2 France, 3 Ireland (the Royal Arms after the union of 1707).

1c

Background and border as 1a. Within the Garter ensigned by an arched coronet having alternately strawberry leaves and pearls, the arms of Denmark. See window sIX, 1c (for Prince George of Denmark the consort of Queen Anne).

Note: Prince George's coat of Denmark is usually differenced by a label of three points ermine.

1d

Background and border as 1a. Within the Garter ensigned by a gold coronet formed alternately of cross formy and fleurs de lis and with a red cap, the Stuart Royal Arms with a label of three points ermine and an escutcheon, Or semy of hearts gules three lions passant in pale azure, crowned or. Beneath in gold letters upon a red background: GUL: DUX GLOVC ob. 1700. At the bottom right-hand corner of the window is a small shield with the monogram T.W. [Thomas Willement].

Note: This coat is for the only child of Queen Anne to survive infancy, William Duke of Gloucester, who died in 1700 aged 11.

2a–2d

A room, the walls of which are brown with pillars and a frieze of white and gold, the floor being of green tiles. To the left Queen Anne is seated upon a gold throne having above a gold tester from which hang furled curtains of red lined with green and fringed with gold. The carpet before the throne, which extends into the other lights, is of gold and black. She wears upon her head a small gold arched crown and around her neck is a collar of the Garter pendant from which is the George. She is clad in a dress of gold with lace sleeves and in a robe of red trimmed with ermine having at the sleeves red jewels set with gold. In her left hand she bears upright a gold sceptre and holds in both hands a paper. To the left of the throne stands Sir Nathan Wright, Lord Keeper of the Great Seal, in a full wig wearing a black suit of the early 18th century, having at the neck white bands and at the wrists white lace. His suit is trimmed with gold. His hose and shoes are also black. Over the suit is a black robe decorated with gold. He holds the purse of a Lord Chancellor, which is of gold and red, decorated with the letter A and R and the Stuart royal arms within the Garter with supporters and from which are pendant gold and red tassels. Below is the motto: Dieu et mon droit. To the right of the throne are the figures of Henry Grey, Earl of Kent, Lord Chamberlain (standing) and Thomas Tenison, Archbishop of Canterbury, John Sharp, Archbishop of York, Henry Compton, Bishop of London, Gilbert Burnet, Bishop of Salisbury and Chancellor of the Garter (all kneeling).

Henry Grey wears a lace cravat and a red robe with white sleeves over which is a blue habit (the mantle of the Garter). He wears a collar of the Garter from which is pendant the George and has at his waist a gold key. In the right hand is borne upright a white star. Tenison, Sharp and Compton wear red robes trimmed with fur over white rochets, while Burnet wears a rochet over which is a blue habit. Pendant from the neck of the rear figure is a red badge upon a blue ribbon.

An inscription is to be found across the base of all four lights. PRIMITUS ET DECIMIS ECCLESIÆ CONCESSIS ANNO DOMINI MDCCIV.

3a

Border and background as sXIII, 3a. Within a floral wreath of white flowers seeded gold and with gold leaves, having on the outside a circle of green, against a blue background, a formal floral design in gold (cypher of Queen Anne).

3b

Background and border as 3a. Within the Garter ensigned by an arched crown with a red cap, against a gold background a red shield bearing thereon upon an open gold arched crown, a lion passant guardant crowned or.

3c

Background and border as 3a. Within the Garter ensigned by an arched coronet having alternately strawberry leaves and pearls, without a cap against a gold background, a silver shield bearing thereon out of a gold coronet a demi lion rampant guardant azure crowned or.

3d

As light 3a (cypher of Prince George of Denmark).

Tracery Quatrefoils

A, B and C as sIX.

The Oliver King Chapel

In the east wall is a window of two lights. In the tracery is coloured glass of a formal floral pattern.

1a

Within the Garter, Quarterly France Modern England impaling the Royal Arms of Spain. These latter arms, which to my mind are possibly of a different design to those of the France and England coat are completely reversed with all the charges facing the wrong way. St John Hope suggests that this is for King Henry VIII and Catherine of Aragon, but this identification must be reconsidered in the light of the reversal. A number of possibilities suggest themselves with varying degrees of probability: it is possible that the France and England impalement is not a part of the original shield.

Was another impalement there, albeit designed the wrong way round so that the whole faced the altar? Alternatively, has the Spanish coat come from another shield and been deliberately cut to fit this one so as to make up a new shield — unlikely as some of the detail upon the coat is likely to be missing — which it is not. Was the Spanish coat originally a dexter impalement? I believe this to be the most likely explanation. But who does it represent? The only candidate I can suggest is King Ferdinand V of Spain. He and Isabella had one son who died without issue and so far as I know had no connection with Windsor or the Garter. Two daughters (Catherine and Joanna), could not have borne the coat to the dexter. My suggestion therefore is that the impalement, as it now exists is made up. This would account for the marked difference in design between the two sides of the shield — and that the Spanish coat was for Ferdinand King of Spain, but with what it was impaled I have no idea.

The arms should be: Quarterly, 1 & 4 Quarterly (i & iv) Gules a castle or CASTILE, (ii & iii) Argent a lion rampant purpure LEON, 2 & 3 Or four pallets gules ARAGON impaling Per saltire, in chief and in base Or four pallets gules and in the flanks argent an eagle displayed sable SICILY; in base, Argent a pomegranate proper GRANADA.

2a

Quarterly of sixteen, 1 Argent a maunch sable HASTINGS, 2 Per pale or and sable a cross engrailed counterchanged POLE, 3 Quarterly, 1 & 4 France Modern 2 & 3 England (parts missing), overall a label of three points argent each charged with a canton gules CLARENCE (York), 4 Gules a saltire argent overall a label of three points company argent and azure NEVILLE, 5 Argent three fusils conjoined in fess gules MONTAGUE, 6 Or an eagle displayed vert (badly damaged) MONTHERMER, 7 Azure - no charges, 8 Or (Gules) three lions passant guardant within a bordure argent HOLLAND, 9 Gules a fess between six cross-crosslets or BEAUCHAMP, 10 Azure - no charges, 11 Quarterly argent and gules in the second and third quarters a fret or overall a bend sable (much faded) DESPENSER, 12 Or three chevrons gules CLARE, 13 Sable two bars argent in chief three plates FITZJOHN, 14 Argent a griffin segreant gules beaked and membered azure BOTREAUX, 15 Azure - no charges, 16 Or two bars gules in chief three torteaux WAKE. Probably for Henry Hastings, Earl of Huntingdon. Elected K.G. 1570, died 1595.

1b

Within the Garter, Argent a cross gules.

2b

Quarterly of twelve, 1 Gules on a chevron argent a lion rampant sable ducally crowned or BROOKE Lord Cobham, 2 Gules on a chevron or three lions rampant sable BROOKE, 3 Argent seven mascules conjoined three, three and one gules BRAYBROOKE, 4 Azure two bars nebuly or DE LA POLE, 5 Gules a fess argent between six crosses patonce or PEVERELL, 6 Argent a chevron between three eagle's legs erased à la quise sable BRAY MODERN, 7 Vair three bends gules BRAY ANCIENT, 8 Argent on a bend gules three rams argent armed and unguled or HALEIGHWELL, 9 Sable a chevron between three bull's heads argent BULKELEY for NORBURY, 10 Gules a fess company counter company argent and sable between six crosses formy fitchy argent BOTELER, 11 Or two bends gules SUDELEY, 12 Bendy of ten or and azure MONTFORT. Probably for William (Brooke) Lord Cobham. Elected K.G. 1584, died 1597.

In the south wall are two windows, each of two lights, the heads of which are decorated as before. Numbering from east to west.

sII

1a

Upper: A gold imperial arched crown. *Middle*: A rose Gules seeded or. *Lower*: Quarterly: 1 Sable semy of cinquefoils a lion rampant argent CLIFTON, 2 Gules three lions passant guardant in pale or ENGLAND, 3 Azure a lion rampant or (Unidentified), 4 Argent a fess between three escallops gules DORTHORPE.

This Clifton coat is a puzzle. A similar coat appears in the windows of Clifton church, Nottingham, but bears: 1 CLIFTON, 2 Azure a lion rampant or, 3 Argent a lion rampant double queued sable CRESSY and DORTHORPE (BL Harleian MS 6829, p. 32).

Note: St John Hope suggests (*Architectural History*, ii, p. 467), that the second quarter is an error. I think that it is part of a made-up shield, and that the present quarters are in the wrong order. He also suggests that the blue shield with the gold lion is for BRAYTOFT, but in my view this is an error. Possibly for GAMALIEL CLIFTON (Canon 1522–41).

2b

Within the Garter, Azure a cross patonce between five martlets or, EDWARD THE CONFESSOR.

1b: Within the Garter, Gules four fusils in fess ermine DINHAM, impaling Gules three arches, two and one conjoined the hood moulds and pillars argent the capitals and bases or ARCHES.

Note: St John Hope, not unreasonably suggests that it is for John, Lord Dinham, elected K.G. ?1485, died 1509. The impaled coat should be for his father who was not a K.G., for he married the Arches heiress. Lord Dinham's stall plate correctly quarters the arms.

sIII

1a

A rose Gules seeded or.

2a

Within the Garter, Quarterly, France Modern and England (a small shield). *Middle*: Within the Garter, Quarterly, France Modern and England (a larger shield).

1b

A rose Gules seeded or.

2b

Within the Garter, Argent a cross gules. *Middle*: Within the Garter, Quarterly France Modern and England within a bordure argent. This is possibly for Henry Stafford, Duke of Buckingham (d. 1483) or for his son Edward (d. 1521). For their use of this coat see Peter J. Begent, *A Noble Place Indeed* (1983), p. 16 and notes.

THE NORTH CHOIR AISLE

nII

A memorial to King Edward IV. This and window nIII consist of four lights only.

1a

A background of quarries bearing the letters E and R in gold. *In chief*: within the Garter ensigned by a gold arched crown with a red cap, Quarterly France Modern and England. Above the crown is a blue circle in which are the letters ER in gold. *In base*: Dexter: within a gold circle against a background party murrey and azure, a rose argent en soleil; Sinister: against a similar background a falcon argent within an open fetterlock or.

1b-1c

Framed by a formal canopy, supported by pillars of white and gold, a room with stone walls and four windows, the wall in light 1b having alternately a murrey and blue decoration with white roses en soleil, whilst that of light 1c has red flowers with green stalks and leaves set against a blue background. The floor of the room is decorated with chequered tiles of black, gold and white. On the left (1b) is King Edward IV, clad in a brown gown over which is a red robe edged with gold and pearls and with an ermine collar. Upon his head is a gold arched crown with a red cap, and in his hands a gold sceptre. He kneels upon blue cushion with gold tassels at a (stone) desk upon which is an open book with gold bindings and a gold clasp. On the right (1c) is Queen Elizabeth Woodville, dressed in robes of the mid-fifteenth century, a gold dress with a girdle and tassels of purple and gold ornamented with pearls. Upon her head is an open crown over a white headdress. Her hands are raised in prayer and before her are a desk and a book.

1d

Quarries as 1a. Within a collar of alternately white roses en soleil and white roses seeded gold, pendant from which is a lion statant argent on a mount vert, the whole ensigned by a crown above which is a blue circle with the letters ER in gold as light 1, Quarterly France Modern and England impaling, Quarterly of six; 1 Argent a lion rampant queue fourché gules crowned or LUXEMBURG, 2 Quarterly (i & iv) Gules an estoile argent BAUX, (ii & iii) Azure semy of fleurs de lis or FRANCE ANCIENT, 3 Barry of ten argent and azure overall a lion rampant gules CYPRUS, 4 Gules three bends argent on a chief per fess argent and or a rose gules URSINS, 5 Paly of six vair and gules on a chief or a label of five points azure ST POL, 6 Argent a fess and a canton conjoined gules WOODVILLE. (These arms, emphasizing her noble descent through her mother Jaquetta, daughter of Peter de Luxembourg, Count of St Pol, were used by Elizabeth after her marriage to the king.) *In base*: Dexter: within a gold circle against a blue background three red flowers with leaves and stems of green. Sinister: within a gold circle against a red background a silver star.

Legend across all four lights: *In piam memoriam Edwari; IV Regis Augusti hujus capellæ conditoris Dec: et Can: P.C. A:D: 1845.*

In the double-headed window tracery is the Garter Badge (St George's Cross within the Garter). The remainder of the tracery contains floral decoration in blue and gold and red and gold. At the head of lights 1a and 1b is a sun in splendour whilst at the head of 1c and 1d is a red flower.

nIII

1a

Background of quarries bearing alternately a rose argent barbed and seeded or and a sprig of broom or. At the top of the light within a blue circle against a red background a rose argent seeded and barbed or. *Centre*: Within a collar of SS having a fringe above and below of green, an impaled coat, to the dexter: Quarterly France Ancient and England overall a label of three points argent each charged with as many torteaux within a bordure argent charged with lions rampant purpure RICHARD OF CONINGSBURGH, impaling Or three bars azure on a chief or two pallets between two gyrons azure overall an escutcheon argent MORTIMER. On the dexter side of the shield is the letter R in gold, the sinister is blank. Below in black letters upon a white scroll fringed with gold and doubled blue is the legend: *Richard Earl of Cambridge married Anne Mortimer. In base*: Within the Garter a shield fringed as above bearing Quarterly France Modern and England a label of three points argent each point charged with as many torteaux impaling Gules a saltire argent NEVILL. On either side of the shield are the letters in gold R and Y. Upon a white scroll doubled red is the legend: *Richard Duke of York married Cecily Nevill.*

1b

Background of quarries bearing alternately a gold open fetterlock and a white hart lodged. At the top of the light within a blue circle against a red background a white hart lodged. *Centre*: within a collar of SS from which is pendant the badge of a white antelope spotted attired gorged and chained gold a shield bearing dexter Gules three lions passant guardant or within a bordure azure flory or HOLLAND DUKE OF EXETER impaling, per fess, in chief Quarterly France Modern and England, in base MORTIMER. The shield is ensigned by a silver helmet barred and decorated in gold turned to the dexter. Mantling of gules doubled or. The helmet bears for a crest, upon a chapeau gules turned up ermine a lion statant guardant crowned or having a collar azure flory or. Below the shield upon a white scroll fringed gold doubled blue *Anne dau: of Rich^{d}: Duke of York married 1st: Henry Duke of Exeter. In base*: dexter, within a gold circle against a red background a white hart lodged sinister within a gold circle against a background per pale murrey and azure a rose argent seeded or barbed vert.

1c

A background of quarries bearing alternately a rose argent barbed and seeded or and barnacles or tied with a cord argent tassels or. At the top of the light within a gold circle against a blue background a pair of barnacles or tied with a cord gules. *Centre*: within a collar having a background of alternate azure and murrey sections the collar itself being formed of alternate suns rayonny or and roses argent seeded or pendant from which against a blue background is a lion argent statant langued gules, a shield bearing dexter: Azure fretty argent a chief or ST LEGER impaling per fess in chief Quarterly France Modern and England, in base MORTIMER, as in light 1b. Above the shield is a helmet as in 2 turned to the dexter. Mantling azure doubled or. For the crest, upon a wreath or and sable a gryphon statant or, the head and wings fretty azure. Beneath upon a white scroll doubled red is the legend: *Anne dau: of Rich: Duke of York mar^{d}: II^{ly} Sir Thos: St: Leger Knt. In base*: dexter, within a gold circle against a blue background a pair of barnacles or tied with a cord gules; sinister, within a gold circle per pale murrey and azure a rose argent seeded or barbed vert.

1d

Background of quarries bearing alternately a wheel or and a water bouget argent. At the top of the light within a blue border against a red background a rose argent barbed and seeded or. *Centre*: within a collar as 1c but without the badge pendant an impaled shield fringed above and below as before and having on each side the letters in gold G.M. Dexter: Or two bars azure a chief gules MANNERS; Sinister: ST LEGER. Beneath the legend upon a white scroll doubled blue: *Anne dau: of Sir Tho: St Leger married Sir George Manners Lord Ros. In base*: within the Garter a shield fringed as before with the letters in gold on either side T.R. Dexter: Or two bars azure on a chief quarterly 1 and 4 azure two fleurs de lis or 2 and 3 gules a lion passant guardant or MANNERS, impaling Argent six fleurs de lis three, two and one azure a chief indented or PASTON. Below is the legend upon a white scroll doubled red: *Thomas Earl of Rutland son of George mar[d]: Eleanor Paston.*

Across the base of all four lights is the legend: *Regiæ stirpis non immemor Joh: Henr: Dux de Rutland, K:G: P:C: A°. Dom: 1845*. (This window was paid for by the Duke of Rutland and depicts his descent from Richard, Earl of Cambridge, son of King Edward III, through the sister of King Edward IV.)

Apex and tracery as nII, save that at the head of lights 1a and 1b is a rose argent and at the head of 1c and 1d a water bouget argent.

nIV

The window is a memorial to King George I.

1a

Border of foliage. Within the Garter ensigned by a gold arched crown, Quarterly 1 & 4 THE PALATINATE, 2 and 3 BAVARIA, overall the insignia of the Arch Steward of the Empire, impaling the Royal Arms of the House of Stuart (see sVIII, 3d). Below, upon a red background: FREDERICK KING of Bohemia Elector Palatine.

1b

Border as 1a but with an additional floral decoration of gold acorns and silver oak leaves. Within a collar of gold and blue flowers and green leaves and ensigned by an electoral bonnet, Quarterly of seventeen, 1 Gules two lions passant guardant or BRUNSWICK, 2 Gules a horse courant argent HANOVER, 3 Or semy of hearts gules a lion rampant azure langued gules LUNEBURG, 4 Azure a lion rampant argent crowned or EBERSTEIN, 5 Argent a wheel gules OSNABRUCK, 6 Gules within a bordure compony azure and argent a lion rampant or HOMBURG, 7 Gules a lion rampant argent crowned or DIEPHOLZ, 8 VACANT, 9 Gules a lion rampant or LAUTERBURG, 10 Azure an eagle displayed argent DIEPHOLZ, 11 Or two bear's paws erased palewise in fess sable HOYA, 12 Barry of six or and gules LAUTERBURG, 13 Argent a stag trippant sable KLETENBURG, 14 Gyronny of eight argent and azure BRUCKHAUSEN, 15 Checky argent and gules HOHNSTEIN, 16 Argent a stag's attire in bend gules REGENSTEIN, 17 Argent a stag's attire in bend sinister sable BLANKENBURG impaling THE PALATINATE quartering BAVARIA. Below, upon a blue background. SOPHIA Electress of Hanover Princess Palatine.

Note: The Diepholz lion (seventh quarter) is often blazoned Or a lion rampant gules.

1c

Within the Garter ensigned by a gold arched crown with a red cap, Quarterly, 1 England impaling Scotland, 2 France, 3 Ireland, 4 Tierced in pairle reversed, Gules two lions passant guardant or BRUNSWICK, Or semy of hearts gules a lion rampant azure langued gules LUNEBURG, Gules a horse courant argent WESTPHALIA (Hanover). At fess point an escutcheon Gules the crown of

Charlemagne or. Below upon a blue background GEORGE King of Great Britain, France and Ireland.

Note: The Crown of Charlemagne was the badge of the Arch Treasurer of the Holy Roman Empire.

1d

Within the Garter ensigned by an electoral bonnet, Quarterly of seventeen, as light 10, overall an inescutcheon of the badge of the Arch Treasurer. Underneath the legend against a red background: GEORGE LEWIS Duke of Brunswick & Lunenberg Elector of Hanover acceeded to the Crown of Great Britain 1714. At the base of this light is the monogram T.W [Thomas Willement].

Across the base of lights 1a to 1d is the legend: *In piam memoriam Georgii Britanniarum Regis; et Matris ejus Sophæ, ex stirpe Electorali Palatina, neptis Jacobi 1^mi: Angliæ et Scotiae Regis, Ernesti Augusti Electoris Brunsvicensis et Luneburgensis Viduæ ad Regni successionem designatæ MDCCI. Dec: et Can: P:C: A: S: MDCCCLIII.*

2a

Within the Garter ensigned by a gold arched crown with a red cap the Royal Arms of the House of Stuart. Below upon a blue background within a gold border: JAMES 1st King of England, Scotland, France and Ireland.

2b–2c

A room with a brown chequered floor, and green hanging curtains with a gold fringe covering the rear wall. To the left stands Sophia, Electress of Hanover wearing a costume of the late seventeenth century, a hat formed of gold work and three ostrich feathers, a dress of gold with purple sleeves and white cuffs together with a lace collar. Over the dress is worn an outer robe of red fringed with gold and lined with ermine. Below, upon a blue background: MAGNÆ BRITANNIAE HÆRES 1701. To the right stands Prince George afterward King George I, wearing a full wig, a waistcoat of cloth, red breeches, white hose and buff shoes with gold buckles and a sword with a gold hilt. Below his left knee he wears the Garter. His coat is of scarlet embroidered at the edges with gold, over which is worn a red robe fringed with gold and with a cape with edges of ermine lined with white. From his neck are pendant two blue and white tasseled cords. Around his neck is the collar of the Garter pendant from which is the George. Below upon a scroll as light 6: IN RECTO DECUS.

2d

Within a decorative collar of purple and green circles and ensigned by an electoral bonnet, Quarterly, 1 & 4 Gules two lions passant guardant or, 2 & 3 Or semy of hearts gules a lion rampant azure langued gules. Upon a scroll as 2a: ALBERT surnamed Magnus Duke of Brunswick & Lunenberg.

3a

A border of blue and white flowers seeded gold with a gold stem and green leaves. An inner panel having a border of gold and red and a white background upon which is a formal floral decoration of gold and white flowers with red tracery. Within the Garter, ensigned by an open crown, Quarterly France Ancient and England. The shield is surrounded by a silver formal floral decoration. Below, pendant from a blue cord against a red background edged with gold: *Edward iii[d] King of France and England and Lord of Ireland.*

3b

Upon a scroll-like shield having a silver border with gold rivets and ensigned by an open jewelled coronet, Gules two lions passant guardant or. Beneath, upon a blue background, having a gold scroll border: *MAUD OF ENGLAND Dau: of King Henry IJ[D] Wife of HENRY the LION.*

3c

Border and panel as 1. Upon a shield similar to 3b, ensigned by an open coronet Barry of ten or and sable. Below, upon a background and border as 3b, *HENRY the LION DUKE of SAXONY, BRUNSWICK & LUNENBERG.*

3d

Background, border and surround as previously. Within a collar formed of chain links of gold and silver interspersed with red jewels set with pearls and ensigned by an electoral bonnet, Gules two lions passant guardant or, impaling, Or semy of hearts gules, a lion rampant azure langued gules. Below, upon a scroll, background and border as 1: OTHO surnamed Puer:Duke of Brunswick & Lunenberg.

Tracery

A, B and C as nV.

nV

The window is a memorial to King George II.

1a

The border is composed of green leaves interspersed with white and purple flowers. Within the Garter and ensigned by an arched coronet with a red cap, the Royal Arms of the House of Hanover until 1801 (displaying an escutcheon but omitting the badge of the Arch Treasurer in the fourth quarter) overall a label of three points argent. Below is the legend in silver letters on blue: *FREDERICK LEWIS PRINCE OF WALES. Obiit vita patris.*

1b

Border as light 1a. Within the Garter the Royal Arms of the House of Hanover until 1801, ensigned by a gold arched crown with a red cap. Below in silver letters on a red background is the legend: *GEORGE the Second King of Great Britain France and Ireland. Acceded 1727.*

1c

Border as light 1a. Within a wreath of laurel leaves interspersed with red and white roses and surmounted by a gold arched crown, the Royal Arms of Hanover impaling quarterly of fourteen: 1 & 14 Per fess gules and argent MAGDEBURG, 2 Argent and eagle displayed sable crowned or PRUSSIA, 3 Or a griffin segreant gules crowned or WOLGAST, 4 Argent a griffin sergeant gules

POMERANIA, 5 Argent a griffin segreant gules WENDS, 6 Or a griffin segreant sable CASSUBIA, 7 Argent an eagle displayed sable CROSSEN, 8 Per pale argent and gules HALBERSTADT, 9 Argent an eagle displayed sable JAGENDORF, 10 Or a lion rampant gules within a bordure company gules and argent NUREMBURG, 11 Gules two keys in saltire wards in chief or MINDEN, 12 Quarterly argent and sable HOHENZOLLERN, 13 Gules a digamma cross argent* CAMIN. Overall on an escutcheon Argent an eagle displayed gules BRANDENBURG. Beneath is the legend in silver upon a red background: *CAROLINE QUEE.*
Dau: of Iohn Fred[k] Margrave of Brandenburg Anspach. Died 1737.
* An heraldic curiosity, unknown in British heraldry, see Charles Norton Elvin, *A Dictionary of Heraldry* (1889), Plate 11, n. 18.

Note: Willement appears to have found some difficulty in correctly displaying the quarters and marshalling of the coats of the Germanic Principalities appearing in this and the next two windows. There are a number of errors, and indeed tinctures vary between the same coats appearing in different impalements. A hint of his difficulty is to be found in the Hanoverian section of his book *Regal Heraldry*.

1d

Border as light 1a. Within a wreath of laurel leaves interspersed with blue and white flowers and ensigned by a gold arched coronet, the Royal Arms of the House of Hanover differenced as in light 9 impaling, Quarterly of eighteen, 1 Azure a lion rampant barry argent and gules LANDGRAVE OF THURINGIA, 2 Gules an escarbuncle and an escutcheon argent CLEVES, 3 Or a lion rampant sable JULIERS, 4 Argent (usually or) a lion rampant sable crowned or MEISSEN, 5 Argent a lion rampant double queued gules crowned or BERG, 6 Argent an eagle displayed sable crowned or PALATINATE OF SAXONY, 7 Or two pales azure LANDSBERG, 8 Sable an eagle displayed argent crowned or PALATINATE OF THURINGIA, 9 Or semy of hearts gules a lion rampant azure crowned or ORLAMUNDE, 10 Argent three bars gules EISENBURG, 11 Azure a lion rampant argent crowned or TONNA, 12 Argent a rose gules barbed and seeded or BURGRAVIATE OF ALTENBURG, 13 Gules plain SOVEREIGN RIGHTS, 14 Argent three beetle's pincers gules BREHNA or ENGERN, 15 Or a fess checky argent and azure MARCK, 16 Gules a pillar argent surmounted by a crown or ROENHILD, 17 Or on a mount vert a cock sable HENNENBERG, 18 Argent three chevrons gules RAVENSBERG. Overall an escutcheon, Barry of ten or and sable a crown of rue bendwise vert SAXONY. Below is the legend in silver letters on a blue background: *AUGUSTA: Dau: of Frederick ii Duke of Saxe Gotha. PRINCESS OF WALES.* At the bottom right-hand side of panel 1d is the monogram TW [Thomas Willement].

Across the base of lights 1a–1d is the legend: *In piam memoriam Regis Georgii II[di] Reginæ Carolinæ, Frederici Walliæ principis et Augustæ principessæ uxoris ejus Dec: et Can: P.C. A.D: 1853.*

2a–2d

These four lights form a single picture of a room, the floor of which is composed of a formal design in blue, green and silver. The wall hangings are of brown and are surmounted by drapery of green and red with a gold fringe: The upper part of the wall consists of arches of stonework interspersed with blue. On the left stands Frederick Prince of Wales, wearing a blue coat edged with gold embroidery over which is a scarlet robe trimmed with gold and ermine and having an ermine cape with gold tassels. He wears a full wig together with a collar with the George. His hose is white and the shoes buff with gold buckles. Beneath is the legend: *Born A:D: 1707 Died A:D: 1751.* In the adjoining light (2b) King George II is dressed in similar style, but with a red coat with blue tassels and holding in the right hand a gold sceptre which rests upon a stool which has gold legs and is covered with blue material. He wears a full wig and the collar of the Garter. His hose and shoes are of white with gold buckles. Beneath is the legend: *Born A:D: 1683 Died A:D: 1760*. In the next light (2c) stands Caroline of Brandenburg and Anspach, dressed in the costume of the late 17th century, her hair set with pearls and surmounted by a small arched crown. Her dress is of purple edged with jewels over an underskirt of cloth of gold. She wears a purple robe fringed with gold and edged and lined with ermine. In her right hand is a silver sceptre tipped with gold. Beneath is the legend: *Born A:D: 1683 Married A:D 1705*. On the right (1c) stands Augusta of Saxe-Gotha, similarly dressed, her hair set with pearls and wearing a blue coat edged with ermine over a dress of cloth of gold set with pearls. She figure wears a blue cloak edged with gold lined with ermine. In her right hand she holds a pink rose. Beneath is the legend: *Married A:D: 1736 Died A:D: 1772*.

3a

Border as 1a. Within a formal gold border against a red background and ensigned by a coronet having a red cap, the cypher in gold and silver of Frederick Prince of Wales. Beneath the legend ICH DIEN. Below against a red background surrounded by a wreath of green, three ostrich feathers argent enfiled by a gold coronet.

3b

Border as previously. Above: Out of a ducal coronet or a horse courant argent in front of a column gules the base argent ensigned by a coronet or from which issues a peacock's tail proper charged with a mullet of six points argent, all between two sickles argent with peacocks' feathers proper attached to the outer edges. Beneath the legend HANOVER. Below within a gold border against a blue background and ensigned by a gold arched crown, the cypher in gold and silver of King George II.

3c

Border as 1a. Above, out of a gold coronet an eagle displayed gules beaked, crowned, membered having in the dexter claw a sceptre and in the sinister claw a sword the hilt or and the blade argent. Upon each wing of the eagle is a kleestengel or and upon the breast on an escutcheon argent a sceptre azure. Beneath is the legend: BRANDENBURG. Below, within a gold border ensigned by a crown as light 2 the cypher of Caroline of Anspach.

Note: For kleestengel see SIV, 2b.

3d

Border as 1a. Above, within a gold border against a red background and ensigned by an arched coronet, the cypher in gold and silver of Augusta, Princess of Wales. Beneath is the legend: SAXE-GOTHA. Below, within a green formal border against a red background out of a gold coronet of strawberry leaves and silver balls a pyrimidal chapeau barry of ten or and sable a crown of rue bendwise vert, the chapeau surmounted by a gold coronet from which arises a panache of green peacocks' feathers, the eyes or.

Tracery

A, B and C as nIV.

nVI

The window is a memorial to King George III.

1a

Border as sIV, 1a. Three shields in pale each ensigned by a bishop's mitre in white and gold. *Upper*: Or a paschal lamb bearing a swallow-tailed pennon charged in the hoist with a cross, all argent, on a chief azure a croisier and a key in saltire or. Beneath the legend: NOVA SCOTIA. 1787. *Middle*: Gules a lion passant guardant or holding palewise in its dexter paw a key or on a chief wavy azure an open book edged or pages argent in front of which is a crosier in bend or a canton argent charged with a cross gules between four crosses formy fitchy sable. Beneath the legend: QUEBEC 1793. *Below*: Per fess indented ermine and gules in chief two palm branches in saltire vert in front of which is a mitre or; in base a crosier in bend or in front of which is an open book the edges of the pages argent. Beneath the legend: CALCUTTA 1814. Across the base of the light is the legend: *INSTITUTUS IN COLONIIS IMPERII BRITANNICI EPISCOPORUM ORDO.*

1b

On a gold cartouche within the Garter and ensigned by an arched imperial crown, the Royal Arms of the House of Hanover between 1707 and 1801. Beneath the legend in silver letters upon a red field: *GEORGE 3 KING OF GREAT BRITAIN, FRANCE AND IRELAND. Defender of the Faith. Acceded 25th Oct. 1760.*

1c

With a cartouche and ensigned, within a collar of jewels of blue set upon gold, the Royal Arms as lb impaling, Quarterly of six; 1 Or a buffalo's head cabossed sable armed and ringed argent crowned and langued gules MECKLENBURG, 2 Azure a griffin segreant or PRINCIPALITY OF WEDDEN, 3 Per fess in chief azure a griffin segreant or and in base vert a bordure argent PRINCIPALITY OF SCHWERIN, 4 Gules a cross formy argent crowned or RATZEBURG, 5 Gules a dexter arm argent issuant from clouds in sinister flank and holding a finger ring or COUNTY OF SCHWERIN, 6 Or a buffalo's head sable armed argent crowned and langued gules LORDSHIP OF ROSTOCK; overall an inescutcheon, per fess gules and or STARGARD. Below, in silver letters upon red: *SOPHIA CHARLOTTE QUEEN. Daughter of Chas Fredk . Lewis, Duke of Mecklenburg-Strelitz died 17th Novr. 1818.*

1d

Border as 1a. Three shields in pale each ensigned by a gold crown. *Upper*: BRUNSWICK, LUNEBURG and WESTPHALIA (Hanover). Overall an inescutcheon gules bearing the gold crown of Charlemagne. Beneath the legend: *HANOVERA REGNI NOMINE ORNATA 1815*. *Middle*: Within a collar of blue on gold letters: *QUIS SEPARABIT MDCCL XXXIII.* Upon a field argent a saltire gules bearing a trefoil slipped vert each leaf charged with a gold arched crown. Beneath the legend: *ORD: S: PATRICII FUND: A:D: 1783*. *Below*: Azure a celtic harp entwined about with a rose, shamrock and thistles of gold. *QUIS SEPARABIT HIBERNIA CUM BRITANNIA UNO INCORPORE JUNCTA A:D: 1801*. At the bottom right-hand side of light 1d is the monogram T.W. [Thomas Willement].

Across the base of lights 1a–1d is the legend: *In piam memoriam Regis dilectissimi Georgii 3ⁱ ;Regina Carolettæ; Frederici Ducis Ebor; et Edwardi Ducis Cantiæ; quorum conduntur exuviæ in coemeterio Regali hujus Capellæ Dec: et Can: P.C. Anno Domini 1852.*

2a–2d

A room with a brown and white floor, the walls covered with green drapery upon which are stone windows which are glazed in blue. On the left stands Frederick, Duke of York, in state robes wearing the mantle of the Garter and having around his neck the collar with the George, holding in his left hand the baton of a Field Marshal. He wears the Garter below the left knee. Beneath, the legend: FIELD MARSHAL AND COMMANDER IN CHIEF. In the adjoining light (2b), King George III is seated, dressed in robes of state made of cloth of gold fringed with ermine, and wearing a robe of red fringed with gold and with a cape and lined with ermine. He is seated in a red-upholstered wooden chair, his feet resting upon a stool of the same materials. He wears the Garter collar and George around his neck and carries upright a gold sceptre in his right hand. He wears the Garter below the left knee. Beneath the legend in gold letters on red: *BORN 24th May 1736 DIED 29th Jany 1820*. In the next light (2c) sits Queen Caroline, wearing a dress of cloth of gold with lace sleeves over which is a robe of purple fringed with gold and with a cape lined with ermine. In her right she holds a gold sceptre. Beneath in gold letters on red: *BORN 19th May 1744 MARRIED 8th Septr 1761*. On the right (1d) stands Edward, Duke of Kent, clad in robes with the collar, George, Garter and sword as previously, holding in his right hand a hat from which issues a bunch of ostrich feathers. Beneath the legend: *FROM HIM PROCEEDS A GEM TO LIGHTEN ALL THIS ISLE.*

3a

Border as 1a. *Above*: within the Garter ensigned by a gold coronet with a red cap, the Royal Arms of the House of Hanover (post 1801) viz: 1 & 4 ENGLAND, 2 SCOTLAND, 3 IRELAND, overall an escutcheon bearing tierced in pairle reversed BRUNSWICK, LUNEBURG, and WESTPHALIA (HANOVER) having at fess point an inescutcheon Gules a wheel argent TEMPORALITIES OF THE BISHOPRIC OF OSNABRUCK; the whole differenced by a label of three points argent the centre point charged with a cross gules (Frederick, Duke of York). *Below*: ensigned by a coronet as above, the arms as above impaling Argent, an eagle displayed sable on each wing a kleestengel argent, crowned, and bearing in the dexter claw a sceptre and in the sinister an orb or, charged upon the breast with the cypher F.R. in gold PRUSSIA. Beneath, in silver letters upon a blue ground *FREDERICA CHARLOTTE ULRICA PRINCESS ROYAL OF PRUSSIA DUCHESS OF YORK died 6th August 1820.*

3b

Above: within a formal border of silver and gold upon an arched crown a lion statant guardant crowned or ENGLAND. Centre, in silver letters upon a blue field, *Dieu et mon droit*. *Below*: within the border as above ensigned by a gold arched crown the cypher of King George III.

3c

Border as 3a. Within a formal border as 3b, against a red background, out of a coronet or a panache of peacocks feathers proper charged with a buffalo's head sable horned and with a ring through the nose argent arising from a closed palisado crown alternately azure, or, gules, argent and sable (crest of Mecklenburg Strelitz). Centre, in silver letters upon a blue field the legend: PROVIDE ET CONSTANTER. Below, within a border and crowned the cypher of Queen Charlotte.

3d

Upon the Royal Arms an escutcheon as light 3a but without the inescutcheon for Osnabruck and differenced by a label of three points argent (EDWARD, DUKE OF KENT) the centre point charged with a cross gules, the outer points each charged with a fleur de lis azure. Below, the arms differenced as above impaling quarterly of eighteen as Window nV for Saxe Gotha. Below in silver letters on blue *VICTORIA-MARIA-LOUISA dau of Francis Anthony Duke of Saxe Coburg Saalfield DUCHESS OF KENT 1818.*

Tracery

A, B and C as nIV.

nVII

The window is a memorial to King George IV.

1a

Border as previously. Ensigned by a gold mitre, Azure a crosier and a key in saltire, in chief, an arched crown or and in base an estoile argent. Beneath, the legend: BARBADOES 1824.

1b

Border as previously. Within a collar of the Guelphic Order and ensigned by an imperial arched crown, the Royal Arms of the House of Hanover post 1815 viz.: 1 and 4 ENGLAND, 2 SCOTLAND, 3 IRELAND. An escutcheon of Brunswick, Lunenburg and Westphalia (HANOVER), above which is placed an imperial crown, at fess point an inescutcheon gules bearing the gold crown of Charlemagne. Beneath in silver letters on a red background the legend: *GEORGE IV, of the United Kingdom of Great Britain and Ireland, King. King of Hanover acceded 29 June 1820.*

1c

Border as previously. Within a wreath of leaves interspersed with red and white roses and ensigned by a gold coronet with a red cap; Quarterly, 1 & 4 the Royal Arms of the House of Hanover post 1801 without the crown and the inescutcheon differenced by a label of five points argent on the centre point charged with a rose gules, 2 & 3 Saxe-Cobourg Saalfeld (as 2d). Overall an inescutcheon as quarter 1 differenced with a label of three points argent the centre point charged with a rose gules. Beneath: The legend in silver letters on a red background: *CHARLOTTE: AUG: only child of Geo: Prince of Wales married to Leopold Prince of Saxe-Cobourg Saalfeld died 6 Nov: 1817.*

1d

Border as previously. Surmounted by a gold mitre, Gules a crosier and a key in saltire in front of which is an open book pages argent edged or, in chief a lion passant guardant and in base a thistle or. Beneath: The legend: JAMAICA 1824. In the bottom right-hand corner of light 12 is the monogram TW [Thomas Willement].

Across the base of lights 1a–1d is the legend: *In piam memoriam Georgii Quarti Regis et Carolettæ Principessae filiae ejus unicae serenissimi Leopoldi Principis de Saxe Cobourg uxoris, quorum conduntur exuviæ in cœmeterio hujus capellæ Dec: et Can: P: A:S: MDCCCLIV.*

2a

Border as previously. Within a collar of the Ionian Order of St Michael and St George and ensigned by a coronet of the Heir Apparent, the Royal Arms of the House of Hanover post 1801 bearing an escutcheon for Brunswick, Luneburg and Westphalia (Hanover) but with a blank inescutcheon, the whole differenced by a label of three points argent. (King George IV as Prince of Wales). Beneath: The legend in silver letters on a red background: *GEORGE Prince of Wales Regent 1811.*

2b–2c

A room with a floor with a formal decoration in blue, green and white, the wall covering brown, the upper part being covered with draperies in red and green fringed with gold. On the left (2b) stands King George IV wearing a narrow ruff and a tabard-like vestment of red powdered with roses, thistles and shamrocks in green fringed with gold and trimmed with ermine. He wears a train of the same material fastened at the neck with gold cords. Around his neck is a collar of the Garter with the Great George and the Garter is fastened below his left knee. His hose and shoes are of white, the latter having golden decorations. In its left hand it holds a white plumed hat with the plumes of ostrich feathers. Beneath is the legend in red letters on a white background: *CROWNED 19 July 1821 DIED 26 June 1830.* On the right (2c) stands Princess Charlotte wearing a dress of white powdered with gold quatrefoils and with a bodice of cloth of gold over which is worn a blue robe edged with gold and lined with ermine. Upon her head is a wreath of leaves and white roses. She leans with her left arm upon a pillar. Beneath, the legend: *BORN 7 January 1796 Married 2 May 1816.*

2d

Border as previously. Within the Garter ensigned by a continental arched crown, the arms of Saxe-Cobourg. Quarterly of eighteen, 1 Azure a lion rampant barry argent and gules LANDGRAVE OF THURINGIA, 2 Gules an escarbuncle or having at the centre an escutcheon argent CLEVES, 3 Or a lion rampant sable MEISSEN, 4 Or a lion rampant sable JULICH, 5 Argent a lion rampant gules crowned azure BERG, 6 Argent an eagle displayed gules PALATINATE OF SAXONY, 7 Or two pales azure LANDSBERG, 8 Sable an eagle displayed or PALATINATE OF THURINGIA, 9 Or within an orle of hearts gules a lion rampant sable ORLAMUNDE, 10 Gules plain SOVEREIGN RIGHTS, 11 Azure a lion rampant per fess or and argent PLEISSEN, 12 Argent a rose gules seeded or BURGRAVIATE OF ALTENBURG, 13 Argent three bars azure EISENBURG, 14 Argent three beetle's pincers gules ENGERN, 15 Or a fess chequy gules and argent MARCK, 16 Per pale, dexter, gules a pillar argent argent crowned or ROENHILD, sinister, Or on a mount vert a cock sable HENNENBERG, 17 Or on a mount vert a cock sable HENNENBURG, 18 Argent three chevrons gules RAVENSBURG; overall an escutcheon, Barry of ten or and sable a crown of rue bendwise vert SAXONY.

Beneath: The legend in silver letters on a red background: *LEOPOLD GEO: FRED:Prince of Saxe-Cobourg Saalfeld.*

3a

Border as sIV. *Upper*: Within a gold border against a red background ensigned by an arched coronet with a red cap, the initials G.P.R. (GEORGE PRINCE REGENT). Beneath the legend: ICH DIEN. *Below*: Upon a base of white and gold surrounded by a formal green wreath, three ostrich feathers enfiled by a gold coronet.

3b

Border as previously. *Upper*: On an imperial crown a lion statant guardant crowned or. Beneath: The legend: ENGLAND. *Below*: Within a gold border against a blue background and ensigned by an imperial arched crown the cypher of King George IV.

3c

Border as previously. Out of a ducal coronet or, a horse courant argent in front of a column gules ensigned by a coronet or from which issues a peacock's tail proper charged with a mullet of six points argent. Beneath: The legend: HANOVER. *Below*: Within a border and background as light 3b ensigned by a gold coronet with a red cap, the cypher of Princess Charlotte of Wales.

3d

Border as previously. *Upper*: Within a gold border, against a red background and ensigned by a continental arched crown the cypher of Prince Leopold. Beneath: the legend: SAXE-COBOURG. *Below*: Within a wreath as 3a and upon a capital, the crest of Saxe-Cobourg as Window IV light 4.

Tracery

A, B and C as nIV.

nVIII

The window is a memorial to King William IV.

1a

Border as previously. Two shields each ensigned by a gold mitre. *Upper*: Argent upon a saltire gules two keys in saltire wards upward or upon a chief gules a paschal lamb bearing a swallow tailed standard argent armed and unguled or the staff and the cross on the standard also or. Beneath: RIPON 1836. *Below*: Argent on a mount vert in front of a banyan tree, on the dexter a kid couchant looking toward the sinister and on the sinister a leopard couchant guardant all proper, on a chief gules (usually azure) a dove volant between two crosses formy or. Beneath: MADRAS 1835.

1b

Border as previously. Within the Garter and ensigned by an imperial arched crown the Royal Arms of the House of Hanover post 1801 with the escutcheon surmounted by a gold crown. Beneath in silver letters upon a blue background: *KING WILLIAM IV. Died 20th June 1837.*

1c

Border as previously. Within a wreath of green leaves with gold and blue flowers and surmounted by a crown, the Royal Arms as in 1b impaling Saxe-Meiningen as in 2d. Beneath the legend in silver letters on a blue background: *ADELAIDE of Saxe-Meiningen. Born 13th Aug^{t}: 1792 died Decr 2nd 1849.*

1d

Border as previously. Two shields each surmounted by a gold mitre. *Upper*: Azure four mullets of eight points in cross argent. Beneath the legend: SYDNEY 1836. *Below*: Sable a crosier and a key in saltire between two eastern crowns in pale or. Below the legend: BOMBAY 1837. At the bottom right-hand corner is the monogram TW [Thomas Willement].

Across the base of 1a–1d is the legend: *In piam memoriam Gulielmi Quarti Regis et Adelaidæ Reginæ uxoris ejus quorum conduntur exuviæ in cœmeterio regali hujus capellæ Dec: et Can: P:C: A:S: MDCCCLIV.*

2a

Border as previously. Within the Garter surmounted by a gold coronet with a red cap, the Royal Arms of the House of Hanover before 1801 viz: 1 England impaling Scotland, 2 France Modern, 3 Ireland, 4 Tierced in pale reversed Brunswick, Luneburg and Westphalia. Overall a label of three points argent the centre point charged with a cross gules and on each of the outer points an anchor azure. Beneath: the legend in silver letters upon a blue background: *WILLIAM HENRY Duke of Clarence Born 21st Augt 1765.*

2b–2c

A room with a chequered brown floor. Against the rear wall a green curtain hangs from a gold rod while open windows are brown showing a blue sky. On the left stands King William IV wearing naval uniform over which is a red robe edged with gold and with a cap and fringe of ermine. His hose is white and the shoes buff with gold buckles. Below his left knee is the Garter. He wears the collar of the Garter and the George about his neck. In his right hand is borne a gold sceptre and his left hand clasps a sword which hangs from the waist belt, the scabbard silver, the hilt gold with blue decorations. Beneath, the legend: *ACCEDED 26 JUNE 1830.* On the right (2c) stands Queen Adelaide clad in a dress of cloth of gold with large puffed sleeves over which she wears a robe of purple edged with gold and trimmed with ermine. On her head she wears a small silver crown and rope of pearls, whilst a triple rope of pearls is around her neck and she wears gold bracelets. In her right hand she holds a sceptre of ivory topped by a gold dove. Below, in silver letters on a blue background: *CROWNED 8 SEPTEMBER 1831.*

2d

Border as previously. Quarterly of eighteen, as nVII, 2d for SAXE-MEININGEN. The shield is ensigned by a gold continental arched crown and pendant from the shield is the Saxon Order of the Crown of Rue. Below: In silver letters upon a blue background: *GEORGE FRED: CHARLES DUKE OF SAXE-MEININGEN.*

3a

Border as nIV. *Upper*: Three crests, the upper against a red background a lion statant guardant crowned or ENGLAND. *Centre*: Against a gold background a lion sejant affronty crowned or holding upright in the dexter paw a sword, the blade argent, the hilt or, in the sinister paw a sceptre or SCOTLAND. *Base*: Against a red background a tower triple towered argent (usually or) from the portal a hart springing argent attired and unguled or IRELAND.

3b

Border as previously. Against an artistic shield shape ensigned by an arched crown against a red background a gold crown of Charlemagne. Below is the legend in silver letters against a blue background: *WILLIAM, KING OF GREAT BRITAIN AND OF HANOVER.*

3c

Border as previously. Against a shield design as before ensigned by an open coronet against a blue background an anchor cabled or. Below: The legend in silver letters against a blue background: *WILLIAM, HENRY DUKE OF CLARENCE LORD HIGH ADMIRAL.*

3d

Border as previously. Three crests of Saxe Meiningen: the upper against a red background SAXONY as nV save that the pillar does not arise from a coronet. Middle: Against a gold background a bull's head cabossed gules, the horns and ringed through the nose argent, crowned with a ducal coronet the leaves or, the rim company argent and gules MARCK. Below: Against a red background a demi griffin erased or langued argent wings elevated displayed gules gorged with a coronet gules JULICH.

Tracery

A, B and C as nIV.

THE SOUTH NAVE AISLE

The Bray Chapel

This polygonal chapel contains ten windows, each of twelve lights. The upper lights are of plain glass. The lower lights are filled with glass designed by Ion Pace inserted in 1882 to complete the memorial to the Prince Imperial. The coats of arms, representing members of the Royal Family, of the Memorial Committee and of the Prince's friends, are set among various Napoleonic emblems against a background of bees and violets, both devices used by the Imperial Family.

The standard of heraldry is poor, the coats of arms being marshalled incorrectly and being accorded to persons who were not armigerous.

In the upper tracery of each window is a floral decoration in silver and gold against a background of either red or blue. Below and on either side is a silver rose against a gold background surrounded by silver leaves.

All of the lights have at the apex a gold coronet having on each side alternately a silver star or a white rose, the borders being formed of open gold coronets alternating with a geometrical design and interspaced with either red, blue or green. Except for lights 2a-3d of window sXVIII, the arms have above and below against a floral background, the letter N within a circle in red, blue or green.

The quarries in each window are composed alternately of bees and of violets in gold.

sXV

1a

Within a wreath of white leaves and roses, Argent three cinquefoils sable (Sir Algernon Borthwick).

Note: These arms are spurious and refer to Lord Borthwick, a member of the Committee (see window sXIX, 2a). Sir Algernon was not granted arms until 20 July 1887.

1b

Azure a Roman eagle displayed head to the sinister, the talons grasping a thunderbolt fesswise or, all within a collar of the Legion of Honour, the badge pendant beneath ensigned by the Napoleonic Imperial crown as used by Emperor Napoleon III (henceforth referred to as Nap. A).

1c

Nap. A.

1d

Within a wreath of white leaves and roses, Argent on a bend azure three stag's heads caboshed or STANLEY. In dexter chief a baronet's badge (Sir John Errington).

Note: These arms are not those usually displayed. Sir John, whose family name was Stanley, assumed the surname of Errington by Royal Licence on 7 August 1877 and from that date appears to have used different arms to those displayed here.

2a

Within a wreath of white leaves and roses, Quarterly, 1 Or an eagle displayed sable, 2 & 3 Azure issuant from the sinister and dexter sides of the shield respectively in each quarter an arm embowed proper grasping five arrows points to the base argent, 4 Or a lion rampant proper langued gules. Overall an escutcheon, Gules charged with a target, point to the dexter proper ROTHSCHILD (Sir Nathan de Rothschild).

Note: This shield should bear the badge of a baronet.

2b

Azure a Roman eagle displayed head to the sinister, the talons grasping a thunderbolt fesswise or, all within the collar of the Legion of Honour the badge pendant beneath. Behind the arms a robe of estate purpure fringed with gold and lined with ermine ensigned by the Napoleonic Imperial crown as used by Emperor Napoleon III with infulae of white and gold (henceforth referred to as Nap. B).

Note: The ermine is usually decorated with bees.

2c

Nap. B.

2d

Within a circlet of the Order of St Patrick (blue bearing the legend QUIS SEPARABIT MDCCLXXXIII) ensigned by the coronet of an earl, Quarterly, 1 & 4 Argent a saltire sable on a chief sable three leaves argent BLACKWOOD, 2 Azure in chief two roses argent in fess a fleur de lis between two mullets or in base three arrows palewise heads in base argent STEVENSON, 3 Gules three pierced cinquefoils ermine on a chief or a lion passant gules HAMILTON (Earls of Clanbrassill), (Frederick Earl of Dufferin).

Note: The circlet of the Order of St Patrick should be blue edged with gold. The arms depicted are not those borne by Earl Dufferin in 1882, which had been changed from the above twice in 1862 and again in 1872.

3a

Within a wreath of white leaves and roses ensigned by the coronet of a viscount, Argent three chevrons gules, a label of three points azure BARRINGTON (George, Viscount Barrington).

3b

Nap. A.

3c

Nap. A.

3d

With a wreath of white leaves and roses ensigned by the coronet of a baron, Quarterly 1 & 4 Or on a chevron gules between, in chief of two crescents and in base an escallop azure, three estoiles argent HENNIKER, 2 & 3 Azure three Corinthian pillars two and one palewise, each bearing upon the top a ball or MAJOR. (John, Lord Henniker).

Note: The quarters are usually marshalled 1 & 4 Major, 2 & 3 Henniker.

sXVI

1a

Within a circlet of the Order of the Bath (red bearing the legend TRIA IUNCTA IN VNO) and within a wreath of green leaves, Gules on a pile between two ostrich heads erased argent, each holding in its beak a horseshoe or a lion rampant gules. In sinister chief a baronet's badge WALLACE (Sir Richard Wallace). Beneath the wreath is the legend ICH DIEN.

Note: The circlet of the Order of the Bath should be red edged with gold.

1b

Nap. A.

1c

Nap. A.

1d

Within a circlet of the Order of the Bath within a wreath of green leaves (see above), per fess the base per pale, in chief Or a dexter hand couped at the wrist grasping a sword erect pommel and hilt gules, the blade entwined with a serpent proper between two lions combatant gules; the dexter base, Vert a buck trippant or; the sinister base, Per pale argent and sable a boar passant counterchanged SULLIVAN (Rear Admiral Sir Francis Sullivan).

2a

Within a circlet of the Order of St Patrick (see above), ensigned by the coronet of a marquess, Quarterly, 1 & 4 Quarterly (i & iv) Argent a bend engrailed between six martlets sable TEMPLE, (ii & iii) Azure three sinister gauntlets or VANE, 2 & 3 Or a bend counter company argent and azure between two lions rampant gules STEWART (George, Marquess of Londonderry).

2b

Nap. B.

2c

Nap. B.

2d

Within a wreath of white leaves and roses, ensigned by the coronet of a marquess, Quarterly 1 & 4 Ermine on a bend azure a magnetic needle pointing to the polar star or PETTY, 2 & 3 Argent a saltire gules a chief ermine FITZMAURICE (Henry, Marquess of Lansdowne).

3a

Within a wreath of white leaves and roses, ensigned by the coronet of a marquess, Quarterly, 1 & 4 Or a saltire and a chief gules, on a canton argent a lion rampant azure BRUCE, 2 & 3 Argent a chevron gules between three chapeau tails to the dexter azure BRUDENELL (Ernest, Marquess of Ailesbury).

Note: The chapeau or bycockets of the Brudenells are an heraldic curiosity — see the article by A. Colin Cole, in *Coat of Arms*, xii, No.85, pp. 2–11.

3b

Nap. A.

3c

Nap. A.

3d

Within a circlet of the Order of St Patrick and ensigned by the coronet of a duke, Quarterly 1 & 4 Argent three fusils conjoined in fess gules within a bordure sable MONTAGU, 2 & 3 Or an eagle displayed vert membered gules MONTHERMER (William, Duke of Manchester).

sXVII

1a

With the Garter and ensigned by a gold coronet with a red cap, the Royal Arms post 1837 charged with an escutcheon of Saxony differenced with a label of three points argent, on the centre point a cross gules and on each of the outer points a heart gules (Prince Leopold, Duke of Albany).

1b

Within the Garter and ensigned by a gold coronet with a red cap, the Royal Arms post 1837 charged with an escutcheon of Saxony differenced with a label of three points argent on the centre point a cross gules and on each of the two outer points an anchor azure (Prince Alfred, Duke of Edinburgh).

1c

Within the Garter ensigned by a gold coronet with a red cap, the Royal Arms post 1837 charged with an escutcheon of Saxony differenced with a label of three points argent on the centre point a cross gules and on each of the two outer points a fleur de lis azure (Prince Arthur, Duke of Connaught).

1d

Within a circlet of the Order of the Bath (see sXI, 1d) ensigned by the coronet of an earl, Quarterly, 1 & 4 Azure a chevron ermine between three escallops argent TOWNSHEND, 2 & 3 Quarterly gules and or in the first quarter a mullet and at fess point a crescent argent VERE (John, Earl Sydney).

2a

Within the Garter, ensigned by the coronet of the Heir Apparent above which, against a green background, are three ostrich feathers passing through a scroll bearing the legend ICH DIEN, all in silver. The Royal Arms post 1837 differenced by a label of three points argent and charged at fess point with an escutcheon, Barry of ten or and sable a crown of rue bendwise vert SAXONY (Albert Edward, Prince of Wales).

2b

Nap. B.

2c

Nap. B.

2d

Within a wreath of white leaves and roses and ensigned by an arched crown with a red cap, Per pale, dexter per fess in chief azure three crowns or SWEDEN, in base azure three bends sinister wavy argent, overall a lion rampant or FOLKUNGA; sinister, Gules a lion rampant or holding upright a long-handled axe or NORWAY. Overall a cross formy of three limbs (the sinister omitted) or, the lower limb charged with an eagle displayed sable VARMLAND. At fess point a cartouche: Per pale; dexter, Argent a vase or VASA; sinister, Azure in chief a bird argent in base a bridge with two towers over water argent PONTECORVO (BERNADOTTE) (Gustav, Crown Prince of Sweden and Norway, later King Gustav V of Sweden).

Note: This shield contains many inaccuracies both as to tincture and charges.

3a

Within a wreath of white leaves and roses and ensigned by an arched imperial crown, with a red cap which within a red circle is a gold chained portcullis, against a blue background the letter V in gold.

3b

Within the Garter ensigned, by the Royal Crest viz. upon an imperial crown proper a lion statant guardant imperially crowned or, the Royal Arms of Queen Victoria viz. 1 & 4 England, 2 Scotland, 3 Ireland.

3c

As 3b.

3d

As 3a, save for the letter R.

sXVIII

The lower halves of lights 1a–1d are filled with stonework. The upper parts of lights 1a–1d have borders and decorated quarries but no arms or other insignia.

2a

Within a wreath of white leaves and roses, ensigned by the coronet of an earl, Quarterly 1 & 4 Argent a fess dancetty sable WEST, 2 & 3 Quarterly or and gules a bend vair SACKVILLE (Reginald, Earl De la Warr).

2b

Nap. B.

2c

Nap. B.

2d

Within a wreath of white leaves and roses ensigned by the coronet of an earl, Quarterly ermine and gules at fess point a crescent argent STANHOPE (Arthur, Earl Stanhope).

3a

Within a circlet of the Order of the Bath and a wreath of green leaves, ensigned by a gold arched crown with a red cap, Per pale; dexter, Or three stag's attires fesswise in pale points to the sinister sable WURTTENBURG, sinister, Or three lions passant in pale sable SWABIA. Overall an escutcheon, Or two pales fusily sable TECK. Beneath the wreath on a scroll is the motto Ich Dein (Francis, Duke of Teck).

Note: The dexter forepaws of the lions should be gules and the escutcheon paly bendy or and sable.

3b

Nap. A.

3c

Nap. A.

3d

Within the Garter, ensigned by the coronet of a duke, Quarterly, 1 & 4 Barry of eight argent and gules a cross flory sable GOWER, 2 & 3 Azure three laurel leaves or LEVESON (George, Duke of Sutherland).

sXIX

1a

Within a circlet of the Order of the Bath and a wreath of green leaves, beneath which is the legend ICH DIEN. Sable gutty d'eau a dolphin naiant embowed or vorant a fish argent, on a canton ermine a mural crown gules SIMMONS (General, later Field Marshal, Sir John Lintorn Simmons).

1b

Nap. A.

1c

Nap. A.

1d

Within a wreath of silver leaves and roses, ensigned by the coronet of a baron, Quarterly, 1 & 4 Quarterly per fess indented argent and sable, in the first and forth quarters a horn sable stringed or FORESTER, 2 & 3 Azure a fess nebuly ermine between three crescents argent WELD (George, Baron Forester).

2a

Within a circlet of white leaves and roses, ensigned by the coronet of a baron, Argent three cinquefoils sable BORTHWICK (Cunninghame, Baron Borthwick).

2b

Nap. B.

2c

Nap. B.

2d

Within a wreath of white leaves and roses, ensigned by the coronet of a baron, Ermine on a bend sable three pheons argent CARLETON (Dudley, Baron Dorchester).

3a

Within a circlet of the Order of the Bath and a wreath of green leaves, beneath which is the legend ICH DIEN and ensigned by the coronet of a baron, Or three water bougets sable ROSE (of Kilvarock), (Hugh, Baron of Strathnairn).

Note: These arms are probably spurious. There are no arms on record for Lord Strathnairn either in England or in Scotland, although as a descendant of Rose of Kilvarock he might have matriculated those arms with a difference in Scotland, but this was never done.

3b

Nap. A.

3c

Nap. A.

3d

With a wreath of silver leaves and roses, ensigned by the coronet of a baron, Argent a saltire gules GERARD (Robert, Baron Gerard of Bryn).

The Beaufort Chapel

In 1506 the polygonal chapel opening from the south-west corner of the nave was appropriated as a chantry by Sir Charles Somerset (1460–1526), afterwards Earl of Worcester, whose tomb lies therein.

The chapel has five windows, each of four lights. At the apex of each is a quatrefoil glazed with a rose gules barbed vert, seeded or en soliel. Within the leaves of the quatrefoil is the motto FAIRE LE DOY and the letter B.

sXXX

Each light is composed of quarries, each charged with a gold chained portcullis, the quarries being interspersed with the motto in bend MUTARE VEL TIMERE SPERNO. A single coat of arms within the Garter or a circlet sable with a formal trefoil pattern in gold, and having on each side a green quatrefoil appears in each light, below which is an inscription.

1a

Within a circlet and having the coronet of an earl, SOMERSET impaling Argent a fess dancetty sable WEST. *Inscription*: Elizabeth West second wife of Charles Earl of Worcester.

1b

Within a circlet and having the coronet of an earl, SOMERSET impaling Or a lion rampant double-queued vert langued gules SUTTON. *Inscription*: Eleanor Sutton third wife of Charles Earl of Worcester.

2a

Within the Garter, ensigned by the coronet of an earl: Quarterly France Modern and England within a bordure company argent and azure, overall a bendlet sinister argent SOMERSET. *Inscription*: Charles Somerset Earl of Worcester K.G. DIED 1526.

Note: He was the illegitimate son of Henry Beaufort, second Duke of Somerset.

2b

Within a circlet sable bearing a formal foliage pattern in gold and ensigned by the coronet of a countess, SOMERSET with an escutcheon of pretence Per pale gules and azure three lions rampant argent HERBERT. *Inscription*: Elizabeth Herbert first wife of Charles Earl of Worcester.

sXXIX

Quarries, mottoes and quatrefoils either side of the shields as in sXXX.

1a

Within the Garter, ensigned by the coronet of a duke, BEAUFORT. *Inscription*: Henry Somerset, Duke of Beaufort K.G. Died 1699.

1b

Within a circlet as sXXX, 2b, ensigned by the coronet of a duchess, BEAUFORT impaling Gules between three cross-crosslets fitchy a lion rampant or langued azure CAPELL. *Inscription*: Mary Capell wife of Henry Duke of Beaufort.

2a

Within a circlet as sXXX, 2b, ensigned by the coronet of a marquess. Quarterly France Modern and England, within a bordure company argent and azure BEAUFORT. *Inscription*: Henry Somerset Marquess of Worcester. Died 1646.

Note: The difference of a bendlet sinister appears to have been dropped by the descendants of the Earl of Worcester who, by the time of the first marquess were using the undifferenced Beaufort coat. Strictly the coat should be described as Beaufort for Somerset, but for convenience it will be referred to as Beaufort.

2b

Within a circlet as before and ensigned by the coronet of a countess, BEAUFORT impaling Argent a lion rampant gules langued azure on a chief sable three escallops argent, a label of three points or RUSSELL *Inscription*: Anne Russell Countess of Worcester wife of Henry afterwards created Marq. of Worcester.

sXXVIII

1a

Background as 2a, ensigned by the coronet of a duke and having on each side a flower, BEAUFORT impaling quarterly, 1 & 4 Gules three stirrups argent SCUDAMORE (ancient), 2 & 3 Or a cross formy fitchy at the foot gules SCUDAMORE. *Inscription*: Henry Somerset 3rd Duke of Beaufort.

Note: He married Frances d. & h. of second Viscount Scudamore.

1b

Background as sXXX. Within a circlet, as sXXX, 2b, on a field paly of four gules and azure a sluicegate chained or. *Inscription*: Henry seventh Duke of Beaufort K.G. repaired this Chapel and the Monuments of his Ancestors. AD 1843.

2a

Background of quarries charged alternately with a gold chained portcullis and a white rose edged with gold, the motto in bend as previously. Within the Garter ensigned by the coronet of a duke BEAUFORT impaling to the dexter, Quarterly or and gules a bend vair SACKVILLE, and to the sinister, in chief Or fretty gules a canton ermine NOEL; in base, Quarterly argent and azure a cross or OSBORNE. *Inscription*: Henry Somerset 2nd Duke of Beaufort K.G.

Note: He married firstly Mary Sackville daughter of the sixth Earl of Dorset, secondly Rachel Noel daughter of the second Earl of Gainsborough, and thirdly Mary Osborne daughter of the second Duke of Leeds.

2b

Background as window sXXX. Within a circlet, as sXXX, 2b, having on each side a quatrefoil vert BEAUFORT with a label of three points argent. *Inscription*: Henry Somerset Lord Herbert eldest son of Henry Duke of Beaufort. ob: vit: pat.

sXXVII

The background of this window is as sXXVIII.

1a

Within the Garter and ensigned by the coronet of a duke, BEAUFORT impaling to the dexter, Quarterly 1 & 4 France Modern impaling England, 2 Scotland, 3 Ireland, overall a baton sinister argent and azure FITZROY; and to the sinister, Quarterly, 1 & 4 Vert three acorns or SMITH, 2 & 3 Argent on a chevron engrailed gules between three stringed horns sable, three mullets pierced argent gules HORNE. *Inscription*: Henry Somerset 7th Duke of Beaufort K.G.

Note: He married firstly Georgiana granddaughter of the first Lord Southampton and secondly Emily daughter of Charles Smith.

1b

Within the Garter and ensigned by the coronet of a duke, BEAUFORT, impaling Ermine a rose gules barbed vert seeded or BOSCAWEN. *Inscription*: Henry Somerset 5th Duke of Beaufort K.G.

Note: He married Elizabeth, daughter of Admiral the Hon. Edward Boscawen.

2a

Within the Garter and ensigned by the coronet of a duke, BEAUFORT, impaling Quarterly, 1 & 4 Argent three bars gules a cross flory sable GOWER, 2 Azure three laurel leaves or LEVESON, 3 Gules three clarions or GRANVILLE. *Inscription*: Henry Charles Somerset 6th Duke of Beaufort K.G.

Note: He married Charlotte, daughter of first Marquess of Stafford.

2b

Ensigned by the coronet of a duke and having on each side a flower, BEAUFORT impaling Quarterly, 1 & 4 Gules between ten crosses formy argent six in chief and four in base, a chevron ermine BERKELEY, 2 & 3 Or a saltire sable BOTETOURT. *Inscription*: Charles Noel Somerset 4th Duke of Beaufort.

Note: He married Elizabeth, sister of Lord Botetourt.

sXXVI

1a

As (i).

1b

Ensigned by the coronet of a duke and having on each side a flower, BEAUFORT impaling Sable two bends argent on a canton azure a bend or HARFORD. *Inscription*: Henry Adelbert Wellington Fitzroy 9th Duke of Beaufort.

Note: He married Louise, daughter of William Harford.

2a

Composed of quarries bearing alternately a gold chained portcullis and a fleur de lis. (No shields or mottoes.)

2b

Background as sXXVIII. Within a Garter, ensigned by the coronet of a duke, BEAUFORT impaling Quarterly 1 & 4 Or a fess between three wolve's heads erased sable HOWE (usually couped and collared gules), 2 & 3 Argent on a bend sable three popinjays or CURZON. *Inscription*: Henry Charles Fitzroy Somerset 8th Duke of Beaufort K.G.

Note: He married Georgiana, daughter of first Earl Howe.

THE NORTH NAVE AISLE

nXIV The War Memorial Window

This is composed of twelve lights and is the first window of the north aisle of the nave, located over the north door. The window was originally glazed to commemorate members of St George's Choir School who fell in the First World War. In 1947 it was altered to include the fallen of the Second World War. Lights 1a–1d are filled mainly by a scroll containing the names of the fallen.
Across Lights 1a–1d

IN MEMORY OF THOSE MEMBERS OF ST. GEORGE'S CHOIR SCHOOL WHO GAVE THEIR LIVES IN THE TWO GREAT WARS.

1914–18		1939–45	
C.W. BATTYE Berkshire Reg	G.B. JOHNSON Norfolk Regt	T.K. BURRIDGE. R.A.	A.D.N. HUNTER Royal Scots Fusiliers & R.F.C.
J.N. BIGGE K.R.R.C.	J.W. LEY Artists Rifles	D.J. COMBER Ghurka Rifles	M.I. JENNINGS Punjab Regt.
H.W. BOSTOCK South Staffordshire Regt.	R.J.A. LIDIARD Royal Fusiliers	D.D. CROFTS Hampshire Regt.	J.A. NORTHEY Cameronians

H.E.L. COX Queen Victoria's Rifles	C.F.K. PIERSON R.F.C.	E.J. DAINTY R.A.	F.B. POMEROY R.A.F.
W.C.H. CREE R.F.A.	D.F. ROBERTS East Surrey Regt	G.M. EDWARDS R.A.F.	M.E. POMEROY Queen's Royal Regt.
G.W. DAMAN Seaforth Highlanders	W.A. SLADE R.F.A.	P.F. FALWASSER R.H.A.	A.P. ROBERTS Royal Scots Fusiliers
C.E. FISHBOURNE R.E.	M.A. SOMERVILLE Rifle Brigade	D.E. GOULD R.A.F	G.W.G. WALKER Lincolnshire Regt.
L.J. HARRISON Lancashire Fusiliers	H.S. SPURLING East Surrey Regt.	M.T. GOULD Royal Irish Fusiliers	W.E.R. TOWNSEND R.A.

For a description of the figures in the main lights see Harrison, pp. 165–6.

THE VESTRY

Two windows in the west wall each of three lights. In the upper tracery of each window are two quatrefoils and the centre of each quatrefoil is Argent a cross or. The background to each window is composed alternately of a gold chained portcullis and a gold and silver double rose. In the upper part of each light is a shield surrounded by the Garter.

I

1a

Royal Arms post 1837, viz: Quarterly, 1 & 4 ENGLAND, 2 SCOTLAND, 3 IRELAND ensigned by the coronet of the Heir Apparent.

1b

Quarterly, 1 & 4 Gules a cross argent between twenty plates five in each quarter saltirewise WELLESLEY, 2 & 3 Or a lion rampant gules ducally gorged or COWLEY.

1c

As 1a but differenced with a label of three points argent. Possibly for Edward, Prince of Wales, later Duke of Windsor, ensigned by an imperial arched crown.

II

1a

As window I, 1a.

1b

Argent a cross gules.

1c

As window I, 1c.
It may be noted that the crowns/coronets have been wrongly affixed.

THE EDWARD IV CHANTRY

Stairway to the Edward IV Chantry

The spiral staircase leading from the north choir aisle is lit by a series of glazed loops. Two of these, which are situated below the chantry floor level, are filled with coloured glass.
Lower: The cusp is filled with yellow glass below which is FRANCE MODERN. A section of yellow and blue divides this shield from one of Argent a cross gules ST GEORGE. A further dividing section of yellow and blue glass divides the bottom shield of Azure a saltire argent ST ANDREW.
Upper: As the lower light save that the cusp is filled with green and the dividing sections comprise mauve glass.

Heraldic Glass in the Edward IV Chantry

The Royal Closet

There is only one shield which is clearly heraldic. It is in the window on the north side.

Bendy of six gules and vert on a fess argent a lion passant guardant between two cinquefoils gules. Probably for THOMAS MAGNUS, Canon 1520–47.

The Inner Room

In a window on the north side.

Light 1: *Upper*: Argent a fess nebuly azure between three crescents jessant-de-lis sable all within a bordure gules. Probably for RICHARD SYDNOR, Canon 1519–34. *Lower*: Within the Garter, Gules four fusils in fess ermine DINHAM impaling Gules three arches two and one conjoined the pillars and hood moulds argent the capitals and bases or ARCHES (see notes re. Oliver King Chapel, p. 233).

Light 2: A rose gules seeded or surmounted by an imperial arched crown or.

Light 3: *Upper*: Quarterly France Modern and England having on each side against a silver background the letters H and R in gold. *Lower*: Within the Garter, Azure a cross flory between five martlets or EDWARD THE CONFESSOR.

THE CHAPTER ROOM

Six windows are filled with heraldic glass. Those in the east wall each comprise four lights. Windows I-IV contain the arms of Canons; windows V and VI the arms of Deans of Windsor. The upper tracery of all six have in the centre, surrounded by green leaves, a bouche shaped shield bearing Argent a cross gules. In the upper corners against a red background appear, in gold, to the left the letter 'S' and to the right the letter 'G'.

I

1a

Upper: Gules a chevron argent between in chief two roses or and in base a fleur de lis argent CURE. Legend: Edward Capel Cure 1884. *Lower*: Quarterly, 1 & 4 Gules three lapwings or TYRWHITT,

2 & 3 Sable a wolf salient or in chief a fleur de lis argent between two bezants WILSON. Legend: Leonard Francis Tyrwhitt 1910.

1b

Upper: Azure semy of cross-crosslets, a lion rampant guardant argent DALTON. Legend: John Neale Dalton 1885. *Lower*: Gules on a cross ermine between four doves argent a book fesswise gules edged and clasped or bearing the Greek letter Theta sable REGIUS PROFESSOR OF DIVINITY, CAMBRIDGE, impaling, Per pale argent and sable on a chaplet four quatrefoils all counterchanged NAIRNE. Legend: Alexander Nairne 1921.

2a

Upper: Argent between two bendlets azure a lion passant bendwise gules, in sinister chief a crescent sable MARSHAM. Legend: Jacob Marsham 1805. *Lower*: Argent three Moor's heads couped in profile proper, wreathed about the temples argent and azure, at fess point a mullet sable surmounted by a crescent or CANNING. *Legend*: William Canning 1828.

2b

Upper: Azure a fleur de lis argent, in dexter chief an annulet or DIGBY. Legend: Charles Digby 1808. *Lower*: Azure six annulets 3, 2 and 1 or, at fess point a crescent argent MUSGRAVE. *Legend*: Richd Adolphus Musgrave 1829.

II

1a

Upper: Argent a fess gules double cotised wavy azure ELIOT. *Legend*: Philip Frank Eliot 1886 [later Dean, see window V, 2b]. *Lower*: Per chevron azure and gules, on a chevron argent between, in chief two open books garnished or in base a double rose argent irradiated or, an annulet ensigned with a cross formy interlaced with a saltire conjoined in base sable TAYLOR. (The charge on the chevron is the mark of the Bridge House Estates in the City of London.) *Legend*: Samuel Mumford Taylor Bp. 1921.

1b

Upper: Or three bars gemels azure, overall on a pale invected ermine a portcullis chained sable BARRY. *Legend*: Alfred Barry Bp. 1890. *Lower*: Argent on a chevron sable between three Cornish choughs proper three crosses formy or DEANE. *Legend*: Anthony Charles Deane 1929.

2a

Upper: Gules an eagle displayed argent langued azure armed or, on a canton argent a chaplet graminy vert GOODALL. *Legend*: Joseph Goodall 1808. *Lower*: Sable a swan, wings expanded, within a bordure engrailed argent, in dexter chief a mullet or MOORE. *Legend*: Edward George Moore 1834.

2b

Upper: Azure semy of cross-crosslets three lozenges or in a chief a martlet argent STOPFORD. *Legend*: Richard Bruce Stopford 1812. *Lower*: Argent a lion rampant gules armed and langued azure, on a chief sable three escallops argent the centre escallop being differenced by a martlet sable RUSSELL. *Legend*: Wriothesley Russell 1840.

III

1a

Upper: Quarterly, 1 & 4 Sable a trefoil slipped between an orle of eight mullets argent PHIPPS, 2 the Stuart Royal Arms viz: Quarterly, (i & iv) Quarterly France Modern and England, (ii) Scotland, (iii) Ireland, all within a bordure company ermine and azure, the azure pieces charged with a fleur de lis or (badly faded). (Arms granted on 7 December 1688 to King James II's illegitimate daughter Catherine Darnley). 3 Paly of six argent and azure overall a bend gules ANNESLEY. Legend: Marquess of Normanby 1891.
Lower: Gules on a pile argent between two crosses flory or a fess wavy between three mullets sable BLACKBURNE. *Legend*: Harry William Blackburne 1931.

1b

Upper: Gules a sword in bend sinister, point in chief, the hilt or, the blade argent, in chief a crescent argent surmounted by a mullet or GEE. *Legend*: Richard Gee 1894. *Lower*: Erminois on a fess azure between three cranes proper a saltire couped between two cross-crosslets fitchy or, in chief a fleur de lis gules for difference CRAWLEY. *Legend*: Arthur Stafford Crawley 1934.

2a

Upper: Quarterly, 1 & 4 Ermine on a chevron sable three fountains CUST, 2 & 3 Argent three cocks gules COCKAYNE, in the dexter chief of the first quarter a crescent or. *Legend*: Henry Cockayne Cust 1813. *Lower*: Argent three bends engrailed gules ANSON. Legend: Frederick Anson 1845.

2b

Upper: Ermine on a fess gules a lion passant or PROBY. Legend: Charles Proby 1814. *Lower*: Quarterly 1 & 4 Or three torteaux a label of three points azure, a mullet argent for difference COURTENAY, 2 & 3 Or a lion rampant azure langued gules REDVERS. *Legend*: Charles Leslie Courtenay 1859.

IV

1a

Upper: Argent a fess dancetty between three roses gules barbed and seeded proper SMITH. *Legend*: Clement Smith 1902. *Lower*: Azure two bars argent VENABLES. *Legend*: Edward Malcolm Venables 1948.

1b

Upper: Sable a fess ermine in chief three poleaxes palewise in fess, the heads argent, the hafts or SHEPPARD. *Legend*: Edgar Sheppard 1907. *Lower*: Argent a fess wavy between three fleurs de lis sable FISHER. *Legend*: James Atherton Fisher 1958.

2a

Upper: Argent three mountain cats passant guardant in pale sable KEATE. *Legend*: John Keate 1820. *Lower*: Quarterly, 1 & 4 Sable a chevron ermine between three martlets or JERVIS, 2 & 3 Per fess wavy gules and azure three suns in splendour all within a bordure engrailed or PEARSON. *Legend*: Hugh Pearson 1876.

2b

Upper: Azure on a chief or a demi lion rampant gules, langued argent MARKHAM. *Legend*: David F. Markham 1827. *Lower*: Paly of six argent and gules on a chevron azure three cross-crosslets or CARPENTER. *Legend*: William Boyd Carpenter 1882.

All the arms in windows V-VI are surrounded by a blue ribbon pendant from which is the Badge of the Register of the Order of the Garter, an office held since the reign of King Charles I by the Deans of Windsor. The badge consists of a closed book with red covers within a gold border with clasps of gold surmounted by two gold quills placed saltirewise, the whole surrounded by the Garter and ensigned by an imperial crown.

V

1a

Azure nine mullets of six points 3, 3, 2 and 1 or, in chief a mullet argent for difference BAILLIE. *Legend*: Albert Victor Baillie, Dean 1917.

1b

Quarterly, 1 & 4 Gules three pierced cinquefoils ermine on a canton argent a trefoil slipped vert HAMILTON, 2 & 3 Argent a lymphad sails furled sable EARLS OF ARRAN. *Legend*: Eric Knightley Chetwode Hamilton Bp. Dean 1944.

2a

Quarterly, 1 & 4 Gules a cross argent between twenty plates five in each quarter saltirewise WELLESLEY, 2 & 3 Or a lion rampant gules ducally gorged or COWLEY, overall at fess point an annulet argent for difference. *Legend*: Gerald Wellesley Dean 1854.

2b

Argent an oak tree eradicated proper CONNOR. *Legend*: George Henry Connor, Dean 1882.

VI

1a

Argent a wolf salient sable collared or WOOD(S). *Legend*: Robin Woods, Dean 1962.

1b

Argent a cross gules between, in each quarter two swords in saltire, the hilts or, the blades proper MANN. *Legend*: Michael Mann Bp. Dean 1976.

2a

Azure on a chevron or between in chief two mullets and in base a pheon point in base argent, a fleur de lis gules DAVIDSON. *Legend*: Randall Thomas Davidson Dean 1883.

2b

Argent a fess gules double cotised wavy azure ELIOT. *Legend*: Philip Frank Eliot. Dean 1891. (See window II, 1a).